Commemorating the Irish Civil War

History and Memory, 1923–2000

Anne Dolan

Trinity College Dublin

D1612741

CAMBRIDGE
UNIVERSITY PRESS

CAMBRIDGE UNIVERSITY PRESS
Cambridge, New York, Melbourne, Madrid, Cape Town, Singapore, São Paulo

Cambridge University Press
The Edinburgh Building, Cambridge CB2 2RU, UK

Published in the United States of America by Cambridge University Press, New York

www.cambridge.org
Information on this title: www.cambridge.org/9780521819046

First published 2003
This digitally printed first paperback version 2006

A catalogue record for this publication is available from the British Library

ISBN-13 978-0-521-81904-6 hardback
ISBN-10 0-521-81904-0 hardback

ISBN-13 978-0-521-02698-7 paperback
ISBN-10 0-521-02698-9 paperback

For my parents and for Jack

Contents

Illustrations

Acknowledgements

This book began as a Ph.D. thesis. I started that as a disgruntled stray on Professor Jay Winter's doorstep at Pembroke College, Cambridge. For taking me in, and for his constant encouragement, I will always be grateful.

I am deeply obliged to the librarians and archivists of Cambridge University Library, the Public Record Office, London, the National Archives of Ireland, the National Library of Ireland, University College Dublin Archives and Library, the Cork Archives Institute, the National Photographic Archive, Fianna Fáil Archives and the Irish Military Archives for all their help and patience. To Commandant Victor Laing of the Military Archives, a special thanks for the tea and biscuits.

I thank the following institutions and holders of copyright for access to collections of papers and permission to quote from them: the Director of the National Archives of Ireland; the Military Archives; the National Library of Ireland; University College Dublin Archives Department (Michael Hayes, Hugh Kennedy, Desmond FitzGerald, Ernest Blythe, Mary MacSwiney and the O'Rahilly papers); the Mulcahy Trust for permission to consult and quote from the Richard Mulcahy papers; Cork Archives Institute (Seámus Fitzgerald papers); Fianna Fáil Archives; and Trinity College Manuscripts Department (Childers papers). I also thank the following institutions and holders of copyright for permission to reproduce photographs: the *Cork Examiner*; the Board of Trustees of the National Library of Ireland; the Military Archives; the Gárda Representative Association; and the *Illustrated London News*.

Thanks are also due to Pat Cremin of the museum at Collins' Barracks, Cork, and to the men and women of the county libraries, county councils and local history societies who replied to my letters with a surprising and much appreciated enthusiasm. I name them individually in the bibliography of this book. To Michael MacEvilly and the late Tess Kearney, who welcomed me into their homes and shared their collections of source materials, I extend my deepest gratitude.

My thanks to all at Cambridge University Press, especially Elizabeth Howard.

I remain indebted to Dr Michael Laffan. He still generously reads my work; he still reminds me why I try to study history. To Dr Deirdre McMahon, to

Professors Keith Jeffery and J. J. Lee, who kindly read drafts with insightful and astute eyes, my sincerest thanks.

Professor Eunan O'Halpin has helped and encouraged in countless ways. For that I will always be grateful.

To my friend and partner in crime Pauric Dempsey, who made travelling around the Midlands searching for monuments a strange joy, my warmest thanks.

I am grateful to William Murphy for being his perceptive, contrary self, and to Gillian O'Brien for all the kindness and support when it was needed most.

My thanks to Joseph Clarke whom I would be lost without.

This book is for my parents, for whom thanks will never be enough.

Abbreviations

ACA	Army Comrades Association
ARCA	Associate of the Royal College of Art
ARHA	Associate of the Royal Hibernian Academy
CAI	Cork Archives Institute
CE	*Cork Examiner*
CID	Criminal Investigation Department
DE, official report	*Dáil debates*, September 1922 –
DE, treaty debate	*Iris Dháil Éireann: official report. Debate on the Treaty between Great Britain and Ireland signed in London on the 6th December, 1921*
DF	Department of Finance
DFA	Department of Foreign Affairs
DJ	Department of Justice
DMP	Dublin Metropolitan Police
DO	Dominions Office
DT	Department of an Taoiseach
EC	European Community
FCA	Fórsa Cosanta Áitiúil
FF	Fianna Fáil
FG	Fine Gael
FJ	*Freeman's Journal*
FS	Free State
GAA	Gaelic Athletic Association
II	*Irish Independent*
IRA	Irish Republican Army
IRAO	Irish Republican Army Organisation
IRB	Irish Republican Brotherhood
IT	*Irish Times*
MEP	Member of the European Parliament
NAI	National Archives of Ireland
NLI	National Library of Ireland
NPA	National Photographic Archive, Dublin

OC	Officer Commanding
OFM	Order of Friars Minor
OPW	Office of Public Works
PG	Provisional Government
PRO	Public Record Office, London
RHA	Royal Hibernian Academy or Academician
RIC	Royal Irish Constabulary
TCD	Trinity College, Dublin
TD	Teachta Dála
UCD	University College, Dublin
UCDA	University College, Dublin, Archives Department
UUP	Ulster Unionist Party

Introduction: Civil war and the politics of memory

Forty-seven years after the end of the Irish Civil War a former Free State soldier wrote to a former Free State senator. He wanted the army to go to Béalnabláth to honour Michael Collins, its first Commander-in-Chief. He made his plea brief and unvarnished, and somehow then he wrote:

regardless of the right and wrong, the civil war is now a part of our history ... The cold eye of the historian in dealing with it will record that to put down the opposition the government were forced to execute 77 men, three times more than did the British in the previous struggle! But will any regard be paid to the human emotion, to the dreadful duty imposed on the army personnel called upon to carry out these executions. At the time I was the camp commandant in charge of Beggars Bush Barracks and as in the other Barracks it fell to our lot to see this gruesome work carried out. It was then that I cursed the fates, the frailty of the leaders, the stupidity of men, or whatever it was that brought the country to this pitch of barbarity. It is impossible to describe the harrowing and the anguish of the soul, of having to see one time comrades in arms brought out and shot to death by a firing squad. And to be aware that these men did not really know what it was all about.[1]

This book is about this letter: Seán Irwin's letter. It is about remembering victory when this was how it felt to win.

   To say what this book is is to say what it is not. It is not a history of the Irish Civil War. War is a past thing, a remembered or forgotten thing. The whys and the wherefores are taken for granted; this is not and was never meant to be a chronicle of scuffles and ambushes. It begins instead at the end of civil war. It begins because no one has accepted a challenge set by J. J. Lee about the legacy of bitterness left by that conflict in Ireland. It begins because 'a definitive verdict must await detailed analysis of the various ways in which the survivors used the memory of the civil war to further their purposes'.[2] This book may be far from providing a definitive verdict, but it is at least a start – an attempt to think in terms of 'the memory of civil war' when no one else has even bothered to count the lives it claimed.

---

[1] Letter from Seán Irwin to Michael Hayes, 3 Nov. 1970, Michael Hayes MSS, UCDA, P53/396 (punctuation as in original).
[2] J. J. Lee, *Ireland 1912–1985: politics and society* (Cambridge, 1989), p. 69.

The memory of the Irish Civil War has been assumed, distorted, misunderstood. It has been manipulated, underestimated, but, most of all, ignored. The nature of the conflict can only be blamed for so much. Historiography has chosen to overlook it and to stop in 1921, because after that it all becomes too 'unsavoury', and most have preferred to leave it to 'some other student of Chaos'.[3] But even accepting the inconvenience of 'chaos', even chaos with Fitzpatrick's capital 'c', the study of the memory of civil war is hindered most by Irish historiography's reticence about the study of memory itself. Although articles and pamphlets are giving way to edited collections of essays,[4] although the bicentenary of 1798 has made memory a suitable endeavour for scholars of the eighteenth century, twentieth-century Ireland has only really considered memory in terms of the Great War. Without Keith Jeffery's work this book could not have been written,[5] but the study of the memory of the Great War, the consensus that has emerged assuming and condemning its neglect, needs to be placed in the context of the traditions that have been accused of neglecting it. Neglect cannot be supposed when the memory of the dead of 1916, the War of Independence and the civil war have not been assessed, when it is only taken for granted that nationalist Ireland gloried in the memory of its martyrs.

At this point there is another caveat. Although the Irish National War Memorial at Islandbridge is a shadowy presence throughout this book, although the commemoration of the Free State soldiers and the Irish soldiers who fought in the Great War might be compared, this is not part of some elaborate republican plot to diminish the importance of the Great War or to write its dead out of Irish history. The Irish Civil War was an eleven-month squabble, a 'quibble of words'.[6] To speak of these two conflicts in the same breath seems almost irreverent. What is being compared is the memory of the dead. All that is questioned are the assumptions made about neglect. Islandbridge prowls through this book because Islandbridge has been perceived as an example of neglect. Islandbridge has been considered exceptional, when no one has cared to examine what was the norm.

At the same time, the impact of civil war cannot be underestimated. There were too many like Robert Barton who would never speak of it,[7] and so the

[3] David Fitzpatrick, *Politics and Irish life 1913–1921: provincial experience of war and revolution* (Dublin, 1977), p. 191.
[4] Jane Leonard, *The culture of commemoration* (Dublin, n.d.); Jane Leonard, 'Lest we forget', in David Fitzpatrick (ed.), *Ireland and the First World War* (Dublin, 1986), pp. 59–67; Laurence M. Geary (ed.), *Rebellion and remembrance in modern Ireland* (Dublin, 2001); Ian McBride (ed.), *History and memory in modern Ireland* (Cambridge, 2001).
[5] Keith Jeffery, 'The Great War in modern Irish memory', in T. G. Fraser and Keith Jeffery (eds.), *Men, women and war, Historical Studies, XVIII* (Dublin, 1993), pp. 136–57; Keith Jeffery, *Ireland and the Great War* (Cambridge, 2000).
[6] Arthur Griffith, *DE, treaty debate*, p. 21 (19 Dec. 1921).
[7] R. F. Foster, 'Remembering 1798', in R. F. Foster, *The Irish story: telling tales and making it up in Ireland* (London, 2001), p. 234.

confused instances of its commemoration become all the more important. Also civil war challenges most of the notions of collective memory. The idea of 'remembering in common' is gone.[8] Even within families, the most basic unit of community, brothers and sisters, parents and children took different sides. Professor Eoin MacNeill, a Free State minister, went proudly to Leinster Lawn, left wreaths at Béalnabláth. He never went to the cross at Benbulben that honoured his dead republican son. It could be argued that pro- and anti-Treatyites were forced to construct communities within community; to define themselves against each other; to take the grand opposition of great nations at war and inflict it on a small and particularly organic society. Perhaps this is why the smaller conflict still smarts, and why it means more to many in the villages of Kerry than something as momentous as the Great War ever could.

Dorothy Macardle's *Tragedies of Kerry* is currently in its sixteenth edition.[9] It was first published in 1924. Republicanism has its *Last post*, its proud lists of patriot dead, its own literature of memory.[10] This book is not a study of republican memory because republicanism has a quite singular approach to its dead. Death, there, is a simpler thing. Men die for Ireland, for the republic. They join Tone, Emmet, Pearse: death is an inspiration to complete the republican task. That is not to diminish the republican experience of civil war. There were too many silences, too many corpses for that. It is merely instead to predicate the more troubled experience of remembering the Free State dead. This emphasis is not part of any elaborate exercise in rehabilitation. The question of what was and was not done in the woods in Kerry is not at issue here. The dead, or rather their commemoration, is the prime concern of this book: how the winners of a war no one wished to fight express whatever there is of pride, sorrow, bitterness, triumphalism, shame. The Free State dead are merely the more evocative examples of this dilemma.

Though victory was later hailed as a triumph for democracy and democratic institutions, winning in 1923 meant little more than safeguarding a compromise, a means to an end.[11] That end, the grail-like republic, mocked the victory. Whatever heroism there was in shooting an off-duty RIC man in the quest, there was none in killing a former comrade who refused to desert it. It was a victory of 'pragmatism over principle', a victory for the 'will of the people',

---

[8] Robert Gildea, *The past in French history* (New Haven and London, 1994), p. 10.

[9] Dorothy Macardle, *Tragedies of Kerry* (Dublin, 1924; 16th edn, Dublin, 1998).

[10] National Graves Association, *The last post* (Dublin, 1932; 2nd edn, Dublin, 1976; 3rd edn, Dublin, 1985; American edn, Dublin, 1986); Richard Roche, *Here's their memory: a tribute to the fallen of republican Wexford* (Wexford, 1966); Nicolás de Fuiteóil, *Waterford remembers* (Waterford, n.d.).

[11] P. S. O'Hegarty states: 'The victory of the people was a victory for democratic government as against a military despotism, a victory for the ballot as against the bullet.' *The victory of Sinn Féin* (2nd edn, Dublin, 1998), p. 101. See also Tom Garvin, *1922, the birth of Irish democracy* (Dublin, 1996), p. 30.

for 'law and order'[12] and for several other overburdened reasons, but it was not a victory with honour.

'In Civil War, alas, there is no glory; there are no monuments to victory or victors, only to the dead.'[13] Todd Andrews spoke as a disillusioned republican. He spoke in the same voice as the men and women who had seen the worst of the war; he spoke in the silence of Stephen Fuller.[14] But, in many ways, Todd Andrews spoke for no one. The faithful republican wore the civil war like a badge of honour on his by-now bloodied Volunteer uniform: another wrong to be righted by another generation's sacrifice. The 'Staters' too paraded their precious state: their monument to victory, every inch built by the hands of Kevin O'Higgins as he cried 'seven hundred and seventy-seven more'.[15] Therefore, the problem arises. After civil war can the winners honour their victory; can they commemorate it; can they raise their flags, cry from their well-guarded rooftops; can they hail their conquering heroes with the blood of their comrades still fresh on their boots? Or does civil war, by its very nature, demand silence? Should the winners cover themselves in shame, bow their heads and hope that the nation forgets 'our lamentable spasm of national madness'?[16] What is a poor victorious state to do, all the time watched by a vigilant empire, all the time wary of an enemy which only stopped fighting but never surrendered its arms?

On another level, winning a civil war presents a different problem of memory. How does a mother, a father, a wife, remember their private, their brigadier general, their son or husband killed in the street, shot by mistake, when they have died in the 'wrong war' against the wrong enemy and when the next government looks on them as traitors? Can a father still say that his son has died for Ireland when he has died to secure a compromise? Does he call his son a hero – his Pearse, his Wolfe Tone? Or does it really matter what he has died for when he is just another dead son? Private grief, therefore, has its part to play. To what extent is remembrance a family's burden? How many of the bowed heads photographed at carefully tended graves shared the distaste Mrs Griffith felt at the abuse of her husband's memory?

---

[12] These phrases were used constantly by the Free State government both during and after the civil war. See, for example, *The Free State – An Saorstát*, 4 Mar. 1922; *The Irish People – War Special*, 6 Aug. 1922.

[13] C. S. Andrews, *Dublin made me* (Dublin and Cork, 1979), pp. 243–4.

[14] Fuller survived the Ballyseedy trap mine, a particularly gruesome incident where Free State soldiers tied nine republican prisoners to a booby-trapped roadblock in March 1923. The only survivor, he never spoke of the event publicly until the 1960s, when he finally gave an interview to Robert Kee. *Ireland: a television history* by Robert Kee, RTÉ Archive.

[15] Speaking in Sligo on 18 Jan. 1925 Kevin O'Higgins, when questioned about the seventy-seven executions, commented: 'I stand by the seventy-seven executions and seven hundred and seventy-seven more if necessary.' 'More Executions', republican handbill, NLI, ILB 300p3, item 6; *IT*, 19 Jan. 1925.

[16] *Kerry News*, 5 Mar. 1928.

In answer, the Free State both acknowledged and ignored the sentiments of Todd Andrews. It erected monuments to the dead, it erected monuments to victory. It often erected the same monument to both. But just as it was expected to, it often chose to forget.

It is this conflict of impulses, this tussle of memory and forgetting that is imperative here. Hence it is addressed at its most public point, at the very point at which it becomes part of the landscape – at the statues and crosses, in the ritual and rhetoric of commemoration. Indeed, it is at the foot of these cenotaphs and crosses that this book poses its central questions. What is particular about the memory of civil war? What is particular to the Irish example when every other European country has inscribed its grief in so many *lieux de mémoire*? What was its legacy? Was the bitterness 'burnished and polished';[17] was it convenient, merely the means to more superficial party political ends?

Chapter 1 turns to the Cenotaph to answer these questions. As the first and most demonstrative expression of Free State sorrow and victory it seems the most appropriate place to start. Chapter 2 addresses the commemoration of, if not the obsession with, Michael Collins: when, where and by whom he was commemorated; when, where and why he was not. Chapters 3 and 4 are the turn of the more obscure: of Arthur Griffith and the men of the Free State army. In their own ways, these chapters make something of an attempt to rescue them from 'the enormous condescension of posterity'.[18] Finally, chapter 5 is for the returning, for the yearly retreat to monument and grave. It examines the use and abuse of memory, the different layers of meaning that commemoration inevitably implies. It considers the politicians who sometimes came, the families who never went away.

[17] Lee, *Ireland 1912–1985*, p. 69.
[18] E. P. Thompson, *The making of the English working class* (4th edn, London, 1980), p. 12.

1   The elephant on Leinster Lawn: a Cenotaph to civil war

We say monument, although it was only a rough model . . . a vast carcass of an idea of Napoleon . . . It was an elephant, forty feet high, constructed of framework and masonry, bearing on its back its tower, which resembled a house, formerly painted green by some house painter, now painted black by the sun, the rain, and the weather . . . One knew not what it meant. It was a sort of symbol of the force of the people. It was gloomy, enigmatic, and immense. It was a mysterious and mighty phantom, visibly standing by the side of the invisible spectre of the Bastille. Few strangers visited this edifice, no passer-by looked at it. It was falling into ruin; every season, the mortar which was detached from its sides made hideous wounds upon it. 'The ædiles', as they say in fashionable dialect, had forgotten it since 1814. It was there in its corner, gloomy, diseased, crumbling, surrounded by a rotten railing, continually besmeared by drunken coachmen; crevices marked up the belly, a lath was sticking out from the tail, the tall grass came far up between its legs . . . It was huge, contemned, repulsive, and superb; ugly to the eye of the bourgeois; melancholy to the eye of the thinker . . .

(Victor Hugo, *Les Misérables*)[1]

On 24 May 1923, the republicans stopped fighting. The Free State had won. In winning it had proved itself as brutal as any British army. It had executed seventy-seven men, sacrificed two leaders, hundreds of soldiers and countless civilians.[2] On 24 May 1923, the Free State had little to celebrate.

Within two months, however, celebration began: the state commissioned its most notable monument to the civil war dead. While some cantankerously

---

[1] Victor Hugo, *Les Misérables*, 2 vols. (London, 1994), II, p. 645.

[2] 'Mulcahy stated that around 540 pro-Treaty troops were killed between the Treaty's signing and the war's end; the Government referred to 800 army deaths between January 1922 and April 1924 . . . No figure exists for total civilian deaths.' Michael Hopkinson, *Green against green: the Irish Civil War* (Dublin, 1988), pp. 272–3. Commandant Peter Young of the Irish Military Archives estimates the total death toll at between 1,500 and 2,000. An alternative estimate is 927. Seán Connolly (ed.), *The Oxford companion to Irish history* (Oxford, 1998), p. 265. The figure of seventy-seven executions is also contested. T. P. O'Neill counts the executions at eighty-one. Thomas P. O'Neill, 'In search of a political path: Irish republicanism, 1922 to 1927', in G. A. Hayes-McCoy (ed.), *Historical Studies, X* (Dublin, 1976), p. 147. 'Seventy-seven', however, is the figure popularly championed by republicanism. Michael Laffan, *The resurrection of Ireland: the Sinn Féin party 1916–1923* (Cambridge, 1999), p. 417. Although Griffith died from natural causes, he was still perceived to have 'died for Ireland'.

called it the 'dire apparition of the Griffith–Collins singularity', most referred
to the manifestation on Leinster Lawn as the Cenotaph.[3] Always written with
the dignity of a capital 'C', this empty or honorary tomb was the Free State's
first answer to the many questions of monuments and memory both public and
private. On 7 July 1923, the cabinet appointed an informal 'commemoration
committee'.[4] Made up of the Ministers for Defence, Local Government and
External Affairs, the Quartermaster General of the Army, and, if necessary,
the Secretary of the Department of Posts and Telegraphs, the committee was
charged with the task of commemorating the anniversaries of Arthur Griffith and
Michael Collins in 'a fitting manner'.[5] With no time to waste on what a competition of sculptors might or might not consider 'fitting', the committee, headed
by Desmond FitzGerald, settled for the rather austere design of the conveniently
close at hand Professor George Atkinson, ARHA, ARCA, headmaster of the
Dublin Metropolitan School of Art and later director of the National College of
Art, Dublin.[6] On Leinster Lawn, facing Merrion Square, a Celtic cross, forty
feet high and eight feet wide, flanked by two panels, each of thirteen feet, was
to be erected on a base platform of three steps. On each panel was to rest a
medallion, carved by Albert Power, RHA, one a profile of Collins, the other of
Griffith; their names to be carved below in Irish and inscribed in English on
the back[7] (see figure 1). A gilt cross was to be inlaid on the Celtic cross and
an inscription, *Do Chum Glóire Dé agus Onóra na hÉireann* ('For the glory of
God and the honour of Ireland'), was to declaim from the centre to every passing Irishman.[8] For one observer its appearance of strength was to represent the
courage of the men it commemorated, the solidity of the state, the resolve of its
government and army.[9] But the monument was a sham. Made of wood and plaster and covered in cement, its medallions were merely painted to look bronze.
It appeared strong but by 10 December 1923 it had already begun to show
the 'effect of the weather'. Seán Lester, Director of Publicity, complained: 'the

[3] C. P. Curran, 'On statues in the air', *Irish Statesman*, 9, 3 (24 Sept. 1927), p. 55.
[4] Cabinet minutes G2/2, c1/129 and c1/130. DT s5734a, Griffith–Collins Cenotaph – general file,
memo by Michael McDunphy to the cabinet, 6 July 1932. The date of commissioning cannot be
ascertained. The earliest references in DF and DT files date to early July 1923.
[5] Cabinet minutes G2/2, c1/129.
[6] Sighle Bhreathnach-Lynch, 'Public sculpture in independent Ireland 1922–1972: expressions of
nationhood in bronze and stone', *The Medal*, 21 (Autumn 1992), p. 44. Theo Snoddy, *Dictionary
of Irish artists – twentieth century* (Dublin, 1996), pp. 17–18.
[7] *II*, 14 Aug. 1923. Snoddy, *Dictionary of Irish artists*, pp. 397–400; Sighle Bhreathnach-Lynch,
'"Executed": the political commissions of Albert G. Power', *Eire-Ireland*, 29, 1 (Spring 1994),
pp. 44–60; Sighle Bhreathnach-Lynch, 'Albert Power, RHA', *Irish Arts Review Yearbook*,
(1990–1), pp. 111–14; Kitty Clive, 'Albert Power, RHA', *The Leader* (7 Nov. 1942), pp. 290–2.
[8] The phrase also appeared on some Great War memorials. It had long been common currency
in nationalist and republican literature. By its appearance on the Cenotaph, it marked a definite
attempt by Cumann na nGaedheal to subscribe to the nationalist tradition from which the Treaty
conspired to exclude them.
[9] *IT*, 14 Aug. 1923.

[College Studios.
Irish Cavalry passing the Cenotaph erected to the memory of Michael Collins and Arthur Griffith.

Figure 1 Irish cavalry passing the Cenotaph erected to the memory of Michael
Collins and Arthur Griffith (courtesy of the National Photographic Archive,
National Library of Ireland).

gilding is coming off in large patches with the result that a shabby effect is
produced'.[10] Unveiled fourteen days before polling in the state's second general election, it had begun to show the signs of wear just like any other forgotten
election poster.

Although the cynicism is less than flattering, the fact that one can be so cynical is indicative of the many and garbled messages that this otherwise rather
bland and short-lived edifice managed to convey. Sighle Bhreathnach-Lynch
expressed surprise that in the midst of civil war the government 'appeared to
find sufficient time and energy to commission a public monument', an expression which is quite remarkable given the reason which she later posits for its
conception.[11] Her surprise is also excessive in the light of several cabinet decisions dating from 20 September 1922. Less than one month after the death
of Michael Collins, the government had commissioned his biography.[12] By

[10] DF file 930, letter from Seán Lester to Mr McGann of the President's Office, 10 Dec. 1923.
[11] Bhreathnach-Lynch, 'Public sculpture in independent Ireland', p. 44.
[12] Cabinet minutes G1/3, PG 10(a), 20 Sept. 1922, item 1; DT s1760a, Michael Collins biographies;
Deirdre McMahon, '"A worthy monument to a great man": Piaras Béaslaí's Life of Michael
Collins', *Bullán: An Irish Studies Journal*, 2, 2 (Winter/Spring 1996), pp. 55–65.

17 October, it had agreed to purchase death masks and bronze busts of Griffith and Collins, both fashioned by Albert Power who would later copy the masks for the medallions on the Cenotaph.[13] The last meeting of the cabinet of the Provisional Government even managed to put time aside to accept a portrait of Griffith from the British signatories of the Treaty.[14] The instinct to commemorate was obviously strong from the start. It is Bhreathnach-Lynch's belief that the Cenotaph was conceived out of the need of a new government 'desperate to establish a secure power base. The speedy adoption of Griffith and Collins as heroes was a move to legitimise the new rulers by creating the impression among the citizens of Ireland that they were being governed in a tradition already established by men considered worthy to be commemorated as heroes.'[15] The accuracy of her conviction is unquestioned. Indeed her precision is confirmed by the labourers 'employed night and day at a high cost' to erect the Cenotaph in time for the first anniversary of the two deaths:[16] the anniversary which was to be as much a showcase of victory and stability as it was a sign of loss.

Kevin O'Higgins spoke of the Provisional Government as 'simply eight young men in the City Hall standing amidst the ruins of one administration... with wild men screaming through the keyholes'.[17] True to Ireland's nationalism of mourning, its frightened successors clutched the bones of their illustrious dead, excusing themselves, justifying themselves, waiting anxiously for the last coat of bronze paint to dry on the fake plaster medallions. Though their sense of security was as spurious as the monument itself, the Free State government commemorated with a haste that indecently decried their knowledge of its power. It was no coincidence that FitzGerald headed the commemoration committee; he had also been instrumental in the commissioning of the Collins biography. He was their most senior propagandist, learning his trade in the difficult War of Independence days. Anxious to mark the first anniversary of the two deaths, eager to exploit it for the coming election, there was a need to be seen to be doing the right thing. The lack of time produced a temporary edifice. Like London's Cenotaph, it was to be a short-lived centrepiece of a victory march; sincerity would replace it with something more permanent as soon as possible. But in Dublin's case minds were changed for different reasons; there was none of the popular regard that altered London's opinion of Lutyens' evocative work.[18]

---

[13] Cabinet minutes G1/3, PG 38(a), 17 Oct. 1922, item 1.
[14] *Ibid.*, G1/3, PG 77(a), 5 Dec. 1922, item 8. DT s1903a, Miscellaneous: portrait of the late President Griffith.
[15] Bhreathnach-Lynch, 'Public sculpture in independent Ireland', p. 45.
[16] DF file 930, letter from the OPW to the Department of Finance, 4 June 1924.
[17] Kevin O'Higgins, *Three years hard labour: an address delivered to the Irish society at Oxford University on the 31st October, 1924*, foreword by Eoin MacNeill (Dublin, n.d.), p. 7.
[18] Jay Winter, *Sites of memory, sites of mourning: the Great War in European cultural history* (Cambridge, 1996), pp. 103–4.

'A monument of the very lightest structure . . . to remain in position for only a short time' became instead 'a structure sufficiently durable to withstand climatic conditions for some years'.[19] The sincerity had waned even before the monument had been completed.

Initially this propriety and sincerity was to cost nothing more than £350, a paltry sum when the state sanctioned a contribution of £50,000 to the First World War Memorial at Islandbridge in 1929, a sum which still exceeded the final cost of the permanent Cenotaph by approximately £30,000 in 1949, much as the 150-acre site by the Liffey dwarfed the few dozen square feet on Leinster Lawn.[20] The final cost of the temporary structure was £833 8s. 4d., a figure which included the expense of the unveiling ceremony and the much begrudged payment of £35 to Atkinson and £20 and £15 to the two OPW architects, M. J. Burke and H. G. Leask respectively, for what was tellingly referred to as 'the onerous task of setting up the Cenotaph'.[21] Finance was firm: such payments to 'established civil servants . . . should not be regarded as precedents': these men were paid solely because of 'the special circumstances of the case'.[22] Finance was further aggrieved when it found these payments amounted to 20 per cent of the entire construction costs. The benefits of commemoration had to come cheap, and, possibly crippled by the burden of the £30 million of material damage and the £17 million that it had cost to finance the civil war, the Department of Finance's niggardly influence on the commemoration committee was justified.[23] But the contradiction remains. Why spend so little on a monument designed to legitimise the authority of the state and then spend so much on one that had come to be associated, however wrongly, by the very enemies of that state with unionism and empire? Every penny of that £833 8s. 4d., like every year that withered that supposedly temporary Cenotaph into the rotting frame of August 1939, seems to suggest that the motives were not strictly pure. But given that a majority of the Dáil deputies had cut their political teeth in the campaign against conscription, one is tempted to suggest that the £50,000 donated in the less than culturally inclusive days of 1929 was as much a gesture to the Protestant capitalism that headed the War Memorial fund as it was a mark of respect for the 49,400 Irishmen who had died in 1914–18 for the freedom of small nations.[24]

---

[19] DF file 930, letter from the OPW to Finance, 4 June 1924.

[20] *Ibid.*, letter from Finance to the OPW, 20 July 1923; DT s4156b, War Memorial Islandbridge, OPW estimate, December 1929; DT s5734c, Griffith–Collins Cenotaph – general file, letter from B. Farrell, OPW to the Secretary of an Department of an Taoiseach, 20 July 1949.

[21] DF file 930, letter from the OPW to Finance, 4 June 1924.

[22] *Ibid.*, letter from the OPW to Finance, 4 June 1924. Finance was also aggrieved by the fact that these payments amounted to 20 per cent of the construction costs of the Cenotaph. DF s200/0017/24, External Affairs – payment to designers of Griffith, Collins, O'Higgins memorial – Messrs Geo. Atkinson, M. J. Burke and H. G. Leask (n.d.).

[23] Hopkinson, *Green against green*, p. 273.

[24] The figure 49,400 appears on the monument at the centre of Islandbridge. However, the figure for strictly Irish deaths is much lower, estimated in the region of 27,000, and 49,400 has become, and

Pure or otherwise, the Cenotaph came of mixed motives. There was pressure to act, to commemorate, spurred if nothing else by the funerals which had paralysed the country a year before. The personalities, too, demanded pageantry; the proximity of their deaths, the tragic double loss, commanded a worthy anniversary. Griffith had laboured since the 1890s, the man of words and inspiration, while Collins, in whose 'name one has written the history of five of the most crowded and most fateful years of Ireland's chequered history', played the hero for those who chose to read those years like an adventure book.[25] The nature of their deaths as much as their lives staked their claim for recognition: the elder statesman, broken by his toil, dying before he saw the full fruits of his labours; the young valiant, assassinated. Both pronounced tragic by a country weaned on martyrdom and wasted lives. However, the very nature of their deaths also prompted their commemoration for another reason. They had not died for the republic and so the doors of the republican pantheon remained closed. They were instead Free State martyrs, in need of a shrine as much to justify their actions as to legitimate the compromise which they had died for. Since their demise newspapers, national and local, had desperately associated them with the long list of heroic dead, eager for their own partisan reasons to bolster the popular legitimacy of the state. Their deaths created the need for a new type of pantheon, an alternative temple where the martyr still died 'for the glory and honour of Ireland', even if pragmatism called it a Free State. Thus the Cenotaph became the physical manifestation of this new martyrdom: an empty tomb for the Free State dead, where Kevin O'Higgins was also symbolically interred in 1927.

Apart from the insecurity of this new pantheon that called for such a physical display of its honour, the security of the state was also buoyed by this plaster Cenotaph. Rulers build monuments, and, in a pointed piece of publicity, the Free State heralded its arrival and its intention to remain. 'It was a piece of statecraft in which the names and reputations of these respected nationalists would be permanently linked with Cumann na nGaedheal.'[26] Shaped like a veritable altar on the lawn of the new parliament, visible to every deputy and senator, every citizen who cared to pass, it was the altar on which the party consecrated its state and its victory. At this point 'party' and 'state' seem indistinguishable terms. The Cumann na nGaedheal Party had been founded to fight the election of 1923; it was made up of 'pro-Treatyites', 'Free Staters'; the party was predicated on the state and the state subsequently consumed by the party. Though funded by the state, the Cenotaph was a gesture of the governing party. A monument to the faithful, it would always stand even if the party fell. But while the Free State

is used here as, a purely canonical figure. David Fitzpatrick, 'Militarism in Ireland, 1900–22', in T. Bartlett and Keith Jeffery (eds.), *A military history of Ireland* (Cambridge, 1996), pp. 379–406.
[25] Kevin O'Higgins, 'Michael Collins, a personal tribute', *II*, 13 Aug. 1923.
[26] Judith Hill, *Irish public sculpture: a history* (Dublin, 1998), p. 153.

government did not have the good grace to raise a fine edifice, its Cenotaph, however feeble, was inspired by republicanism almost as much as it was a rebuke to its republican opponents. The Cenotaph shared Leinster Lawn with a statue of Prince Albert, a relic of a British rule which the new monument was eager to overshadow. On a symbolic level it lessened the political potency of the prince and of his wife Victoria, whose statue dominated the Kildare Street side. It relegated the trappings of empire, asserting an independent Ireland in the face of those who said the 'Staters weren't nationalists'.[27] Of course, that the wood-and-plaster cross looked ridiculous in the light of the Saxe-Coburgs' splendour suggested a symbolism of a thoroughly different kind.

Not only were the 'Staters' nationalists, they were also good Catholics and good Irish-Irelanders as well. Art historians have criticised the stylised Celtic cross with its connotations of religion and the Gaelic revival, damning the monument as 'a triumph of ideology over taste'.[28] But it is unfair to expect a bold artistic leap of faith from a state eager to assert its own nationalist credentials in the face of a possibly armed opposition which took pleasure in pronouncing it pro-British and which periodically accused it of pandering to Protestants. If the Cenotaph was, as the *Irish Times* chose to believe, a spiritual conception 'symbolic of the faith of the men commemorated', if the new type of Irish hero had to have his 'personal religious beliefs publicly reaffirmed', then the art historian should consider the private and political expediency of 1923 as well as the aesthetics.[29] Yet even on an aesthetic level, how could the new state afford to forgo the regalia of the revival? 'An obvious symbol of the party's cultural aspirations was chosen' one critic complains.[30] How could it be otherwise from a generation schooled in the Gaelic League, from a government whose cabinet included Eoin MacNeill, a professor of early Irish history and a co-founder of the League, from a government eager to cloak its compromise in nationalism?

The monuments to the dead of the First World War

were built as places where people could mourn. And be seen to mourn. Their ritual significance has often been obscured by their political symbolism which, now that the moment of mourning has passed, is all that we can see. At the time, communal commemorative art provided first and foremost a framework for and legitimation of individual and family grief.[31]

In the case of the Cenotaph 'all that we can see', all that the art historians can see, is an expression of narrow Roman Catholicism. They do not see that the faithful in mourning seek solace in the familiar; that 'their sorrow was bound to dwell

[27] Bhreathnach-Lynch, 'Public sculpture in independent Ireland', p. 45.
[28] Hill, *Irish public sculpture*, p. 153.
[29] *IT*, 14 Aug. 1923; Bhreathnach-Lynch, 'Public sculpture in independent Ireland', p. 45.
[30] Hill, *Irish public sculpture*, p. 153.   [31] Winter, *Sites of memory*, p. 93.

on traditional devotional art and sculpture'.[32] Just as guilty, the historian seeks context, and all that he sees is the election that lurks in the background. He sees the Cenotaph as the perfect party political broadcast, covered in every national and several local newspapers beside columns of electioneering.[33] Undoubtedly it was a glorious propaganda opportunity, one which passed through the minds of Cumann na nGaedheal strategists. But that presumes that a state feels no loss, that politicians do not grieve. Not only had the government lost its two most dynamic and resourceful figures, a loss which became painfully obvious in the staid years of policy that followed, it had lost, at the least, two colleagues, and in many cases two friends. There was a genuine impulse to honour these two dead men. To deny these statesmen their grief, their heartfelt sorrow, is unjust.

Like many of Europe's Great War memorials, the Cenotaph, kept firmly behind the high railings of Leinster Lawn, was set apart, a place to grieve, detached from the everyday that had left civil war behind.[34] It was not in St Stephen's Green; it did not join O'Connell Street's rich monumental pageant. Leinster Lawn was a type of retreat: from the grandeur of Nelson's Pillar and the O'Connell and Parnell monuments; from the lavish amounts that the nineteenth century was wont to spend; from the enthusiasm of 1898; from republican rage that might grow bold on maybe drunken Saturday nights.[35] But while these same high railings always conspired to keep the public out, especially the vandalising republican kind, the monument remained a place of public sorrow. Although this may seem melodramatic, given that 'the moment of mourning is past' and few now notice the present Cenotaph as they hurry along Merrion Square, the drama seemed more real to the 50,000 who had lined the streets to watch a passing funeral, to the countless who had queued to pay their last respects as the bodies of Griffith and Collins lay in state. But even if many queued just to see these 'great men' once or to check in enmity that they were really dead, even if the funeral throng was swelled by those who merely wished to see the spectacle, this monument recognised that a nation had mourned, that 50,000 had taken to the streets whether in curiosity or in grief.[36] It was a place for

---

[32] *Ibid.*, p. 92.   [33] For example *II*, 11 Aug. 1923.   [34] Winter, *Sites of memory*, p. 96.

[35] The centenary of the 1798 rebellion and the battalion of pikeman statues which it prompted from around the country caused one observer to declare that in 1898 'the country appears memorial mad'. Roy Foster, 'A Trevelyan lecture to commemorate the 200th anniversary of the Irish rising of 1798', Cambridge University (4 Nov. 1998), since published as 'Remembering 1798', in R. F. Foster, *The Irish story: telling tales and making it up in Ireland* (London, 2001), pp. 211–34. For earlier nineteenth-century memorials see Homan Potterton, *The O'Connell monument* (Cork, 1973); Gary Owens, 'Nationalist monuments in Ireland, c. 1870–1914: symbolism and ritual', in Raymond Gillespie and Brian P. Kennedy (eds.), *Ireland: art into history* (Dublin, 1994), p. 106.

[36] Gabriel Doherty and Dermot Keogh, ' "Sorrow but no despair – the road is marked": the politics of funerals in post-1916 Ireland', in Gabriel Doherty and Dermot Keogh (eds.), *Michael Collins and the making of the Irish state* (Dublin, 1998), p. 193.

the people to lament the hope that had been lost with these two men, the men who had swayed many to accept the Treaty; to remember the news that moved 'Ireland as nothing has moved her in living memory'.[37] It was the means to recall a fallen statesman, to contemplate the sorrow of a hero taken by the hand of a treacherous countryman.

Yet the Cenotaph, in recalling Collins, also recalled the folly of the 'last mad year of wantonness',[38] the year that killed the man 'who won the war',[39] the year that killed the 'glorious unity' of the last five years. Thus it was a monument to civil war, a reminder of its losses and excesses, a constant rebuke, so that the 'madness from within' would never escape again.[40] And while it was described as the 'Griffith–Collins Cenotaph' this monument to civil war was also a monument to all who died in that war: all who died for the Free State at least. In its own way it was like London's Cenotaph:

by announcing its presence as the tomb of no one … [it] became the tomb of all who had died in the war. In the heart of London, in Whitehall, in the middle of the street adjacent to the Houses of Parliament – the seat of Government – Westminster Abbey, and Horse Guards Parade, it brought the dead of the 1914–18 War into history.[41]

This makeshift Cenotaph on the lawn of Leinster House was a monument to the nameless hundreds who were never honoured, even if by default rather than design. On the day of the dissolution of the Dáil, one day after W. T. Cosgrave announced the unveiling of the Cenotaph to that chamber, the veteran Sinn Féiner, Seán Milroy, stood and spoke of the 'saviours of the nation'. He announced that they

should not forget who it was that made it possible for the nation to be carried into safety from the dangers through which it passed. The rank and file of the Army have done that. They have given this nation stability and security and they have given it a chance of being a place in which it is safe to indulge in the Ten Commandments, and they have made it unsafe and unfit for the assassin and bandit … we should not allow them to think that we did not appreciate fully the great work that they have done for the nation. I hope that when the history of this period is written the fidelity, the valour, and the steadfastness of the rank and file of the national Army will be remembered as one of the brightest things in this period of Irish history.[42]

Another TD, D. J. Gorey, rose to lament the loss of Seán Hales, the passing of one of 'the noblest men I ever knew', while Cosgrave remembered 'great sacrifices' and 'sympathy', and 'hard work' done by 'those who took up arms in

---

[37] *FJ*, 23 Aug. 1922.   [38] O'Higgins, 'Michael Collins, a personal tribute'.

[39] *DE, treaty debate*, p. 20 (19 Dec. 1921).

[40] General Richard Mulcahy quoted in *The madness within*, RTÉ 1 documentary, produced by Colm Magee, screened 21 Jan. 1998.

[41] Winter, *Sites of memory*, p. 104.

[42] *DE, official report*, IV, col. 2005 (9 Aug. 1923); *II*, 10 Aug. 1923.

defence of the State, both in the Army and in the other organisations which have made it possible for us to secure both life and property in the State'.[43] Thus three days before the unveiling of the Cenotaph, a day before the announcement of the unveiling in the national press, a nation read reports of a Dáil being dissolved; it read nothing of Griffith and Collins, just tributes to the rank and file, tributes to the dead that the Cenotaph would honour but never name.

On 11 August 1923 the country opened its daily papers to learn that on Monday the 13th the gates of Leinster Lawn would open and admit President Cosgrave's invited guests.[44] At 1.00 p.m. he would stand before them and speak. Silence would follow and then, to the strains of a military salute, the President would unveil the state's first monument. Inside Leinster Lawn there was to be room for up to 2,000 people: 2,000 people who had invitations, who knew when and where to assemble without prompting from the national press.[45] Hence the notices were for the uninvited, for those who would hopefully come and watch in the streets, for those whose spontaneous attendance would ensure a spectacle. But appearing with admirable eclecticism in journals ranging from *An t-Óglách* to the *Irish Builder*, these notices were also for those who could not and would not attend.[46] They advertised triumph to ally and enemy alike, telling of pageant and honour, selling the wares of a seemingly strong and established state. Abetted by the *Irish Independent*, which turned a short Publicity Department statement into a three-column feature, the government assailed a vast national readership with promises of pomp and circumstance.[47] An important event was to happen in an important state – 'Look on my Works, ye Mighty, and despair!'

However, like seasoned hawkers, the government left little to chance. Building upon the instinct of heroisation which had manifested itself in 'Grand Memorial Booklets', in the Department of External Affairs' expensive and less than successful 'Griffith–Collins Album',[48] and in the beginnings of what was to become the biographical bandwagon, the Publicity Department dispatched photographs of Griffith and Collins to every provincial newspaper and slides to

[43] D. J. Gorey, *DE, official report*, IV, col. 2006 (9 Aug. 1923); W. T. Cosgrave, *DE, official report*, IV, col. 2002 (9 Aug. 1923).

[44] Government Publicity Department Statement, *IT*, 11 Aug. 1923. Invitations were issued in the President's name, Hugh Kennedy MSS, UCDA, P4/1733; NLI, ILB 300p9, item 14.

[45] *II*, 14 Aug. 1923. All newspaper reports both before and after the event quote 5,000 as the number present, but it is unlikely that Leinster Lawn could have accommodated 5,000. Also the following sources refer to only 2,000: DT s5734a, Griffith–Collins Cenotaph – general file, memo by Michael McDunphy to the cabinet, 6 July 1932. This figure is reinforced by a memorandum dating from 7 Aug. 1923, which refers to seating for 2,000 with standing room for a further 500. Desmond FitzGerald MSS, UCDA, P80/303(9).

[46] *An t-Óglách*, 3, 13 (new series), (11 Aug. 1923), p. 9; *Irish Builder*, 65, 16 (11 Aug. 1923), p. 606.

[47] *II*, 11 Aug. 1923.

[48] DF s0046/0039/25, External Affairs – Griffith–Collins Album, cost of publication.

every cinema.[49] Instructed to feature in time for the joint anniversary, the pictures 'duly appeared in the great majority of the papers to which they were sent', while the slides 'were very favourably received by the Picture Houses'.[50] An apparent success, they were deemed worthy of Finance's highly prized £74 5s. 0d. With senses thus bombarded, the populace was primed for the ceremonies on Leinster Lawn, primed for the crucial general election that two more weeks would bring.

'Wary of a replay in the autumn', the government was desperate to secure a stronger mandate at the polls.[51] De Valera was saying too much, making too many noises about the Pact Election, calling the government a 'usurping junta'.[52] Eleven thousand republicans were still detained in Free State jails and a Public Safety Bill, passed on 2 July 1923, resolved to keep them there. An Indemnity Bill, passed a month later, protected the forces of law and order in their pursuit of even more. Standing for Clare again, in a campaign powerfully reminiscent of the 1917 by-election, de Valera promised that 'nothing but a bullet will stop me'.[53] De Valera had to be arrested. He was an embarrassment. In letters from America he was assuming Scarlet Pimpernel proportions, evading capture and gaining a notoriety that implied that 'his responsibility for the bloodshed will be forgotten'.[54] And that above all could not be allowed. Most of the Sinn Féin candidates were on the run, but only de Valera provoked the need for the Publicity Department to 'prepare the public mind' for his arrest with 'a little campaign on his personal responsibility – the death of his dupes etc.'.[55] The Cenotaph became imperative. De Valera had to be taken; the election had to be won convincingly. Standing wronged and yet victorious on Leinster Lawn at the foot of a monument to the two men de Valera could be blamed for killing seemed the requisite 'preparation' for the 'public mind'. He was finally arrested two days after the ceremony.

The spectacle began at 11.00 a.m. A large congregation, echoing the chorus of prayer offered earlier that morning at each military barracks, attended solemn requiem mass at the Pro-Cathedral. Relatives and friends knelt alongside

---

[49] *The Free State – An Saorstát* advertised its 'Collins Memorial Number' between vols. 1, 30 (9 Sept.) and 1, 36 (21 Oct. 1922); *United Irishman*, by its title an appropriation of Griffith's memory, heralded the 'Griffith and Collins Memorial Booklet', 1, 3 (1 Mar. 1923), while in 1, 19 (23 June 1923), it advertised editions of *The resurrection of Hungary* and *Griffith's fiscal policy for Ireland*. George A. Lyons, *Some recollections of Griffith and his times*, found favour in both *An t-Óglách*, 1, 9 (new series), (16 June 1923) and *United Irishman*, 1, 17 (9 June 1923).

[50] DF file 930/2, Commemoration of the death of Griffith and Collins, letter from F. T. Cremins, Department of Publicity to the Secretary to the Minister for Finance, 28 Aug. 1923.

[51] Kevin O'Higgins quoted in Tim Pat Coogan, *De Valera: long fellow, long shadow* (London, 1993), p. 356.

[52] *Ibid.*   [53] *II*, 24 July 1923.

[54] DT s1369/15B, Whereabouts of papers relating to imprisonment of Stack and de Valera, 1923–4, Seán Lester to W. T. Cosgrave; comments of Lindsay Crawford appended, 9 Aug. 1923.

[55] *Ibid.*

ministers and foreign consuls, while the President, the Governor General Timothy Healy, General Mulcahy, the Attorney General Hugh Kennedy and several military officers played the humble servers at the ceremony.[56] But despite the relative grandeur of the setting and the exclusivity of its congregation, this was merely one of many masses offered throughout the country for the repose of the souls of the two dead men. Masses had begun on 8 August, and they continued for another ten days after the unveiling ceremony.[57] Athlone, Kenmare, Sligo, Dun Laoghaire, Bundoran, Limerick, Bray and several churches throughout Dublin offered prayers, and each crowded church bespoke the sincerity of a nation's grief. In Belfast and Derry bishops presided over requiem masses, leading their flock in what was as much a political act in the six troubled counties as it was an act of commemoration or prayer. But apart from the anxious North, even the 'heathens' felt sorrow and paid their respects. *An t-Óglách*, in its own tellingly Catholic way, seemed surprised that 'their fellow Irishmen who differed from them in religion also remembered – services were held in many non-Catholic churches – even in the Synagogues'.[58] Thus the country prayed to its chosen gods, and the country prayed for days. Solemnity gripped the nation and the procession moved to Merrion Square.

At noon the gates of Leinster Lawn opened and, as every daily newspaper seemed altogether too keen to report, the best of Irish political, intellectual, commercial, professional, literary and artistic life mingled: a veritable 'nation not a rabble'.[59] Rubbing shoulders with those who had applied or who had had tickets thrust or bestowed upon them, they took their seats behind the reserved front rows which were soon filled from a separate entrance. Representatives of the army, the judiciary, and the Civic Guards sat with senators and state dignitaries; ministers mingled with Dáil deputies; consuls from France, Belgium, Italy, Argentina and America joined guests from Liverpool, Glasgow, America and Rome.[60] The *Irish Times* called a haughty type of attention to a group of 'Working men visitors and their wives from the North of England',[61] their lowly blue collars proof apparent that in these seats, as in this new nation, 'there was no precedence'.[62] And it was the same for religion. A strange new ecumenism welcomed every creed to Leinster Lawn. The Superior of the Christian Brothers sat with bishops of the Catholic and Protestant faiths, and in their midst was

---

[56] *FJ*, 14 Aug. 1923; *CE*, 14 Aug. 1923.
[57] *II*, 13 and 14 Aug. 1923; *FJ*, 11 and 14 Aug. 1923; *IT*, 14 Aug. 1923; *CE*, 14 Aug. 1923; *An t-Óglách*, 1, 14 (new series), (1 Sept. 1923), p. 12.
[58] *An t-Óglách*, 1, 14 (new series), (1 Sept. 1923), p. 12. For Jewish services, see *II*, 14 Aug. 1923.
[59] George Gavan Duffy, May 1922, quoted in National Archives of Ireland, '*A nation and not a rabble': Ireland in the year July 1921–June 1922* (Dublin, n.d.), frontispiece.
[60] *FJ*, 14 Aug. 1923.
[61] *IT*, 14 Aug. 1923; *II*, 14 Aug. 1923. The group had been invited by the Minister for Industry and Commerce, Joseph McGrath, to complement their visit to Irish workplaces.
[62] *IT*, 14 Aug. 1923.

Rabbi Gudansky, a seemingly magnanimous figure, absolving Griffith of his allegedly anti-Semitic sins of earlier years.[63] This 'Rev. Gudansky' would even 'have a memorable prayer offered in the Cynagogue if requested to do so'.[64] It was ecumenism but no one really knew the right words.

Relatives sat close to the front and just before 1.00 p.m. the President, accompanied by a guard of honour, and a coterie of special guests entered from Leinster House. Collins' sister, Mary Collins-Powell, came with Eamon Duggan, an honoured guest now because he was the last remaining pro-Treatyite signatory of the 1921 agreement. The Governor General followed with Sir John and Lady Lavery. They proceeded to take up their positions directly in front of the monument beside Professor Michael Hayes, Speaker of the Dáil, Judge Cohalan of New York, Diarmuid O'Hegarty, Clerk to the Executive Council, General Cullen, ADC to the Governor General, and Hannah Collins, sister of the dead Commander-in-Chief.

At 'precisely one minute past 1 o'clock' President Cosgrave stood at a dais before the monument and the crowd hushed.[65] With a clear and distinct voice he broke the 'profound silence':[66] 'In the name of the Irish nation and by the Irish nation commissioned and empowered, we offer here a symbol of Ireland's reverence and sorrow, of Ireland's pride and gratitude, to the memory of two heroic men.'[67] From the very first clause the President betrayed himself. All the reverence and sorrow, the pride and the gratitude perished in the triumphalism of his first fifteen words. 'Commissioned and empowered', his party had suddenly become the Irish nation, reading its thoughts, acting in its name. Eleven months of war and the loss of these two men had seemingly taught it that it 'had only to examine my own heart and it told me straight off what the Irish people wanted'.[68] The power was now Cumann na nGaedheal's, and here in the nation's silence de Valera was officially stripped of his clairvoyant privilege. Thus victorious, the President turned to commune with even loftier spirits: 'Scornful alike of glorification and obloquy, Arthur Griffith and Michael Collins, following the path of duty, led forth their people from the land of bondage.' Unknowingly this pair of latter-day Moses had led their people into this strange Israel, from slavery to dominion status, by signing a Treaty fashioned according to the 'designs of Providence' with a capital 'P'. This deification, close to the type of blasphemy that is typical of all Irish nationalism since the Easter 'sacrifice' of 1916, beatified their actions and achievements rather than the men themselves. Free from the republicans' 'selfishness and vain glory', they 'grasped an

[63] *Ibid.* Griffith had lent tacit support to Fr John Creagh's anti-Semitic campaign in Limerick in 1904.
[64] DT s8358, Griffith–Collins commemoration 1923, letter from Philip Sayers to Diarmuid O'Hegarty, 8 Aug. 1923 (spelling from original).
[65] *II*, 14 Aug. 1923.   [66] *FJ*, 14 Aug. 1923.   [67] *Ibid.*
[68] Eamon de Valera, *DE, treaty debate*, p. 274 (6 Jan. 1922).

opportunity so rare in time and circumstance . . . and by an act of courageous decision they endowed this nation at once with liberty and with power to sustain it'. In other words, they signed the Treaty, and this 'opportunity', this 'courageous decision', became their glory. In honouring them one honoured the compromise and the state it left behind. Yet in these words Cosgrave merely echoed the sentiments of Kevin O'Higgins, who felt that 'the tempered judgment of posterity' would find 'the height of Michael Collins' greatness or the depth of his love for his people . . . at the moment on the night of 6th December, 1921' when he 'took pen in hand and signed the Anglo-Irish Treaty'.[69]

But while the President's first three sentences courted the scorn of these modest men for the sake of the glory of the Treaty and the state, the three which followed spoke more of 'reverence and sorrow'. 'A year ago, within the space of two weeks, came the awful tragedy of their death.' The regret seems sincere, the sense of loss unquestioned. He continued: 'They gave their lives in doing their duty to Ireland, and this was the death that they had always looked for and desired. They died before the fruit of their labours could be tasted by them in this life, but many a patriot before them had gone bravely to death with less success in sight.' As his words tumbled out, loss and regret became quickly tangled in a web of patriotism and duty. Tragic death had become noble death, 'always looked for and desired', no longer 'awful'. By dying, they had done their 'duty to Ireland'; they had sanctified the Free State with their blood, establishing it as something which great men thought worthy to die for. Yet when a man admits that in signing a Treaty he has signed his own death warrant, it is difficult to accept that his demise at the hands of a fellow Irishman on a back road in Cork was the one he 'had always looked for and desired'. But three months after civil war, in a fragile state eager to legitimate itself to friend and foe, a needless assassination and the death of a tired body in a less than romantic Dublin hospital were soon tailored by rhetoric to resemble 'many a patriot before them'. However, unsatisfied with mere legitimisation, rhetoric went further. Going to their deaths with more 'success in sight', these paragons of the virtues of compromise had achieved more than their illustrious republican predecessors. Dead republicans, it seems, were vanquished too.

'The tragedy of the deaths of Arthur Griffith and Michael Collins lies in the blindness of the living who do not see, or refuse to see, the stupendous fact of the liberation these two men brought to pass.' Again, like fools drawn to the golden calf rather than the guiding light of Free State salvation, the republicans were upbraided for their sins. But true to type, like all benevolent deities, 'the men to whom we are here paying the homage of memory and gratitude were men with big hearts and generous souls. They would themselves resent it were this occasion to be used for bitterness or vilification toward those who have sought

---

[69] O'Higgins, 'Michael Collins – a personal tribute'.

to blast the fruit of their endeavour.' Had Collins not died, like the country's own personal Jesus, with the words 'Forgive them' on his lips? Was it not the place of the righteous to spread the good news, to turn the other cheek? There was to be no 'bitterness or vilification', just the denigration of the words 'those who sought to blast the fruits of their endeavour' and the sentence: 'Personal vanity, assertion of the individual jealousy, and the bitterness that springs from such mentality – these are the great renders and destroyers, and these have no place in the Ireland of Griffith and Collins.' The cheek may have indeed been turned, but the hand of friendship extended was as well armed and as eager to strike as its war-wounded partner. There were conditions to obey to enter this kingdom of Heaven, this 'Ireland of Griffith and Collins'. Their lives proclaimed an example which the pilgrim had to follow: 'the lesson of work indefatigable, of sacrifice of self, of tolerance wide and generous for disagreement in opinion, but intolerance most stern of attack upon the safety of the nation or upon the rule of the people'. Disagreement would be tolerated but disobedience would not:

the crown of these two beloved lives will be the paramount rule of a united people in this land – united in individual obedience to the authority of the whole, however sections may differ in political programmes or dissent from majority judgment as to what is wisest and best for the nation at a particular time.

Doffing his cap to aspirations of unity within the twenty-six, and the intimated thirty-two counties, the President's was an empty gesture. In the jails still full of republican prisoners, in the Northern Parliament, in the light of a later mutiny by the converted, it was all mere talk. In fact Cosgrave's last two sentences made sure it could be nothing more:

A year ago . . . an attack brought Ireland to the brink of what might have been her final ruin as a nation. But the Irish people stood true to the memory and counsels of their dead deliverers, and now, with gratitude and pride, if with reverence and sorrow, the Irish people calls to mind, and will again call to mind in the years to come, as long as Ireland is Ireland, the wisdom and courage of these two men, Griffith and Collins, the architect and the master-builder of our nation.

Ending in triumphalism, with a vision of the nation on its knees turning to its saviours, its 'dead deliverers', the President exiled all who thought that this Free State was not Ireland: all who thought the 'architect' and 'master-builder' had left a mere dominion that was treason to the word 'nation'. These men were to be remembered as long as 'Ireland is Ireland', for what they had done and for what Cosgrave, not de Valera, was about to do.

It had taken the President just under nine minutes to say these words.[70] The newspapers called his speech 'affecting', 'effective', 'touching'; it was 'an

---

[70] *FJ*, 14 Aug. 1923.

historic oration', a 'great tribute to the Patriotic dead', and many eyes were seemingly 'dimmed while he spoke'.[71] But however effusive this praise may seem, the commendation has to be put in the context of the fact that each newspaper dwelt longer on the clarity of Cosgrave's voice than on the meaning of his words. He was 'eloquent', 'he spoke with clear enunciation' in a resonant and 'at times thrilling voice which carried to the limits of the gathering'.[72] Each newspaper printed every word he spoke. The *Irish Times* made no comment but the fact that he was clearly heard.[73] The *Cork Examiner* called it brief, eloquent and, yet again, clear.[74] On two occasions the *Freeman's Journal* applauded his voice, a sentiment which the *Irish Independent* heartily endorsed.[75] None but the London *Times* went so far as to say that the 'glowing words' were 'in excellent taste'; none went so far as to subject his brief oration to objective analysis.[76] But in a sense it is foolish to expect them to. They all agreed with every word he said and what else could they have realistically expected him to say: why question, why comment? They spoke of dignity, never disapproval, of 'a time of solemnity not of speeches'; and they tailored their praise accordingly, muting what would, on happier occasions, have been a more ringing imprimatur.[77] Invited in large numbers to observe from the special press enclosure within Leinster Lawn, journalists watched. Before them, many of their own editors in their Sunday best were part of the pageantry. After all, to the government, Healy of the *Irish Times*, Harrington of the *Irish Independent*, Hooper of the *Freeman's Journal* and Crosbie of the *Cork Examiner* 'are more important personally to the State than many of the other people who will no doubt receive invitations'.[78] Publicity was all. The state provided the spectacle, and the papers repaid the debt writ large in acquiescent column inches.

The newspapers said exactly what the state wanted them to say. They published aerial photographs provided by the government, while certain sentences even dared to recur verbatim.[79] Each described the unveiling, the President pulling the appropriately patriotic green rope which released the white covering from the monument. Each recounted the shrill notes of 'The Last Post' played by army buglers; the large laurel wreath laid by Cosgrave at the base of the monument; the wreaths from General McMahon on behalf of the army, from the Laverys 'in proud memory of the glorious and beloved dead', from Liam Devlin, owner of the hotel in Parnell Square where Collins had often met and hid with his infamous Squad.[80] All spoke of the four and a half minutes of silence

71 *Ibid.*; *II*, 14 Aug. 1923.   72 *CE*, 14 Aug. 1923; *II*, 14 Aug. 1923; *FJ*, 14 Aug. 1923.
73 *IT*, 14 Aug. 1923.   74 *CE*, 14 Aug. 1923.   75 *FJ*, 14 Aug. 1923; *II*, 14 Aug. 1923.
76 *The Times*, 14 Aug. 1923.   77 *II*, 14 Aug. 1923.
78 DT s8358, Griffith–Collins commemoration 1923, letter from Seán Lester to M. McDunphy, 4 Aug. 1923.
79 *IT*, 14 Aug. 1923; *FJ*, 14 Aug. 1923; *II*, 14 Aug. 1923, *CE*, 14 Aug. 1923.
80 *II*, 19 Mar. 1924.

which followed, the four military aeroplanes which circled overhead, breaking that silence, and the large guns in the Phoenix Park which fired their respectful salute across the city, instructing the troops to fix bayonets and present arms. All told of buglers sounding the general salute, of John Kells Ingram's 'The memory of the dead' with its 'Who fears to speak of '98' bringing matters to a suitably nationalist close.[81]

Joined in a union of adjectives, four national newspapers and the London *Times* considered themselves impressed, touched, struck by the historic ceremonies 'appropriate in their solemnity, orderliness and manifestation of affection for the great dead'.[82] But while the *Freeman's Journal* spoke of the 'partly civil and partly military' ceremony which 'was at once simple yet superb; brief yet comprehensive', *An t-Óglách*, the journal of the Irish army, was a little more honest:[83]

The ceremony in connection with the unveiling of the Cenotaph to the memory of Arthur Griffith and General Michael Collins was as simple as it was impressive. One felt throughout that he was participating in a great National act of Faith and Hope. It is only fitting that tributes of this kind on the part of the nation to its mighty dead should be of a military character, and should be entrusted to and carried out by the Army of the nation. The Army today typifies the living reality of the ideals for which our bravest sacrificed themselves. It is the first Irish Army the nation has had since the disaster of Kinsale. It is in every sense the Army of the people, composed of and led by the sons of the people. It is maintained by the nation for the avowed purposes of defending its right to shape its own destiny according to its own ideals. It is accepted as such the world over. The existence of the Army today is the Nation's surest guarantee of the recognition of that right. The participation of the Army in these memorial ceremonies is the pledge of the living to the dead that this right shall be maintained by the full strength of and all the resources of the nation.[84]

Though reading like an attempted verbal coup, assailing the state's bid for ceremonial glory, this army bombast was closer to the reality of 13 August 1923 than the newspapers were prepared to concede. Apart from the nine-minute speech, the four and a half minutes of silence and the brief concession of wreath laying, the 2,000 people seated in Leinster Lawn and the thousands gathered round the city were merely guests at what was effectively a show of military strength.

Yet, given that two of the four positions on the committee charged with commemorating the anniversary 'in a fitting manner' were taken by General Richard Mulcahy, Minister for Defence, and by Seán Ó Muirthile, Quartermaster General of the Army, the militarism was not only inevitable but essential.[85]

[81] 'The memory of the dead', or more popularly, 'Who fears to speak of '98?', in John Kells Ingram, *Sonnets and other poems* (London, 1900), pp. 104–6.
[82] *II*, 14 Aug. 1923.   [83] *FJ*, 14 Aug. 1923.
[84] *An t-Óglách*, 1, 14 (new series), (1 Sept. 1923), p. 2.
[85] Cabinet minutes G2/2, c1/130, 7 July 1923; *ibid.*, c1/129, 3 July 1923.

From early morning obedient uniformed men imposed the military will. Military police marshalled proceedings inside the grounds 'with all the efficiency and all the urbanity of trained stewards', while outside the Dublin Metropolitan Police regulated traffic and herded people eager to get a better look.[86] Their corralled enthusiasm was to be rewarded not necessarily by the unveiling, which could not have taken more than twenty minutes, but by the army pageant which complemented the altogether brief formalities on Leinster Lawn. Thousands of troops, gathered from the country's battalions, were assembled in the Phoenix Park. Joined by a regiment of Civic Guards, the procession crossed the Liffey and paraded through the city.[87] Snaking its impressive way, it engulfed Parliament Street, Dame Street, College Green and Nassau Street, consuming attention with the relish of its colour, its music and its pageantry. A full hour before the ceremony 'was occupied by the marching of military contingents' and 'the period of waiting was enlivened by the strains of a military band, which played airs appropriate to the occasion'.[88] With salutes and aeroplanes and guns, the army dominated the solemn spectacle of the unveiling ceremony. Even the notes of the military buglers' 'Last Post' were what rendered the event 'doubly impressive indeed mournful'.[89] But when 'what was mournful in the day's ceremonial passed away', it was the army which strode victoriously on, returning triumphantly through the city back to barracks to 'the blare of the brass in stirring military marches'.[90]

In truth the unveiling had been a mere civil interlude in what had been established as a military showpiece from early that morning. But the soldiers' morning prayers for the repose of the souls of the two leaders were but a prelude to the military parades which invaded every barracks to coincide with the unveiling on Leinster Lawn. At 1.00 p.m. the men paraded and presented arms at all headquarter posts throughout the country. They stood to until 1.15 when, to synchronise with the salute of the heavy artillery in the city, the general salute was sounded and the troops presented arms.[91] The Civic Guard was also conscripted for the countrywide spectacle and the eight hundred who paraded at the Guard Depot at the Phoenix Park in Dublin were mimicked by the small bands of men stationed in the Killeshandras and Fermoys and Mullingars throughout the country.[92] Even civilian masses in the days that followed were not safe from parading troops and Civic Guards who came to pray with the people they had sworn to protect.

Not content with ubiquity, the army and the state were eager to impress their omnipotence. Army power and efficiency were stressed at every turn: a comfort

[86] *IT*, 14 Aug. 1923.
[87] No precise figure exists for the number of troops that took part in the 1923 ceremony. Two thousand took part in 1924.
[88] *FJ*, 14 Aug. 1923; *II*, 14 Aug. 1923.   [89] *II*, 14 Aug. 1923; *CE*, 14 Aug. 1923.
[90] *FJ*, 14 Aug. 1923.   [91] *II*, 14 Aug. 1923.   [92] *FJ*, 14 Aug. 1923; *CE*, 14 Aug. 1923.

to the loyal, a riposte to those who could still consider rebellion. The 'immense muster of military officers' which thrilled Merrion Square at the unveiling was praised for its 'precision and regularity'.[93] Taking their places 'with a smart piece of drill work, which, with the steadiness and fine carriage of the men, was good enough for any Army', the *Irish Times* redeemed these bands of men criticised for their inexperience and their greed for the 'King's shilling'.[94] But apart from waxing lyrical about the efficiency of men, the *Irish Times* recounted tales of guns that could hush a city, and whispered the wondrous names of mysterious fighter planes. 'Four aeroplanes circled over the city, and gave general emphasis to the great victories of Griffith and Collins in bringing to Ireland the mastery of her own affairs and equipment of every description for her own defence.'[95] 'The great victories' were echoed in every marching step, in every sputtering 'fast-flying Bristol Fighter' and DH9. 'The great demonstration of affectionate remembrance' instilled with 'the spirit of the triumph which has resulted for their native land from the massive and enduring work of the two immortals mourned and honoured today' was felt for the next nine days in the official period of mourning inaugurated by the ceremony on Leinster Lawn. Each day officers and men paraded at general headquarters at midday for the general salute in memory of the dead.[96] On the tenth day, 22 August 1923, the anniversary of Michael Collins' death, mourning ended with a victory march:

Irish troops on the 'Fifteen Acres' – Infantry, Cavalry, Artillery, Special Services – serried masses of men in green uniform [were] drawn up in Review formation – bayonets flashing and accoutrements glinting in the brilliant sunshine between showers ... The time of mourning is past and the Army has mustered from the four corners of the country for the first *Bothar Buadha* parade – in proud memory of those twain who first set their feet upon the Road to Victory.[97]

With aeroplanes and heavy artillery on the parade ground at the Phoenix Park and with bands and buglers at the ready, the President's arrival commenced the ceremony of the blessing of the flag of the Irish army. The proud parading soldiers then marched their way through the city, saluting the guarded Cenotaph, to the cheers of 'enthusiastic crowds'.[98] Cork, Limerick, Carlow, Waterford, Athlone, Tralee, Templemore, Dun Laoghaire, Galway and Sligo saw similar scenes, all witnessing this 'apotheosis of the wartime army', this last triumphant hurrah of a carefully staged victory march which had taken its first steps before a hurriedly moulded plaster monument on Leinster Lawn.[99] But while the army announced that 'the Griffith–Collins commemoration will close

[93] *II*, 14 Aug. 1923; *FJ*, 14 Aug. 1923.   [94] *IT*, 14 Aug. 1923.
[95] *Ibid.*; *CE*, 14 Aug. 1923.
[96] *FJ*, 14 Aug. 1923; *An t-Óglách*, 1, 14 (new series), (1 Sept. 1923), p. 13.
[97] *An t-Óglách*, 1, 14, (new series), (1 Sept. 1923), p. 13.   [98] *Ibid.*; *II*, 23 Aug. 1923.
[99] John P. Duggan, *A history of the Irish army* (Dublin, 1991), p. 106.

tomorrow ... with the first *Bothar Buadha* [Road to Victory] Parade in Dublin', the Civic Guard and the DMP disobeyed the military orders and marched.[100] On 23 August 1923, 300 Civic Guards wended their way through the city, placing a wreath on the Cenotaph before marching to the graves of the dead men in Glasnevin Cemetery. The following day 200 DMP men repeated the ritual, this mark of respect masquerading as victory, this show of strength disguised as something solemn.[101]

Though the army enacted its 'Road to Victory' march, the title which was soon assigned to the ceremony at the Cenotaph itself, the government performed its own victory play at the unveiling with its cast of invited guests. Act I spoke of sovereignty, foreign consuls playing their dutiful parts, proving the Free State was indeed a nation. The second act bespoke approval. Religion assented by its episcopal presence, while Dr Fogarty's published commendation recalled for all the excommunication of the foe.[102] 'An assemblage entirely representative of the whole nation' brought the drama to a close as the great and the good, the George Russells, the John McCormacks, led the nation by example to their seats and paid homage to the state.[103] But as the curtain closed on this pageant, this gathering of pro-Treatyite players left a bitter postscript to the civil war; they left a legacy of triumphalism which could only serve to make the memory of the war even more divisive. Yet who could begrudge them their triumphalism? Three months after war it was necessary: understandable if a little unwise. Arms were hidden, not surrendered; jails were still full of republican prisoners; they would remain full for another ten months. Fear needed triumph just as the people needed triumph: a gesture to show that the civil war had purpose, that the sacrifices made had not been in vain. Most of all the government yearned for glory and all the legitimacy that triumph wields. It needed to thwart its enemy and de Valera knew it. The Cenotaph embodied a desire which he had recognised as early as May 1923: 'peace by understanding would be for the best in the national interest – but our opponents want a "triumph"'.[104] Nine months later that desire had reached a venomous pitch: 'I think we ought to say again and again, you could have won – the fight was there for you to win, you should have won, why didn't you? – the answer is because you put up the white flag! ... 50,000 ready to die for the MacSwiney Republic! No! We couldn't take 50,000 prisoners much less find 50,000 to die for Mary.'[105] Wilful and victorious in August 1923, the government rubbed the republican nose in a public pageant of anti-Treatyite defeat.

---

[100] *II*, 21 Aug. 1923.

[101] *Iris an Ghárda*, 1, 28 (3 Sept. 1923), pp. 2–9; *FJ*, 23–5 Aug. 1923; *II*, 23–5 Aug. 1923.

[102] *FJ*, 14 Aug. 1923; *II*, 14 Aug. 1923.   [103] *FJ*, 14 Aug. 1923.

[104] De Valera to Monsignor Hagan, 19 May 1923, Hagan MSS, quoted in Dermot Keogh, *The Vatican, the bishops and Irish politics 1919–39* (Cambridge, 1986), p. 119.

[105] DT s585, Attempted reorganisation of people of old Sinn Féin tendencies, 1924, letter from W. T. Cosgrave to Richard Mulcahy, 1 Feb. 1924.

Eager to see the humiliation,

The general public assembled without the railings of Leinster Lawn, and were marshalled by men of the DMP into thick lines, which stretched from Leinster Street along Merrion Square as far as the entrance to Government Buildings. A great number of them could not obtain more than a glimpse of the proceedings, but they stood on, patiently and reverently, all through. The windows of all houses commanding a view of the Lawn were filled, and the roofs of many houses were occupied. A big crowd swarmed over the roof of Government Buildings.[106]

Swelled by the thousands of visitors for Horse Show Week, the 'great throng which had gathered from all parts of the country' waited and watched, undiminished by inclement weather.[107] The curious and the converted cheered, listening to the strains of 'Who fears to speak of '98' and the nationalism its playing attempted to appropriate, and watching the national flags rise in triumph on Government Buildings from the respect and remorse which half-masted them. They stood in silence even though many could not have seen the Cenotaph or heard the President's speech; they stood in solemnity and sorrow, without another monument, comforted by the ceremony of remembrance which said that war was truly over. 'They stood on patiently and reverently' because throughout they were patrolled by the police, because 'a sergt. and 10 constables' were 'posted at intervals along Merrion Square . . . to be in a position to deal with any person misconducting or acting in a disorderly manner'.[108] In tens and forties police patrolled. Dissent was not countenanced by any but the *Irish Times*. Breaking the vow of silence which the other newspapers had taken, it told of a 'small crowd of women who long before the hour for the ceremonies to commence showed that they were there to "interrupt"'.[109] Quickly 'removed' by the vigilant police, these women were undoubtedly part of the vociferous, and predominantly female, Prisoners' Defence Association whose members' protests on behalf of republican prisoners were by now a familiar sight at the gates of city jails. However, this was the only voice the republicans raised that day. The enemies of the state said nothing, their silence echoing the prayers which republican prisoners said on their knees in Free State prisons at the news of Collins' death. Tom Barry remembered that morning in Kilmainham Jail: 'There was a heavy silence throughout the jail, and ten minutes later from the corridor outside the top tier of cells I looked down on the extraordinary spectacle of about a thousand kneeling Republican prisoners spontaneously reciting the Rosary for the repose of the soul of the dead Michael Collins.'[110] The republicans' surviving newspapers chose to ignore the ceremony rather than risk the unpopularity of criticising an act of mourning. Caught between

---

[106] *FJ*, 14 Aug. 1923.   [107] *The Times*, 14 Aug. 1923; *II*, 14 Aug. 1923; *FJ*, 14 Aug. 1923.
[108] DT s8358, Griffith–Collins commemoration 1923, memo on 'police arrangements', n.d.
[109] *IT*, 14 Aug. 1923.   [110] Tom Barry, *Guerilla days in Ireland* (Dublin, 1949), p. 180.

contempt and respect, the republic was silent, content to let the state mourn in peace.

Although 'mourning in victory', the state did mourn.[111] Marching past the Cenotaph, the soldiers grieved, recalling 'the soldier, friend and comrade who had been with them in many a hard-fought fight, but whom a cruel fate had snatched away from them'.[112] And while it was unlikely that Collins had actually fought side by side with any of them, he was still their leader, their first Commander-in-Chief lost to them, an army built on rank and hierarchy and the need to be led. He was mourned by the Dublin Brigade, some of whom were members of his 'Squad' in the War of Independence: the Brigade, which according to one of the many versions of his dying words, was charged with burying him.[113] Though mythologising had left nothing more than an archetype, this 'Chief' was loved and mourned, missed by the young soldiers brought on stretchers to Leinster Lawn to represent the injured men, who attempted, despite their injuries, to join the general salute. He was missed by the 'four old comrades of General Collins [who] had marched up, and, with all the military dignity of such an occasion, mounted guard, one at each corner of the memorial, leaning with lowered heads over their reversed rifles'.[114] Unrehearsed and unprovoked, these men acted out of a genuine grief, a grief which much of the day's orchestrated triumphalism conspired to hide.

Conspire though it might, the day could not conceal the sense of loss. Related as 'pathetic' or 'touching' incidents, writ large in newspaper headings with an exactitude which seemed more eager to titillate than to empathise, the private sorrow of these men's families and friends was rewritten as public spectacle. By accepting the invitation they bartered their privacy; their sorrow sold for the sake of the stability of the government. But, as was the case with London's Cenotaph, their grief turned what was ostensibly conceived as a public monument into a site of private mourning. Invited to witness their relatives thus posthumously honoured, it became instead a pilgrimage to a personal shrine. The Collins family was represented by Seán Collins, brother of the late general, by his sisters Hannah, Mary Collins-Powell, Katie Sheridan and Margaret Collins-O'Driscoll, along with several nieces, nephews and cousins.[115] Griffith was mourned by his son Nevin, his daughter Ita, his sister, two brothers, Frank and William, and his two brothers-in-law, Frs Leo and Peter Sheehan, OFM.[116] Mrs Griffith refused to attend. She objected to the Cenotaph and wished 'her husband's name erased from such a senseless show'. To her it was nothing but a 'stunt...not at all in concord with his [Griffith's] life of sacrifice and

---

[111]   Emmet Dalton, 'Comrade's moving story of Michael Collins' last fight', *FJ*, 22 Aug. 1923.
[112]   *FJ*, 23 Aug. 1923.
[113]   'Let the Dublin Guards bury me' was used as the title of the cinematic news item covering the funeral of Collins. *Topical Budget*, Irish Film Archive, item no. 575–1.
[114]   *IT*, 23 Aug. 1923.   [115]   *IT*, 14 Aug. 1923; *FJ*, 14 Aug. 1923.   [116]   *IT*, 14 Aug. 1923.

honesty'.[117] She wrote a year later: 'money enough was wasted on that horror with its pagan emblem. I have never found out who made money on it – anyway it's a disgrace to them & I'm glad to see the medalions [sic] are chipping badly.'[118] While she wanted these objections 'at once published ... in the daily press', she chose to grieve privately at a mass celebrated by her brothers at Clontarf on the anniversary of Griffith's death and by laying wreaths with her children at her husband's grave.[119] One newspaper reported that a wreath was laid on her behalf at the Cenotaph, but it was not part of the ceremony and was not reported elsewhere.[120] She was never to go to Leinster Lawn, too wary of the motives of a government which taxed the pension it had only grudgingly granted her. She never used the 'perpetual ticket of admission to the Cenotaph' which Cosgrave posted to her within days of the ceremony.[121] It gave her access to Leinster Lawn whenever she wished; she never went. But she sent her children; she sent them every August. She sent them eager that they should not be overshadowed by what she considered the place-hunting Collinses; that 'AG's son should have a look in'.[122] There they watched their father honoured, their sadness conscripted to the service of Cumann na nGaedheal. Eleven-year-old Ita Griffith began to cry when the portrait medallion of her father was unveiled. Her brother Nevin stood fatherless and pitiful in his national costume. Now the head of the family, his hand was shaken with 'much emotion' by the brother of Michael Collins, even though this new patriarch still wrote 'To Daddy' with a child's innocence on the wreath he had laid on his father's grave the day before.[123] The *Irish Independent* chronicled every impulse of their grief, parading them as the little fatherless victims of de Valera's evil. Not so easy to exploit, the Collins family was solemn and silent. One newspaper mentioned the 'pathetic figure' of Kitty Kiernan, but she did not attend.[124] Another mistook Lady Lavery for the fiancée of the dead Commander-in-Chief. The mistake was pointed out by a rival newspaper the following day as an 'amusing case of mistaken identity'.[125] While Lady Lavery may have 'derived ironic pleasure' from the error, it is difficult to imagine that the same was true of Kitty

---

[117] Copy of a letter sent anonymously on behalf of Mrs Griffith to General Richard Mulcahy and Ernest Blythe, 30 July 1923, Desmond FitzGerald MSS, UCDA, P80/303(8).

[118] Department of an Taoiseach s33913, Griffith and Collins – ownership and erection of memorials at graves, letter from Maud Griffith, 17 July 1924. (It is not clear who the letter is addressed to. It merely opens 'A cara'.)

[119] Copy of a letter sent anonymously on behalf of Mrs Griffith to General Richard Mulcahy and Ernest Blythe.

[120] *FJ*, 14 Aug. 1923.

[121] DT s8358, Griffith–Collins commemoration 1923, memo by W. T. Cosgrave, 28 Aug. 1923.

[122] Letter from Maud Griffith to Desmond FitzGerald, n.d., Desmond FitzGerald MSS, UCDA, P80/5112(9).

[123] *II*, 14 Aug. 1923.   [124] *Ibid.*

[125] Unidentified press cutting, Aug. 1923, Lady Lavery Scrapbooks; quoted in Sinéad McCoole, *Hazel: a life of Lady Lavery 1880–1935* (Dublin, 1996), p. 106.

Kiernan.[126] Lady Lavery's prominent presence is indeed fuel for those who wish to stoke the fires of Collins' philandering:[127] she was seated in the front row, she laid one of the few wreaths at the Cenotaph. But whatever the nature of the association, the day was for the woman to grieve. It just seemed cruel that the same newspaper implied that Lady Lavery would have looked more wistful if she had known she had been mistaken for the less 'charming' 'Miss Kitty'.[128] Yet grief was not restricted to the Lady Laverys, or to the families of these men. Sobbing reportedly broke the four and a half minutes' silence, and at the end of the ceremony men and women walked to the Cenotaph to offer prayers at the state's new altar.[129] Grief was genuine, despite the manipulations.

But the manipulators also mourned: their prayers on Leinster Lawn were augmented by trips to Glasnevin Cemetery in the days that followed. They went as friends, as comrades, as the bereaved; amongst them Colonel Joseph O'Reilly and Eamon Duggan.[130] They added tributes to those placed there by the public, their tokens lying next to the wreaths and flowers that were laid by a solemn and unprovoked civic grief. Those flowers, like the presence of the thousands at the unveiling of the Cenotaph, bespoke a sincerity and an ardour which would always guarantee the success of the government's commemorative endeavours. Commemoration seemed instinctive, the natural expression of a people schooled in the centenary of 1798 and the beatifying masses for the dead of 1916; it was instinctive even if erecting monuments was not. And commemoration was political: rewriting 1798 as a quest for faith and fatherland, redrafting 1916 as circumstances required. However, none was as political as the monument on Leinster Lawn, commemorating the figures of an Irish divide for which the Parnell split was a mere bloodless rehearsal. But enthusiasm for the Cenotaph, though partisan, never waned. It wrote letters, asking for Leinster House to be renamed 'Griffith Buildings' to mark the unveiling. It wrote poems, short, purposeful, sombre poems, elegies to the occasion, like one man's proud 'At the Cenotaph'. Enthusiasm even sold photographs, pictures of the ceremony advertised at two shillings each: costly little mementoes bought because the day must have been great.[131]

'In the heartfelt tribute of the people's minds honour was done to Arthur Griffith and Michael Collins ... their work for Ireland is remembered. The sacrifice of their lives is remembered too.'[132] Thus spoke the editor of the *Irish Independent*, who, having looked into the people's minds, found merely honour

126 McCoole, *Hazel*, p. 106.   127 *II*, 15 Aug. 1923.
128 Unidentified press cutting, Aug. 1923, Lady Lavery Scrapbooks; quoted in McCoole, *Hazel*, p. 106.
129 *CE*, 14 Aug. 1923.   130 *II*, 15 Aug. 1923.
131 Letter to the editor, *II*, 10 Aug. 1923; advertisement, *II*, 15 Aug. 1923; 'At the Cenotaph', *II*, 13 Aug. 1923.
132 *II*, 14 Aug. 1923.

there. What he did not see as he lamented the end of the 'age of great monuments' was the enthusiasm that greeted what he correctly called an austere memorial. He felt many people would criticise the Cenotaph for its design, though never its purpose: 'no doubt a more beautifully wrought memorial might have been designed'.[133] No doubt indeed, yet why was an attempt made to make miniature reproductions of a piece of sculpture which even the most diplomatic could only describe as 'not imposing'?[134] Like many of its predecessors built in the enthusiastic wake of the 1798 centenary, the Cenotaph was a triumph of purpose over design.[135] Lacking splendour and even permanency, it was not a thing of beauty, yet a nameless company saw a market for souvenir reproductions of an edifice of peeling wood and plaster.[136] Like cheap, badly hewn copies of the guillotine, the souvenir Cenotaph would be sold for its symbolism instead of its aesthetics. It would have a market because it was 'more than a tribute to the dead. It stands as a proof that the work to which they gave their lives has been carried to success';[137] it would sell to the enthusiastic merely by association.

Yet, thanks to the Department of Finance, it would never sell. There were no objections to the idea mooted to George Atkinson by the agent of the anonymous manufacturing firm in early 1924. Atkinson was willing to submit his design to reproduction 'subject to the approval and permission of the government'.[138] Indeed his request for the extension of the copyright was not unfavourably met by the experienced publicist FitzGerald, and enquiries were circulated to the Office of Public Works, the Department of Finance and the cabinet. By 10 April 1924 Finance was prepared to 'grant the present application on the understanding that a similar permission would be given to anyone else applying for it', showing a rare alacrity for the cautious ministry.[139] Yet, 'as a question of policy' was deemed to be involved, the matter was brought before the Executive Council, where the Minister for Finance, Ernest Blythe, pronounced that he was 'not ready' to deal with the issue.[140] The minister was unprepared, and the matter did not arise again. That the government was prepared to consider the enterprise at all was proof that the Cenotaph was something more than a mere monument to the dead. The state seemed happy to barter all the orchestrated solemnity of the crumbling structure, selling it into a talismanic slavery to adorn

---

[133] *Ibid.*   [134] *The Times*, 14 Aug. 1923.
[135] Owens, 'Nationalist monuments in Ireland', p. 106.
[136] DT s5734a, Griffith–Collins Cenotaph – general file, letter from George Atkinson to Desmond FitzGerald, 4 Mar. 1924. The first report of the monument peeling dates from 10 Dec. 1923, DF file 930.
[137] Editorial, *FJ*, 14 Aug. 1923.
[138] DT s5734a, Griffith–Collins Cenotaph – general file, letter from George Atkinson to Desmond FitzGerald, 4 Mar. 1924.
[139] *Ibid.*, letter from Arthur Codling to Diarmuid Ó hÉigceartaigh, Secretary of the Executive Council, 10 Apr. 1924.
[140] *Ibid.*, agenda of the Executive Council, 14 Apr. 1924.

the mantelpieces of the faithful. But the government was only eager to promote this portable piece of victory as long as it was convenient. When the issue required attention, when it prompted 'a question of policy' to be discussed and decided, it disappeared from government files because the Minister for Finance simply was not, and never bothered to be, ready.[141]

But while the minister procrastinated, the government opted for ambiguity. Director of Publicity, Seán Lester, having watched passing Londoners salute their Cenotaph, felt that 'it would be a desirable thing if we could arrange to have a similar honour done to the Collins–Griffith Cenotaph Memorial'.[142] Though shamelessly aping the former oppressor, this sin of imperialism was deemed worthwhile because

The honouring of the memory of Collins and Griffith in such a way would have a psychological effect on public opinion. Anything that can be done to preserve a reverent affection for the late Commander-in-Chief and the late President will tend to strengthen the position of the State ... If the military and members of the police force saluted as they passed it would be an example for civilians and would give us an opportunity of influencing civilians through the press.[143]

Tempted by Lester's promises of strengthening the position of the state, the Department of Defence quickly capitulated and within two months of his late October suggestion, the ministry issued General Routine Order Number 56, which instructed 'all Officers, NCOs, and men to salute when passing the Cenotaph or to raise their hats if in civilian dress'.[144] Thus the soldiers of Ireland were ordered to salute a monument which, by Seán Lester's own admission, was already falling apart.[145] Already affected by the weather in December 1923, the medallions were peeling badly by March 1926. But a government that once promised to replace it as quickly as sincerity could manage, now refused to lift what would have been a costly finger. Arthur Codling of the Department of Finance had no desire 'to be fussy in the matter' but he recognised that the neglect of the monument was 'the sort of thing that busybodies like to call attention to when overlooked by a public department'.[146] Unafraid of the 'busybodies', the government, and more notably the Office of Public Works, acknowledged Codling's anxiety and did nothing at all.

Nineteen twenty-seven changed their minds. Kevin O'Higgins was murdered and the government were haunted by the spectre of 1922. Requesting another

---

[141] *Ibid.*

[142] Department of Defence A10426, Saluting of the Cenotaph by soldiers, Seán Lester to C. B. O'Connor, Secretary Department of Defence, 17 Oct. 1923.

[143] *Ibid.*

[144] *Ibid.*, Adjutant General's Department, General Routine Order No. 56, Saluting; *An t-Óglách*, 1, 20 (new series), (15 Dec. 1923), p. 27.

[145] DF file 930, Seán Lester to Mr McGann of the President's Office, 10 Dec. 1923.

[146] *Ibid.*, Arthur Codling to Sir Philip Hanson, OPW, 3 Mar. 1926.

show of strength in the face of the weakness that let gunmen kill the Vice-President, the state turned again to the crumbling piece of wood and plaster and added an unpopular martyr to its tarnished tomb. Although the memory of O'Higgins was linked with the monument at the August 1927 ceremony, this association was only confirmed in 1928 when a rectangular plaque, or 'medallion' as the files called it, of the dead minister was added to the memorial.[147] Placed directly beneath the cross, between the medallions of Griffith and Collins, the addition was marked by a silent ceremony. There was no speech to signify the attachment of this last painted plaster mould, no fine words uttered over the heads of this ill-matched trinity, sanctified on the state's slowly rotting cross. There were just the marching troops, the artillery, the bands, and the ministers entering Leinster Lawn together, in the same show of strength they had been ordered to perform in 1927.[148] There was just the garish plaster which held the medallion in place with its white newness mocking the weathered surrounds. Again it was a solemn occasion, a symbolic rebuke to match the stringent Public Safety Bill which the murder also provoked. But the fact that the attachment of the medallion coincided with the scaling down of the pageant was indicative of a marked shift in the government's position since 1923. This shift was perceptible in the tardy approach of the government to the commissioning of the medallion itself. The decision to do so was only taken on 13 July 1928, over a year after O'Higgins' death and a mere thirty-six days before the scheduled ceremony; and then the task was only assigned verbally to the sculptor Oliver Sheppard by his friend, Senator Oliver St John Gogarty. For a fee of £50 he constructed a larger-than-life profile, based on the death mask of the minister which he had independently cast. Approval came only on 9 August, and while all concerned seemed quite happy to settle for the exhibition of the medallion at the ceremony on the 19th, it was affixed in time as Sheppard had planned.[149]

Much had changed since 1923, even more since the foundation of Fianna Fáil in 1926 and its entry, at the government's behest, into the Dáil a year later. It was a different Cumann na nGaedheal which stood before the Cenotaph on Leinster Lawn in August 1928: an uneasy Cumann na nGaedheal not altogether sure why it was really there. The nature of O'Higgins' death called for this ceremony in the same way that it demanded and received the token of a lavish funeral that dominated the streets of the capital and closed all government departments.[150] Yet while the government mourned the loss of another of its

---

[147] The nomenclature is maintained here.
[148] DT s5484, Griffith–Collins commemoration ceremony 1927, letter from M. McDunphy to each minister, 18 Aug. 1927.
[149] DF s200/0006/28, Commemorative ceremony 1928 – addition of medallion portrait of the late Vice-President, Mr Kevin O'Higgins to Cenotaph.
[150] DT s5478, Kevin O'Higgins' death.

more dynamic figures, the President's graveside oration hinted at what would become by 1928 the government's ambivalence. Though praising the efficiency of his work and crediting him with the now commonplace messianic forgiveness of his killers, Cosgrave declared, with a type of honesty scarce in such orations, that O'Higgins was 'insensible at times towards the emotions of others'.[151] What the President had tried to say politely was that Kevin O'Higgins was not very popular. He may have topped the polls; he may have been an efficient, even respected politician; but he was never popular.[152] He was one of the most ardent pursuers of republicans during the civil war. And he had more cause than most. The knowledge that 'father was shot because of me' doubtless contributed to his advocacy of a stringent policy of law and order.[153] While the republicans repaid him with an enmity which was rivalled only by their feelings for General Richard Mulcahy and the Dublin Brigade, the people in general were just as ungrateful. His Intoxicating Liquor Bill provoked by his 'duty to inculcate a sense of public responsibility into the reluctant natives' was yet another means of his own haughty alienation.[154] To the rather timid Cosgrave, he was always a threat, ever eager to fill his leader's ill-fitting presidential shoes. To J. J. Walsh, O'Higgins had 'won much respect, much hatred, and little popularity', a damning sort of praise from a colleague with which a reluctant public would only ever grudgingly concur.[155] He had been brutally gunned down on his way to mass. Each of the twelve bullets that hit him turned this hate figure into a type of hero, a status which Kevin O'Higgins, 'a soul incapable of remorse or rest', would never have achieved by himself.[156]

After four years of a type of peace, assassination could again shock, turning 'the strong man of the government', the 'Irish Mussolini', into a bleeding body in the street, to be mourned by a wife and two young children.[157] His assassination also shook the government out of what was not complacency but was certainly the assumption that such violence had ended. After all, mainstream republicanism was 'slightly constitutional' now; the 'Soldiers of Destiny' had marched out of the shadows of their wilderness years behind de Valera's new political standard.[158] In many ways O'Higgins' death brought back 1923, because in many ways his death was an act of civil war. It was a threat from within

[151] DT s5983/11, President's Cosgrave's oration at the grave of Kevin O'Higgins, 13 July 1927.
[152] Brian M. Walker (ed.), *Parliamentary election results in Ireland, 1918–92* (Dublin, 1992), p. 120.
[153] Simone Tery, 'As others see us III – Ireland honours the memory of Kevin O'Higgins', *Irish Statesman*, 9, 6 (13 Oct. 1928), p. 109; *IT*, 25 Jan. 2002.
[154] J. J. Lee, *Ireland 1912–1985: politics and society* (Cambridge, 1989), p. 153.
[155] J. J. Walsh quoted in Lee, *Ireland 1912–85*, p. 153.
[156] 'The municipal gallery revisited' from *The tower*, W. B. Yeats, *The collected poems of W. B. Yeats* (New York, 1956), p. 316.
[157] Lee, *Ireland 1912–85*, p. 153; Terence de Vere White, *Kevin O'Higgins* (Dublin, 1986), p. 180.
[158] Speech by Seán Lemass, *DE, official report*, XXII, col. 1615 (21 Mar. 1928).

to the security of the state and the government had to reassert itself. The implementation of Public Safety and Electoral Amendment Acts was one way; the fearful response of a state under siege. Another way was triumphalism: the symbolic placing of O'Higgins in the state's empty tomb, a little over a month after his murder, at the August 1927 ceremony. In a speech written by O'Higgins' close friend, Desmond FitzGerald, Cosgrave spoke of the 'shadow of calamity' and of 'our deep sorrow to include in our remembrance the name of Kevin O'Higgins'. Then his tone changed. His next sentence asserted that

It is fitting that we should pause in our work once a year and meet at this place to commemorate the founders of our State and in doing so to renew our faith in our country's glory and destiny by a contemplation of the lives of those heroic men. For their lives are an inspiring message to us who are left to carry on the work . . . We cannot think of our New Ireland, vibrant with new life and new hope, full of faith born of responsibility in her destiny, – we cannot think of this New Ireland without instinctively thinking of Arthur Griffith. And we cannot think of Arthur Griffith without thinking of Michael Collins.[159]

'Glory' and 'destiny' and 'hope': pompous words indeed for a man who had just buried his Vice-President, who had survived a vote of no confidence thanks to the disappearance of a drunken Deputy Jinks five days before.[160] But this speech, like the attachment of the medallion of O'Higgins to the Cenotaph a year later, was part of the same need for legitimisation and security which prompted the original hurried monument in 1923.

However, such honour required the necessary heroisation. Only the greatest men were worthy, otherwise all were demeaned. Thus greatness by association followed. An anonymous and undated piece from a government file attempted to complete the arduous task which the assassins began: the challenge of turning an unpopular politician into a martyr. Comparing O'Higgins to Lincoln and Carnot, the writer later opted for more profitable connections:

O'Higgins like Collins and Griffith, has sacrificed his life in testimony of his belief in the sanctity of his country's bond. He believed, as they did, in his country's destiny and, like them, he saw with clear vision that it could only be accomplished by treading the hard ways of peaceful reconstruction and daily sacrifice. These three men were ready to face obloquy and ingratitude and even death itself in the realisation of their ideals. Ireland will respond to their example as other nations have done in like circumstances and the strength of their beliefs shall be the measure of their country's endeavour, to bring their ideals to fruition.[161]

To be fair to the government, however, it was merely trying to reap the rewards of an investment made by O'Higgins himself. Throughout his career he claimed

---

[159] Speech at the Cenotaph, Kathleen McKenna Napoli MSS, NLI, MS 22,626, 21 Aug. 1927; *Gárda Review*, 2, 11 (Oct. 1927), pp. 1080–1.

[160] F. S. L. Lyons, *Ireland since the famine* (London, 1973), p. 500.

[161] Department of an Taoiseach s5478a, Kevin O'Higgins' death, undated and unsigned.

to be a disciple of Collins,[162] a declaration which his wife heartily endorsed in an interview in 1928 as she retold how 'the picture of Michael Collins was always in front of him'.[163] Collins' words were also cited in what was, even by Shakespearean standards, his impressive array of last words. The *Irish Statesman* declared that his 'death is for Ireland a loss as irreparable as that of Michael Collins' and appropriately for such a loss it read like the 'beautiful passages of the epic legends of Ireland'.[164] But the associations were as hollow on the lips of his wife and his colleagues as they were on his own. While he may have envisaged 'Mick' waiting for him in heaven 'on a damp cloud with a harp, arguing about politics',[165] no one cared to mention that privately O'Higgins referred to Collins as 'that pasty-faced blasphemous fucker from Cork'.[166] In Collins and O'Higgins 'it is difficult to think of two more potentially incompatible personalities', but dead men cannot choose their companions and both suffered by the comparison.[167]

O'Higgins was not a Collins or a Griffith, and no amount of fine words or plaster medallions could make it otherwise. From the beginning it was all incongruity: a death that called for honour but mocked the martyr by the method. When Cosgrave stood at the Cenotaph on 21 August 1927 and conjured up the memory of Kevin O'Higgins, he paid the murdered minister the state's greatest tribute. Yet this tribute amounted to a mere paragraph, a hackneyed eighty-five words from a politician going through the motions. With a brevity that took solemnity to its extremes, it seemed a grudging honour. No doubt there was grief; there was an appropriately weeping wife and sorrowing family, a cabinet with bowed heads robbed of another dynamic colleague, if not a friend. Relations were often strained with Cosgrave; with Mulcahy there was not even the pretence. Patrick Hogan and Desmond FitzGerald were perhaps the only ones to count as more than colleagues to be treated on 'formal terms'.[168] But, throughout, the motives seemed mixed. The ceremony in 1927 took place three and a half weeks before the election that was to change Free State politics for ever: four days before the Dáil was dissolved, five days before J. J. Walsh, the Minister for Posts and Telegraphs, left the country and the party, ten days after Fianna Fáil had entered the Dáil. For the first time, the opposition had to enter the Dáil, obliged to abandon the luxury of abstention to take up its thorny place in the government's side. Forcing its adversaries through the doors of the chamber, Cumann na nGaedheal had to contest an election that had more than numerical consequences for the Dáil's rows of empty seats. Winning and losing had more immediate consequences now, and Cumann na nGaedheal was determined to fight. The ceremony at the Cenotaph in 1927 was yet another

[162] Lee, *Ireland 1912–1985*, p. 153.   [163] Tery, 'As others see us', p. 109.
[164] *Ibid.*, pp. 108–9.   [165] De Vere White, *Kevin O'Higgins*, p. 242.
[166] Garvin, *1922*, p. 101.   [167] Lee, *Ireland 1912–1985*, p. 153.
[168] De Vere White, *Kevin O'Higgins*, pp. 168, 154, 157, 161, 120.

party political broadcast: a plea for a sympathy vote, an indictment of an opposition tainted with the common cause of the dead minister's killers. Floss Long wrote to her cousin Piaras Béaslaí, 'I'm sure his death won more sympathy for the Government than anything that happened for a long time',[169] and the government was intent on capitalising on it. But while this may seem callous, especially in the light of the avuncular sorrow of Timothy Healy and George Russell's rather melodramatic outburst that the loss of O'Higgins was felt 'with a deeper emotion' than 'any Irish leader since the death of Parnell', the ceremonies of 1927 and 1928 give no reason to be kind.[170] The silence of 1928 is damning. With the election won, the wreath was laid; the new medallion was uncovered but not unveiled; and throughout the President never said a word. What the newspapers called 'impressive simplicity' reads more like confusion, like an essay in embarrassment by a government no longer sure of why it was still standing at a piece of rotting plaster.[171]

On 20 August 1928 the *Irish Independent* ran three pictures of the ceremonies at Leinster Lawn. On the same day, on the same page, the paper published thirteen pictures of the Tailteann Games. The *Irish Independent* was always the most enthusiastic reporter of the ceremonies at the Cenotaph, but the Tailteann Games made better news. In many ways the daring deeds of leaping Irishmen were a welcome distraction for a government which, three days before the ceremony at the Cenotaph, had not yet decided what form that pageant was to take.[172] The Games, despite the retrospective sneers at the concept of an 'Irish Race Olympics', were part of the vision of Ireland that Cumann na nGaedheal was so eager to promote. There was no confusion, just running and jumping for the sheer joy of being Irish in an Irish Free State. Standing at the Cenotaph was a different matter. Now there were fifty-seven Fianna Fáil deputies lying in wait, ready to seize upon every carelessness and exploit every circumstance. According to J. J. Lee, after the September 1927 election, the government, despite its increased representation, 'retreated psychologically into opposition as Fianna Fáil now stalked Cumann na nGaedheal and hunter became hunted'.[173] To exhaust the metaphor completely, by standing on Leinster Lawn in 1928 the government made itself an easy target.

Yet the government had no choice. It had to go to the Cenotaph, on the one hand, because it was obliged to, and, on the other, because it wanted to. The death, rather than the man himself, forced it to dust down its morning suit and prepare for pageantry. But the government could have merely repeated the performance of 1927: another token speech, a march, a few photographs, a

---

[169] Floss Long to Piaras Béaslaí, 8 Aug. 1927, Piaras Béaslaí MSS, NLI, MS 33,963(15).
[170] De Vere White, *Kevin O'Higgins*, p. 233.   [171] *II*, 20 Aug. 1928.
[172] Department of Defence file 2/16304, Griffith–Collins–O'Higgins anniversary 1928, *Bothar Buadha* parade.
[173] Lee, *Ireland 1912–1985*, p. 155.

couple of inches in the next day's paper. Instead it chose to add O'Higgins to this pantheon, to add a medallion, to link his memory, as solidly as a piece of plaster can, to this totem of Free State security and sacrifice. The decision to do so may have been dilatory, but it was made none the less.

It was made because the government had a point to prove. In fact the government had several points to prove. It had uncaptured killers to rebuke with armoured cars and weeping wives and a dignity that dared them to murder at will. It had a burgeoning opposition to better, and like the Unionists at Stormont who would later stand under their statue of Edward Carson, this was a triumphalism that protested that bit too much.[174] Yet none of this considers the fact that perhaps the government was moved by a genuine sorrow, by a wish to honour the man who had been instrumental in creating its precious state of law and order. Thousands had, after all, repeatedly voted for the man and lined the streets for his funeral, and here they were again to see him immortalised in plaster. Whether these people came out of shock or sorrow or the love of spectacle; whether the government commemorated him out of grief or of obligation, it is impossible to tell. One is merely left with a reticence writ so large that it brushes away much of the sincerity and sorrow before it. By honouring O'Higgins, the government seemed more eager to honour itself, to show that it had survived the election and the shock of opposition, to prove that one of its number was worthy of such a distinction and that this hallowed cabinet had such glories to bestow. Here was another 'great' man willing to die 'for the glory and honour' of the Irish Free State, another member of Cumann na nGaedheal prepared to make the great sacrifice that republicans seemed to have a monopoly on.

Hammering that plaster medallion on to the Cenotaph ensured the eternal association of O'Higgins with the party and with the memory of Griffith and Collins, linking the four in an uncomfortable union that served to damage all. Retreating into a civil war mentality that grasped anything that 'will tend to strengthen the position of the State',[175] the government again turned to the memories of its first dead leaders, and like pilgrims rubbing a relic they faced down their foes at the foot of the Cenotaph. But the association of O'Higgins with this monument to civil war confirmed his death as an act of civil war, tracing a parallel that could only rest uneasily with the strands of republicanism that had just conceded to the strictures of its earlier defeat. It also incriminated Fianna Fáil, linking this death to the past deaths and all the guilt and blame that took refuge in the vague republicanism which now fostered this new party. Yet if the parallel which was being drawn between O'Higgins' murder and the deaths of Griffith and Collins was on the symbolic level of the addition of another civil

---

[174] Gillian McIntosh, 'Symbolic mirrors: commemorations of Edward Carson in the 1930s', *Irish Historical Studies*, 32, 125 (May 2000), pp. 93–112.

[175] Department of Defence A10426, Saluting of the Cenotaph by soldiers, Seán Lester to C. B. O'Connor, Secretary Department of Defence, 17 Oct. 1923.

war casualty to a civil war monument, that which was being drawn between the lives and ideals of these three men strayed beyond the subtleties of symbolism. O'Higgins' medallion made him the same as Griffith and Collins; casting him as the man who had carried on their work, lived according to their wishes, and died with the same earnest thoughts of freedom and Ireland on his mind. The truth was altogether different, and perhaps because it knew this, Cumann na nGaedheal took an appropriate vow of silence on 19 August 1928. O'Higgins, like the government he had come to epitomise, had not carried on their work, a fact that had not gone unnoticed by the Cumann na nGaedheal TDs who chose to defect to Fianna Fáil. Granted, both Griffith and Collins had the good fortune to die before being tested by Collins' 'freedom to achieve freedom', the promise turned catch-phrase which was to haunt Cumann na nGaedheal for its political life. But O'Higgins was no longer a republican who had accepted a Treaty; O'Higgins had been for a long time just a Treatyite. To associate him with these men in a way demeaned them. The 'man who won the war' and the once inspirational elder were now joined by the arch advocate of Commonwealth, a less than fetching addition to the government's roll of martyrs as it vied for national loyalty against 'the Republican Party'. But while this may seem harsh given that Griffith's dual monarchism was conveniently overlooked, given that neither he nor Collins had to endure the five years which turned a means into an end, O'Higgins was still an unsuitable companion for the only heroes that the less than charismatic Cumann na nGaedheal could boast. They may have been divisive figures, but to the faithful Griffith and Collins were inspirational, even mythical. O'Higgins was not. At worst he was hated, at best considered efficient, and the legacy of his unpopularity merely tainted them all.

However, if O'Higgins compromised the memory of Collins and Griffith by association, the government was compromising itself with this return to what had become by 1928 a shrine to what it had failed to achieve. No longer living up to the promise of either Griffith or Collins or the expectation of 6 December 1921, having discarded the illusions of unity in the hidden pages of the Boundary Commission, the government was finding it difficult to pretend. Civil war had 'drastically altered' its perception of the Treaty. What began as a 'stepping stone' 'became instead a monument to the dead'.[176] That Irishmen had killed Irishmen to defend it 'reinforced the inhibitions of Free State ministers against tinkering with, let alone dismantling, the treaty which they had fought [for] and won'.[177] It had been consecrated with too much blood to change it. But now that there was an eager opposition promising to achieve the things it had not done, the government, in these days before the Statute of Westminster, stayed

---

[176] Ronan Fanning, *'The four-leaved shamrock': electoral politics and the national imagination in independent Ireland* (Dublin, 1983).
[177] *Ibid.*

silent. Although the army advised that an address, however short, be given at the ceremony, the President told the Minister for Defence that nothing would be said and nothing unveiled.[178] It may be merely uncanny, but it seems strange to consign to chance the coincidence that the year chosen to reduce the scale of the ceremony was also the first year that the government could be humiliated by the inconsistencies of the party and the pageant in the Dáil.[179] Although the opposition said nothing, fearful of the shadows the gunmen still cast over them, respecting the grief that prompted this honour, their silence allowed the government to dictate its own disgrace.

The question of whether the government honoured O'Higgins in order to reap the cynical rewards of a dead minister or whether it stood on Leinster Lawn out of the deepest sense of sorrow is overshadowed, however, by the monument itself. By 1928 the Cenotaph was an insult. It was an affront to the vaunted Griffith and Collins who had been promised all manner of eternal glories in the troubled days of grief and civil war and political expediency; an offence to their families who watched the state's supposed regard rot before their eyes, who saw the annual ceremony now even denied the dignity of a few presidential platitudes. It was also an insult to Kevin O'Higgins, an insult to the wife who remembered him 'feeding their child and telling her he would love her eternally'.[180] Although he was not the Christ that the words 'you must forgive them as I do. They did not know what they were doing' might imply, the dying man, to whom a ten-year-old boy was allegedly willing to give his blood, deserved more than a plaster medallion on this festering Free State Calvary.[181] Cumann na nGaedheal, however, did not seem to think so. It was happy to stand at this doctored memorial, happy to pay £170, £20 more than the year's original allowance for the entire structure, to meet the political reality which murder had made reminiscent of 1922 and 1923.[182]

Caught between the indifference which overlooked the decay, and the impulse to honour and to benefit from that honour, the Cenotaph was perishing at the hands of Cumann na nGaedheal's ambivalence. Because the party was now as precarious as the monument it had once built to bolster its strength and security, each one of the £50,000 donated to the Great War Memorial seemed to thumb its nose at the decaying edifice on Leinster Lawn.[183] Admittedly there were civil

[178] Department of Defence file 2/16304, Griffith–Collins–O'Higgins anniversary 1928 *Bothar Buadha* parade, memo and note of telephone conversation between the Minister for Defence and the President, 16 Aug. 1928.

[179] Although Fianna Fáil was attending the Dáil at the time of the 1927 ceremony, it took place a mere ten days after they had entered the Dáil for the first time and four days before the Dáil was dissolved.

[180] Tery, 'As others see us', pp. 109–10.   [181] *Ibid.*, p. 110.

[182] DF file s200/0006/28, Commemoration ceremony 1928 – addition of medallion portrait of the late Vice-President, Mr Kevin O'Higgins to Cenotaph, T. Cassidy, OPW to the Secretary of the Department of Finance, 4 July 1929: this amounts to the entire cost of the 1928 ceremony.

[183] DT s4156b, War Memorial Islandbridge.

war debts and the constant pressures of inadequate budgets, there were graver concerns and worthier claims on government time and money, but surely the same rules should have applied to the memorial at Islandbridge? Why was the construction of a permanent Cenotaph constantly postponed when so much money could be found for a monument to the Great War; when even Cosgrave had to admit that 'It is idle . . . to ignore the fact that there is a certain hostility to the idea of any form of War Memorial'?[184] It would be nice, but a little naïve, to believe that this donation came from hearts sorrowing for the 49,400 men who had died for the nationalism of John Redmond, the rights of small nations, the empire, the adventure, the wages. But a government that feared the shadow that a Great War Memorial would cast from the once mooted Merrion Square site on to Leinster House, and possibly on to the Cenotaph, did not make such donations. Kevin O'Higgins' comments in the Dáil were proof of that:

You have a square here, confronting the seat of the Government of the country . . . I say that any intelligent visitor, not particularly versed in the history of the country, would be entitled to conclude that the origins of this State were connected with that park and the memorial in that park was connected with the lives that were lost in the Great War in France, Belgium, Gallipoli and so on. That is not the position. The State has other origins, and because it has other origins I do not wish to see it suggested, in stone or otherwise, that it has that origin.[185]

O'Higgins' two brothers had fought and one had died in the Great War; he had insisted on laying a wreath at the Cenotaph in London when Cosgrave was unable to attend.[186] He was possibly more inclined than most in the Dáil to the War Memorial cause. The more volatile outside the Dáil would make no concessions at all. Yet even he could still utter these words. He could utter them because even the seemingly mild-mannered Cumann na nGaedhealers were dissatisfied, complaining that too 'many Irishmen are showing their admiration of the late Earl of Ypres and his supporters in the English Army'.[187] He was simply trying to appease as many as he could. Affording a convenient degree of invisibility, the wilds of Islandbridge presented the cabinet with a chance to re-treat to the utilitarianism which had more noble exemplars in the memorial halls and hospitals of the cities and towns of post-war Europe. Work on the project was divided equally between former members of the British and Irish armies, addressing the question of unemployment,[188] and quieting the memories of de-mobilisation and the recent army mutiny. It was a nod in the direction of Ulster

---

[184] *Ibid.*, W. T. Cosgrave to Sir Andrew Jameson, 2 Dec. 1929.
[185] *DE, official report*, XIX, col. 400 (29 Mar. 1927).
[186] DF s200/0024/26, Wreath laid on the Cenotaph, London by President; DT s3370a, Armistice Day commemorations.
[187] DT s4156, War Memorial Islandbridge, letter from John Sweetman, Kells, Co. Meath, to the 'Government', 10 Aug. 1925.
[188] DT s4156b, War Memorial Islandbridge.

Unionism, a gesture to Southern Protestantism which did not seem to involve genuflecting to Rome. Most of all it was a type of appeasement, a generous kind of thank you to Sir Andrew Jameson and Henry Guinness, one a leading member of the memorial committee and, more importantly, director and governor of the Bank of Ireland, respectively. The government remembered the bank's loans of £100,000 a fortnight, of £2,750,000 that had kept the desperate Free State afloat in 1922.[189] Judging from O'Higgins' statement, it remembered the money more, more than the men who had given their lives in 'France, Belgium, Gallipoli and so on'. When the donation was eventually made, republicanism jumped eagerly to the obvious conclusions:

the old English Garrison, pampered and nursed by the present Free State Government, have votes; and it is through them Mr Cosgrave hopes to secure another five years in office. The secret circular from the Unionists to their fellow-Masons soliciting funds to return Mr Cosgrave at the next election, and Mr Cosgrave's grant of £50,000 out of the Irish people's money for their English Memorial Park, throws off the mask of Irish Nationality under which the members of the Free State Government have hitherto tried to deceive the Irish people in their platform utterances.[190]

On the basest of levels, the government had more to gain from Islandbridge: settlement of favours past, the prospect of favours still to come. A new Cenotaph would merely be a costly sermon to the converted.

Given that they were converted, a new Cenotaph could wait. If anyone asked, a monument constrained by the budget of 1928 would be more degrading to these fine men than a memorial which could still at least claim to be temporary. On 16 July 1928, three days after the decision to commission a medallion of O'Higgins, Sir Philip Hanson of the OPW pleaded the case for permanent bronze medallions.[191] With ears deafened by the inconvenient talk of such expense, the government instead chose to capture O'Higgins in the glories of plaster of Paris. One day after the 1928 ceremony a Board of Works architect announced 'that owing to the condition of the Cenotaph early steps must be taken to have the monument erected in a permanent form'.[192] His concerns were noted by the President's Department and a report on the condition and expected life of the monument was requested from the Office of Public Works. The reply confirmed that the inner frame was suffering the effects of mildew. By ventilating the interior to minimise the risk of dry rot, and by continuing the periodic repainting and patching which had become part of the Cenotaph's ritual, the OPW estimated that under normal climatic conditions it would retain

[189] Ronan Fanning, *The Irish department of finance 1922–58* (Dublin, 1978), pp. 84–7.
[190] *Republican File*, 9 Jan. 1932.
[191] DF file s200/0006/28, Commemoration ceremony 1928 – addition of medallion portrait of the late Vice-President, Mr Kevin O'Higgins to Cenotaph, department memo, 16 July 1928.
[192] DT s5734a, Griffith–Collins Cenotaph – general file, note by P. J. Banim to the Secretary of the Executive Council recording a conversation with Mr Williams, 20 Aug. 1928.

its present appearance for at least five more years.[193] Assured 'that the cost will be small', Finance gave its willing approval to this ventilation.[194] After all, £6 7s. 4d. was a small price to pay for five more years.[195]

Alienated from the ideals of the men commemorated, the government seemed to retreat in miserly embarrassment from the memorial. But like most of its decisions in its final years of power, this retreat was fraught with indecision. After three months' exposure it had become obvious that the new O'Higgins medallion could not survive. With £50 thus squandered, the OPW advocated the replacement of all three medallions with gilded cement and sand castings.[196] Another £36 4s. 5d. was spent to tide things over: another pittance to postpone the expensive inevitability of a new memorial.[197] It seemed as if the government had forgotten graveside speeches and deification; as if it had lost the will to commemorate when commemoration required a monument as grand as anything the past or the English could provide. Yet throughout there remained something more than the embarrassed running repairs and the furtive retreat from ceremony. There was a type of shame in the inaction: republicanism was raising money for a fifty-foot round tower for Liam Lynch; even the people of Inchicore could raise £9,000 for a statue of the Virgin Mary.[198] There was shame and in shame an inherent type of fervour that could not bear the thought of being outdone. The decision to add a medallion of O'Higgins bespoke the persistence of the will to taunt; prodding civil war wounds with all the malice of the victor. In August 1928, a donation of £5 5s. 0d. towards the erection of a 'Griffith–Collins Memorial' was refused because 'I take it the memorial when erected in permanent form will be at the expense of the State'.[199] The memorial was to be erected; it was 'when' not 'if'. The will remained, especially among the party faithful whose Rathmines (Kevin O'Higgins') branch had collected the sum in question for a memorial which had seemingly shed its patron; it remained, as the obsessions of the Blueshirt-ridden party of the 1930s were to prove. But if there was still will, there was also arrogance. The presumption that the state would bear the cost of a monument which had come to symbolise the victory of one of its parties had the inherent insolence of a party which had come to identify itself exclusively with power. Sited on the lawn of Government

[193] *Ibid.*, letter from T. Cassidy, Secretary of the OPW to the Secretary of the Department of the President, 18 Sept. 1928.
[194] DF file s200/0006/28, Commemoration ceremony 1928 – addition of medallion portrait of the late Vice-President, Mr Kevin O'Higgins to Cenotaph, letter from T. Cassidy, Secretary of the OPW to the Department of Finance, 4 July 1929.
[195] *Ibid.*
[196] *Ibid.*, letter from T. Cassidy, Secretary of the OPW to the Department of Finance, 22 Nov. 1923.
[197] *Ibid.*, letter from T. Cassidy Secretary of the OPW to the Department of Finance, 4 July 1929.
[198] *Illustrated London News*, 176, 4572 (17 May 1930), p. 888.
[199] DT s5734a, Griffith–Collins Cenotaph – general file, letter to P. J. Banim from Mairead Murphy, Acting Secretary of Cumann na nGaedheal, 25 Aug. 1928; note from Banim to McDunphy, 27 Aug. 1928.

Buildings, this tribute to the state's first President, the state's first Commander-in-Chief and one of the state's ministers, built by the hands of a Cumann na nGaedheal government, had become a monument not only to its grief but also to its success. Settled behind the high railings of Leinster Lawn it would remain, however decrepit, a totem of the party, a mark of political colonisation as potent as any statue of Queen Victoria.

In 1930, a worried voice was raised in the letters page of the *Irish Statesman*: 'when Fianna Fáil or the Republican Party come into power they will probably, as the result of preceding circumstances, yield to a patriotic impetus and destroy all monuments commemorating the founders of the Irish Free State'.[200] Two years later, this concerned citizen was forced to confront his fears. But while de Valera had led the promised revolution at the polls in February 1932, towns were not renamed nor statues torn down, as the threatened excesses of Fianna Fáil were tempered by the urgencies of its own ambition. Much as it may have angered de Valera to sit in the shadow of a monument to 'traitors', his party left the Cenotaph alone, letting it fester like an indictment of the last ten years. Nothing was done, merely a departmental note made of the projected life-span – the date in September 1933 when 'the Cenotaph, which many people regard as ugly', was predicted to fall down.[201] Yet September 1933 passed, as did 1934 and 1935. The monument weathered the years and Fianna Fáil added inactivity to its predecessor's indecision. At this point it would be easy to retreat to the shadows of Coogan's de Valera, the man whose bitterness and begrudgery left Collins' grave without a headstone.[202] But however he was damned by his rather biased biographer, de Valera's response to the Cenotaph must be considered in the light of circumstance and not according to the whims and conspiracies of *bien pensant* opinion.

Circumstance provided 10,000 republicans standing in the Knockmealdown Mountains watching Moss Twomey, a man wanted by the police, a man who refused to recognise de Valera and his 'mongrel Free State', unveiling a monument to Liam Lynch.[203] It provided an IRA bomb that destroyed an equestrian statue of George II in St Stephen's Green. De Valera had split republicanism when he founded Fianna Fáil and worsened that split when he entered the Dáil; to the extremists he had given in and turned his back on the republic, however much his party may have professed its faith bareheaded at republican plots, at Bodenstown, at a cross to Noel Lemass. Rebuilding a Cenotaph would merely have been grist to this increasingly volatile republican mill. But circumstance also provided economic war: a legitimate excuse, mitigating against the

[200] T. Hennessy, letter to the editor, *Irish Statesman*, 13, 19 (11 Jan. 1930), p. 374.
[201] DT s5734a, Griffith–Collins Cenotaph – general file, memo on the History of the Cenotaph by Michael McDunphy, 6 July 1932.
[202] Tim Pat Coogan, *Michael Collins: a biography* (London, 1990), pp. 416–32.
[203] *Tipperary Star*, 13 Apr. 1935.

propriety of constructing any monument to any man regardless of his republican hue. However, economic war was also a convenient façade, covering malevolence or indifference according to one's views of de Valera and Fianna Fáil. Yet in a way it seems too easy to cast de Valera as the villain of the piece, narrow-minded and bitter, letting the memorial decay in vindictive spite of the men who had once thwarted him. Such bitterness can only be judged by his government's inactivity, but why should this inactivity be any more damning than that of its predecessors? If Cumann na nGaedheal was profane enough to neglect its own shrine to 'Ireland's reverence and sorrow',[204] is it realistic to expect Fianna Fáil to repair and replace a monument which triumphalism had turned into a talisman of party and Free State; which Blueshirtism would turn into a rallying point for revenge? Bitterness undoubtedly played its part, the instinct to commemorate the state's first dignitaries lost in the memories of taunted republicanism and the echoes of 'seventy-seven' and 'Ballyseedy' in the Dáil.[205] Yet bitterness was only part of a greater indifference. Personally de Valera had more faith in the testimony of the written word. His attachment to the Cuchulainn statue in the GPO and the busts of Brugha and Stack in the Dáil were trifling affairs compared to his investment in the Lord Longford and T. P. O'Neill account of his life.[206] The government too had more important things to do. Dismantling treaties and fighting economic wars took precedence over the fortunes of a piece of rotten wood and plaster.

It is worth referring to the opinion of F. S. L. Lyons. Held so dearly for so long, it deserves further consideration. If the civil war was 'an episode which has burned so deep into the heart and mind of Ireland that it is not yet possible for the historian to approach it with the detailed knowledge or the objectivity which it deserves',[207] how did a Fianna Fáil government, without the historian's detachment or the distance Lyons enjoyed when writing in 1971, make the decision to rebuild a monument to the men who had supposedly sacrificed the republic;[208] to the man eagerly, if wrongly, blamed for the seventy-seven executions of 1922–3? It would be cynical to say that the party built for its own benefit, seeming to forgive because it was good for publicity, honouring because it might humiliate the negligent Cumann na nGaedheal. There was, of course, always the possibility that the Fianna Fáil government was simply sick of the sight of the festering mess on the lawn of Leinster House. Yet publicity did play a part, if not in this particular role then in one dictated by the fear that failure to replace the monument would be construed as a particularly insidious type of malice.

---

[204] *II*, 14 Aug. 1923.   [205] Noël Browne, *Against the tide* (Dublin, 1987), p. 228.
[206] Lord Longford and T. P. O'Neill, *Eamon de Valera* (London, 1970).
[207] F. S. L. Lyons, *Ireland since the famine* (London, 1971), p. 460.
[208] DT s5734a, Griffith–Collins Cenotaph – general file.

But the new Cenotaph was also a rebuke. Rebuilt as a retort to those who had been convinced by Cumann na nGaedheal's portrayal of Fianna Fáil as the gunman's party of choice, the memorial bespoke another Fianna Fáil. Men who built monuments to their enemies were not the assassins or the anarchists of Cumann na nGaedheal posters. Instead they were statesmen, paragons of democratic virtues who called the Cenotaph as a character witness, an alibi for the days and nights when IRA explosions took seven British lives in 1939. This monument to the men that the Moss Twomeys could never forgive was to stand like a symbolic reinforcement of the Offences Against the State Act, passed into law one month before the decision was made to rebuild the Cenotaph. Like the suppression of the IRA commemoration at Bodenstown, like the other ceremonies and anniversaries that were increasingly falling into the hands of extreme republicanism, it was to serve as another reminder that Fianna Fáil was no longer part of the IRA, no longer part of the rage of 1922.

Whether the party was playing with symbolism to rid itself of a troublesome ally or whether it simply had the misfortune to be in power when the temporary Cenotaph finally collapsed, the fact that the decision to rebuild the monument was made gives credence to Michael Hayes' belief that friendships defied the bitterness of civil war.[209] Whatever the motive, it was a magnanimous act; an act which puts Lee's questions about the legacy of civil war bitterness into perspective. He compares civil war in Ireland and civil war in Finland. In Finland, a country with a similar population, 25,000 died in the civil war of 1918. Of that 25,000, 8,300 were executed and 9,000 died in prison camps. By 1937 former Finnish enemies served together in government. Ireland's seventy-seven executions and even the most exaggerated estimate of 5,000 casualties fail to compare. Yet 'the legacy of the more modest inheritance lasted longer in Ireland':

this lay more in a retrospective need for bitterness than in the nature of civil war itself. Indeed, as other distinguishing features between the main parties become more difficult to discern, only memory continued to divide them. It may be that the image of the civil war had to be burnished and polished, and the fires of hatred stoked, to foster the illusion that fundamental differences remained between the parties.[210]

Somewhere between the burnishing and the polishing and the traditional consensus of a country still scarred by the divisions of 1922, the Cenotaph rises like a reproof. A challenge to a historiography gorged on the notion of 'civil war politics', its construction calls for more than the formulaic retreat to a persistent and inherent bitterness which only began to dissipate with the inter-party government or the foundation of the Progressive Democrats in December 1985.

[209] Michael Hayes, 'Dáil Éireann and the Irish Civil War', *Studies*, 58 (Spring 1969), p. 22.
[210] Lee, *Ireland 1912–85*, p. 69.

Much as the apparent magnanimity of a Fianna Fáil-built Cenotaph might discourage one from such formulaic retreats, the less-chosen path follows a deceptive course. Meandering between 1932 and July 1939, when the decision was finally taken to replace 1923's rotten structure, there is much upon the journey to raise the hackles of 'civil war politics'. Between 1932 and October 1935 the monument was ignored. Decay was rampant, unchecked because of indifference, bitterness or economic war, unchecked because Blueshirtism could not be conceded even the slightest symbolic victory. In truth, the years 1935 to 1939 pose the same problems. Reports were commissioned and reports were ignored. Cracks, fungus, broken steps, a tilting cross, constant pleas from the OPW to demolish the entire structure – nothing moved the government which postponed a decision on the matter four times between 19 October 1937 and 9 August 1938. It would be easy to say that bitterness deafened Fianna Fáil ears, that a malevolent revenge took pleasure in watching decay devour a monument to the 'traitors' who had been foolishly promised posterity. But bitterness does not explain why de Valera consulted Collins' brother[211] or why he heeded Seán Collins' response:

I have been speaking to some of Michael's old comrades about this matter and having given the Board of Works view of the instability of the present structure they were all unanimous in stating that they would much prefer to see it go into decay, rather than to remove even such a flimsy token of commemoration to the work of men who had served their country . . . so well. As these are somewhat the views of the members of Michael's family whom I have had the opportunity to consult, you will, I know understand how impossible it would be to allow my name appear [sic] as consenting to the removal of the cenotaph.[212]

Bitterness does not explain why this letter should convince 'the Republican Party', with the weight of at least seventy-seven martyrs on its back, to strengthen the base of the monument and erect a new cross.[213] 'Civil war politics' would have pulled it down, brothers, families, comrades, consultations aside. If bitterness burned with the fervour suggested by F. S. L. Lyons, then nothing should have saved the Cenotaph, nothing should have induced Fianna Fáil to build, to consort with Fine Gael about the construction of a permanent memorial to the 'traitors' of 1922.

Although the decision to meet representatives of Fine Gael was only taken when the OPW had vetoed alterations, when the cross stood 'one foot out of the perpendicular' and prey to the whims of the next gust of wind,[214] the terms of reference for the discussion promised the inclusion of the opposition party at

---

[211] DT s5734a, Griffith–Collins Cenotaph – general file, letter from Seán Collins to Eamon de Valera, 16 Aug. 1938.
[212] *Ibid.* (punctuation as in the original).   [213] *Ibid.*, cabinet resolution, 23 Aug. 1938.
[214] *Ibid.*, copy of report by Joseph Connolly, chairman of the Commissioners of Public Works, submitted to members of the government by the Minister for Finance, 28 May 1939.

every stage of the design process. The Taoiseach and Seán Moylan, Fianna Fáil TD for Cork North, met Desmond FitzGerald and Michael Hayes on Friday 28 July 1939. The following Monday the Minister for Finance instructed the OPW to submit 'a design for a permanent memorial including a cross'.[215] The OPW was anxious that the cross, and all it stood for, should remain an integral part of any new design.[216] On the face of it, all was peace and reconciliation; former enemies discussing a memorial to the figures that once divided them, men once called killers consulting the families of the dead.[217] In less than one hundred words a statement informed the press that the memorial was to be replaced: dignity tripping from the tongue of these terse few words that seemed to say that civil war politics were at an end. But just as the scaffolding erected at Leinster Lawn was merely there to 'indicate that work is in hand or is contemplated',[218] there was something false about the meeting and the statement, something contradictory about Fianna Fáil's entire approach to the memorial. To begin with, the meeting with Hayes and FitzGerald was held privately. Voters were never told, because cries of 'seventy-seven' still carried too much weight at some election hustings to risk the revelation. Voters had no need to know because news of collusion with the enemy over the bones of Collins, Griffith and O'Higgins would have fallen on stony ground in the Ballyseedys, at the masses on 8 December, in the Rory O'Connor Fianna Fáil Cumainn, and in the extremes of Fianna Fáil which did not share their leader's opinion of the IRA. Although the motives for this secrecy might explain the brevity of the press statement, they do more to endorse Lee's opinions, to explain something of the nature of civil war bitterness in Ireland. Behind closed doors politicians could discuss the civil war and ruminate over the commemoration of one side's dead. Outside, in the Dáil, in the streets, it was different; there was a memory to be 'burnished and polished', fostering 'the illusion that fundamental differences remained between the parties'.[219] But if politicians preserved their friendships, as Michael Hayes believes,[220] if de Valera and FitzGerald and Hayes could discuss the past, the people that these, amongst other men, had once charged with the actual fighting of the war did not have the luxury of such pliant memories. For many there was nothing but silence: the quiet return to a republican or an army grave that could never speak of the horrors seen and the horrors done.

But memory was not as malleable as the noble leaders might pretend. Gestures were made with one hand, then taken back with the other. De Valera took

---

[215] *Ibid.*, letter from the Minister for Finance to the OPW, 31 July 1939.

[216] *Ibid.*, OPW report, 27 June 1938.

[217] *Ibid.*, memorandum of the meeting of the Taoiseach with the members of Fine Gael, 31 July 1939.

[218] DT s5734a, Griffith–Collins Cenotaph – general file, letter from P. J. Raftery, Assistant Secretary, OPW, to the Secretary, Ministry for Finance, 11 Aug. 1939.

[219] Lee, *Ireland 1912–1985*, p. 69.   [220] Hayes, 'Dáil Eireann', p. 22.

control. He discounted the notion of a competition for the design. That was all right for the Garden of Remembrance with its cheerily neutral promise to honour all who died for Ireland. This was Leinster Lawn, the seat of power; the men honoured were once the enemy. Nor would it be relocated; the dangerously public and popular St Stephen's Green was no place for a monument to the leaders of a Free State.[221] The new constitution said it was Éire after all. De Valera discussed the matter personally with the chairman of the Board of Works, the virulently republican former Fianna Fáil minister, Joseph Connolly.[222] Stipulating, deciding, de Valera presented Fine Gael with a design only after he had altered and fashioned it to his own tastes. He reduced H. G. Leask's three-panelled design to a little over twenty feet. It would include nothing but a plain cross and three plaques. He even stipulated the removal of the lettering: the dedication to the men it was supposed to honour. And it would cost no more than £2,700.[223] Fine Gael could have its monument but, like Collins' headstone, only on de Valera's personal terms. Commemoration would be conceded but only without the clamour of ceremony, only if Fianna Fáil was seen to give and Fine Gael submissively and silently to receive.

Throughout, the Taoiseach was consistent in this apparent inconsistency. He completed Cosgrave's initiative to provide busts of Collins and Griffith for the privacy of the Taoiseach's office but stopped the state ceremony at the Cenotaph;[224] he permitted the Collins family to erect a monument over the grave of Michael Collins, but only with restrictions on the materials, the inscription and the amount spent, only with the promise that there would be no public subscription, no publicity and no one present at the blessing.[225] Coogan puts it all down to bitterness, a personal paranoia that kept de Valera trembling in the shadow of Collins for the rest of his life, but this does nothing to explain the concessions, however grudging. It does not ask why a Cumann na nGaedheal government let the Cenotaph rot or why it failed to mark the grave of Collins, the man it had promised to honour eternally. Although de Valera commemorated his enemies with an asceticism that undermined the gesture, although he had to wait until the Anglo-Irish Agreement of 1938 had torn the last sentences of Collins' and Griffith's Treaty to shreds, his actions, however shaped by bitterness, defied bitterness. The decision to rebuild the Cenotaph may have been a nod in the direction of the cross-party unity which 'the Emergency' demanded, its manifest maturity a sign of statesmanship, but the decision bespoke something more than

[221] DT s5734a, Griffith–Collins Cenotaph – general file, memorandum for the cabinet from the Department of Finance concerning the Cenotaph, 27 Feb. 1940.
[222] *Ibid.*, letter from Maurice Moynihan to the Minister for Finance, 31 July 1939.
[223] The cabinet was presented with this design by H. G. Leask, Keeper of National Monuments, on 27 Feb. 1940. *Ibid.*, report by H. G. Leask, 19 Aug. 1940; memo of the meeting between J. Connolly, OPW and Eamon de Valera, 24 May 1940.
[224] Hill, *Irish public sculpture*, p. 153.   [225] Coogan, *Michael Collins*, pp. 428–30.

the mere accommodation of a possibly troublesome opposition. The decision implied an end to bitterness.

For some, however, even the implication was too much. An anti-Treatyite government may have made its first recognition of the legitimacy of pro-Treaty memory, but ingrained in some political hearts and minds was a bias that continued to 'burnish and polish'. While any efforts to begin work on the monument were vetoed by a Department of Defence fearful of giving 'a particular advantage to an attacking body of troops', German or English,[226] certain members of Fine Gael took the opportunity to exploit the inactivity for all its political worth. P. S. Doyle, a Fine Gael TD for South Dublin, raised the matter four times in the Dáil between June 1944 and October 1947.[227] Abetted by an article by the 'Special Representative' in the *Sunday Independent*,[228] and resolutions from Dublin City Council and a newly formed Fine Gael Central Branch,[229] Doyle found his greatest ally in John A. Costello. Having put an aggressive question to the Minister for Finance, Costello was dismissively told to take the matter up with his own Chief Whip.[230] The public urgency of Doyle and Costello, their impatience with the excuses of war and finance and the lack of materials, belied the real feelings and the direct involvement of the Fine Gael Party, whose representatives 'did not indicate that the erection of a new Cenotaph was regarded by them . . . as a matter of urgency',[231] and whose leader had just sent written acceptance of the new design.[232] Costello did not heed the hidden meetings, the concessions; he disregarded Fianna Fáil's rejection of a plan to site the monument on Merrion Square simply because Mulcahy 'and his colleagues were opposed to the erection of the Cenotaph on any other site than Leinster Lawn'.[233] Costello continued to play to the gallery.

Apart from acceding to Fine Gael's wish to maintain its symbolic colonisation of the seat of power, de Valera and his cabinet made one other parting bequest. On 16 September 1947 a decision was made to alter the design of the monument. Orders for 'a column or obelisk, including provision for a cross and for portrait

---

[226] DT s5734a, Griffith–Collins Cenotaph – general file, letter from Commandant Lucas Ó hÉigeartaigh, Officer in Command of Defences, to T. S. C. Dagg, Department of Finance, 22 July 1940.

[227] *DE, official report*, XCIV, col. 1418 (28 June 1944); *ibid.*, XCVIII, col. 165 (11 Oct. 1945); *ibid.*, CI, col. 449 (21 May 1946); *ibid.*, CVIII, col. 366 (15 Oct. 1947).

[228] *Sunday Independent*, 5 July 1942.

[229] *II*, 18 Sept. 1944; DT s5734b, Griffith–Collins Cenotaph – general file, letter from Thomas McNeill, Clerk of the City Council to the Government Secretary, 8 Jan. 1946.

[230] The question was answered on the minister's behalf by his secretary, O'Grady. *DE, official report*, CVI, cols. 774–5 (28 May 1947).

[231] DT s5734b, Griffith–Collins Cenotaph – general file, letter from J. E. Hanna, Department of Finance to the Secretary of the Department of an Taoiseach, 18 Feb. 1946.

[232] *Ibid.*, letter from Richard Mulcahy to an Taoiseach, 7 July 1947.

[233] *Ibid.*, memorandum for the government from the Office of the Parliamentary Secretary to an Taoiseach, 10 Sept. 1947.

plaques of the late Arthur Griffith, Michael Collins and Kevin O'Higgins' were made[234], orders for an image that traditionally spelt power,[235] an image that might, given Fine Gael's insistence on the siting, mute the associations with the party's martyrs. Art historians consider that the change was prompted by the report, which accompanied the original design, with its claims that a Celtic cross was out of place on Leinster Lawn, that it was no longer possible to produce such crosses to the standard of their ancient predecessors.[236] It is difficult to believe that Fianna Fáil only grasped the ramifications of an artist's misgivings eight years after its ringing endorsement of the design in 1939. The circulation of a memorandum to the cabinet on 10 September 1947,[237] a mere six days before the decision was taken, recalling Fine Gael's affinity with the Leinster Lawn site, seems, even accounting for Fianna Fáil's appreciation of all things aesthetic, a little more plausible. A petty rebuke of the opposition perhaps, but the bequest of an obelisk by a party buoyed by the success of neutrality and the satisfaction of such a public moral victory over Churchill, thwarted Fine Gael's attempt to continue to assert its own version of political legitimacy. The obelisk was an image of power and statesmanship, not mourning: 'a symbol of state authority which any Dáil could endorse'.[238]

Presented with a Dáil question from P. S. Doyle[239] and a resolution from the Cork Central Branch of Fine Gael,[240] Costello, the leader of the new inter-party government, was reminded of what was once the urgency of his own opposition. But, once prompted, Costello readily recalled his crusading zeal. Not to be outdone by de Valera, he insisted on handling the issue personally, answering Dáil questions and circulating memos on the history of the monument, because he was 'anxious that all the members of the government should have some knowledge of the history of the matter'.[241] He tussled with an indolent Finance, sending minutes 'in rather stiff terms',[242] demanding that 'all action necessary ... should be taken as expeditiously as possible and that the matter should be dealt with as one of the greatest urgency at every stage'.[243] Pressed by 'several complaints regarding the delay',[244] it was the Taoiseach who met the commissioner of the OPW, the Taoiseach who scrutinised the designs, the Taoiseach

[234] *Ibid.*, memorandum of cabinet meeting, 16 Sept. 1947.

[235] Hill, *Irish public sculpture*, p. 153.   [236] *Ibid.*

[237] DT s5734b, Griffith–Collins Cenotaph – general file, memorandum to the cabinet from the Office of the Parliamentary Secretary to an Taoiseach, 10 Sept. 1947.

[238] Hill, *Irish public sculpture*, p. 155.   [239] *DE, official report*, CX, col. 1323 (12 May 1948).

[240] DT s5734c, Griffith–Collins Cenotaph – general file, letter from W. G. Kennefick, Secretary of the Fine Gael Cork Executive to John A. Costello, 3 May 1948.

[241] *Ibid.*, memorandum for the government by the Department of an Taoiseach, 5 May 1948.

[242] *Ibid.*, memo from N. S. Ó Nualláin to the Secretary to an Taoiseach, 4 Feb. 1949.

[243] *Ibid.*, memo from M. Ó Muimhneacháin, Taoiseach's Office to the Department of Finance, 9 Feb. 1949.

[244] *Ibid.*, letter from the Secretary of the Department of an Taoiseach to the Secretary of the Department of Finance, 4 Feb. 1949.

who restored the inscription which Fianna Fáil had dared, in its eagerness to neutralise the monument, to erase. There was to be no mistake; the monument would be 'worthy of the purpose for which it is to be used'.[245] In truth the Cenotaph was to be Costello's monument.

Set in the centre of a re-landscaped Leinster Lawn a slender, tapering sixty-foot granite obelisk, capped by a gilt bronze flame, would stand on a circular sloping base adorned with four bronze wreaths that framed medallions of Griffith, Collins and O'Higgins and an inscription tablet bearing the words *Do Chum Glóire Dé agus Onóra na hÉireann* ('For the glory of God and the honour of Ireland').[246] A gold inlaid cross would be the only other feature of the OPW's principal architect, Raymond McGrath's, austere design.[247] Costello and his inter-party cabinet promptly sanctioned the scheme: the design, the re-planning of the garden, the estimate of £20,000. Clann na Poblachta, the party which balked at Richard Mulcahy and his civil war record, now acquiesced in honouring the men who had supposedly caused the war, forgiving, it would seem, under the guiding hand of a reputedly impartial Taoiseach. But Costello's purity is not enough to explain this peaceful concord. Seán MacBride and his republican ilk may have been moved to honour by a genuine respect for the dead men, a respect which can be traced to the *An Phoblacht* obituaries of 1922[248] and to the grudging gestures of Fianna Fáil. MacBride had clearly come a long way since his days of hearty objections to a treacherous Fianna Fáil daring to commemorate Cathal Brugha. But while esteem could apparently remember what Griffith once inspired, what Collins had once achieved, it could never forgive the Richard Mulcahy of 1923. Alternatively the Clann may have thought little of honour and esteem, capitulating instead to the whims of a stronger partner in government who insisted on including the less popular Kevin O'Higgins. Whatever the reason for Clann na Poblachta's consent, the Cenotaph conspires to question Costello, at least Costello as the man 'untainted by civil war memories'.[249]

Between the acceptance of the design on 26 July 1948 and the completion of the monument in October 1950, Costello had shown a degree of haste which, in terms of the Cenotaph, could only be considered indecent. On every level the urgency bespoke purpose. Sixteen years of Fianna Fáil and de Valera, sixteen years scavenging in a political wilderness that yielded nothing more than the futility of Blueshirtism, had taken its toll on Fine Gael. Rising like a trophy of power, the Cenotaph bellowed the return of Fine Gael; the shout all the louder

---

[245] *Ibid.*, letter from the Office of an Taoiseach to the OPW, 27 Feb. 1950.
[246] *Ibid.*, letter from B. Farrell, OPW, to the Department of an Taoiseach, 20 July 1949.
[247] The medallions and the bronze flame were the work of the sculptor Laurence Campbell; the inscriptions were the work of Colm Ó Lochlainn.
[248] *Poblacht na hÉireann War News*, 39, 15 Aug. 1922; *ibid.*, 47, 24 Aug. 1922.
[249] Lee, *Ireland 1912–1985*, p. 299.

because of the indignity of coalition. Powerful parties build monuments, in this case with a haste that hoped Fine Gael would still be in office to reap the benefits of its completion. But if haste denoted the party's will to reassert its claims on power, the urgency also registered Costello's personal claims to power and recognition. Thrust into the spotlight which de Valera had cast on the position of Taoiseach, Costello was forced to perform. Without the baggage of 1916 and reprieved executions, without the mystery or the provocation of de Valera, the relatively anonymous and uncontroversial Costello had to manufacture tangible bequests to the nation. He left a monument which associated him with a time of power and opportunity, a monument which linked his name with the oft-spoken greats of more exciting years who shared his distinction of defeating de Valera. But even if the Cenotaph was not erected out of a sense of inferiority and personal aggrandisement, Costello's urgency and involvement link the monument to his other great bequest to the nation: the declaration of a republic.

In September 1948, the leader of Fine Gael, the supposedly conservative and Commonwealth party, declared that Ireland would become a republic. In the months that followed, he scrutinised plans, approved inscriptions, beseeched and implored for the erection of a monument to the men who had supposedly signed away the republic, to Griffith the dual monarchist, to O'Higgins the advocate of Commonwealth. In many ways his urgency seemed to associate these men with his action, adding their imprimatur to that of the men of 1916 which the appropriation of Easter Sunday 1949 had guaranteed for his somewhat premature and contentious declaration. His eagerness, in many ways, was an attempt to vindicate them. Here at last was the republic, declared by a Fine Gael man, a man of the party of Griffith, Collins and O'Higgins. Now they could be republicans again instead of 'traitors' and 'Free Staters', now appropriately honoured with their permanent memorial, which had fittingly relegated the statue of Prince Albert to a shadowy corner of Leinster Lawn.[250] They were, after all, the men who had bequeathed the freedom to achieve this long awaited freedom, and Fine Gael had waited long enough to make the most of Collins' awkward claim.

Spurious though the connection may be between the declaration of the republic and the erection of this beleaguered monument, this question mark over Costello as the man 'untainted' by civil war bitterness remains. While the apparent vindication of his predecessors raises a tentative doubt, other questions asked both in and outside the Dáil evoke greater misgivings. Notwithstanding a quibble as to the pagan origins of the obelisk form, quickly dissipated by a photograph of the Pope in close proximity to the obelisk in St Peter's Square,[251] and an objection made by Con Lehane, a Clann na Poblachta TD,

---

[250] DT s5734c, Griffith–Collins Cenotaph – general file, memorandum from the Department of Finance to the cabinet, 15 July 1948.
[251] Hill, *Irish public sculpture*, p. 155.

to the extravagance of £20,000 when 'want and destitution could still be found in many places in Dublin', [252] bitterness was the main charge. The first assault was made on 2 May 1950. Seán MacEntee contrasted the activity on Leinster Lawn to the postponement of work on the Rotunda Garden of Remembrance designated by Fianna Fáil, on the prompting of the Old IRA, to commemorate all who died for Ireland.[253] Encouraged by the Fianna Fáil TD, Lehane suggested that the Cenotaph be re-dedicated to 'all those who gave their lives to break the connection with England'. He was ignored, but his departing 'all you are concerned with is instigating and maintaining bitterness' presaged the tone of the exchanges which followed.[254] A debate on the estimates for the Office of Public Works on 12 July 1950 provided a forum for the virulence which had been incited by articles in Fianna Fáil's *Irish Press*.[255] M. F. Kitt, a Fianna Fáil TD for Galway North, provided a fitting prologue to the onslaught of his colleague, deputy Henry Colley. Recalling MacEntee's earlier theme, Kitt spoke of 'conniving' to erect a memorial to Fine Gael 'leaders' while 'forgetting the men who died for the Republic'[256], grist to a mill which Colley would grind with all the passion of 1922. Angered by the erection of a temporary infants' clinic on the site of the proposed Garden of Remembrance, Colley began:

It has surely come to a pretty pass if we have to hide behind infants' swaddling clothes to protect ourselves when we are trying to let down the memory of the 1916 men ... there has been no hesitation about the memorial on Leinster Lawn to the founders of a partitioned State while the memorial to the real founders of the State, the 1916 men, about whom there should be no questions whatever has been deferred, to use the Parliamentary Secretary's expression ... The erection of the Cenotaph is going ahead. Immediately the Government took office they saw to that. In fact it looks like a deliberate attempt to try to recreate the whole civil war spirit.[257]

Next he attacked the republicanism of Clann na Poblachta: the shame of 'people who protested to be staunch republicans' erecting monuments to 'the founders of a partitioned State'.[258] Bowing out with the charge of extravagance, he compared the original Fianna Fáil provision of £2,700 for the monument with the £30–35,000 figure which various deputies and press articles now associated with the Cenotaph.[259] Taking Colley's place, Lehane rose and began his epilogue – a plague on both your houses:

[252] *Sunday Press*, 4 Dec. 1949; *DE, official report*, CXVIII, cols. 2395–6 (15 Dec. 1949); *IT*, 23 Jan. 1950.
[253] *DE, official report*, CXX, cols. 1438–41 (2 May 1950).
[254] *Ibid.*, cols. 1439–40.   [255] *Irish Press*, 12, 15 and 26 July 1950.
[256] *DE, official report*, CXXII, cols. 1394–5 (12 July 1950).
[257] *Ibid.*, cols. 1400–1.   [258] *Ibid.*, col. 1401.
[259] DT s5734a, Griffith–Collins Cenotaph – general file, report by H. G. Leask, 19 Aug. 1940; memo of the meeting between J. Connolly, OPW, and Eamon de Valera, 24 May 1940. Files relating to the final cost are withheld in the National Archives. Estimates, however, amounted to £20,000. *DE, official report*, CXVIII, cols. 2395–6 (15 Dec. 1949).

I deplore that decision [to erect the Cenotaph] because the memorial is purely sectional in its significance, erected to the three leaders of one Party in the British-engineered civil war. I deplore the decision because it is calculated to recreate the bitterness engendered by that civil war... Unfortunately, on too many occasions from members of the Party opposite [Fianna Fáil] have we seen deliberate attempts to provoke that bitterness, to maintain it and to intensify it. I deplore the decision, and I think the Government by that decision have, to an extent, played into the hands of those sections of the Fianna Fáil Party who realise that they have no political existence other than that based on the bitterness they can create.[260]

Questioning the sincerity of Fianna Fáil opposition in the light of the party's decision to erect the Cenotaph while in power, Lehane's references to unity and the generations born after the civil war, his pleas to abandon past bitterness and dissension, his belief in the Dáil as a place to 'heal' rather than 'reopen civil war scars',[261] naïvely presaged the Taoiseach's lengthy and more realistic response.

Without mention of the extravagance of his own party bias or the hospital building programmes that his government repeatedly postponed, Costello stressed that he was merely the innocent carrying out plans initiated by the previous Fianna Fáil government.[262] Virtuous, he vigorously renounced bitterness: 'So far from endeavouring in any way to foment the feelings or the spirit of the civil war or to revive bitterness, the whole policy of this Government, and the real reason for its foundation, has been to put an end to that bitterness and to this personal strife.'[263] While Richard Mulcahy might have had something else to say about this motley union of the dissatisfied convened to dethrone de Valera, the Taoiseach had politely pointed out what Lehane had been trying to say. Colley, while undoubtedly aggrieved by the delay of the Garden of Remembrance, was playing politics with the garden and the Cenotaph. He was 'burnishing and polishing' the bitterness to the detriment of the maverick Minister for Health, Dr Noël Browne, whose temporary infant care units erected on the precious Rotunda Gardens were undoubtedly causing dead republicans everywhere to spin in their unsettled graves.

Following an unsuccessful attempt by Colley to engage the Taoiseach in a second round two days later, MacEntee stepped into the breach. A bastion of apparent magnanimity, he spoke of the good faith of Griffith, Collins and O'Higgins, of how the 'good they did this country entitles their memory to our honour and respect', of how his party sanctioned the erection of the memorial because it was big enough to recognise that

the Irish people and the Irish nation is one, and that there has to be an element of give and take in these matters; so that what is dear to one heart, not so dear to another, nevertheless might be realised in order to preserve the essential unity of our nation. It was in that spirit that men whose brothers who had been done to death, that men who had been

[260] DE, official report, CXXII, cols. 1406–7 (12 July 1950).   [261] Ibid., col. 1407.
[262] Browne, Against the tide, p. 114.   [263] DE, official report, CXXII, col. 1432 (12 July 1950).

deprived of the right to earn a livelihood because they would not take the test under the old Free State Constitution, decided to give effect ... to the decision of the Cumann na nGaedheal Government which they had displaced in 1932.[264]

With the simple 'it is regrettable ... that our successors were not inspired with the same feelings',[265] MacEntee advanced his charge for the high moral ground. In a haze of Pearses, Brughas and conjured images of an idyllic Garden of Remembrance where the young might realise the cost of their freedom, he bemoaned the precedence which the Cenotaph had taken over the memorial garden 'to the men who had died faithful to the Republic'.[266] That the Garden had been overlooked by Fianna Fáil from 1935 to 1948 seemed to have slipped the deputy's mind. Because Fine Gael were not being seen to return the favour of Fianna Fáil's grudging concession of the Cenotaph, because it had allowed Noël Browne to put sick children before dead republicans, the party was pursuing the 'republican dead with malevolent hatred even beyond the grave'.[267] But Seán MacEntee did 'not wish to create any bitterness'.[268] He spoke not as a politician, 'not because we want to make Party political capital out of this', but as a 'friend' and a 'comrade' of the republican dead; 'the men with whom we had chatted and joked'.[269] Yet whoever he was pretending to be, MacEntee was ignored. Nothing was said, just the damning, and still fitting, indictment of deputy Lehane: 'I do not think I ever listened to anything so nauseatingly dishonest in all my life.'[270]

Other voices were raised. Republican 'friends' and 'comrades', undoubtedly biased but free of the slur of party politics which maligned the sincerity of MacEntee's objections, gathered and issued resolutions. To the Nortons Malthouse Garrison (1922), an association of civil war veterans, the Cenotaph was a 'deliberate attempt to distort history', a danger to unity in the days ahead.[271] The committee of the Four Courts Garrison and the national executive meeting of the IRA Veterans' Association decried the party political monument, calling for the grounds of the 'People's Parliament' to be adorned with a memorial to the men who had died for the republic.[272] None were as critical as T. P. Murphy, a Mayo man who wrote to the editor of the *Irish Press*. Attacking the Taoiseach for 'simulating sweet reasonableness' and for playing upon the 'decency and propriety' of Fianna Fáil, he accused the Cenotaph and its builders of injuring the memory of the republican dead by honouring the two men 'whose names ... spell the last act of a tragedy for Ireland'.[273] All spoke with the zeal of bias, some suggesting the inclusion of the men 'who so nobly

---

[264] *DE, official report*, CXXII, cols. 1989–90 (14 July 1950).   [265] *Ibid.*, col. 1990.
[266] *Ibid.*, cols. 1991–4.   [267] *Ibid.*, cols. 1994–5.   [268] *Ibid.*, col. 1994.
[269] *Ibid.*   [270] *Ibid.*, col. 1992.   [271] *Irish Press*, 12 July 1950.
[272] *Ibid.*, 15 July 1950; DT s5734c, Griffith–Collins Cenotaph – general file, resolution of the National Executive of IRA Veterans' Association held at Gort, 29 July 1950, sent to the Taoiseach's Office.
[273] *Irish Press*, 26 July 1950.

carried on the fight to 1947', men who had conspired against the law of the state since the banning of the IRA. All spoke of unity, but a unity based on submerging Free State memory. While the *Irish Times* praised the good example of party leaders on both sides of the Dáil, these more public, and possibly more sincere, reactions vindicated the article's other conclusion.[274] For many of the men who had fought in the civil war, thirty years was still a short time in the memory of a nation.

On 9 July 1952 Liam Cosgrave asked the new Fianna Fáil Minister for Finance when the Cenotaph was due to be completed.[275] The terse response, that work had been finished since October 1950 when Cosgrave's own party was in power, is somehow a fitting epilogue to the history of this troubled monument. None of the deputies who had so eagerly exchanged names of martyrs and claims of honour and dishonour could even bother to look out the window of their own parliament building, the chance to play politics having passed. Never unveiled, it would always be merely a silent honour. After the objections there could be no speeches or ceremonies; after the declaration of the republic there could be no more talk of Free State. Lost in the need for a unified past, lost in the biographies and memoirs that stopped at 1921, the Cenotaph was ignored in the hope that what it stood for might be forgotten. Following events in Northern Ireland in 1968 and 1969 there could be no reminders of a divided South.

Most Dubliners probably know nothing of the Cenotaph, where it is, or who it honours. Today they could be excused for thinking it a novel feature of the new Dáil car park which completely obscures it from view. In a confident republic there is no place for a Free State Cenotaph. The 'peace process politics' of the 1990s imply a different kind of compromise, a simplified one, because a detached South observes Northern Ireland from a rather comfortable remove, one distorted by the fact that 'we are all revisionists' and perhaps republicans now. The Cenotaph shames, no longer because it is a monument to civil war, but because it reminds the South that it fought the wrong war. Never a memorial to a valiant struggle for a thirty-two county republic, it remains a monument to 'a quibble of words' which never really mentioned the North.[276] For the celebration of the foundation of a state, it is a strange and embarrassed totem of independence. Dwarfed by its surroundings and obscured by cars and prohibitive railings, this ill-fitting Cenotaph is a monument to unease – an unease with a past that no longer seems to suit.

[274] *IT*, 15 July 1950.   [275] *DE, official report*, CXXXIII, col. 421 (9 July 1952).
[276] Arthur Griffith, *DE, treaty debate*, p. 21 (19 Dec. 1921).

2   'History will record the greatness of Collins'? Michael Collins and the politics of memory

On 21 June 1923 six people were photographed before a plain wooden cross on a back road in West Cork. Five were soldiers; one was the sister of Michael Collins.[1] They had gathered for a 'pathetic ceremony' to mark the place where brother and comrade had died ten months before.[2] The soldiers told tales of a last stand, impressing an already proud sister. They prayed and quickly left this lonely place.[3] A four-foot cross, roughly hewn and crudely lettered with white paint, was all they left behind. It read *I gcuimhne Micíl Uí Choileáin ár n-ard Taoiseach grádhmhar d'éag ag troid anseo ar son na h-Éireann* ('In memory of Michael Collins, our beloved leader who died here fighting for Ireland') and the date of death, nothing else. It was cheap and badly made, but joining a small chorus of anonymous willow crosses, that cheapness, the lack of speeches, bespoke a genuine grief. Erected by Frank Bolster, a commandant in the Free State army, but once one of Collins' infamous 'Twelve Apostles', the cross was a private gesture, a soldier's token to a lost leader. Yet even if Bolster was playing the 'big fellow', parading his grief for the *Cork Examiner*, improving his own position by this display of closeness to Collins, he was still doing, or at least being seen to be doing, what others had promised and failed to do. Graveyard eulogies had yielded nothing; Béalnabláth was still a lonely unmarked place; Bolster's gesture, however crude, however heartfelt, was something.

Over one year later there was another gathering at Béalnabláth. Another cross was to be unveiled, another ceremony at the roadside. Only with 300 troops, seventy Civic Guards, the President of the Executive Council and a profusion of people and pressmen it was all a little different. 'A very impressive spectacle' eclipsed the 'pathetic ceremony',[4] while opportunism waved tricolours and replaced private grief. Wooden and willow predecessors were cast aside, making way for a large limestone cross, haughty and tasteless, atop its spacious platform.

As they marched back and forth, saluted, stood to attention, fired shots, sounded the 'Last Post', it was apparent that this cross belonged to the army

---

[1] The soldiers were: Commandant Kingston; Commandant Frank Bolster, C.O. Kinsale; Commandant Cronin, Inspector of Staff GHQ; Commandant Scott, Cork; and Captain Meade.
[2] *CE*, 22 June 1923.   [3] *Ibid*.   [4] *CE*, 23 Aug. 1924.

General view of the scene at the blessing of the Collins Memorial in the Valley of the Blossoms, County Cork, on Friday, 22nd inst.

[Photograph by courtesy of the " Freeman's Journal."

Figure 2 The unveiling of the memorial cross at Béalnabláth, *An t-Óglách*, 30 August 1924 (courtesy of the Military Archives).

(see figure 2). And maybe because Collins died a soldier's death, because he died the first leader of the Free State forces, the army had more right than any other to appropriate this 'sacred spot'.[5] But as Eoin O'Duffy, the general officer commanding the forces, the man transferred from the police to quell mutiny, tore the tricolour from the cross it became clear that this monument at Béalnabláth was as much a token for, as from, the army. It would be unfair to deny that it was 'an enduring tribute' from the troops,[6] an expression of the grief of the rank and file, but it would be naïve to take O'Duffy and his officers at their newspaper-fashioned word. Though they felt the loss of their fallen 'Chief', and felt it with a greater passion than any mere private who only knew tales of the man they knew intimately, theirs was a more practical grief, prostrating itself before power, politics and an elusive popularity. This was not a simple cross at the roadside. Grief's simple crosses were like Bolster's: they were not equipped with their own rostrum; they were not a mere prop on a stage set for future political speeches. With firing parties and marching bands they conquered Béalnabláth in the name of the Irish Free State. They created a place of oratory, not sanctity.

[5] Eoin O'Duffy, *II*, 23 Aug. 1924.   [6] *FJ*, 22 Aug. 1924.

In 1924 an IRAO pamphlet protested that

in the name of 'discipline' the large majority of the old soldiers of 1916–21 have been driven out of the army. May we suggest that the time has not yet come for us in Ireland to be ruled by formulas. Discipline is necessary, but at times it can cover stupidity, tyranny and injustice. What discipline, as it is understood now, had we in 1916–21? We had an army of Volunteers disciplined by love of country and readiness for self-sacrifice. 'Soldiers must not meddle in politics'. We have heard no such formulas from our soldier-patriot, Michael Collins, when we were fighting with him for Irish freedom against the British. Till the national ideals are satisfied we are patriots, not politicians. *There seems to be no place in the Army of Ireland for the old spirit to-day*, although the full ground of Irish freedom and unity is not yet won ... We can only succeed in the future by giving free play to the old revolutionary spirit. We are all still revolutionaries, *or should be*, because our freedom is still not complete.[7]

On 22 August 1924 Eoin O'Duffy stood on the new army-built platform at Béalnabláth and taunted Tobin and Dalton with the word 'discipline'.[8] They were told that the Collins in whose name they had mutinied was not only the army's most loyal soldier and leader but that he was also 'the best disciplined man in the GPO in 1916'.[9] There was no mention that he may have put a gun to Desmond FitzGerald's head at one point in the GPO.[10] To spite them Collins 'obeyed every order', he 'encouraged a spirit of comradeship and goodwill', he was even called a 'strict disciplinarian'. Honouring him became a matter of completing 'the work that was at their hand faithfully and well, to have respect for themselves and the uniforms they wore, and to give unqualified loyalty to the State for which he died'. O'Duffy made no excuses: a military man, his speech was written for a military audience, for the 300 men before him, for the mess room discussions of the newspaper coverage. That Collins had only worn a uniform for the last weeks of his life no longer mattered. Béalnabláth was a platform for the words 'unqualified loyalty', a means to stake a final claim for the memory of the first Commander-in-Chief. The IRB, the IRAO, Kevin O'Higgins, General Richard Mulcahy, Joseph McGrath, each had summoned a version of Michael Collins to their side during the mutiny, but at the place made 'sacred by the blood of General Collins' O'Duffy marked the spot with a cross and claimed the memory of the man for the 'disciplined', 'loyal' army of the Irish Free State. The mutineers had questioned the government's commitment to Collins' stepping stone approach to the Treaty; they had questioned the

---

[7] Irish Republican Army Organisation, *The truth about the army crisis* (Dublin, n.d.), pp. 15–16 (emphasis from original).
[8] General Liam Tobin and Col. C. F. Dalton presented the ultimatum on behalf of the IRAO.
[9] *CE*, 23 Aug. 1924; *II*, 23 Aug. 1924; *FJ*, 23 Aug. 1924; *An t-Óglách*, 2, 15 (30 Aug. 1924), pp. 10–13.
[10] Coogan, *Michael Collins*, p. 40.

government's loyalty to Collins; they had challenged its nationalism. This cross was the government's response:[11] honouring Collins, it snatched him back from the men who branded it traitor in his name.

Yet Béalnabláth was all contradiction: from the monument itself to the people who erected it, to those who attended its unveiling. Nothing was as simple as it was supposed to seem. Honour was coupled with exploitation, mourning with a scheming practicality that could know nothing of grief. Appropriately, the cross itself began the deception. O'Duffy spoke of it marking 'that spot made sacred by the blood of General Collins'. No one contradicted him, even though his 'sacred spot' was forty yards away on the other side of the road.[12] The chosen site was apparently more convenient, more amenable to large gatherings, more comfortable for political rallies. In this there was nothing particularly Irish. Accuracy was not prone to standing in the way of practicality, especially when many who came to 'mourn' did not seem to care or know enough to recognise the mistake. Yet somehow it would be harsh to blame them for their ignorance; all evidence of the actual place of death was moved to support the fallacy. A small round-topped cone of cement, white, apart from a small black cross, had once stood where Collins fell mortally wounded.[13] It had replaced Bolster's wooden cross, which, much weathered, had retreated to the sacristy of the chapel at Collins Barracks, Cork.[14] It was not vandalised as some eager to see conspiracy are wont to contend.[15] The cement cone now stands to the right of the monument at Béalnabláth, demure in the presence of a wealthier grief, conscripted to support the Free State version of events. Nothing was left to mark the actual place of death, a place once lovingly commemorated by a simple cross cut into the roadside grass.

There was nothing simple about the new monument. Enclosed and elevated, with steps and railings; that which made it a platform for oratory also made it a detached place of private grief.[16] Set apart from the world, it was a place to mourn, even though the 'massive platform' conveniently lent itself to guards of honour and gesticulating O'Duffys.[17] It was a place to mourn and, by design, a place to pray, but with its crucified Christ in relief and its own kneeler, it was no longer clear whether the supplicant was prostrate before Christ or Collins.

---

[11] To coincide with the unveiling, Victoria Barracks, Cork, was renamed Collins Barracks. *FJ*, 22 Aug. 1924. It subsequently became known as Michael or Micheál Barracks to distinguish it from Dublin's Collins Barracks. Dan Harvey and Gerry White, *The barracks: a history of Victoria/Collins barracks* (Cork, 1997), p. 115.

[12] Only the *CE*, 23 Aug. 1924 and the *Cork Weekly Examiner*, 30 Aug. 1924 admitted that the cross was erected on the opposite side of the road. Patrick Twohig, *The dark secret of Béalnabláth* (Cork, 1997), pp. 274–5.

[13] This cone was erected by a local committee. No details of the committee are available. Meda Ryan, *The day Michael Collins was shot* (Dublin, 1989), p. 197.

[14] The cross is now in the Military Museum, Cork.

[15] Twohig, *The dark secret*, p. 274.

[16] The railings were added by February 1925.   [17] *CE*, 23 Aug. 1924.

Immortalised at the Cenotaph, Collins was deified at Béalnabláth, the place where he shed his blood to take away the sins of the Free State, where, fatal head wound aside, he had allegedly enough sense of the messianic to utter 'Forgive them'.[18] Yet, when men spoke in terms of 'our faith in Mick Collins',[19] it seems unfair to question the instinct to sacralise him, especially when sacralisation was often all they had to offer, when it disguised the fact that he had died in a shoot-out that the most naïve soldier would have shunned, when sacralisation would never let the republican forget his Nietzschean crime.

However, at Béalnabláth the sacred was embraced by profanity at every turn. For ninety weeks the cross had loitered in the shed of the brother of Dublin sculptor Michael Shortall – ninety weeks that had changed it from an unwanted gift to a cheap solution. In February 1923, the Governor General, Timothy Healy, acting on behalf of an anonymous 'Irish lady in New York',[20] suggested the erection of this cross over the grave of Michael Collins in Glasnevin Cemetery.[21] The Army Council declined the offer in March, refusing to countenance the erection of a monument while the grave was still in use for military casualties, refusing because they had yet to even pay for the grave.[22] Healy had been careful in his negotiations with the Cemeteries Committee when they brought up the price of the grave. He told them nothing of the man this cross was to honour, nothing in case the committee would 'use my desire to do homage to a great memory as a leverage to screw a perhaps high demand' from the government for the plot.[23] Healy may have been well trained as far as the Department of Finance was concerned, but his guile counted for little as long as the Department failed to pay. The cross, already carved to Healy's specifications, was consigned to the dust and indignity of Shortall's brother's shed. When the Shortalls became restive, when they asked for their money, the army took the cross instead.[24] Tim Pat Coogan identifies the 'lady' as Hazel Lavery, a convenient assumption

---

[18] 'Forgiveness with dying breath', *II*, 24 Aug. 1922.

[19] John A. Pinkman, *In the legion of the vanguard* (Dublin, 1998), p. 95.

[20] Letter from Timothy Healy to General Richard Mulcahy, 22 Feb. 1923, Ernest Blythe MSS, UCDA, P24/152(4); Memo by Diarmuid Ó hÉigceartaigh to each member of the Executive Council, 12 Dec. 1923, Ernest Blythe MSS, UCDA, P24/152(1). Her anonymity was on her own insistence.

[21] Letter from General Richard Mulcahy to Timothy Healy, 17 Feb. 1923, Ernest Blythe MSS, UCDA, P24/152(2); DF s004/0013/24, Proposed acquisition of burial plot for deceased members of the national army, letter from the Cemeteries Committee to Timothy Healy, 17 Feb. 1923.

[22] Collins was buried in a large army plot in Glasnevin Cemetery. Memo by Diarmuid Ó hÉigceartaigh to each member of the Executive Council, 12 Dec. 1923, Ernest Blythe MSS, UCDA, P24/152(1); DF s004/0013/24, Proposed acquisition of burial plot for deceased members of the national army, letter from the Cemeteries Committee to Timothy Healy, 17 Feb. 1923 and letter from General Richard Mulcahy to President Cosgrave, 3 Mar. 1923.

[23] DT s3424, General Collins' grave – erection of cross, letter from T. M. Healy to Richard Mulcahy, 22 Feb. 1923.

[24] DT s3424, General Collins' grave – erection of cross.

at a time when biographers of Collins and the biographer of Lady Lavery have just realised the premium of their subjects' private lives.[25] Coogan considers the refusal as a dignified retreat from a potentially scandalous situation, despite the fact that Timothy Healy, Eamon Duggan, the meticulously Catholic W. T. Cosgrave and Collins' own brother, Seán, had already approved the acceptance of the cross and its inscription with nothing more than a name and date of death.[26] He states that the mention of an 'American lady' alerted Mulcahy to Lady Lavery's Chicago origins[27] even though all correspondence refers to an 'Irish-born' lady living in New York and nothing of Mulcahy's doubts. He also forgets to mention that Timothy Healy also requested anonymity in the matter. Are we not, using his logic, to draw the same conclusions here?[28] Yet whether Coogan is right or wrong, whether the lady in question was indeed Lady Lavery or whether she was another admirer of Michael Collins, this woman's token was too human, too profane for the now-hallowed ground of Béalnabláth. However, there was something more profane about the men who erected the cross; men who had dared to do so in the name of the Irish Free State government and army. In the wake of the mutiny a gesture was needed. In Michael Shortall's brother's shed there was a cheap remedy; whether it was the token of a lover no longer mattered. The anonymity that might once have denoted scandal became a type of convenience. A hero could be sacralised, soldiers appeased. No one needed to know that the cross was once paid for by a woman's love or regard or affection, that a miserly government would so callously reap the rewards of another's benevolence.

While it is tempting to revel in the irony of the sanctimonious honouring their saint with a forbidden token, there is something less palatable about the hypocrisy of Béalnabláth. In the light of the Cenotaph it is probably foolish to expect anything better, but there is something particularly dispiriting about the cross's apparent Pauline conversion. Profane became sacred, not by miracle or metamorphosis, just meanness. Costing nothing, it was quickly forgiven its supposedly adulterous sins. Although it may be possible to dress up its parsimony in the guise of a post-war practicality which would have appealed to Collins the Minister for Finance, the response of the government to the cost of erecting and unveiling the cross begs one to question the sincerity of its grief. While the September payment of £75 17s. 0d. to Messrs John Cullen & Co. for transportation and placing, and the payments of £22 10s. 0d. for storage and £26 1s. 0d. for carving to Michael Shortall, were readily borne by

[25] Coogan, *Michael Collins*, p. 428; McCoole, *Hazel.*
[26] Letter from Timothy Healy to General Richard Mulcahy, 22 Feb. 1923, Ernest Blythe MSS, UCDA, P24/152(4).
[27] Coogan, *Michael Collins*, p. 428.
[28] Letter from Timothy Healy to General Richard Mulcahy, 22 Feb. 1923, DT s3424, General Collins' grave – erection of cross.

the army and promptly sanctioned by the Minister for Finance, eyebrows began to be raised when November brought more bills.[29] The £110 5s. 0d. for sand, gravel and limestone coping yielded nothing but Finance's pointed remark that the minister hoped 'that the responsible authorities satisfied themselves before committing the public funds to this expenditure that the prices proposed to be charged were fair and reasonable'.[30] Payment ensued when the Army Finance Office hinted that the Executive Council's tardy approach to the monument left no time to invite tenders.[31] However, an embarrassed Department of Finance exacted its revenge six months after the unveiling ceremony when another £125 12s. 5d. was sought to cover the cost of railings for Béalnabláth. Admonished for not submitting its bills in a prompt and orderly fashion, the army's wrist was duly slapped.[32] But while there was no dignity in begging for the money to honour its first Commander-in-Chief, there was also no dignity in the army's attempt to shirk the costs of his commemoration. Even the soldiers loyal and true had put a price on their honour. It was just a pity that the soldiers balked at something as paltry as the £47 17s. 4d. imbibed at the unveiling ceremony.[33] For the price of tea and sandwiches the army shamed itself, passing on the bill to the Department of External Affairs like a guilty schoolboy shirking blame. But External Affairs just passed it back in a similarly juvenile fashion, thumbing its nose at the army and chiding it with the comment that 'no distinguished visitors' and 'foreigners were entertained on the occasion'.[34] Mr Dermot O'Leary's much-travelled invoice was finally paid by the Army Finance Office on 18 December 1925.[35] Having apparently taken sixteen months to meditate on the quality of O'Leary's sandwiches, the army added insult to the injury of its leisurely contemplation. Deducting a petty £2 12s. 0d. from the amount due, the army had forgotten that 'O'Leary was the only one willing to undertake the catering', 'that several others approached refused',[36] forgotten that, in a predominantly

[29] DF s004/0264/24, Cost of erecting a memorial cross at Béalnabláth Co. Cork to the late General Collins, letter from D. O'Sullivan, Army Finance Office to the Secretary of the Department of Finance, 4 Sept. 1924.

[30] *Ibid.*, letter from the Department of Finance to Thomas Gorman, Army Finance Officer, 27 Nov. 1924.

[31] *Ibid.*, letter from Thomas Gorman, Army Finance Officer to the Secretary of the Department of Finance, 15 Jan. 1925.

[32] *Ibid.*, letter from the Secretary of the Department of Finance to the Army Finance Office, 28 Feb. 1925.

[33] DF s005/0057/24, Claim of Dermot O'Leary, dry canteen, Collins Barracks, Cork, for catering on the occasion of memorial service at Béalnabláth, letter from Thomas Gorman, Army Finance Office to the Department of Finance, 22 Sept. 1924.

[34] The Army Finance Office attempted to establish the payment of the costs of the Bodenstown ceremonies as a precedent for offloading the costs of the Béalnabláth affair. *Ibid.*, letter from S. P. Breathnach, Department of External Affairs to the Department of Finance, 11 Dec. 1925.

[35] *Ibid.*, letter from J. Hanna, Department of Finance to the Army Finance Office, 18 Dec. 1925.

[36] *Ibid.*, letter from Thomas Gorman, Army Finance Office to the Department of Finance, 22 Sept. 1924.

anti-Treatyite area, this man had risked being called a collaborator just so the army could honour Michael Collins. He had endured the unpopularity of the work and risked the patronage of more regular and reliable clients: the army took a year to cheat him out of £2 12s. 0d.

In the case of James Hennessy, owner of the land on which the cross was erected, the army took almost two years. Claiming £95 for the purchase price of the site and for trespass and damage to his lands, Hennessy was finally paid £20 in June 1926: £1 for the land and £19 compensation for the damage caused by troops.[37] Two years had weakened his admittedly overpriced resolve, but even his opportunism could not excuse the army, which paid the Chief State Solicitor ten shillings more to process the case than the £1 they paid Hennessy for the land. That the Chief State Solicitor was only paid his £1 10s. 0d. in November 1928 is merely another piece of damning evidence.[38] Yet the army had its accomplices. General Eoin O'Duffy was not alone on the platform at Béalnabláth. President Cosgrave was lurking there; a reluctant acting Minister for Defence, silent, content to let O'Duffy and the army chaplains speak the post-mutiny words he could not risk saying himself[39] (see figure 3). Because he had lost two cabinet ministers and seven TDs over the mutiny,[40] because O'Higgins served more as a threat than a Vice-President, it was important for him to be at Béalnabláth – important because only the President and the Minister for Defence could make a convincing profession of faith. A lesser mortal would have been an insult to the army, proof that its beloved Collins had truly been betrayed.

It may be callous to question Cosgrave's motives in this way. He had, after all, 'stood bareheaded and silent' as Seán Collins described his brother's death;[41] he sympathised with the Collins family; he shared his colleagues' grief. He had at least bothered, for whatever reason, to be there. The other ministers remained in Dublin, happy to let the words 'his memory will be ever cherished, revered and honoured by the people of all creeds and classes' stick in their throats in the comfort of the Pro-Cathedral instead.[42] It was easier to attend an anniversary requiem mass in Dublin than to stand in the rain on the side of a road in Cork. Regardless of their grief, honouring Collins had become a matter of convenience. His name could strengthen a weak paragraph in a speech; his memory had its occasional uses. Travelling to Béalnabláth was apparently

[37] DF s004/0264/24, Cost of erecting a memorial cross at Béalnabláth Co. Cork to the late General Collins, letter from Thomas Gorman, Army Finance Office to the Secretary of the Department of Finance, 7 June 1926.

[38] Ibid., note from the Department of Finance sanctioning the payment of £1 10s. 0d., 24 Nov. 1928.

[39] The memorial was blessed by Frs O'Neill and McCarthy, chaplains to the forces. CE, 23 Aug. 1924.

[40] Walker, Parliamentary election results in Ireland, p. 116.

[41] II, 23 Aug. 1924.   [42] Cork Weekly Examiner, 30 Aug. 1924.

MICHAEL COLLINS COMMEMORATED AT THE SCENE OF HIS DEATH : THE MEMORIAL AT BEALNABLATH UNVEILED.

Figure 3 The unveiling of the memorial cross at Béalnabláth, *Illustrated London News*, 30 August 1924 (courtesy of *Illustrated London News*).

beyond the call of duty issued at his graveside in Glasnevin in 1922. Travelling was inconvenient, and trips to Cork cost money.

Yet travelling to Béalnabláth was not the pilgrimage it might seem. Just as Cosgrave's motives were mixed, so too were the instincts of the local politicians and councillors who wended their way to West Cork. To the plethora of Cork rural and urban district councillors, to M. J. Hennessy and John Prior, Cumann na nGaedheal TDs for Cork East and West respectively, even to Senator J. C. Love, Béalnabláth offered the chance to be seen, and to be seen to be doing the right thing by the party faithful. Even the president of the South of Ireland Cattle Trade Association was there to reap the rewards.[43] Genuine grief may have brought them there, but being there would do them no harm in the next local election. The mutineers had cried 'Collins' because it was more laudable than unprincipled pique about poor pensions and demobilisation.[44] The lesson was not lost on the men who relied on Collins' neighbours and notoriety for their political survival. Of course this may be entirely unjust, a blind assumption that position and politics corrupt, but it would be equally short-sighted to presume that every head that bowed at Béalnabláth was lowered to honour and to pray. The crowds that came to the unveiling, crowds of indeterminate number,[45] of such volume that the President was forced to abandon his car and walk the last mile to the monument,[46] deserve to be questioned. They need to be chased from their hiding place, from the homogeneity of the very word 'crowd'.

The townland of Béalnabláth was not given to large gatherings. The prospect of speeches and marching soldiers and the President of the Free State was too great a novelty to miss. Men, women and children came. They came on foot, wearily on bicycles, crowded on the back of farmers' drays.[47] They came because, for once, there was importance, because they had a chance to be part of it, because Dublin had buried Collins and this was Cork's turn. Whatever their opinion of Collins, they came because they were curious. The *Irish Independent* said that 'all were deeply affected'.[48] Undoubtedly some or most were: the 'silence ... broken occasionally by the sobs of women and girls' was proof of that.[49] But the six-week spectacle of camping troops at Béalnabláth was also proof of something else.[50] There was fear of hatred still.

Curiosity was not the preserve of the loyal. Sympathies were mixed in West Cork; the county had bred the killers as well as Collins. Men and women who had brought food and drink to the ambushers as they lay in wait,[51] men and women who could never vote for Cumann na nGaedheal, still came to Béalnabláth. Curiosity may have been enough for some, but they were also local people, people who had to go on living and working in the same community as the friends and family of Michael Collins.[52] They owed them that much, and in

[43] *CE*, 23 Aug. 1924; *Realt a Deiscirt*, 23 Aug. 1924.
[44] Ronan Fanning, *Independent Ireland* (Dublin, 1983), p. 47; Duggan, *A history of the Irish army*, pp. 131–5.
[45] No figure exists for the attendance at Béalnabláth.   [46] *II*, 23 Aug. 1924.   [47] *Ibid.*
[48] *Ibid.*   [49] *Ibid.*
[50] Troops camped there from 21 July to 1 Sept. 1924. DF s004/0264/24, Cost of erecting a memorial cross at Béalnabláth Co. Cork to the late General Collins.
[51] Ryan, *The day*, p. 76.
[52] James Mackay, *Michael Collins: a life* (Edinburgh, 1996), p. 298.

a way they owed Collins more. Of all those who died, Collins was one of the few to retain a type of republican respect. His picture always hung beside de Valera's on the wall of Ned Barrett's 'very republican' family home.[53] Even in 1974 *An Phoblacht* could write 'if those two [Collins and Boland] had survived the legitimacy of Dáil Éireann might have been saved'.[54] The years 1919–21 could never be taken away from Collins, and death meant that he was never tainted by the atrocities or the executions. There remained a faith that Collins could have ended the war, could have made things different, a faith because, unlike the others, he was one of their own. Even the most extreme Liam Lynch conceded, albeit grudgingly, that 'nothing could bring home more forcibly the awful unfortunate national situation at present than the fact that it has become necessary for Irishmen and former comrades to shoot such men as M. Collins who rendered such splendid service to the Republic in the last war against England'.[55] On hearing of his death one republican cried 'Ireland is lost';[56] another, Erskine Childers, walked silently to his desk and raised the voice of *Poblacht na hÉireann* in praise of him.[57]

The less articulate said it in different ways. Two sisters went to Béalnabláth the day after the shooting. There they found a once-starched but now blood-ied linen collar. They picked up empty bullet cases, spent cartridges, anything they could find, and for twenty years they kept them safe in their 'rabid Republican' home.[58] Another treasured Collins' handkerchief;[59] others took what they could from abandoned vehicles, useless things, but now secret relics under local republican beds. Two members of the ambush squad also returned.[60] They found Collins' cap and his revolver and, bringing them to their leader Tom Hales, they buried the hat and prayed for the man who once wore it.[61] Collins had said of Hales that 'More than any man, I would have valued his support.' Hales acknowledged the compliment, kept the badge from the cap, and murmured something about 'a souvenir of a friend'.[62] British soldiers brought home German helmets because they were relics of bravery, tokens seized from a hated and defeated enemy. They were never given a dignified burial or hidden from the prospect of an admiring glance. Collins' relics were different. They were wrapped up in shame and sorrow and hidden, hidden be-cause republicanism regretted what it had done. The new, young republicans, baptised in the euphoria of the truce, may have celebrated at the news of his death, may have daubed Dublin walls with 'Move over Mick and make room

[53] Ryan, *The day*, p. xi.   [54] *An Phoblacht*, 23 Aug. 1974.
[55] Letter from Liam Lynch to Liam Deasy, 28 Aug. 1922, Military Archives, lot 4/3.
[56] Margery Forester, *Michael Collins – the lost leader* (London, 1971), p. 342.
[57] Frank O'Connor, *An only child* (London, 1961), p. 232.
[58] Twohig, *The dark secret*, p. 181.   [59] *Ibid.*, p. 114.
[60] Jim Kearney and Timmy Sullivan.   [61] Ryan, *The day*, pp. 30–2.
[62] *Ibid.*, p. 31. Jim Kearney, a member of the ambush squad, also kept the cap's front strap.

for Dick': 'But those soldiers of the Republic who had been his comrades-in-arms did not share their elation. There can have been few times of war in which the death in battle of the opposing Commander-in-Chief has aroused such personal sorrow as Republicans felt at the passing of Michael Collins.'[63] Sonny O'Neill, the man generally believed to have fired the fatal shot, only muttered 'May the Lord have mercy on his soul',[64] and kept his secret for almost thirty years. He died wishing to meet Seán Collins, wishing for the forgiveness of the Collins family.[65] Another member of the ambush squad, Jim Hurley, confronted Seán Collins in 1923. Crying like a child, all he could say was 'How could we do it?' In 1965, according to his dying wish, Hurley was buried in Clonakilty churchyard beside Seán Collins.[66] There were republicans at Béalnabláth in 1924, but there was no need for the encampment of soldiers. In 1924, Béalnabláth was a monument to republican regret.

Béalnabláth was also a monument to grief. The extended Collins family came, mourning also the anniversary of a cousin, another Michael Collins, fatally wounded one day before his more famous Commander-in-Chief.[67] Friends came: Elizabeth and Margaret Hales; sisters of the man who had led the ambush; sisters of the Free State Brigadier General murdered by a brother's companions.[68] They came because here allegiances meant nothing, because this was a place for old acquaintances. It was 'not about the affairs of State or the Army, but about the past, their past, his past'.[69] It was about a past before civil war. Here there was nothing but the loss of him, nothing but the loss of a man once admired. Unlike the Cenotaph, and despite the marching soldiers, Béalnabláth remained a public place. Though the land had been bought and grudgingly paid for with Free State money, the monument belonged to the men and women who stood bareheaded there, to the endless names that the next day's newspapers recalled. Grief could not be controlled or orchestrated, and like the anniversary masses attended by those 'who were not in consonance with Michael Collins's views', it obstinately refused to be contained.[70] Wreaths, crudely numbered at 'two lorry loads' by the *Freeman's Journal*,[71] spelt out this stubborn sadness: some erudite, some simply 'to a dear friend'.[72] One, purple for remembrance, left by the women of Cumann na mBan, spoke plainly of Cork's affection.[73] Béalnabláth was then a place of sorrow and sorrow knew nothing of the words 'republic' or 'Free State'.

---

[63] Forester, *Michael Collins*, p. 342.
[64] Known as Denis 'Sonny' Neill or O'Neill. Ryan, *The day*, p. 127.
[65] Mackay, *Michael Collins*, p. 299; Coogan, *Michael Collins*, p. 421.   [66] *Ibid*.
[67] Ryan, *The day*, p. 59.   [68] *Realt a Deiscirt*, 23 Aug. 1924.   [69] Ryan, *The day*, p. 85.
[70] *II*, 23 Aug. 1924.   [71] *FJ*, 23 Aug. 1924.   [72] *Realt a Deiscirt*, 30 Aug. 1924.
[73] The wreath was presented on behalf of GHQ staff of Cumann na mBan by President B. Conway. *CE*, 23 Aug. 1924. This was the strictly pro-Treatyite Cumann na mBan, who operated under the name Cumann na Saoirse except in the case of County Cork. Lil Conlon, *Cumann na mBan and the women of Ireland 1913–25* (Kilkenny, 1969), p. 297.

But if sorrow was labouring under a misapprehension, it was merely symptomatic of a greater confusion. The commemoration of Michael Collins was, and is, a bewildering thing. He died within two months of the outbreak of civil war, yet Free State memory is obsessed with him. He died a 'great soldier', having failed the only combative test he ever took. However, it could be said that he lends himself well to obsession. He was a young and, relative to his cabinet peers, an attractive man. His past was the stuff of legend, his unlived future a rod to beat mediocrity's back. He was glamour and adventure to 'the most conservative-minded revolutionaries that ever put through a successful revolution';[74] he was redemption for the Flogging Bill and the executions and the trap mine in Ballyseedy Wood. He died before he had done enough to damn himself; he was potential unfulfilled and his memory was at the mercy of every man who invoked his name. In this respect there was no confusion: he was the best the Free State had to offer. He was a leader with an illustrious past. Other dead soldiers were an admission of incompetence, of military failure. The confusion rests rather with the acts of commemoration. Following his death there was urgency and activity, then nothing: nothing for years; nothing until men aged, until the centenary of his birth, until a film gave life to another generation of myths.[75]

Every act encompassed something of motive and emotion; little was innocent of either. Death evoked many responses; answers to some of the questions and absences left by his death. The government was prompt: quick to capitalise, quick to mourn. A bust and a biography were commissioned; an attempt was made to purchase a death mask, all within two months of Collins' death.[76] But in its haste to bask in the reflected glory of its dead hero, the government was punished: a fool rushing in to be rewarded by a sculptor's tardiness and an author's grievance. A combination of errors, accidents and negligence resulted in Albert Power's failure to produce the mask and bust, which he agreed to undertake in October 1922.[77] It was suggested that he lacked sympathy with his subject, that his republicanism clouded and continued to cloud his vision until 1936 when the mask was eventually presented to the National Museum and the bust to the National Gallery. Oliver St John Gogarty, who mediated between the sculptor and the government, made Power's feelings clear in 1925:

[74] Quoted in de Vere White, Kevin O'Higgins, p. 142.
[75] This is purely in terms of monuments. 'Collins', the biography industry, is an entirely different matter.
[76] The cabinet decision was taken concerning the biography on 20 Sept. 1922, cabinet minutes, PG10(a); on 11 Oct. 1922 concerning the death mask, PG34(a); and on 17 Oct. 1922 for the bust, PG38(a). Consultation relating to the mask and the bust does, however, date from 10 Oct. 1922. DT s1827b, National leaders: busts, death masks, statues.
[77] DF 365/6, Portrait busts of Griffith and Collins by Albert Power; letter from M. McDonnchadha to FitzGerald, Desmond FitzGerald MSS, UCDA, P80/1027; DT s1827b, National leaders: busts, death masks, statues.

there appears to me to be some lack of sympathy in Power for the memory of General Collins. Therefore I think that if the commission for the second bust were to be given to a sculptor with a masterful capacity for embodying dignity and force, a better statue would be the result. Where sympathy is wanting we can only look for a likeness and not a creation in bronze of what Collins represented and of what his character and memory deserves.[78]

Power did not have the same struggles with the many republican commissions he undertook.

But somehow Fianna Fáil seemed to manage to find the sympathy which the artist could not; a strange discovery if the legacy of civil war bitterness was as potent as popularly believed. De Valera's government paid £220 for the bust, maintaining the commission as part of a grander scheme to provide busts of a series of revolutionary leaders. Extreme republicanism did not seem to care that a Fianna Fáil government was paying for the Collins bust. It thought the treacherous Collins was now a fitting companion for Fianna Fáil. It was simply more offended that the turncoats dared to included Cathal Brugha in their plans. Cumann na nGaedheal had been willing to pay £300 for the bust:[79] a rare spasm of generosity from a government given to erecting cheap or preferably free monuments. The explanation may lie in Cumann na nGaedheal's collective grief. Alternatively it may be explained by the fact that the bust was originally destined for the floor of Leinster House. There it would laud over the Dáil, casting a cold eye over political enemy and ally alike, never letting either forget that Cumann na nGaedheal had won the war and was claiming the credit for all that could be achieved in peace. That the bust never reached Leinster House may be appropriate if this was indeed the intention;[80] that it never reached Leinster House must have satisfied those who resorted to shouting a discordant 'seventy-seven' whenever Dáil discussions took an inconvenient turn, those who repeatedly inferred that de Valera and his party were as spiteful as some Cumann na nGaedheal electioneering implied. That de Valera, as Taoiseach, sat in an office beneath copies of the Cenotaph medallions of Griffith and Collins was a less publicised fact. Five pounds' worth of sculpture had adorned the leader's wall since 1926: five pounds' worth of cheap legitimisation that would remind every Taoiseach of his debt to Cumann na nGaedheal.[81]

De Valera made no attempt to remove them, though within two months of taking power he ordered plaques of Cathal Brugha and Austin Stack to lessen

[78] DT s1827b, National leaders: busts, death masks, statues, letter from Gogarty to Diarmuid O'Hegarty, 15 May 1925.
[79] DF 365/6, Portrait busts of Griffith and Collins by Albert Power; Desmond FitzGerald MSS, UCDA, P80/1027.
[80] The bust was delivered to Oriel House in November 1936. It was inspected and taken from there to the National Gallery. DT s1827b, National leaders: busts, death masks, statues, letter from P. J. Raftery, Office of Public Works to the Department of Finance, 11 Nov. 1936.
[81] Ibid., letter from Philip Hanson, OPW to Arthur Codling, Department of Finance, 13 Apr. 1932.

the liability.[82] Muted, the medallions remained. And why should they not? Why should de Valera's government not order and pay for a bust of Michael Collins? 'Perhaps this action was motivated by a desire to heal civil war wounds, albeit in a small way. On the other hand, it may have been an attempt by him [de Valera] to appropriate all the heroes!'[83] That neither Stack nor Cathal Brugha's family were given to singing de Valera's praises had not deterred his party from appropriating their memory. Mary MacSwiney made republicanism's feelings clear in a letter to Seán T. O'Kelly: 'Are you going to do what is right and just, or become a second murder-gang, like the Cosgrave-Mulcahy Ministry? On your heads be the responsibility! We do not recognise the people's right to surrender their independence. You did not once, but you have come to limit yourself by their mandate.'[84] To Mrs Brugha and to most of the republicans Fianna Fáil had left behind in 1926, de Valera was now as much a traitor as any Griffith or Collins. 'It is better to die nobly ... than live a slave' was the de Valera of 1923.[85] A captive of Free State politics in the 1930s, he could find no favour with Mrs Brugha now. She refused him the use of the death masks for the sculptures, just as she refused pro-Treatyites permission to attend her husband's funeral in 1922.[86] When republicans stole a plaque to Brugha which de Valera had planned to unveil on a government building, *An Phoblacht* could only mournfully ask 'Where are those friends of the fallen heroes now?'[87] Seán MacBride explained the theft to an IRA rally in Kilkenny: it was an insult to Brugha's memory to associate him with an institution of a state he refused to recognise.[88] Yet nothing stopped de Valera. The National Health Insurance offices still became Brugha Buildings just as Fianna Fáil intended.[89] There was something of worth in any hero, any Brugha, any Collins. His government could buy a bust of Collins because in the early 1930s de Valera needed to be all things to all men: Brugha for the recalcitrant republicans; Collins for those who did not trust him yet. But perhaps, as Cumann na nGaedheal may have intended, the bust of Collins came more from a desire to impress where it mattered – politically. Leinster House was not a public place. Béalnabláth was graced with

---

82 DT s1827b, National leaders: busts, death masks, statues. When the Taoiseach was interviewed in his office journalists nearly always referred to the presence of the Griffith and Collins medallions in the background. Thanks to Dr Deirdre McMahon for this reference.

83 Sighle Bhreathnach-Lynch, 'Face value: commemoration and its discontents', *Circa*, 65 (Autumn 1993), p. 34.

84 Letter from Mary MacSwiney to Seán T. O'Kelly, Mary MacSwiney MSS, UCDA, P48a/139.

85 Eamon de Valera's address to the republican army following the death of Liam Lynch, 12 Apr. 1923, *Daily Bulletin*, 13 Apr. 1923; Florence O'Donoghue MSS, NLI, MS 31,242.

86 Publicity Department pamphlet, 9 July 1922, NLI, LOp117, item 91.

87 *An Phoblacht*, 8 Oct. 1926.   88 *Irish Press*, 9 July 1934.

89 Sighle Bhreathnach-Lynch, 'Commemorating the hero in newly independent Ireland: expressions of nationhood in bronze and stone', in Lawrence W. McBride (ed.), *Images, icons and the Irish nationalist imagination* (Dublin, 1999), p. 154.

a cross that cost nothing; Leinster Lawn was bedecked with a crumbling piece of wood and plaster.

Cumann na nGaedheal began to take something for granted: commemoration could be cheap. Renaming a barracks or two was economical and efficient; it kept the soldiers happy, it worked wonders for the legitimisation of pro-Treatyite authority.[90] However, conferring Collins' name on a landmark could only be as successful as old habits allowed; change took time to become common usage. The public mind required public acts of commemoration. Collins' uniform was quickly installed in the National Museum;[91] it joined the cap once buried by Tom Hales but soon excavated by a farmer's uneasy conscience.[92] Together they were left in this communal place, a place free to enter, where commemoration came for the price of a glass case. The uniform and the cap cost nothing more than their original manufacture; the death mask, when it arrived in 1936, a mere £20.[93] Commemoration could be cheap. It could be cheap because cheap did not always have to signify the Cenotaph's type of indignity. Ordinary things did not cost much and now there was nothing else left: a coat, a cap, a piece of handwriting – anonymous, unimportant, but fragments now of a greatness that was gone. Each acquired a value beyond material means and all were treasured for the want of him. Things touched or used or worn had become relics of him, the fascination feeding the memory of his worth, thriving on the hushed voices reduced to a whisper by a type of awe. The instinct was public, but the instinct was also private. Kitty Kiernan kept a button from his coat,[94] Lady Lavery, some shamrock from the grass at Béalnabláth.[95] Joe O'Reilly took a lock of his hair[96] and began using Collins' room at Portobello Barracks.[97] In 1924 he attempted to buy the furniture from this room simply because 'I wish to have them in memory of Mick'.[98] He could not afford the £22 2s. 10½d. he was

---

[90] Royal Barracks, Dublin, and Victoria Barracks, Cork, were both renamed Collins Barracks, the former in 1922, the latter in 1924, as stated earlier, to coincide with the unveiling of the Béalnabláth monument.

[91] The uniform, cap and overcoat were presented to the National Museum on 27 Jan. 1923. DT s2927a, Uniform of the late General Collins – presentation to the National Museum. The uniform which Collins was wearing when he died was taken to Argentina by a doctor from Shanakiel Hospital in Cork where the body was originally taken. Coogan, *Michael Collins*, p. 449; Mackay, *Michael Collins*, p. 293. Another uniform, an earlier Volunteer uniform belonging to Collins, was later presented to the museum by Bridget O'Connor in mid-1953. Richard Mulcahy MSS, UCDA, P7b/206.

[92] Mr Long, owner of the land, entrusted it to the local priest, Fr Coffey, who took it to Military HQ in Bandon. From there it was taken to Dublin. Twohig, *The dark secret*, pp. 261–2.

[93] DT s1827b, National leaders: busts, death masks, statues.

[94] Mackay, *Michael Collins*, p. 278.

[95] Kept in an envelope labelled 'where Michael fell', the shamrock had been sent to her by Hannie, Michael's sister. McCoole, *Hazel*, p. 101.

[96] Ryan, *The day*, p. 121.

[97] DF f200/16/24, Application of Col. O'Reilly to purchase furniture used by the late Gen. Collins in Portobello Barracks, letter from Col. Joseph O'Reilly to W. T. Cosgrave, 1 Apr. 1924.

[98] *Ibid.*

asked to pay or the assurance sought that he would not 'alienate any of these articles'.[99] The government offended him, then taunted him with the promise that there was money to be made out of sentimentality: 'the sentimental interest connected with it ought to have the effect of increasing its value'.[100] Several letters later the bed, table, chairs, washstand, jug and basin were bought by Collins' sister Margaret for £18 9s. 1d.[101] The government had spent more in civil servants' time than the tired furniture was once worth, but it had learned nothing.[102] It still felt there was 'no reason to sell them to her'[103], no reason because it understood nothing of sorrow. A uniform or a death mask could be flaunted in a museum, flaunted to its advantage. Battered furniture was not suitable for show cases; in government terms it was worthless. Commemoration could be cheap, but it still had to serve a purpose.

The biography would do both.[104] Beginning amid the instincts of a brother's pride, it quickly became, in government hands, 'a worthy monument to the life-work of a Great Man',[105] reflecting well upon the Free State version of events. The cabinet had had one amongst its number worthy of the acclaim of biography, and it was commissioned with the intention of basking in the glory of the weighty tome. Anxious that 'some chancer "on the make"' should not come 'butting in and dealing with our dead hero in a way that none of us would like', Commandant General Piaras Béaslaí was a convenient if not a popular choice of author.[106] Gearóid O'Sullivan, adjutant general of the Free State army, responded to Béaslaí's selection thus: 'The person you suggest *would not do at all*. Literary Generals are not always endowed with sufficient keenness and greatness of mind to appreciate the enormous virtues and vices combined in one person.'[107] Diarmuid O'Hegarty, secretary to the Provisional Government and later the Department of an Taoiseach, also shared this opinion. More objected to his capabilities, others to his knowledge of Collins. But he was acceptable to the Collins family and, more importantly, he was already on the payroll.[108] Forcing him to submit each chapter to a review committee, the government remained

---

[99] *Ibid.*, internal Finance memo, 16 Apr. 1924.

[100] *Ibid.*, letter from J. J. Healy, OPW, to Brennan of Finance, 5 May 1924.

[101] *Ibid.*, transference of articles to Mrs Collins-O'Driscoll, 27 Aug. 1925.

[102] Coogan, *Michael Collins*, p. 425.

[103] DF f200/16/24, Application of Col. O'Reilly to purchase furniture used by the late Gen. Collins in Portobello Barracks, undated memo.

[104] Of all the Collins biographies this particular work has been selected for examination because it was the only one to have been actively commissioned as a commemorative act.

[105] DT s1760a, Michael Collins biographies, letter from Piaras Béaslaí to McDunphy, 26 Oct. 1922.

[106] Letter from Piaras Béaslaí to Gearóid O'Sullivan, 4 Sept. 1922, Piaras Béaslaí MSS, NLI, MS 33,915(7).

[107] DT s1760a, Michael Collins biographies, letter from O'Sullivan to Cosgrave, 12 Sept. 1922.

[108] Seán Collins told Cosgrave of his preference for Béaslaí in early September 1922. *Ibid.*, memo from McDunphy to W. T. Cosgrave, 7 Sept. 1922.

relatively content at least until he spoke the words 'serialisation' and 'profit'.[109] The precious biography was not to be pawned, 'not to be published in serial form'.[110] It was not for blackened newspaper hands, nor eyes fed on weekly westerns, greedy for the next instalment. Only the government's reluctance to alienate Collins' relatives retrieved the situation. Béaslaí had intended 'that the lion's share of the money [royalties] should go to the Collins family'.[111] Insulted by the government's attitude, Seán Collins threatened to withhold his family's co-operation.[112] Though serialisation was never mentioned again, the government gave in: Béaslaí and Seán Collins alone would settle publication details. But in this giving in the government gave up. Relations with Béaslaí deteriorated, culminating in his demotion and resignation from the army. He went on his way to finish the biography in his own time, a victim somewhat of a change of heart. By March 1924 'we can scarcely justify having on the payroll of the Army a "General" whose only occupation is writing the life of the late Commander in Chief'.[113] It was fine in 1922: there was no army mutiny, no one using Collins' very name to curse what the government had become. The biography may have been cheap and convenient, but the government was frightened once the legacy was questioned. Afraid, it opted for ambivalence, washed its hands of the book and left Béaslaí to make his profit.

The two-volume biography, *Michael Collins and the making of a new Ireland*, went on sale in November 1926. It sold and sold and its further editions sold. If the advertisements were to be believed, no good Irish home could be complete without it: 'It is a book of international importance . . . but its special appeal is to all Irishmen and Irishwomen who love their country, and no private bookcase in Ireland will be complete without a copy of this great work.'[114] But prior to publication the success was not always so sure. Béaslaí sent extracts to the *Cork Examiner* and the *Manchester Guardian* and was happy to accept the £150 the *Examiner* sent him in return.[115] He had learned his lesson a year earlier in 1925 when he tried and very quickly failed to get £12,000 from an

---

[109] The committee consisted of O'Sullivan, O'Hegarty and Kevin O'Shiel, Assistant Legal Advisor. *Ibid.*, Provisional Government minute, 21 Sept. 1922. See also Deirdre McMahon, ' "A worthy monument to a great man": Piaras Béaslaí's Life of Michael Collins', *Bullán*, 2, 2 (Winter/Spring 1996), pp. 55–65.

[110] Letter from the Publicity Department to Piaras Béaslaí, 31 Oct. 1922, Piaras Béaslaí MSS, NLI, MS 33,930(14).

[111] DT s1760a, Michael Collins biographies, letter from Béaslaí to Eamon Duggan, 3 Nov. 1922.

[112] *Ibid.*, letter from Seán Collins to W. T. Cosgrave, 7 Nov. 1922.

[113] *Ibid.*, letter from W. T. Cosgrave to Joe McGrath, 15 Mar. 1924.

[114] *The Star*, 5 Jan. 1929. See also *An t-Óglách*, 5, 19 (13 Nov. 1926), p. 17 and the 'Advance publicity booklet' (Dublin, n.d.), NLI, p2467, item 18.

[115] Letter from D. McGrath, to Béaslaí, 21 June 1926, enclosing £75 as the first of two instalments for his articles, Piaras Béaslaí MSS, NLI, MS 33,930(2).

American publisher.[116] While Béaslaí had learned to temper his rather greedy expectations, he had reason to believe that the memory of Collins would be a sure saleable commodity. He knew of all the precedents.

While the government went out of its way to make political capital out of its dead leader in 1922, others went the way of material gain. Collins was marketable: even before his death he had been offered £10,000 from a London agent and $20,000 from the *New York World* for his memoirs.[117] After his death the government was forced to monitor the instincts of the more salacious press. 'The secret history of Michael Collins' by a 'Bodyguard' had the dead leader cavorting across the pages of the *World's Pictorial News*, vanquishing Englishmen on the back of a white charger. Although the story galloped untrammelled across England, the government placed an embargo on the sale of the journal in Ireland for the duration of the series of articles; it had no wish to give 'great pain and annoyance to the friends and relatives of the late General Collins'.[118] It had no wish to make Collins, or indeed itself, look like a character in a cheap novelette. A series of articles by Hayden Talbot in the *Daily Express* prompted Joseph O'Reilly to send the editor his objections: the articles were 'lies, pieced together from gossip... I have to believe either that my dead Chief was what Talbot calls "romancing" or that Talbot is a liar and a forger... it is just such matter as a stranger to Ireland would fake up from gossip and hearsay.'[119] Béaslaí made similar objections to Talbot's endeavours: the articles were 'bogus', 'the life story... a forgery'.[120] However, Béaslaí's concerns may have been coloured by Talbot's threat to pre-empt his own biography. But Béaslaí's book was only the beginning. While Mary Banotti wrote that 'there was no mention of him [Collins] in the history books. There was never a mention of his name in the discussion of national life',[121] J. J. Lee, one page later in the same book, stated that:

it cannot credibly be claimed that Michael Collins has been neglected by historians and biographers. If anything, the contrary is the case. For one whose public career was compressed into a few short years, and who died at the age of thirty-one, he has attracted intense biographical attention by Irish standards. More words have probably been written about him than about Eamon de Valera, whose public career spanned sixty years. Far

---

[116] Letter from Diarmuid Lynch, New York, to Béaslaí, 7 Aug. 1925, Piaras Béaslaí MSS, NLI, MS 33,930(4).

[117] Piaras Béaslaí MSS, NLI, MS 33,916(1); McMahon, '"A worthy monument"', p. 55.

[118] Letter from Piaras Béaslaí to James Tevan, special correspondent, *World's Pictorial News*, 5 Oct. 1922, Piaras Béaslaí MSS, NLI, MS 33,915(8).

[119] Letter by Joseph O'Reilly to the editor, *Sunday Express*, 15 Sept. 1922, Piaras Béaslaí MSS, NLI, MS 33,915(7).

[120] Letter by Béaslaí to the editor, *Daily Express*, 5 Sept. 1922, *ibid.*

[121] Mary Banotti, 'Introduction', in Gabriel Doherty and Dermot Keogh (eds.), *Michael Collins and the making of the Irish state* (Dublin, 1998), pp. 17–18.

more work has been devoted to him than to Arthur Griffith, founder of the original Sinn Féin, and leader of the Treaty delegation.[122]

From the elegiac to the downright prurient, biography has queried Collins and clarified him. There is little left to pick from the bones of the carcass, just versions and revisions, challenges and rebuttals. His name on a cover is a guarantee of commercial success, more so now that his filmic persona has fostered a whole new fascination. It seems easier to take a seat on the lucrative bandwagon than to turn historiographical attention to someone new.

But there was always money to be made from the instinct to commemorate, a profit to be reaped from the public fascination, and many were willing to count the spoils. What cheap newspaper supplements were quick to begin, artists, sculptors and even novelists fervently completed.[123] Sir John Lavery sat with the corpse for three days and painted 'Love of Ireland', a portrait of the lying-in-state of Michael Collins. It was shown in the artist's house thirteen days after the Commander-in-Chief's death. Most newspapers reacted kindly, commending the artist and the patriotic sentiment he had captured. Only the *Morning Post*, not renowned for its art criticism, dared to tell its readers why the press had been summoned to Cromwell Place to view a portrait which was never to be exhibited in England[124] – publicity for the forthcoming sale of colour reproductions of the painting. But then Sir John was not new to this type of profiteering. His portraits of Griffith and Collins, executed in early 1922, were already available to the public in print form at fifteen and twenty shillings from 'a reputable Dublin agent'.[125] There was honour and commemoration and a nice little profit on the side, and profiting from Collins was nothing new to the Laverys. Hazel had dined out on the strength of her association with Collins on several occasions,[126] often enough perhaps for her husband to subsequently donate many of his Irish paintings to the state.[127] This may be somewhat unfair, given that the Laverys were not alone in their apparently mercenary approach to commemoration. Within days of the funeral a roaring trade in photographs had begun: commemoration by postal order for anything from two to twelve shillings.[128] Busts and medallions appeared and were eagerly exhibited; copies were sold advertising the talents of the artist but then all was redeemed by the

---

[122] J. J. Lee, 'The challenge of a Collins biography', *ibid.*, p. 19.

[123] *The Free State – An Saorstát* and the *United Irishman* eagerly advertised supplements regarding Collins.

[124] *Morning Post*, 5 Sept. 1923; Hugh Kennedy MSS, UCDA, p4/1927.

[125] Advertisement from *The Free State – An Saorstát*, 25 Mar. 1922.

[126] See McCoole, *Hazel*.

[127] DT s5503, Sir John Lavery – proposed presentation of paintings to the state. He presented thirty-four paintings to the state in 1935. Snoddy, *Dictionary of Irish artists*, pp. 252–7.

[128] A number of advertisements appeared in the following newspapers: *Irish Independent, Cork Examiner, Free State – An Saorstát* and *Young Ireland*.

dignified gesture of donating the original to the state.[129] One particular bust, completed by Francis William Doyle Jones in 1923, was vigorously exhibited in both London and Dublin. As a well-executed, topical piece of art that had allegedly captured the public imagination it did his tender for the lucrative Wolfe Tone Memorial no harm at all.[130] This may seem callous, too critical of what were legitimate responses to a public's wish to grieve. Artists and writers deserved to be paid; that they were was merely indicative of a people's hunger for commemoration.

However, the government no longer shared its people's appetite. 'In 1922 Collins had been the lost leader of the new Free State; by 1924 his legacy was altogether more uncomfortable and ambivalent'.[131] He had been used against the government, wielded by the mutineers, and as time passed his 'freedom to achieve freedom' returned to haunt it. He had promised more than it had accomplished; to invoke his memory now was to recall how much it had failed him. Béalnabláth was a concession to a mutinous army that had to be appeased. There would be no more elaborate shows, just passing references, nothing that would draw attention to the failed Boundary Commission or to the fact that the government preferred the safety of the dominion shore to Collins' slippery stepping stone approach. At every turn the government thwarted enthusiasm. In 1924, commemorative stamps of Griffith and Collins were considered and dismissed;[132] a medal of Collins and Griffith to be distributed to school children on the anniversary of the Treaty was also rejected, rejected even though 'anything which helps to place Griffith and Collins in their proper niche in Irish history will tend towards stability'.[133] A scheme to sell reproductions of Sarah Harrison's portrait of Collins was also spurned in 1927, scorned in the belief that 'if a genuine public demand exists, private enterprise might be expected to reproduce the picture in a form suitable for meeting such demand'.[134] In 1928, the chance to purchase artist's proofs of Lavery's portraits of Griffith and Collins was promptly passed up.[135] There would be no more extravagance; there was simply too much shame.

---

[129] Joseph Higgins completed a wooden study of Collins in 1922, while F. W. Doyle Jones's bust of Collins appeared at the exhibition of the Royal Academy in London in 1923. After appearing in Dublin the bust was in great demand and even reproductions of its photograph were eagerly sought by American and British colonial newspapers. Theodore Spicer-Simson's medallion and its model, completed 1922, were deposited in the National Gallery of Ireland.

[130] *An t-Óglách*, 1, 7 (new series), (19 May 1923), p. 3.

[131] McMahon, '"A worthy monument"', p. 59.

[132] Sample designs for commemorative stamps of Griffith and Collins, Hugh Kennedy MSS, UCDA, p4/601, 25 Mar. 1924.

[133] DT s4011, Proposed Griffith–Collins medal, letter from Séan Lester, Director of Publicity to the Secretary, Department of Education, 21 Aug. 1924.

[134] She had donated the portrait to the government, which placed it in the Council Chamber. DF s200/0001/27, Proposed reproduction of Miss Harrison's portrait of General Collins for sale to the public, memo to the Minister for Finance, 3 Jan. 1927.

[135] DT s5739, President Griffith and General Collins: artist's proofs by Sir John Lavery, 1928.

Yet the government's retreat from commemoration belied a more persistent public affection for the dead Commander-in-Chief. Urban and county councils renamed roads;[136] the party still cherished Collins and christened branches in his honour;[137] the Association of the Old Dublin Brigade presented the Collins Memorial Cup for billiards in 1929;[138] a Michael Collins Golfing Society was even established in 1931.[139] The gestures may have been small, but they were none the less heartfelt. One army commandant, Padraig Ó Colgain, proposed the erection of a Collins Memorial Stadium 'as a memento to the great soldier of the Gael'.[140] Ó Colgain envisaged each corp and battalion of the army financing a section of the edifice, and, judging by his colleagues' letters of support to *An t-Óglách*, the rank and file shared his enthusiasm for the project. One soldier lamented that 'if only all our commanding officers took an interest in this scheme, it certainly would not fail through lack of support, as we are all only too anxious to commemorate the memory of our late Commander-in-Chief'.[141] The idea was discarded in 1926.

But this anxiety also haunted Collins' closest friends. Sir John Lavery had given Kitty Kiernan a portrait of Collins. Exhibited on an easel, it dominated her family home. She named her son Michael Collins Cronin; her nieces and nephews marked their prayer books with his mortuary cards.[142] She was buried as close to Michael Collins as Glasnevin Cemetery would allow.[143] Piaras Béaslaí kept the flag which was once draped over Collins' coffin.[144] That he let it grace the coffin of Gearóid O'Sullivan said more than any eulogy; there was honour simply by association.[145] But grief was not the preserve of those who knew Collins intimately. When he died 'men and women who had never met him felt a sense of personal loss'.[146] They had crowded to the hospital, to government buildings, to newspaper offices, anywhere for word of him. One woman was pictured kneeling in the street, prayer her only refuge from the shock of the news. And this regard remained. The attendance at ceremonies

[136] There are roads named after Collins in Dublin, Cork and Galway.
[137] In 1998 there were nineteen Fine Gael branches named after Michael Collins.
[138] Piaras Béaslaí MSS, NLI, MS 33,946(15).
[139] Richard Mulcahy MSS, UCDA, P7B/87(64) and (65).
[140] *An t-Óglách*, 3, 23 (14 Nov. 1925), p. 11.
[141] Letter to the editor from Corporal Patrick Hannan, A Company, 8th Infantry Battalion, *ibid.*, 4, 18 (15 May 1926), p. 18.
[142] León Ó Broin (ed.), *In great haste: the letters of Michael Collins and Kitty Kiernan* (Dublin, 1983), p. 222; Margot Gearty, 'Michael Collins: the Granard connection', in Doherty and Keogh, *Michael Collins*, p. 44.
[143] Batt O'Connor also requested to be buried beside Collins. Justin Nelson, *Michael Collins: the final days* (Dublin, 1997), p. 73.
[144] Thanks to Commandant Victor Laing.
[145] Gearóid O'Sullivan, 'Gearóid O'Sullivan – friend and ally', in Doherty and Keogh, *Michael Collins*, p. 51.
[146] Forester, *Michael Collins*, p. 341.

throughout the 1920s was proof of that. Regard, however, met its greatest challenge when Collins was conscripted into the Blueshirts. He was denigrated every time a country dance or a football match turned into a bout between the shirted followers of Eoin O'Duffy and the local village republicans. Conjured up to dignify a confused and ragged fascism, the anniversary of his death in 1933 was intended to afford an opportunity to march Mussolini-like on Dublin. This association with this pathetic caricature of the March on Rome left Collins' memory battered and dejected, at the mercy of a movement that used the memory of civil war to score cheap points in what was largely an economic game. There was too much training and drilling, too many songs of 'marching to the fray' to truly commemorate Collins.[147] In a Blueshirt's mouth 'the call of the mighty departed' was a call back to war; to strike at 'the viper whose venom withers our substance', a call in Collins' name that a war-weary people no longer wished to answer.[148] There had been too much death to build monuments to a harbinger of war.

But perhaps the people had lost their will for monuments. In the 1930s de Valera had, after all, out-Collinsed Collins. Since 1932 he had clambered across Collins' stepping stones, casting articles of association aside, grasping at this 'freedom to achieve freedom' until freedom was a republic in all but name. Collins had been vindicated, but eclipsed. It was left to those closest to him to redeem him, to wrest him from the clutches of Blueshirtism, from the gloom of de Valera's indomitable shadow. Until 1932 it had almost been taken for granted that the state would erect monuments and honour him. There was none of the compunction or necessity that provoked republicanism to found its own National Graves Association in 1926 to ensure the commemoration of the republican dead. Republican monuments and ceremonies had long been the preserve of small local committees, of men and women scrimping and saving to keep the memory of a local Volunteer alive. For the Free State side, and particularly in the case of Michael Collins, this was a new and rather humbling experience. Without the structural framework of a National Graves Association, there was never the same impetus to build. In dying for the Free State there was an assumption that the state would enshrine the memory of the dead. After the civil war republicanism never made that assumption; after the Sinn Féin split in 1926 it never could. Pro-Treatyites did persist, however; that they persisted where honour was most political, and possibly most familiar, is probably no surprise. In January 1944 three portraits, one of Collins, one of Griffith and one of O'Higgins, were unveiled by the Most Reverend Michael Fogarty, Bishop of Killaloe, in the lobby of Leinster House. They had been painted by Leo Whelan and paid for by public subscription. Two hundred and twenty-six donors were listed in the booklet commemorating the day's events: 226 names that read

[147] 'March of the Comrades', by 'A Comrade', *United Irishman*, 20 May 1933.   [148] *Ibid.*

like a who's who of Fine Gael and Fine Gael supporters – five Cosgraves, three Costellos, two Hayes and a couple of Mulcahys for good measure.[149] In redeeming Collins, Fine Gael was also redeeming itself. Hanging portraits in the Dáil, in the bastion of democracy, they were buying back the respectability that they had squandered on the flirtation with O'Duffy. They were buying back Collins, reasserting his moderation and his dignity with the repute that a portrait endeavours to paint.

Yet the pictures had been hung with the permission of a Fianna Fáil government and it was with words such as 'mutual tolerance' and 'profound feelings of admiration' that they were unveiled.[150] In 1928 Cosgrave 'thanked heaven the bitterness of civil war had now subsided, among the rank and file at any rate. Now even the Republicans have a bigger conception of nationality.'[151] Whatever prompted him to thank his celestial betters so effusively, whether he was distracting attention from Kevin O'Higgins' corpse or merely saying what he thought the press and the people wanted to hear, it was clear by 1944 that this bitterness had also subsided amongst the higher echelons of Fianna Fáil. Although the portraits had been paid for with Fine Gael money, they joined a collection of pictures commissioned by a Fianna Fáil government. Depicting the members of the 1921 cabinet, these pictures of pro- and anti-Treatyites were hung together in Leinster House, evocative of a stronger past and a bitterness overcome. There were still the Oliver J. Flanagans: men who saw a fiendish Fianna Fáil plot to cover the Dáil in images of de Valera when the portraits of Griffith, Collins and O'Higgins were merely removed for cleaning. There were still those who wished to 'continue with their prolonged parliamentary squabbles about who started, who won, and who lost the civil war... too old to fight now... they were content to pester one another about each other's motives for the rest of their lives'.[152] There was a familiarity about the anger, the well-worn catch phrases. Many of these men were too old and too stubborn to learn new ones, and many, like Flanagan, who only entered the Dáil in 1943, showed themselves only too keen to learn. And so they turned every fight into the old fight and like hardened combatants they would start another round. But it was easy to fight ten or twenty years later in the comfort of Dáil Éireann. 'Where were all these brave warriors when we needed them?' was all Seán MacEoin needed to say in response to their heated exchanges.[153] Most of the real 'warriors' had heeded Yeats' words: 'Let us not casually reduce that great past to a trouble of fools, for we need not feel the bitterness of the past to discover

---

[149] 'Memorial to the founders of the Irish State', NLI, Ir 94109m15. Ernest Blythe MSS, UCDA, P24/2431. Desmond FitzGerald MSS, UCDA, P80/499.
[150] *Ibid.*
[151] Simone Tery, 'As others see us – I. Interview with President Cosgrave', *Irish Statesman*, 9, 3 (22 Sept. 1928), pp. 48–9.
[152] Browne, *Against the tide*, pp. 228–9.   [153] *Ibid.*, p. 229.

the meaning for the present and the future.'[154] Most had realised 'that modern Ireland has no time for the bitterness or quarrels of that period and that there is far too much work to be done in Ireland today and all of us, on all sides of the House, have to look to the future'.[155] The Collins Memorial Fund and the monument at Sam's Cross were proof of that.

The Collins Memorial Fund was established in 1956 following the visit of President Seán T. O'Kelly to an exhibition of the work of the sculptor Seamus Murphy. Confronted by a large marble bust of Collins, O'Kelly was noticeably moved. 'Mick, that's Mick alright' and some whispered words of admiration were heard, then nothing but an eager insistence to become patron of a fund to purchase the bust for the nation. This was 'a spontaneous expression of feeling from the head of State towards his legendary adversary in the civil war',[156] an expression that, for him, the bitterness was over. The 1950s were apparently O'Kelly's time to reflect on his past, time to make amends. As President, he unveiled many of the decade's sudden crop of republican statues and monuments. Bandon, Bruff, Soloheadbeg and Newcastlewest[157] were part of the sudden '*statuomanie*', the sudden realisation of a generation of men and women who in their fifties, sixties and seventies wanted their stories told, their comrades remembered.[158] Age had brought an urgency, a familiar and almost desperate human response: the plea to posterity before death. At each ceremony O'Kelly spoke of 'unity'. He claimed that 'the passage of time' had brought him to 'a different perspective'.[159] He even admitted that 'the sufferings, sacrifices and bitterness of the Civil War could have been avoided'.[160] He did not seem to care that some of the statues he stood at depicted IRA volunteers with guns pointing purposefully North, that there was a clear discrepancy between his speeches and the statues' symbolism (see figure 4). Newcastlewest's Eire, depicted handing on the mantle from dying Volunteer to boy soldier, was not the stuff that peace and reconciliation were made of, but it seemed to make little difference to O'Kelly.[161] At seventy-four years of age, he was ready to make his peace, and to make his peace with Michael Collins. Seán MacBride and the still more militant General Tom Barry echoed the President's sentiments. They joined the list of trustees of the Collins Memorial Fund; they joined Jack Lynch,

---

[154] W. B. Yeats quoted by Donogh O'Malley, *DE, official report*, CCVIII, col. 844 (11 Mar. 1964).
[155] *Ibid.*, col. 843.
[156] Dermot Foley, 'The rose in the stone', *Cork Review*, 4 (Oct. 1980), p. 18.
[157] The Soloheadbeg monument, Co. Tipperary, was unveiled on 28 Jan. 1950; the Bruff memorial, Co. Limerick, two years later. The one in Bandon, Co. Cork, was unveiled in 1953 and the one in Newcastlewest, Co. Limerick, in 1955.
[158] Maurice Agulhon, 'La statuomanie et l'histoire', in Maurice Agulhon, *Histoire vagabonde*, 2 vols (Paris, 1988), vol. I, pp. 137–85.
[159] *Limerick Chronicle*, 18 Oct. 1952.
[160] Speech by Seán T. O'Kelly at Cumann Tír Conaill, 1965, Seán Ó Lúing MSS, NLI, MS 23,516.
[161] Letter from John Cussen, Newcastlewest, 22 July 1998. Hill, *Irish public sculpture*, p. 172.

Figure 4 Republican memorial, Bruff, Co. Limerick.

Fianna Fáil deputy and later leader of the party.[162] By 1958 the necessary £1,000 had been raised and the bust was deposited with the Municipal Gallery, Dublin,

[162] Other trustees included: P. Hogan, TD, Ceann Comhairle; Sen. P. F. Baxter, Chairman of the Senate; Brendan Corish, Minister for Social Welfare; Declan Costello, TD; Joseph McGrath;

by June.[163] Seán T. O'Kelly saw 'a memorial not alone to Michael Collins and his work for Ireland but to the men and the soldiers who assisted him in the work of bringing independence to the greater part of our land'.[164] To some it was simpler. One woman who visited the exhibition walked straight to the Collins sculpture. She looked up at the face, genuflected and left.[165] She cared nothing for art; she merely saw the face of her dead hero, and mourned. Only now she was not alone; a strand of republicanism was prepared to concede that this pro-Treatyite had died for Ireland too.

The same concession was made seven years later at Sam's Cross, Clonakilty, only this time 15,000 people bore witness to the republicans' beneficence.[166] The family of Michael Collins joined Tom Hales, the man who had led the Béalnabláth ambush in 1922; Collins' allies stood shoulder to shoulder with Liam Deasy, once commandant general of the anti-Treaty IRA.[167] Together they watched General Tom Barry unveil a rough piece of impenetrable granite, unmarked but for a simple bronze medallion that etched out Collins' unforgotten face, his date of birth and his haunting date of death.[168] A local committee had milked the vanity of local pride and the money had bought them this 'day of reconciliation'.[169] One subscription came with a note: 'I was with him in Frongoch in 1916 and was a colleague of his in the Second Dáil. We disagreed afterwards but I always held him in esteem as one of the greatest Irishmen of his generation.'[170] It was written by Séamus Fitzgerald, once a Sinn Féin deputy, then still an ardent Cork Fianna Fáil activist. The newspapers were not merely coining a convenient phrase; the committee's intentions were noble. The place that bore him should be proud of him; he was theirs and always would be. Yet by claiming him thus, they gave him back all the possibility that his years away from Clonakilty had taken from him. The committee chose the republicans'

Ald. R. Briscoe, TD, Lord Mayor of Dublin; Ald. S. Casey, TD, Lord Mayor of Cork; Padraig O'Keefe, General Secretary GAA; Archdeacon Thomas Duggan, PP VF Kinsale; Thomas McGreevy, Director of the National Gallery, Dublin; R. F. Dalton. Anthony Barry, TD acted as honorary secretary. Collins Memorial Fund Appeal, NLI, p2467, item 8.

[163] DT s1827b, National leaders: busts, death masks, statues, etc. A copy of the bust is on display in the Cork Sculpture Park.

[164] Seán T. O' Kelly MSS, NLI, MS 27,688(iii), Letter from O'Kelly to Seamus Murphy, 1 June 1956.

[165] Foley, 'The rose', p. 17.

[166] *CE*, 19 Apr. 1965 estimated an attendance of 15,000. An estimate of 20,000 was preferred by the *II*, 19 Apr. 1965. The ceremony was also attended by representatives of the Old IRA, the Gárdaí, the Military Police and a guard of honour from the 11th Battalion of the FCA.

[167] *CE*, 19 Apr. 1965.

[168] The stone was crafted by Maurice Murphy, Drimoleague, the medallion sculpted by Seamus Murphy.

[169] The committee was made up exclusively of West Cork men and was chaired by James L. O'Keeffe, Skibbereen.

[170] Letter from Séamus Fitzgerald to Pádraig Walsh, 3 April 1965, Séamus Fitzgerald MSS, CAI, PR/6/640.

sacred Easter Sunday, it chose Tom Barry, it chose no inscription to offend. At Sam's Cross there was no 'mobilization of bias':[171] Michael Collins could be all things to all men.

It was described as 'a memorable ceremony', and perhaps because it was the largest 'Free State' commemoration since the unveiling of the Cenotaph it was entitled to the praise.[172] But it was deemed memorable for another reason. Tom Barry made a plea rather than a speech. He said he was honoured to be there, honoured because the committee had sacrificed nothing to the whim of party politics, because it has 'studiously avoided raking up the embers of our tragic civil strife'; he was proud because he remembered Collins as 'one of the chief architects of the fight for Irish freedom'.[173] But most of all Barry was weary of the bitterness:

it is not for us here to go into the rights or wrongs of the civil war when Michael Collins met his tragic death. Many of you here were on opposite sides. Let us leave it that each of us, like I did myself, believed in the correctness of our choice. I concede that those who were on the opposite side believed that their decision was the right one too. But let us end all futile recriminations of an event which happened over 43 years ago, and which divided brother against brother, neighbour against neighbour. Here at this monument, erected to commemorate for all time the greatness of the contribution made by Michael Collins in our struggle for freedom, let us bury the dead past of dissensions. He whom we knew hated civil war and all its sad consequences, would have us all do so. We who have grown old and are nearing the end of our road have this final contribution to make, so that the young people of Ireland can march on together to our ultimate freedom and build a better life for themselves and for the coming generations.[174]

The speech was not merely the ramblings of an old man slithering towards death under the weight of his guilt for the men he may have killed or the killings he may have encouraged. Barry never seemed the guilty type. It was no coincidence that three months earlier a Southern leader had met a Northern Premier for the first time since the Craig–Collins pacts; that one week after this meeting Eddie McAteer and his Nationalist Party entered Stormont as the official opposition. Always one to concede that the job had never been truly finished in 1922–3, Tom Barry's vision of marching on 'to our ultimate free-dom' harked back to the years of 'glorious unity', the thrill of the common enemy of 1919–21 that had fuelled the largest part of his unveiling speech. For Barry it was time to forget the past divisions because he still thought in terms of that elusive 'fourth green field'. There was none of the pacifism of Europe's Great War ceremonies that promised 'never again'; Barry's speech, like the

---

[171] Quoted in Steven Lukes, 'Political ritual and social integration', *Sociology*, 9 (1975), p. 305.
[172] Meda Ryan, *The Tom Barry story* (Dublin, 1982), p. 164.
[173] *CE*, 19 Apr. 1965. The speech was also published in the *II*, 19 Apr. 1965 and the *IT*, 19 Apr. 1965. Barry was also presented with a replica of the monument by the committee.
[174] *Ibid*.

belligerent symbolism of the republican monuments in Bruff and Shankill, was another call to arms[175] (see figure 4). For others the monument could represent the same unity but another option: reconciliation by negotiation, a nationalist party in Stormont, advancement by political means. In the same fashion Seán T. O'Kelly's eager sponsorship of the Murphy bust of Collins had diverse motives in a 1958 troubled by a reinvigorated IRA and the shame of the reopened Curragh detention camp. The deaths on New Year's Day 1957 of Fergal O'Hanlon and particularly Seán South, a reputed paragon of the Legion of Mary, had stirred nationalist sympathies and brought four Sinn Féin deputies into the Dáil. Even Fianna Fáil could concede; there was virtue in compromise. As seventy West Cork congregations prayed for Collins on that Easter Sunday morning,[176] the once reluctant plenipotentiary was being reborn in the image of Seán Lemass.

But this was naïve even then. The Lemass–O'Neill meetings achieved little but enthusiasm bred of the falsest hopes. Lemass had shelved the question of discrimination against the Northern minority: 'he had come dangerously close to the *bête noire* of republican politicians, "recognition" of the Stormont administration'.[177] Tom Barry was tired of civil war bitterness because now more than ever it added insult to every incessant daily injury that constituted Catholic life in the North. By January 1964 it had become necessary to form the Campaign for Social Justice in Northern Ireland. It was no longer defensible to wallow in that splendid Southern isolation that preferred to stoke the embers of civil war bitterness than to face a Northern question that had realistically been ignored since the first shots of that wasteful conflict. Northern Ireland was collapsing into a basic struggle for civil rights; it was no longer credible to hide behind the paralysis of civil war. 'More than four decades of partition had bred a certain insensitivity among all but the most dedicated Southern nationalists to the plight of their Northern compatriots.'[178] Squabbling over who shot Michael Collins did nothing for a Northern Catholic without a job and burned out of his home.

Yet if Barry was weary of the bitterness, he saw hope in the unity that such commemoration could evoke.[179] Though his urgency toyed with notions of cross-party consensus, with the promise of factions forgotten for the greater Northern good, his faith in the unifying dimension of commemoration was not

---

[175] Winter, *Sites of memory, sites of mourning*, p. 95; Seán Farrell Moran, 'Images, icons and the practice of Irish history', in McBride (ed.), *Images, icons and the Irish nationalist imagination* (Dublin, 1999), p. 175. The monument in Shankill, Co. Roscommon, depicted the Volunteer in three stages: ready for battle, defeated and once again prepared to fight. It was unveiled in September 1963.

[176] *CE*, 19 Apr. 1965.

[177] John Horgan, *Seán Lemass: the enigmatic patriot* (Dublin, 1997), p. 279.   [178] *Ibid.*

[179] Tom Barry was also presented with a replica of the monument at the ceremony. Ryan, *Tom Barry*, p. 165.

lost upon the more moderate contingent. Opening its coffers with a grandeur easily afforded by Joseph McGrath at his head office in the Irish Sweepstakes Buildings in Ballsbridge, the Michael Collins Memorial Foundation loosed its high hopes upon a 1966 primed for the fiftieth anniversary of the Easter Rising.[180] While guests dined on lobster and quaffed champagne, 'Irish men and women from any of the four provinces without distinction of creed, class or politics'[181] were gallantly invited to avail of a trust fund initially conceived to educate 'some bright boys'.[182] Commemoration, unity, youth and education: an admirable mixture to all who contributed anything from a few shillings to twenty thousand pounds.[183] But this blind eye that the Foundation promised to turn to the creed, class and politics of its young beneficiaries could not seem to overlook its forty-year-old adversaries.

On the face of it, the Foundation was a noble idea, born in 1964 out of Seán Collins' concern for the wealth that was burning a hole in McGrath's pocket.[184] Meetings had been held and men eager to do honour to Collins squabbled over the form a memorial should take. They felt thwarted by the plans for the Clonakilty monument, and talk of the Clonakilty committee's 'parochial narrow way' begot grandiose, almost *World's Pictorial News*-esque, schemes for equestrian statues in St Stephen's Green.[185] But the meetings were overshadowed by the controversy that surrounded the publication of *Facts about Ireland*, an official guidebook prepared by the Department of External Affairs. Collins had been left out, and if one looks with Tim Pat Coogan's eye for conspiracy, then it was de Valera who did the excluding.[186] It caused grumblings in the Dáil, and Fine Gael, under Oliver J. Flanagan's eager tutelage, admonished Fianna Fáil impishly from its high moral ground, castigating a bitter and small-minded government.[187] McGrath regretted this. He regretted that the book had been criticised 'entirely in a party spirit and for a party purpose'.[188] For him, Collins 'transcended anything in terms of "party"'.[189] Much as he may have hounded republicans as head of the CID, McGrath's contributions to these early

[180] Material relating to the Collins Memorial Foundation, launch, 14 Jan. 1966, Richard Mulcahy MSS, UCDA, P7/D/248.

[181] Foundation Appeal, *ibid*.   [182] Seán Collins quoted in Coogan, *Michael Collins*, p. 431.

[183] Recorded donations range from 2/6 to £20,000. Early county totals display the Cork–Dublin bias of donations, but nine counties failed to reach as much as £10. Leitrim raised the lowest amount, £2 10s. 0d. Contributions from Canada and America amounted to £23,000 by the end of Jan. 1966. Richard Mulcahy MSS, UCDA, P7/D/248.

[184] Coogan, *Michael Collins*, p. 431.

[185] Inaugural meeting of Provisional Committee, 17 June 1964. Seán MacEoin became the provisional chairman. The committee was comprised of Cosgrave, McGrath, Mulcahy, Brennan, McMahon and Costello. The secretary was Ita McCoy. Richard Mulcahy MSS, UCDA, P7/D/248.

[186] Coogan, *Michael Collins*, p. 431.

[187] For example *DE, official report*, CCVIII, cols. 519–21 (10 Mar. 1964).

[188] Inaugural meeting of Provisional Committee, 17 June 1964. Richard Mulcahy MSS, UCDA, P7/D/248.

[189] *Ibid*.

committee meetings bespoke a genuine impulse to make amends. He had employed former anti-Treatyites throughout his time at the Irish Sweepstakes. A convenient outbreak of amnesia when there was all that money to be made had suddenly made it a lot easier to get along, a lot easier to forget who might have killed Noel Lemass. But whatever the motives then, McGrath now invited Liam Deasy, former commandant general of the anti-Treaty forces, to join the committee. When Deasy's initial acceptance gave way to a refusal on the grounds that he could only join the committee 'if the name of Liam Lynch were associated with that of Collins in the intention of the memorial', McGrath only emitted the weary opinion that Deasy 'had been got at'.[190] And perhaps he had. Seán T. O'Kelly had. Perhaps punished for his £25 patronage of the Seamus Murphy bust, his £5 donation to the Foundation was quickly retracted with a snivelling 'He'd be furious if he knew I agreed.'[191] 'He' naturally was de Valera or at least Coogan's mafioso embodiment of de Valera. There is of course the possibility that Coogan prefers not to consider: O'Kelly, known for his frugality, might have simply thought better of his earlier extravagance.

Once McGrath had been told that he had only a few months to live, indecision ended. He approached de Valera in early 1966 and with a plaintive 'My days are numbered and there's no differences in the grave' he asked the President to become patron of what was now to be an educational foundation.[192] De Valera allegedly responded thus: 'I can't see my way to becoming Patron of the Michael Collins Foundation. It's my considered opinion that in the fullness of time history will record the greatness of Collins and it will be recorded at my expense.'[193] This has become one of the most controversial statements in modern Irish history, primarily because there is no written proof that it was ever made and it is recorded with a lyricism that belies the rigours of thirty years and the memories of two, three or even four people. And Coogan's approach does nothing to help. He writes biography with all the purpose of a morality play, his subjects sacrificed to some burning hierarchy of good and evil. It is possible that de Valera made this statement, that he rejected patronage of the Foundation because at eighty-five years of age he was still consumed with the bitterness that once called on men to wade through their comrades' blood.[194] If one needed proof of his alleged bitterness, all one has to do is consider his treatment of Collins' grave. In February 1935 Seán Collins made it clear that his family wished to erect a monument over Michael's grave in Glasnevin.[195] Four months later Frank Aiken's Department of Defence grudgingly conceded

---

[190] Ibid.   [191] Coogan, Michael Collins, p. 431.   [192] Ibid., p. 432.   [193] Ibid.

[194] St Patrick's Day 1922, DT s26, Anglo-Irish Treaty, 1921: expressions of opinion including intelligence reports on public attitudes and recommendations for government action, Jan.–June 1922.

[195] DF Supply 1939 s004/0009/39 – permission to Mr Seán Collins to erect monument over grave of his brother, the late General Michael Collins, in the army burial plot in Glasnevin Cemetery, Seán Collins to Frank Aiken, 13 Feb. 1935.

that 'the erection of monuments other than those erected by the State is not permitted but in view of the representations made on behalf of your family... the Minister will offer no objection to the erection of a monument if it is still your intention to do so'.[196] In 1939 it was still Seán Collins' intention to do so.

The Dublin Cemeteries Committee, not de Valera, knitted a web of the reddest tape and objected to the proposed monument encroaching on the paths by a mere three inches, capitulating only when Aiken intervened in March 1939.[197] While the Collins sisters contemplated recourse to the courts, Seán persisted, meeting de Valera personally on two occasions, once to propose his case, once to hear the Taoiseach's judgement.[198] The Collins family could have their cross, but there would be no public subscriptions, no publicity. The cross would be carved from limestone, plain without marble or ostentation. Nothing would cost more than £300. The inscription, which had to meet with de Valera's approval, could be in Irish on the front and must state that the family alone had erected the cross. The cross could be blessed and if necessary the chaplain could have the services of an altar boy, but 'Nobody but yourself can be present.'[199] Seán Collins, the priest, the altar boy and the gravedigger witnessed the erection of the cross over the grave of Michael Collins. A photograph, merely taken by a passing tourist, shows only a brother noble in his family's misery, a solitary witness to a Taoiseach's petty and damning spite. But de Valera need not have worried. Seán Collins inscribed the cross with nothing more than his family allowed any committee to carve on any other monument: *I ndil-chuimhne ar Mhícheál Ó Coileáin a rugadh an 12adh lá de mhí Dheireadh Foghmhair, 1890 agus d'éag an 22adh lá de mhí Lughnasa, 1922 – Go dtugaidh Dia suaimhneas síorraidhe dá anam* ('In loving memory of Michael Collins who was born on 12 October 1890, and who died on 22 August 1922 – May God grant him eternal peace').[200] 'Erected by his brothers and sisters' was carved, as de Valera wanted, below. It was never Seán Collins' intention to upset the Taoiseach, or to use his brother's memory to rally the nation against Fianna Fáil or indeed against anyone. He just wanted his brother's grave marked, his brother remembered. Even Tom Barry recognised that 'Seán's main object in life, since the civil strife, was to bring together again those who were divided'.[201] De Valera simply could not see this.

It has been described as a 'mean and sordid story'.[202] Oscar Traynor, the man charged with enforcing de Valera's wishes, would probably have agreed. Several years later he apologised to the Collins family; the order had been the

[196] *Ibid.*, letter from the Secretary, Department of Finance to Seán Collins, 3 June 1935.
[197] *Ibid.*; DF Supply 1939 s102/2/39, memorandum for the government, 6 Mar. 1939.
[198] Coogan, *Michael Collins*, p. 429.
[199] For de Valera's conditions see Coogan, *Michael Collins*, pp. 429–30.
[200] The inscription was translated into Irish by Piaras Béaslaí at the request of the family. Piaras Béaslaí MSS, NLI, MS 33,666(10) and MS 33,966(10).
[201] *CE*, 19 Apr. 1965.   [202] MacKay, *Michael Collins*, p. 308.

hardest of his life to implement.[203] De Valera's actions cannot be excused. But it might be somewhat short-sighted to see them only on Coogan's unsourced black-and-white terms. The last time a Fianna Fáil government was confronted by the prospect of a major Collins commemoration a shirted organisation, up to 30,000 strong, had threatened to march on Dublin and seize the power de Valera had coveted for so long.

The year 1934 brought more Blueshirts and disturbances at Béalnabláth. In 1939, as Europe gave way to the vagaries of shirted movements, de Valera could not risk a gathering of any kind. With extreme republicanism increasingly alienated from him, being seen to commemorate Collins could have been a potentially perilous act. De Valera was all too aware of the IRA mentality that struck in times of crisis; there could have been no 1916 without World War I. As he began to grapple with the intricacies of neutrality, as he watched the latest embodiment of 'England's difficulty is Ireland's opportunity' kill seven and injure more than 200 English men, women and children, he could not take the chance of antagonising republicanism further still. Coogan never mentions this, nor that in the same year the opening of Islandbridge was postponed because of 'the tenseness of the international situation... and the consequent ferment here'.[204] That de Valera was 'furious and visibly upset' by the news of Collins' death, that his office in Suffolk Street flew its flag at half-mast, simply does not help Coogan's argument.[205] These are not excuses, just something to consider. Something to consider together with the thought that ten years of Cumann na nGaedheal power had left the grave not only unmarked but neglected.

True, a Cumann na nGaedheal government had bought the grave, but only eventually and after much haggling.[206] In May 1925 the army admitted 'that the present appearance of the Plot is such as to reflect some discredit on the Army'.[207] Seán Collins met with W. T. Cosgrave in February 1923. He was upset because there was nothing to distinguish his brother's grave from all the rest.[208] By May 1931 little had changed, there was no way of knowing where any soldier, even Collins, was buried.[209] Cosgrave's concerns that it 'should be left

---

[203] Coogan, *Michael Collins*, p. 431.

[204] DT s4156, War Memorial Islandbridge, report of meeting of Major Tynan and A. P. Connolly of the British Legion and Eamon de Valera, 28 Apr. 1939.

[205] Quoted in MacKay, *Michael Collins*, p. 286; Forester, *Michael Collins*, p. 342.

[206] DF s004/0013/24, Proposed acquisition of burial plot for deceased members of the national army.

[207] DF s004/0098/25, Army burial plot – Mount Prospect Cemetery, Glasnevin – sanction for maintenance by the army, letter from the Secretary of the Department of Defence to the Department of Finance, 1 May 1925.

[208] Dáil Éireann departmental file 5/83, Correspondence and receipts for funeral expenses in connection with the deaths of President Griffith and General Collins, letter from the Secretary to the President to Richard Mulcahy, 23 Feb. 1923.

[209] DF s004/0013/24, Proposed acquisition of burial plot for deceased members of the national army, Department of Finance memorandum, May 1931.

for consideration in the future when the subject can be solved free from the heat of the conflict [which caused] his death',[210] was all very well, but for Collins' family it was not enough. In ten years the Cumann na nGaedheal government had done nothing. Rhetoric had brought no monument to rival Parnell's, nothing to challenge O'Connell's. Privately Cosgrave conceded that what Cumann na nGaedheal could provide would not be worthy of the man: 'My own impression is that it is not advisable just now that if a monument were put up it sh[ould] need be a good one & in some degree worthy of the dead'. He knew his government and perhaps his party had neither the will nor the money to prove him wrong.[211] A few flowers on the grave were not enough, especially when one of the party's own supporters pointed accusingly to the money spent on the dead of the Great War, when he wrote to the newspapers that

to pay tribute to Collins' memory was all right in certain constituencies at election time, but to spend money in commemorating him in bronze or stone would not meet with the approval of their money-bag, empire-building friends. Therefore as far as they are concerned, the grave of Michael Collins must remain unmarked.[212]

De Valera was apparently in good Cumann na nGaedheal company.

Joseph McGrath may have had a wistful dying vision of the Collins Memorial Fund, hoping that it would 'bridge the gap' and bring together again those who were divided.[213] But the committee's correspondence reveals that de Valera was not the only one to deal in undying bitterness. Bride O'Rahilly was charged with assembling articles for a fundraising supplement to be issued with the *Irish Independent*. She was an eager worker, enthusiastic about the Foundation. By February 1967 all she could say was: 'I was glad to be finished with it as there was a terrible lot of labour and disillusionment with it. The personnel of the Committee damned it from the start and made the job a hundred times more difficult'.[214] While she was 'very conscious of not confining the whole endeavour to one side' the very names that tripped from the committee minutes thwarted her at every turn.[215] Representing a committee which was chaired by Seán MacEoin and which included Richard Mulcahy, she thought it pointless to approach the Fianna Fáil-bred *Irish Press*.[216] Left with the legacy that simmered

---

[210] DT s3913, Griffith and Collins – ownership and erection of memorials at graves, memo by W. T. Cosgrave, 9 Apr. 1931.

[211] *Ibid*. (punctuation as in original).

[212] 'The unmarked grave' by John Roche, *The Nation*, 3 Aug. 1935.

[213] Letter from Bride O'Rahilly to Dan Nolan, 26 Apr. 1966, O'Rahilly MSS, UCDA, P102/553(6).

[214] Letter from Bride O'Rahilly to Dan Nolan, 2 Feb. 1967, *ibid.*, P102/553(22).

[215] Letter from Bride O'Rahilly to Dan Nolan, 26 Apr. 1966, *ibid.*, P102/553(6).

[216] The committee or governing body was listed as follows: Lt Gen. Seán MacEoin (chairman); Joseph McGrath; Gen. Richard Mulcahy; Nevin Griffith; John A. Costello; Seán Collins TD; Liam Cosgrave TD; Maj. Gen. Joseph Sweeney; Eamon Martin; Lt Gen. Michael J. Costello; Lt Gen. Liam Archer; Dr Niall O'Rahilly; Stephen D. Barrett; Sen. Prof. James Dooge; and Roderick Connolly. Richard Mulcahy MSS, UCDA, P7/D/248.

in every syllable of their names, she was stranded with the once pro-Treatyite *Irish Independent*, left without option, even though she knew that this newspaper 'is still not acceptable to a great many who are reluctant to forget the past'.[217] Although Mulcahy and MacEoin cannot be blamed for the resilient bias of others, for the unforgiving memories of those who 'would not allow their names on the Committee',[218] they can be blamed for the manner in which they turned the Foundation into a crusade, into a means of settling old scores and rewriting an uncomfortable history. Theoretically there was nothing wrong with ensuring 'that the name and memory of Michael Collins shall be venerated and perpetuated, and his services to the Irish nation adequately and appropriately commemorated',[219] but the spirit in which many of the donations were made merely fed the fears which the *Irish Times* expressed when the Foundation announced that its first bursary was to be bestowed on a scholar of modern Irish history. While the paper hoped that the Foundation would not 'be turned into a mere search for a counter-propaganda to what is beginning to become the official view of those tumultuous times',[220] the donors rubbed their gleeful hands and sent ragged pound notes to waft 'some fresh air through the fog and murk of recent historical writing'.[221] Together with his pound, Jack Moriarty sent his good wishes, with the belief that 'were I old enough then – would [de Valera] be alive today. I have a faint idea that he would not.'[222] None asked for an honest retelling; they merely wanted a more balanced fight. Frank Pakenham and Dorothy Macardle had to be countered.[223] Piaras Béaslaí tried with later editions of the Collins biography, but there was too much unease with Béaslaí within Fine Gael, prompted mainly by Richard Mulcahy, for that ever to be enough.[224] As a result, the Foundation had 'a responsibility to see that history is not written as it is at present as if Dev was the one that saved us all from worse than death'.[225] There was no place for the 'modesty' that has 'let Dev and Co. get all the awards'.[226] Money was sent, eager, in its grubby envelopes, to infuse another generation with old men's hates.

---

[217] Letter from Dan Nolan to Bride O'Rahilly, 25 Apr. 1966, O'Rahilly MSS, UCDA, P102/553(2–5).

[218] Letter from Bride O'Rahilly to Dan Nolan, 26 Apr. 1966, *ibid.*, P102/553(6).

[219] Recommendations of the sub-committee, Collins Memorial Foundation, Sept. 1965, Richard Mulcahy MSS, UCDA, P7/D/248.

[220] 'Veritas', *IT*, 16 May 1967.

[221] Richard Connolly enclosed £1 with this letter to Richard Mulcahy, 28 Apr. 1966, Richard Mulcahy MSS, UCDA, P7/D/248.

[222] Letter from Jack Moriarty to Richard Mulcahy, n.d., *ibid.* (punctuation as in original).

[223] Frank Pakenham, *Peace by ordeal* (London, 1935); Dorothy Macardle, *The Irish Republic* (London, 1937).

[224] McMahon, '"A worthy monument"', pp. 62–3.

[225] Letter from Edith MacNeill to Richard Mulcahy, 16 Jan. 1966, Richard Mulcahy MSS, UCDA, P7/D/248.

[226] *Ibid.*

Much as it may have liked to cultivate the impression, Fine Gael's ground was not particularly high or moral. Supporters in London squabbled; one strand of ten, later six, having failed to dominate several other Irish groups in the city, formed a Michael Collins Society and erected a hideous statue of the Virgin Mary in his honour at St Anne's Church in Whitechapel.[227] Kevin Smith, chairman of this spurious but allegedly 'non-political and non-sectarian' organisation, invited the Irish ambassador, Con Cremin, to attend the unveiling on 7 June 1964. The ambassador, having consulted numerous Irish associations in London, refused to attend.[228] Smith, he had been told, was 'a self-publicist' and 'a trouble-maker'; none of the members of the organisation had even been born during the civil war,[229] and the statue was ill-conceived and would 'encourage divisive influences'.[230] That Collins had only tenuous connections with this parish did not help Smith's plight; that the murder of Sir Henry Wilson was planned there did nothing to endear it to an Irish ambassador eager to contain relations with Her Majesty's government. The parish priest accepted Cremin's explanation. Fr Crawley even suggested delaying the ceremony 'to obviate risks of friction'.[231] It is clear from the ambassador's reports that he genuinely desired to 'obliterate all traces of political division among the Irish in London'.[232] But the £30 plaster statue was erected, Smith complained of the ambassador's absence to the press, and Seán MacEoin and his cronies accused the government of refusing to honour 'the greatest leader which it was the good fortune of this nation to have'.[233] That the government was merely protecting itself and, in a sense, the country, from an association with a 'crank' meant nothing to MacEoin and Fine Gael.[234] In their haste to score political points they never bothered to consider the facts. It was just another chance to berate the government, to bellow brazenly across the Dáil that 'you are a miserable lot of begrudgers'.[235] Collins' protectors played politics with all the grace of drunken fishwives.

But they need not have bothered; their grace was wasted on a people that no longer seemed to care. Fundraisers for the Collins Memorial Foundation

---

[227] Letter from Kevin Smith to Seán Lemass, DT President's Office 97/9/1634. DFA, Secretary's Office 1995 release p367, Michael Collins Society, London, letter from Con Cremin to Hugh McCann, Secretary of the Department of External Affairs, 7 Jan. 1964.

[228] These associations included the Council of County Associations, the Association of Old IRA and Cumann na mBan, the United Ireland Association and the Corkmen's Association.

[229] DFA, Secretary's Office 1995 release p367, Michael Collins Society, London, Con Cremin quoting the Old IRA Association to the Department of External Affairs, 19 Dec. 1963.

[230] Frank Aiken, *DE, official report*, CCX, col. 808 (9 June 1964).

[231] DFA Secretary's Office 1995 release p367, Michael Collins Society, London, letter from Cremin to McCann, 21 Jan. 1964.

[232] *Ibid.*, letter from Con Cremin to the Department of External Affairs, 19 Dec. 1963.

[233] Richie Ryan, *DE, official report*, CCX, col. 809 (9 June 1964).

[234] DFA Secretary's Office 1995 release p367, Michael Collins Society, London, letter from Cremin to McCann, 15 Jan. 1964.

[235] Richie Ryan, *DE, official report*, CCX, col. 810 (9 June 1964).

complained that 'the response from Ireland has been very bad',[236] that 'the youth here don't even know his name'.[237] Sixty thousand pounds fell far short of the expectations that flirted with the fancy of a quarter of a million. Collins got lost in the haze of 1966, the fiftieth anniversary of the Rising, which had been turned into a campaign to secure de Valera his second presidential term.[238] And Collins, like much that had been considered sacred in the years 1916 to 1922, was lost in the hate that erupted on the streets of Northern Ireland in 1968 and 1969. In April 1969 Mulcahy refused to have anything to do with a planned memorial to Collins and Griffith: 'There is no help of any kind that your committee can expect from me.' He could not promise to avoid or refrain from future controversy.[239] By April 1969 the memorial committee was tired of party quibbles anyway; riots were becoming routine and the first Northern death was only three months away. 'And in any case, the politicians are not particularly interested in our scheme.'[240] The past was becoming not merely 'a foreign country' but an increasingly uncomfortable one.[241]

The republic was hungry for another generation's sacrifice but this time the broken bodies of its victims and martyrs were not the stuff of legend and ballad: they were the televisual diet of a country grown complacent in the comfort of its isolation. There was no place for commemoration when it recalled, however much Fianna Fáil tried to refute it, that the civil war had nothing to do with Northern Ireland. There was shame that the South had merely fought amongst itself. There was an arms trial and the threat of war between North and South. In 1971 Patrick Lindsay was interrupted at a debate on the Treaty at the Literary and Historical Society, UCD. As he spoke of the freedom the Treaty brought, a student reminded him that sixty people had been killed in the past two years in Northern Ireland. All Lindsay could say was that the Treaty was between Britain and the South; it did not apply to Northern Ireland.[242] They had quarrelled over an oath, over a republic that no one could define. The North had never been relevant. At the same debate Seán MacEntee scrambled for a reply: the 'men who signed the Treaty were as patriotic as any who gave their lives for their country on the battlefield or on the scaffold'.[243] They were all brave; they had all died for some great generic Ireland and that made everything all right. Bitterness forgotten in the face of an awkward question.

---

[236] Letter from Bride O'Rahilly to Dan Nolan, 25 Mar. 1966, O'Rahilly MSS, UCDA, P102/553(1).
[237] Letter from Edith MacNeill to Richard Mulcahy, 16 Jan. 1966, Richard Mulcahy MSS, UCDA, P7/D/248.
[238] Horgan, *Lemass*, p. 284.
[239] Letter from Richard Mulcahy to P. J. Herbert, chairman of the Griffith and Collins Memorial Committee, 29 Apr. 1969, Richard Mulcahy MSS, UCDA, P7c/2(14).
[240] Letter from P. J. Herbert to Mulcahy, 6 May 1969, *ibid.*
[241] David Lowenthal, *The past is a foreign country* (Cambridge, 1985).
[242] 'What Collins saw in the Treaty', *Irish Press*, 14 Mar. 1971.
[243] Notebook 3, 15 Mar. 1971, Michael Hayes MSS, UCDA, P53/326(3).

And nothing followed. Ceremonies made pleas for an end to Northern violence but there were no more monuments; nothing until the centenary of Collins' birth, until thirty years of violence began to yield to talk of Northern peace. The only exceptions to this nothing was the renaming of a bridge in Cork city the same day one was dedicated to Eamon de Valera, and one plaque safely tucked away in London on a house in West Kensington where Collins had lived in 1914 and 1915. But then it changed.[244] In 1990, Merrion Square was graced with a bust of Collins, tactful in its civilian attire though more evocative of an exuberant Boris Yeltsin in its execution.[245] A stamp was issued, notably as part of the dignified and democratic 'Statesmen of Ireland' series.[246] Commemoration was rehabilitated because Collins, the compromising statesman, had a certain peace process appeal. Even the publicity poster for Neil Jordan's film *Michael Collins* was altered to suit these changing tastes. Originally showing Collins leaping over a barricade with rifle in hand, it became Collins in civilian attire in full rhetorical flight on an election platform.[247] In the same way the opening of the cottage in which leading republicans had gathered to discuss the end of civil war in 1923 made a certain sense in a turbulent 1978.[248] The rebel turned negotiator was now to have his day. Commemoration began to take tentative commercial steps: the *Irish Times* added Collins to its familiar range of bronze busts and Foxford Mills produced a 'Collins Centenary Rug' to match the one the Foxford nuns had presented to Collins in July 1922, which, bloodstained, had been kept by nurse Nora O'Donoghue from Shanakiel hospital.[249] But while remembrance took this somewhat surreal woven turn, Woodfield, Collins' birthplace, was flaunted as the noble, well-meaning alternative.

Reconstructed by a team of local voluntary workers and £25,000,[250] the home of Michael Collins, reborn as the Collins Heritage Centre, was opened by President Hillery to the drenched applause of four to five thousand people. It had none of the morbid fascination of Béalnabláth; it was the beginning, the birthplace, with nothing of the divisive end. Liam Collins, Michael's nephew, wanted it that way. Adamant that 'no assistance that could be linked in any way

---

[244] The plaque was unveiled to the accompaniment of a stage presentation of his life and death commissioned by Hammersmith and Fulham Libraries Department. Coogan, *Michael Collins*, pp. 15, 434; Letter from Neil Fitzpatrick, Cork Corporation, 29 May 1998.

[245] The bust was commissioned from Dick Joynt and erected by the Office of Public Works in 1990.

[246] An Post, *Postage stamps of Ireland: 70 years 1922–1992* (Dublin, 1992), p. 35.

[247] *IT*, 19 Oct. 1996.

[248] *IT*, 24 Oct. 1978; letter from Carrie Acheson, secretary Knockanaffrin republican cottage restoration committee to Capt Jack Carroll, Mount Street, Sept. 1977, FF/258, Fianna Fáil Archives. Wall's cottage in Knockanaffrin, Co. Waterford, was opened by Jack Lynch.

[249] The original was presented to the National Museum in 1965: Twohig, *The dark secret*, p. 178.

[250] The workers were mainly comprised of members of Cumann Seanchais Cloich na Coillte (Clonakilty Historical Society).

to politics would be accepted',[251] he dictated the terms and provided the £25,000 himself. Politicians were welcomed to the unveiling but there would be 'nothing party political, nothing sectional, nothing of historical point-scoring'.[252] And the politicians came, eager revellers in a rich and representative pageant. There were three former Taoisigh – Jack Lynch, Liam Cosgrave and Garret FitzGerald – party leaders, church leaders, the British ambassador, the president of the GAA, TDs, senators, councillors, MEPs and a gaggle of presidential election candidates. There was an enthusiasm, a need to be there, and maybe because it was the 'event that swept aside the divisions of the past 70 years', the ardour was not misplaced.[253] Civil war bitterness was apparently at an end, even though Cosgrave declared it so in 1928, and despite Tom Barry's pleadings in 1965. Civil war bitterness was at an end again. It would have another end in 1985, another in 1991 and another in 1998 at the re-erection of a monument to Noel Lemass.[254] There was prestige in defying the ravages of the past, in rising above it in a wave of civility that conferred a superiority on every generation, on every declaration. One report revelled:

It was easy to get carried away by it all as Alan Dukes rubbed shoulders with Brian Lenihan, Jack Lynch took his place with Liam Cosgrave and Garret FitzGerald, Mary Harney sat with Prionsias de Rossa, Mary Robinson shook hands with Austin Currie. Here on the one platform was the full spectrum of Irish political life, behaving in a civilised friendly manner, preaching reconciliation and understanding of the past. Had anything like it ever been seen in this country before?[255]

Without being facetious, this happened most days in Dáil Éireann; it was not their war. The differences of these men and women had nothing to do with a Treaty or an 'oath of allegiance'; they were accustomed to 'rubbing shoulders', to behaving in 'a civilised friendly manner'. They were representatives of parties that had moved on from the torments of 1922. To congratulate them for this advance was something of a disservice to the maturity of many of their predecessors. Presumably there was more to Irish politics in 1990 than a seventy-year-old Treaty.

Together they listened to an oration by former EC Commissioner, Peter Sutherland. He applauded the occasion, how its laudable ecumenical vision was a refreshing change from 'the patriot graves...exploited more than honoured'.[256] He continued: 'Irish commemorations have often, too often, been occasions where narrow tribal allegiances are proclaimed and the dead are invoked to justify barbarous actions and events that defile their memory and the

[251] *IT*, 15 Oct. 1990.   [252] *Ibid.*   [253] *II*, 15 Oct. 1990.
[254] The year 1985 marked the foundation of the reputedly mould-breaking Progressive Democrats; 1991 heralded the election of Mary Robinson who declared at her inauguration that she represented the end of civil war politics.
[255] *Southern Star*, 20 Oct. 1990.
[256] *IT*, 15 Oct. 1990; *II*, 15 Oct. 1990; *Southern Star*, 20 Oct. 1990.

honour and dignity of their country.'[257] In many ways he was correct. Extreme republicans had exploited and continued to exploit their dead, and Fianna Fáil and Fine Gael were often happy to pay the commemorative piper for a fitting party tune. But in truth Peter Sutherland was no better. In a haze of compliments, he made four claims about Michael Collins. Firstly, Collins had a mandate for whatever violence he employed, because 'those who are carrying out vicious and sordid acts of murder and pointless violence in Northern Ireland today must never be allowed to invoke the name or the authority of those who took part in the War of Independence and least of all Michael Collins to justify their crimes'.[258] Many who voted for Sinn Féin in 1918 may have disagreed. Secondly, Collins knew when to give in; he possessed the pragmatism to negotiate and to compromise. The IRA should take note, Sinn Féin should be encouraged. One newspaper editorial even went so far as to say that 'the negotiating of the peace was more important to him than executing his campaign of warfare': an uneasy vision of the once reluctant plenipotentiary. Thirdly, Collins would have 'found it in his heart – with that reservoir of generosity and imagination which he certainly possessed – to salute the brave who...fought in Flanders and the Somme'.[259] And, finally, Collins would approve of Ireland's entry into the European Union. Peter Sutherland had no way of knowing this. He had no way of knowing any of these things, just as extreme republicanism had no way of knowing if it could count Collins or any of his contemporaries amongst its number. Because old adversaries could agree on a version of the past, because they could all pay lip service to a platform that espoused a paragon of forward-looking pluralism and pragmatism, it was still an abuse of the past as valid or, more fittingly, invalid, as the abuse that continues to reap its violent rewards. 'Old hatreds can no longer be used to fan present divisions', but new lies cannot merely paper over the cracks.[260]

But the cracks were even evident at the ceremony. While much was made of the healing presence of Sile de Valera, the absence of the Taoiseach, Charles Haughey, was merely fuel to the fire that had supposedly gone out. Although protocol dictates that President and Taoiseach do not generally attend functions together, Fine Gael TD Monica Barnes and several correspondents of the Southern Star were not satisfied. Apparently 'Mr Haughey had a marvellous chance to appeal to the youth, to help bury the Civil War hatchet by attending last Sunday's ceremony. His promised private visit in the future is only closing the stable door when the horse has bolted. Once again Mr Haughey has done his own thing and has been found wanting'[261], wanting even though he had offered to take the monument into state care,[262] even though the Collins family

---

[257] Ibid.   [258] Ibid.   [259] II, 15 Oct. 1990.   [260] Ibid.
[261] Southern Star, 20 Oct. 1990.
[262] Liam Collins decided to retain ownership of the site, though it would be bequeathed to the Office of Public Works as a national monument.

enunciated nothing of this disgust. Monica Barnes was sure that 'civil war politics could have ended yesterday if Mr Haughey had put outdated bitterness to one side and attended the Michael Collins centenary commemoration'.[263] That Monica Barnes placed such faith in the healing powers of Charles J. Haughey is her own affair; that she used the commemoration to do that which it was supposedly designed to end is another matter. Swathed in ecumenism she had nothing but the bitter word.

Then came the film. By the end of 1996 Neil Jordan's life of Michael Collins had changed everything.[264] While some facts were altered for the benefit of cinematic effect and Jordan's rather inadequate homage to *The Third Man* and *The Godfather*, others were sacrificed to suit Northern metaphors. 1922 became 1994; Michael Collins became Liam Neeson; Michael Collins became Gerry Adams; and all the time press conferences were told 'this is history'.[265] It quickly broke Irish box office records. It touched those who knew nothing of Béalnabláth or Woodfield, statues or graves, commemoration or neglect. Memory became the currency of posters and t-shirts, telephone cards and statuettes; it was vital, commercial, popular, even alive.[266] Kilmainham Jail now exhibits Collins' cane, his scapulars, his brush, a letter to Hazel Lavery and a lock of his hair: he was never imprisoned there. Granard suddenly rediscovered its links with the 'Big Fella' and a refurbished and renamed Michael Collins bar and Kitty Kiernan restaurant were opened to thirsty and hungry patrons and pilgrims alike at the old Kiernan family hotel.[267] Béalnabláth became popular; Woodfield became a place to visit, to etch one's name on the modest stone walls. Yet none of the names pre-date the film, and they seemed chiselled in a naïvety drawn to the brightness of a Hollywood image instead of a historical figure. But this is not the fault of the signatories. And a film cannot be damned because it has had more effect than over seventy years of commemoration and scholarship. It cannot be condemned when it prompted a people to remember, when it brought calls for a Collins statue in O'Connell Street,[268] when the writing and rewriting of biography became its greatest postscript. However, it can and was criticised because one man's myth was made at another's expense. De Valera lurches through the film, a fiendish force of intransigent darkness whose tearful cowardice baits boys to do his murderous dirty work. De Valera did not kill Michael Collins or have him killed, although throughout the 1920s he

---

263 *IT*, 15 Oct. 1990.
264 The premiere was held in Dublin on the 6 Nov. 1996. The proceeds were divided between the Michael Collins Memorial Foundation and the Cope Foundation, Cork. Premiere programme, Michael MacEvilly private collection.
265 Neeson also said 'we feel it's historically accurate', *IT*, 5 Nov. 1996.
266 *II*, 4 Dec. 1996; *II*, 25 Aug. 1998; *Evening Herald*, 19 Apr. 1999.   267 *IT*, 20 Aug. 1998.
268 *Sunday Independent*, 22 Feb. 1998. A similar call for the replacement of the pillar with a Collins statue was made rather more mutely in 1966. Two eccentric letters to the Taoiseach were received and promptly ignored. DT s4523, Nelson's Pillar.

had to answer questions asked on election platforms like 'On the day Michael Collins was killed where was de Valera?'[269] Angry letters to editors about libel, requesting apologies, even from one of de Valera's armed guard on that day in Béalnabláth, never seemed to make any difference.[270] But as glamorous premieres turned eager Fine Gael and even Fianna Fáil heads, no one seemed to mind. Síle de Valera was one of the few voices in the wilderness, but with glib articles such as 'Dev and Collins were good pals' she did her cause no favours.[271] No one is saying that Neil Jordan is not entitled to his opinion, but there is something problematic in choosing and reshaping a man to meet the measure of our modern tastes. Jordan has spoken of his frustrations with de Valera's vision of Ireland; he and many of his generation were sickened by the stultifying spectre of 'cosy homesteads' and 'comely maidens'. Collins presents them with possibility. To speak up for de Valera is to speak as a conservative, to be castigated as one who yearns or defends a past that no longer appeals. De Valera left no surprises. Collins, on the other hand, left a life unlived, years of possibility tailored to fit our pluralism, our hopes for Northern Ireland, even, seemingly, our visions of Europe. We cannot overcome the bitterness of civil war simply by agreeing that there is now someone to deify and someone to blame. We cannot change the past because the past no longer suits us.

There is of course the possibility that myths and meanings should clash, that they should contest. Pieter Geyl's study of the many and varied Napoleons is eloquent proof of the virtues of diversity and disparity.[272] The intensity of the response to Jordan's work, however, has left little room for anything, be it truth, myth or downright lies. The type of exchanges which the film provoked, especially between Jordan and Eoghan Harris, entertaining though they may have been for the reader, were little more than childish squabbles over whose screenplay was the most historically inaccurate.[273] But film has always provoked a heated response. Hitchcock's *Juno and the paycock*, thought offensive to Catholicism and nationalism, was seized and burned in Limerick in the early 1930s;[274] *Beloved enemy* opted for the happy ending: no death, no risk of encouraging the rumour that Emmet Dalton may have killed Michael Collins.[275] And of course it is not a strictly Irish problem: *The life and death of Colonel Blimp, Objective Burma, The bridge over the river Kwai, Sword in the desert, Danton, JFK, Land and freedom, Schindler's list, Braveheart, Saving Private*

[269] Canon Coholan speaking at Bandon, *CE*, 13 Sept. 1927.
[270] Letter to the editor, *CE*, 15 Sept. 1927. De Valera himself refuted the accusation at an election address in Donegal. *Kerry News*, 19 Sept. 1927.
[271] Síle de Valera, 'Dev and Collins were good pals', in Nelson, *Michael Collins*, pp. 115–17.
[272] Pieter Geyl, *Napoleon for and against* (London, 1949).
[273] For example, Neil Jordan, 'Tally ho! Mr Harris', *IT*, 23 Oct. 1996.
[274] Kevin Rockett, Luke Gibbons and John Hill, *Cinema and Ireland* (London, 1987), p. 53.
[275] *Beloved enemy* directed by H. C. Potter was screened in 1936. Kevin Rockett (ed.), *The Irish filmography – fiction films 1896–1996* (Dun Laoghaire, 1996), pp. 349–50.

Ryan, The patriot[276] – the list could go on and on. Film will always upset or offend or at least provoke the historian. In a sense it should. Historical accuracy does not lend itself well to the confinement of two or three hours, to plot and drama and the demands of studio bosses for the prescribed number of action and romantic scenes. In most cases the inaccuracies are just more entertaining.

When Constantine Fitzgibbon littered one of his novels with accounts of Collins cavorting in countless beds, Richard Mulcahy tried to persuade the Minister for Justice to refuse Fitzgibbon his naturalisation papers.[277] As Neil Jordan can probably testify, there is still a high price to be paid for daring to dabble with the conventional memory of this 'great man'. That one of the more consistent criticisms of Jordan's Collins was his cursing and his drinking is proof still of the saintly vision that remains. Those who believed that Collins has 'taken too long to emerge from the black shadows of the past' have largely welcomed the film.[278] They would possibly never concede that Collins was afforded a particularly accommodating exile. No matter how much one may subscribe to the sanitising force of Fianna Fáil power on the history of the civil war period, those 'black shadows' lent themselves well to commemorations and monuments, to articles and orations, to possibly more biographies than for any other individual in Irish history. Shadows seemed instead the refuge of Collins' anti-Treatyite foes. General Liam Lynch may have his round tower in the wilds of the Knockmealdowns, but not one person in the four nearest villages could say where it was, or knew anything of Liam Lynch. Only republicanism's most intemperate now seem to care to journey there even though 10,000 or 15,000 people came to see the tower unveiled in 1935.[279] Liam Mellows has his statue in Eyre Square; prominent, dignified, but remembering only the Volunteer of 1916, not the Irregular of 1922. Rory O'Connor merely has his corner in Glasnevin's republican plot. The shadows could never contain Collins. They were instead the shroud of the Free State dead, the 'legion of the vanguard' that marched on its anonymous way, forgotten largely but for the sorrow of its families' grief.[280]

---

[276] Philip French, 'Hypocrisy, not history, fuels attacks on films', *The Observer*, 23 July 2000; Robert Darnton, *The kiss of Lamourette* (London, 1990), pp. 37–52.

[277] Constantine Fitzgibbon, *High heroic* (London, 1969); Risteárd Mulcahy, *Richard Mulcahy (1886–1971): a family memoir* (Dublin, 1999), p. 94.

[278] *Southern Star*, 20 Oct. 1990.

[279] *Tipperary Star*, 13 Apr. 1935; *An Phoblacht*, 21 Sept. 1973.   [280] Pinkman, *In the legion*.

3   The forgotten President: the awkward memory of Arthur Griffith

I got two books of Mr Collins life 'with the compliments of the Phoenix Co' so please
thank the sender for me. (Somehow I don't think you had the thought) they are put aside
till *AG's* son is of an age to think things for himself – I could not read either – a friend
looked out the part I wanted the Sinn Féin Ard Fheis of May 1922 to read what you said
of the agreement and you nicely slide over, the General's method of getting it behind
AGriffith's back, he had no inkling till the paper was laid before him in Mansion House,
it was mean and underhand way of working his own will and proved beyond all that
Collins had no idea of statesmanship... Why drag in my boy's mention the word *damn*
(a friend told me of it) I did not believe he said it till I asked he laughed and said 'You
are surprised, Yes I did' – my reply was, 'now I know you are human, but don't learn
any more of Mr Collins language', that I hear you never refer to in all the book his vile
expressions, I only heard him talk once and can never forget, people told me that was
his usual way of expressing himself, AG once said *damn*, the whole press printed it &
you go out of your way to drag it into your book did you forget it was not my boy's
life you were writing? It was low and mean & I think it a *great insult to his memory*
Were I Mrs S[heehy] S[keffington] Madam [de Markievicz], or Maud G[onne] or any
of these women I would have a meeting at once and just say what I think, but I am too
quiet & have to take all the stabs into my sad despair, & wait till judgement Day, to have
my *husband's record heard before all the world*, it is my only comfort in my desolate
home, made so by most of AG's *friends* – I'll hear more from time to time about the
book I suppose, but I won't read it, I have as much as I can bear without adding to the
burden.[1]

Maud Griffith wrote this letter to Piaras Béaslaí in December 1926, one month
after the publication of his biography of Michael Collins. She was angry,
jealous: a mere foul-mouthed 'soldier' had been preferred over 'my boy', over
'my President'.[2] She felt that her husband had given his life for Ireland with no
reward, to be forgotten within four years, or to be remembered only for calling
Erskine Childers 'a damned Englishman'.[3] In her view he was not appropriately

---

[1] Letter from Maud Griffith to Piaras Béaslaí, 6 Dec. 1926, Piaras Béaslaí MSS, NLI, MS
33,930(14) (emphasis and punctuation from original).
[2] DF f13/3/26, Griffith settlement – payment of annuity, letter from Maud Griffith to W. T. Cosgrave,
quoted in a letter from Cosgrave to Ernest Blythe, 5 May 1925.
[3] *DE, treaty debate*, p. 416 (10 Jan. 1922).

appreciated or commemorated. This chapter is the shortest because in the midst of her unpunctuated fury she may have had a point.

While Maud Griffith was content to wait for the glories that 'judgement day' would bestow upon her husband, this chapter has to settle for the less exalted little that happened in the years after his death. It may seem strange to speak of him as a forgotten president given the honour hammered together on Leinster Lawn, given the eagerly commissioned effigies, the Albert Power bust and death mask that wended their tardy ways into museums and galleries with those of their companion Commander-in-Chief.[4] There were portraits, worthy and noble in exhibitions, copied and cheap on barracks walls.[5] Griffith featured in biography, in souvenir booklets; his own works were republished and sold.[6] A bridge, a road and a barracks were renamed; the men of Manchester built him a hall; Cumann na nGaedheal once eagerly christened some fledgling branches after him; Fine Gael still honour him with six.[7] There was commemoration and he was pantheonised; his name was even useful to mention in advertisements for eyeglasses.[8] But while there was something to be gained from boasting that one was once optician to a president, for a government eager to establish its own credibility in 1922 and 1923 the first President had to be left behind. Years of protest had proved his nationalism, yet he had been seen to weaken in London; he had allowed himself to be tricked and had given in. He would always be remembered as the first to sign the Treaty. Near the end of his life, his cabinet colleagues allegedly referred to him as 'an old fogey'; before his death he could be found, the President of the Second Dáil, sitting alone in his office 'with not even a secretary or a typist available to him'.[9] In 1922 and 1923 it was necessary, even desirable, to remember that 'his life was given for Ireland as truly as if he had laid it down on the field of battle'.[10] After 1923 it was not. He was no longer the great man that this desperate state required.

Republicans may have respected him once, but in August 1922 prisoners in Portobello barracks were reported to have cheered the news of his death.[11]

---

[4] DT s1827b&c, National leaders: busts, death masks etc.; DF 365/6, Portrait busts of Griffith and Collins; by Albert Power; Desmond FitzGerald MSS, UCDA, P80/1027; Sighle Bhreathnach-Lynch, 'Face value: commemoration and its discontents', *Circa*, 65 (Autumn 1993).

[5] Lily Williams' early portraits of Griffith were exhibited in the Dublin Municipal Gallery of Modern Art. A copy of one of them hangs in the Military Archives, Cathal Brugha Barracks.

[6] *The two leaders* (Dublin, 1922). Advertisements appeared for *Griffith's fiscal policy for Ireland* and *The resurrection of Hungary* in, for example, *United Irishman*, 23 June 1923.

[7] The Arthur Griffith Irish National Club was opened in St Patrick's Parish, Manchester, in Nov. 1922. *Young Ireland*, 4 Nov. 1922. Letter from Patrick O'Meara, Policy and Research Officer, Fine Gael, 8 July 1998.

[8] E. J. Kearney advertisement, *United Irishman*, 1 Mar. 1923.

[9] Statement by Patrick Moylett, quoted in John M. Feehan, *The shooting of Michael Collins: murder or accident?* (Dublin, 1982), p. 80.

[10] DT s8358, Griffith–Collins commemoration 1923, draft article for American press by John Chartres, July 1923.

[11] *Evening Herald*, 12 Aug. 1922.

Although this was refuted with stories of prisoners kneeling and praying, the republicans would never forgive him.[12] There were even fears in the hospital that republicans had poisoned him.[13] Laudable obituaries in *The Nation* and in *Poblacht na hÉireann War News* could not hide what was truly felt: 'the life of the Republic is greater than the life of Mr Griffith'.[14] 'The Hidden Hand of the Great Irregular struck him down ... The angel that guards the destiny of Ireland revealed to him his great error, his sin against the nation, and for sorrow he died.'[15] But Griffith had been equally unforgiving; there was none of the great wave of last lenient words that would allegedly flow from Michael Collins' lips ten days later. In his last interview, given from his hospital bed, Griffith rejected a peaceful solution to the civil war: 'every door has been closed on conciliation ... it must be fought out to the end'.[16] He died 'embittered by the ingratitude of his countrymen, after a life of service',[17] with nothing more auspicious uttered over his head than 'take up that corpse at once'.[18]

In civil war he was portrayed by the government as a noble statesman who had given his life for the good of Ireland; in peace he was unmentioned, nothing but the occasional reference to the slur on Erskine Childers. If he was remembered, it was for his early work, his journalism, his economic theories, fighting the good South African fight. His eloquent defence of the Treaty was quickly overlooked. Griffith had committed the country to dominion status and it was not wise for the government to champion the dual monarchist in their midst. There were too many like Robert Barton saying that 'Griffith was not a republican. His ideal was the King, Lords and Commons of Ireland.'[19] And there were too many within the government who knew he was right. When army mutineers called for action, this was not the man for the government to summon to its side. The dual monarchist was quietly cast aside.

Suggestions of commemoration came to nothing. Government Buildings did not become Griffith Buildings as one writer to the *Irish Independent* had wished.[20] There was no stamp, just a sample of one for ten shillings that would have rarely been used anyway.[21] There would be no educational medal, as mooted by the government Publicity Department.[22] After the army mutiny the government had no desire to reward schoolchildren with a medal for being able to spell dual monarchy or compromise. There was no lavish presentation

[12] *Republican War Bulletin*, 22 Aug. 1922.
[13] Oliver St John Gogarty, *As I was going down Sackville Street* (London, 1954), p. 199.
[14] *Poblacht na hÉireann War News*, 39, 15 Aug. 1922.
[15] 'A great repentant', *The Nation*, 19 Aug. 1922.
[16] James D. Phelan, *Travel and comment* (San Francisco, 1923), pp. 244–5.
[17] *Ibid.*   [18] Gogarty, *As I was going*, p. 199.
[19] Robert Barton's replies to queries from Mr Boyle (n.d.), Robert Barton MSS, TCD, MS 7834(10).
[20] Letter to the editor of the *Irish Independent*, 10 Aug. 1922.
[21] Hugh Kennedy MSS, UCDA, p4/601.   [22] DT s4011, Proposed Griffith–Collins medal.

of his possessions, just private papers in a strong room, later packaged and partially destroyed. Seán Lester's suggestion to collect them was noted, eagerly sidelined and quickly discarded.[23] It was only British politicians who showed themselves eager to remember him. To some this seemed fitting; to the Free State government it could only ever be damning. Paul Henry had etched a charcoal portrait of Griffith lying in state. It was intended for a Dublin gallery but was bought instead by the British signatories of the Treaty and 'Presented to the Government of the Irish Free State' in his honour, as the inscription said. The British had suggested that Eamon Duggan, the last remaining pro-Treatyite signatory, should be associated with the purchase, but this could not be allowed. In the tentative days of December 1922 even this tenuous association had to be rejected. 'It should be regarded as a gift from the British signatories alone.'[24] It was bad enough that the British were so fond of Griffith as to wish to honour him. The government had no desire to mire itself even further in minds already convinced of its treacherous faults. The portrait was hung in the Ceann Comhairle's office, a worthy place, but a place where the public would never see the dedication.

Other portraits were picked up along the way. One was bought for the office of the High Commissioner in London in 1924. It was not strictly commemoration; the Commissioner wanted pictures of 'distinguished Irishmen' on his walls – it seemed the right sort of thing for a Commissioner to do.[25] An artist's proof of a John Lavery portrait was purchased by the state and hangs in the Department of Foreign Affairs. It was bought as part of a scheme to provide portraits of prominent members of the first and second Dála.[26] It was bought in 1955 by a Fianna Fáil government despite the fact that a largely Fine Gael-funded initiative had placed three portraits of Griffith, Collins and O'Higgins in the Dáil in 1944. George A. Lyons sent his small subscription to Joseph McGrath in 1942. He also sent this letter:

Please accept the enclosed small subscription towards the Griffith–Collins memorial portraits next to my regret that the subscription is so small is my regret that the proposed memorial is to take such an inadequate form. 20 golden years ago I suggested to Mr Cosgrave that a sculptural memorial should be erected in front of the Dáil to the memory of the founders of the state in place of the present Imperial monstrosity which stands there. Mr Cosgrave then replied, 'Twenty years hence will be time enough to launch the project'. Well 20 years after the project has shrunk into this little measure with

23 DT s9190a, Arthur Griffith – personal papers.
24 DT s1903a, Miscellaneous: portrait of the late President Griffith, copy of memo to cabinet, 7 Dec. 1922.
25 DF s0071/0011/24, Authority for expenditure on provision of pictures of distinguished Irishmen on the walls of the High Commissioner's office.
26 DT s15134a, Leinster House provision of portraits of prominent members of the first and second Dála and other leaders of the struggle for independence.

a...couple of posthumous portraits. I am an enthusiastic admirer of the Leo Whelan portraits but even *he* can devine [sic] little inspiration from posthumous studies and I may say that the Nation is not without portraits of the dead patriots...I am still of opinion that a State-aided memorial of a truly courageous and dignified character should have been embarked upon and I trust that the project has not been abandoned. Posterity is a fugitative [sic] entity.[27]

For a man who had admired Griffith, as Lyons had, the portrait was not enough. Lyons had written his memories of Griffith in 1923;[28] he had been promised then a monument worthy of the man he had eulogised. And now there was only a mediocre painting. For those who admired Griffith there would only ever be this disappointment.

In many ways they were foolish to expect matters to be otherwise. Griffith had not proved a successful subject of earlier government initiatives. A memorial album, short and filled with pictures, had been published on 28 February 1923. Each of its 25,000 copies paid homage to Griffith and Collins, and all of the £635 0s. 10d. it cost seemed to suggest that the government wanted something in return. It had been commissioned by the government Publicity Department after all. Having contributed to the bankruptcy of its publishers, Martin Lester Ltd, it had sold less than half of its print run in August 1923. By October 1925, 'despite a special effort to push this book', despite reviews which commended it to 'every Irish man and woman who desires to understand the character and ideals of the men who found Ireland a province and left her a nation', the Talbot Press, to whom sales had now been entrusted, was left with 7,863 copies on its hands. No one wanted to pay the shilling price to read of Griffith and Collins; no one even wanted to pay the half price of 6d. The Talbot Press reported uneasily that 'further sale was practically dead in this country. There was no possibilities of effective sales in USA. The book was more or less out of date and not now topical.'[29] Although they conceded that 'the object was not, of course, primarily to make a profit, but really for propaganda purposes',[30] the total receipts of a mere £394 2s. 11d. still galled the Department of Finance when it considered the £635 it had spent. Ferenc Deák, Frederich List and *The resurrection of Hungary* were not the stuff bestsellers were made of. And with more than two hundred precious pounds gone down the drain, the government would not make the same mistake again. Renaming a barracks was not costly; renaming a street on the outskirts of Dublin, renaming a bridge, amounted to

[27] Letter from George A. Lyons to Joseph McGrath, 30 June 1942, George A. Lyons MSS, NLI, MS 33,675/A/2/(81) (spelling and punctuation as in original).
[28] George A. Lyons, *Some recollections of Griffith and his times* (Dublin, 1923).
[29] Report by S. P. Breathnach, Department of External Affairs to the Department of Finance, 11 Aug. 1925, DT s0046/0039/25, External Affairs – Griffith–Collins album – cost of publication.
[30] Letter from J. Hayes, Department of External Affairs to E. O'Neill, Department of Finance, 24 Mar. 1927, *ibid*.

nothing more than a new road sign, a small change on a map.[31] There was no need or no will for anything else.

Thus commemoration fell to those closest to him. An appeal was made for funds for a high altar for the new parish church on that cheaply renamed Griffith Avenue, 'a tribute of love' to honour him, a token of regard from 'Arthur Griffith's personal friends'.[32] This plea was made in October 1927; by this time the committee of his closest companions already knew that commemoration depended on them alone. They were stalwarts of the older days; they were the men and, unusually, the two women who remembered the days before 1919. Under the names Seán Gall, P. J. Ingoldsby, L. Rooney, J. F. Shouldice, Charles Moran, P. J. Duffy, Mícheál Ó Loingsigh, Mary Saurin and Margaret Wheatley, the appeal was made. The altar would 'stand above and beyond party'; it would embody his 'devotion to the cause of all the people of his country'.[33] It was for the Griffith of 'patient toil', who wrote through 'obscurity and privation',[34] the Griffith before civil war, before party and politics had claimed him for their own. This was the Griffith his wife honoured; the altar was the only monument she ever endorsed. It was erected in 1928, ready for the opening of the new church, built on the shilling and pound donations, on the five-pound good grace of the Rathgar and Rathmines Cumann na nGaedheal branches who saw beyond the utilitarianism of their colleagues in government.[35] For many it was fitting that the altar would stand in a church of St Vincent de Paul. The monument was built for the Griffith who toiled in penury for the freedom of his country, for the betterment of his fellow men. This was not the Griffith of the top hat and tails of government that his erstwhile colleagues were now lampooned for by Fianna Fáil. It was a monument instead to humility, fitting in a church dedicated to the saint most closely associated with the plight of the poor. The monument was religious, and unashamedly so; five or six times a day a priest would stand at this altar and say that God so loved the world that he gave his only son. Five or six times a day Griffith would be sanctified: a man who so loved his country that his blessed heart 'broke for Ireland'.[36]

However, there was never such blasphemy again. But then there was not much opportunity. Ceremony waned and talk of biography was only encouraged to counteract a boisterous Fianna Fáil. In the beginning there were hints that it might have been different. Within six days of his death, Darrell Figgis wrote to Maud Griffith to announce that he 'believed Griffith wanted him to write his

[31] Wellington Barracks was renamed Griffith Barracks, a main thoroughfare on the outskirts of Dublin city became Griffith Avenue, and North Gate Bridge became Arthur Griffith Bridge. *The Star*, 10 Aug. 1929.
[32] 'Memorial to Arthur Griffith', NLI, LOp115, item 56; John Devoy MSS, NLI, MS 18,132.
[33] *Ibid.*   [34] *Ibid.*
[35] DT s5734a, Griffith–Collins Cenotaph – general file; *The Freeman*, 18 Aug. 1922. Information also from Fr Boland, parish priest, Church of St Vincent de Paul, Griffith Avenue, Marino.
[36] *Good Counsel Magazine* (Autumn 1966).

official "life" '. He wanted her permission because it was important to 'make [the] book a piece of literature of its own merit – to stand among the books of the world'.[37] The earth had barely settled on her husband's grave. Two days later she replied. She was

making other arrangements...I should be very sorry to say anything to hurt you... while I fully recognise your high literary ability and your desire to place Arthur's life adequately before the world, I do not think that you are the proper person to undertake this work, and I am satisfied that you are mistaken in interpreting him as indicating a desire that you should do so.[38]

What her arrangements were never became clear. They became less clear as she grew more and more upset by the response of her husband's colleagues to his death. George A. Lyons' memories of Griffith and some newspaper articles and reminiscences were all that 1923 brought. Anniversaries prompted periodic rememberings, but nothing more substantial than an article or two, to be forgotten with the next day's editions. Only in 1930 were there mutterings requiring something more:

It is now eight years since Arthur Griffith died and yet, so far as we are aware, no attempt has been made to provide the public with an authoritative biography of that great Irishman...nothing has been done towards placing on record the services of Griffith to his country. It is a pity, because a new generation is growing up in Ireland which knows little of the man who played such a dominating part in the struggle which brought the Saorstát into being. A well-written and adequate biography of the founder of Sinn Féin is indeed overdue, and we would make a special plea that the Government should endeavour to have a start made upon this important work.[39]

But while Cumann na nGaedheal remained in government it did not share its supporters' enthusiasm for Griffith. Fianna Fáil were doing more than enough to point out their inadequacies in the Dáil without commissioning and paying an author to remind the people that Griffith only wanted a 'King, Lords and Commons' after all. Nor were memories of Piaras Béaslaí and the Collins biography particularly endearing. Wilful authors were frankly more trouble than they were worth. Change only came after 1932, only after another electoral defeat in 1933 and a damning third in 1937. Change came after Frank Pakenham's *Peace by ordeal*, after Dorothy Macardle's *The Irish Republic*.[40] There were too many scribbling to de Valera's dictation; there was now a need for a Free State version of events. Oliver St John Gogarty's *As I was going down Sackville Street* was simply not enough. To one observer he had 'made a complete hash of the thing in

[37] Letter from Darrell Figgis to Maud Griffith, 18 Aug. 1922, Desmond FitzGerald MSS, UCDA, P80/302(1).
[38] Letter from Maud Griffith to Darrell Figgis, 20 Aug. 1922, *ibid.*, P80/302(2).
[39] *The Star*, 2, 4 (25 Jan. 1930), p. 4.
[40] Pakenham, *Peace by ordeal*; Macardle, *The Irish Republic*.

his rather mediocre book',[41] but, in fairness to Gogarty, he was not trying to write a biography of Griffith. While James Crosbie of the *Cork Examiner* suggested to Piaras Béaslaí that he should step into the breach in 1937, it took another five years before orders were issued from the elder statesmen of Fine Gael to find, as Crosbie had suggested, 'someone in a position to do the life of Griffith... straight away'.[42] W. T. Cosgrave wrote to Desmond FitzGerald and Michael Hayes in February 1942. He was on the point of making an agreement with Seán Milroy to write a biography of Griffith, but having learnt from the mistakes made with Béaslaí, he wanted to maintain control. Hayes and FitzGerald would make satisfactory arrangements to check the work. A former Cumann na nGaedheal TD, Milroy was at least one of their own; he had also 'expressed his willingness to abide by any plan made to enable him to start and complete the work'.[43] He knew better than Béaslaí, he knew what had been written by Pakenham and Macardle, he knew that there was now as much if not more at stake than when Béaslaí was charged with putting pen to paper in September 1922. Cosgrave finished his letter to both men in the following terms: 'I realise at once the onerous character of this undertaking and I would scarcely venture to ask your co-operation in it but that it is for such an important work on behalf of the country.'[44] The intention was clear from the start. There was just one error in the letter: this was important work on behalf of Fine Gael. If there was any doubt, Cosgrave made his meaning clear in a letter to Milroy two months later:

Desmond [FitzGerald] and I had some words with Pakenham on his sources of information and my language to him was strong. The Government through their Secretary wrote to me saying they were considering or had decided – I forget which – to publish. I demurred very emphatically and that was the end of that. As you will readily understand this is confidential. In dealing with these people I have been meticulously careful to observe discretion.[45]

It was simply all about the best way of 'dealing with these people'.

Reports on Milroy's progress began with airy assumptions that this would be merely the first book of many, that each of these many would be 'as various as their writers and as the different times in which they are written'. But with these concessions made, the report made its intentions clear: 'The first Life written now, some twenty years after his death should fulfil certain fixed requirements.' Apparently it should be clear that Griffith 'could joke about some

[41] Letter from James Crosbie to Piaras Béaslaí, 11 Nov. 1937, Piaras Béaslái MSS, NLI, MS 33,930(2).
[42] *Ibid.*
[43] Letter from W. T. Cosgrave to Desmond FitzGerald and Michael Hayes, 26 Feb. 1942, Michael Hayes MSS, UCDA, P53/217(1) and Desmond FitzGerald MSS, UCDA, P80/1137.
[44] *Ibid.*
[45] Letter from W. T. Cosgrave to Seán Milroy, 20 Apr. 1942, Michael Hayes MSS, UCDA, P53/217(4).

of his earlier views, and even deeply deplored them. Any biography will have to bring out that fact.'[46] To all intents and purposes the facts seemed irrelevant. Griffith was merely a means to an end. For his followers to disavow some of his earlier ideas was one thing, to depict the man himself laughing and deploring his own beliefs was quite something else. Buoyed up by Joseph McGrath's millions, Hayes and FitzGerald became 'trustees for the publication of the life of Arthur Griffith' in February 1944,[47] and Milroy was sent the cheques, the £200, the £250 that McGrath donated 'to keep the pot boiling'.[48] The phrase was perhaps more appropriate than McGrath may have flippantly meant. This 'life of Griffith' would not have been out of place with any of the best 'pot boilers' that fiction could produce. This is perhaps an unfair assessment, but this triumvirate of Fine Gael nobility wanted nothing more than that the book be 'largely factual'.[49] To be entirely factual would have merely defeated the greater purpose.

When Milroy died in 1946 the pot boiling was offered to Liam Ó Briain, another Fine Gael man.[50] He refused and the research stopped until November 1949 when Padraic Colum agreed to take up Milroy's mantle. Ostensibly 'a work of piety', 'a monument to a devoted man',[51] it remained, as W. T. Cosgrave had said in 1942, an 'onerous . . . undertaking'.[52] The delay had made the intention even clearer. Michael Hayes was just a little more polite: 'it will be necessary to make Griffith's position as a force and an influence clear and to show how right he was on the Treaty issue in 1921'.[53] Paddy O'Daly, once major general in the notorious Kerry Command, was just more brutally honest: 'We got a job of cleaning up a lot of dirt in 1922 and we certainly made a bad job of it as the dust from the same dirt heap is still blinding a lot of the people.'[54] A cantankerous Cosgrave made his position clear: 'his main purpose is to ensure my name is not mentioned';[55] while Mulcahy, as Minister for Education in September 1951, just could not 'afford to be wrong in anything I say about Dev'.[56] Arthur Griffith seemed to be the last thing on any of their minds. That

---

[46] Letter from Michael Hayes to W. T. Cosgrave, 9 Dec. 1943, *ibid.*, P53/217(7).

[47] Letter from Liam Burke, Secretary of Fine Gael to Michael Hayes, 22 Feb. 1944, *ibid.*, P53/217(9).

[48] Note from Joseph McGrath to Michael Hayes, 1 June 1945, *ibid.*, P53/217(20).

[49] Letter from Michael Hayes to W. T. Cosgrave, 9 Dec. 1943, *ibid.*, P53/217(7).

[50] Letter from Michael Hayes to Liam Ó Briain, 21 Aug. 1947, *ibid.*, P53/222(12).

[51] Letter from Padraic Colum to Michael Hayes, 16 Feb. 1955, *ibid.*, P53/222(155); letter from Padraic Colum to Michael Hayes, 1 Dec. 1950, *ibid.*, P53/222(27).

[52] Letter from W. T. Cosgrave to Desmond FitzGerald, 26 Feb. 1942, Desmond FitzGerald MSS, UCDA, P80/1137.

[53] Letter from Michael Hayes to Padraic Colum, 5 Aug. 1950, Michael Hayes MSS, UCDA, P53/222(8).

[54] Letter from Paddy O'Daly to Michael Hayes, 11 July 1949, *ibid.*, P53/222(3).

[55] Letter from W. T. Cosgrave to Padraic Colum, 18 Mar. 1953, *ibid.*, P53/222(114).

[56] Letter from Richard Mulcahy to Michael Hayes, 5 Sept. 1951, *ibid.*, P53/222(54).

they appeared to be right in 1921, 1922 and 1923 was all that mattered. The 'persistent efforts of anti-Treaty writers', the books 'which contained all the usual dope', were to be thwarted at all costs.[57] 'For too long the falsification of history by Fianna Fáil propagandists has gone unchecked.'[58] Brugha was to be depicted as a mere part-time revolutionary. Emphasis was to be placed on the fact that 'during the whole time of the troubles, he [Brugha] kept on his business, and he did not, like Collins and Mulcahy, devote his whole time to the work of the Volunteers'.[59] There was to be no reference to Collins looking as if he wanted to shoot himself after he signed the Treaty. 'This should not be quoted of a man with the religion and courage of Collins.'[60] Monitored with military precision – 'I don't like the reference to a public house' – this Griffith would do nothing to embarrass Fine Gael.[61] There were even questions raised concerning Colum's use of Frank Pakenham's *Peace by ordeal* as a source. Pakenham was believed, after all, to be practically in the pay of Fianna Fáil. But for all their labours, they fooled no one. Listeners to Radio Éireann heard how

the biographer throws all semblance of impartiality to the winds . . . each page (from the 1921 period onwards) is devoted to the problem of proving de Valera a complete fool, or possibly a knave, Erskine Childers to be a suspect person, and Brugha a blood-thirsty megalomaniac, Austin Stack a half-wit, and the rest of the Republicans to be a stupid people whose silly loyalty to principle when expediency was called for did them no honour. Really Mr Colum! Or should one accept without question that Padraic Colum is responsible for the sneers, the jeers and the ridicule that are showered on the Republicans in this book? . . . Who has most to gain by lauding Griffith and vilifying de Valera and all who remained loyal to the Republican ideal? . . . it is made clear to us that this biography is based more or less on a narrative written by the late Seán Milroy at the behest of a number of prominent supporters of the Free State. In addition to this unpublished work, Mr Colum has leaned heavily on the unpublished papers of the late Desmond FitzGerald. As well as this, the preface contains this phrase: '. . . the ones who induced me to become a biographer, the friends of Arthur Griffith, Joseph McGrath, W. T. Cosgrave, Richard Mulcahy, the most zealous of all in obtaining, arranging and caretaking of material, Michael Hayes'. All these people are excellent sources for anyone writing a life of Griffith or indeed writing anything about the period. But, who would deny that at least three of them are among the most one-sided people in the land when it comes to discussing the Treaty, the events that led up to it, and especially all that followed it. And who can blame them for this? They were all involved personally in these tragic happenings; it is only natural that they should keep silent on facts that do not support their

---

[57] Letter from Michael Hayes to Padraic Colum, 14 Feb. 1952, *ibid.*, P53/222(59); *ibid.*, 17 Sept. 1952, P53/222(73).

[58] *Fine Gael Digest*, special Ard Fheis issue, 1960; Michael Hayes MSS, UCDA, P53/245.

[59] Memo from Michael Hayes to Padraic Colum, 20 Aug. 1952, Michael Hayes MSS, UCDA, P53/222(69).

[60] W. T. Cosgrave's comment on the draft, n.d., *ibid.*, P53/222(160).

[61] Letter from Michael Hayes to Padraic Colum, 17 Sept. 1952, *ibid.*, P53/222(73).

own side. It is of course hardly necessary for me to add that their opposite numbers of
the Republican side are just as one-sided, and the views of all of them should be treated
with extreme care and caution. This Mr Colum did not do. Seán Milroy could hardly be
called an impartial observer and Desmond FitzGerald could hardly be expected to be
just when writing of Eamon de Valera. But Mr Colum puts forward their statements as if
they were accepted facts. No one who knows anything about the period will take much
notice of the curious fables that pass as history in this book, but, unfortunately, it may
well fall into the hands of people who, knowing nothing of the background, will take
much of it as truth and so help perpetuate untruths that should have died years ago.[62]

The review was damning and in that sense worthy of this lengthy extract.
It was also reprinted in full in *Revolt – voice of young republican Ireland* just
in case anyone missed the broadcast, in case anyone was likely to forget the
old allegations and the old fight.[63] That no one seemed interested should have
upset Fine Gael even more. To the party's disgust Colum sold the syndication
rights to the *Manchester Express*. That he had done so was merely 'because
our own has not the interest or the enterprise to try to secure' them.[64] The
Manchester Express was not exactly on a par with Fleet Street's finest. And
to add insult to injury, publishers showed the same reluctance. Publisher after
publisher read the manuscript and refused it. Harvard University Press sent an
honest appraisal of America's disinterest: 'there is no book-buying Irish public
here, the interest in Ireland has lapsed'.[65] London flatly declined. Perhaps Seán
Ó Lúing's *Art Ó Gríofa*, published in 1953, was to blame for this reluctance.[66]
It was a more accomplished life of the former president but, written in Irish, the
book was never a realistic rival for an English text. It was 1957 before Brown
and Nolan of Dublin obliged, 1959 before the book was published. That Colum
was difficult, that his work was 'the most murderous job' the copyeditor had
ever undertaken, did not, admittedly, help matters.[67] But the enthusiasm of his
once ebullient backers had also waned. Exasperated at the years he had spent
on the project, Colum protested: 'I should have thought that his friends would
have put some energy into doing this.'[68] Griffith's 'friends' had merely realised,
in the intervening years, the magnitude of this 'onerous' and unrewarding task.

In many ways they must have known that it was a foolhardy act. By then,
Griffith had long been stolen from them. From early in its tenure Cumann na
nGaedheal was taunted by the ghost of Griffith; memories soured when he
became the rod to beat the government's back. His economic theories were
constantly quoted; his protectionism and self-sufficiency summoned to Fianna

[62] Copy of the review of Colum's biography by Proinsias MacAoghusa, broadcast by Radio
Éireann, *ibid.*, P53/224(29).
[63] *Ibid.*   [64] Letter from Padraic Colum to Michael Hayes, 9 Aug. 1951, *ibid.*, P53/222(52).
[65] Letter from Padraic Colum to Michael Hayes, 16 Sept. 1954, *ibid.*, P53/222(144).
[66] Seán Ó Lúing, *Art Ó Gríofa* (Dublin, 1953); Padraic Colum, *Arthur Griffith* (Dublin, 1959).
[67] Letter from Frank Keane to Michael Hayes, 9 Oct. 1956, Michael Hayes MSS, UCDA,
P53/222(179).
[68] Letter from Padraic Colum to Michael Hayes, 28 Oct. 1955, *ibid.*, P53/222(176).

Fáil's side as it assumed the mantle of economic defender of the nation.[69] The barbs were constant. They were irritating in 1927: Cumann na nGaedheal had 'sold out' on Griffith.[70] By 1930 they were insinuating that to judge 'by recent speeches by Mr FitzGerald and Dr O'Higgins, if Griffith lived and spoke today he would be liable to be sent to jail for sedition'[71], possibly not too preposterous a suggestion, given that a former Cumann na nGaedheal minister admitted that 'the ideals of Arthur Griffith were scrapped without mercy'.[72] By 1931 Fianna Fáil's devotion was even celebrated in verse: de Valera was the defender of Griffith's ideals; Cumann na nGaedheal had betrayed its famous son. 'Straws in the wind' by J. O'F. began its protectionist rant with 'Once Griffith said some pleasant things... Now de Valera follows him...'.[73] By the anniversary of his death in 1932, the *Irish Press* were taunting: 'Today the party which speaks of Arthur Griffith as its founder have formed their national and economic policies on just those false principles he gave a life's work to expose.'[74] But while Griffith may have found his economic spiritual home in the cosy homesteads of Fianna Fáil, although it was the clever thing to do at an opportune time, there was an element of Fianna Fáil that still bore a grudge. Furthermore, extreme republicanism took a more condescending view: 'Republican he may not have been but he loved his country, and the realisation of what he had done when he yielded to the blandishments and threats of the English... must have broken his heart. His story is one of the saddest in the annals of Ireland.'[75] De Valera had been persuaded in January 1922 that his own prestige would outweigh loyalties to both Griffith and Collins; despite the Treaty vote he presumed to be re-elected President of the Irish Republic. Griffith was 'never forgiven for having pinched Dev's clothes. Dev was the only one who was permitted to perform that particular sartorial trick.'[76] Griffith the awkward predecessor was claimed when convenient but, in truth, forgotten by all.

Because 'there is practically nothing known about Griffith amongst the younger generations. It is quite clear that the school book historians, the Department of Education and people responsible for documentaries such as "Facts about Ireland" have succeeded in reducing this great man to a non-entity in the

---

[69] T. K. Daniel, 'Griffith on his noble head: the determinants of Cumann na nGaedheal economic policy, 1922–32', *Irish Economic and Social History*, 3 (1976), pp. 55–65; William Murphy, 'In pursuit of popularity and legitimacy: the rhetoric of Fianna Fáil's social and economic policy 1926–34', unpublished MA thesis, University College, Dublin (1998).

[70] Seán Ó Muimneacáin, *The Nation*, 16 Apr. 1927.

[71] Seán Lemass quoted in the *IT*, 10 Feb. 1930. Thanks to William Murphy for this reference.

[72] J. J. Walsh, *Recollections of a rebel* (Tralee, 1944), p. 72.

[73] *Catholic Bulletin*, 21, 12 (Dec. 1931), p. 1142.   [74] *Irish Press*, 12 Aug. 1932.

[75] *Wolfe Tone Weekly*, 1, 11 (13 Nov. 1937), p. 2.

[76] Tom Garvin, 'Dev and Mick: the 1922 split as social psychological event', in Gabriel Doherty and Dermot Keogh (eds.), *Michael Collins and the making of the Irish state* (Cork, 1998), p. 153.

minds of most';[77] because he is 'scandalously neglected by historians and half-forgotten by the country at large',[78] by 1968 'those of us who revere his historic name' felt obliged to redeem him.[79] Redemption amounted to a plaque on his home, paid for by fifty citizens of Dublin North East. It simply read: 'From 1910 until his death in 1922 this was the home of Arthur Griffith patriot and statesman. His monument, an Ireland free.' It was the work of a few friends, Fine Gael supporters admittedly, but friends none the less. Watched by Griffith's son and daughter and a host of Fine Gael acolytes, Richard Mulcahy unveiled the plaque on 13 September 1968. The pupils of all the local schools had been invited together with all the Dublin branches of Fine Gael. There was no desire to invite the possibly more like-minded Fianna Fáil. Standing on 'holy ground', a moderate crowd was told of the 'extraordinary selflessness' of 1903 and 1904. It heard nothing beyond 1919.[80] There had been a civil rights march in Dublin the day before; petrol bombs had been thrown at the British embassy.[81] Mulcahy had learned his Northern lesson, but so too had his political colleagues. The committee was 'disappointed at the mere handful of elected representatives who bothered to turn up'.[82] But the committee was still optimistic; it was 'counteracting the deliberate playing down of the great achievements of Arthur Griffith';[83] it was 'quite pleased with the crowd', 'happy in thinking that a reawakening' had begun.[84] Yet their enthusiasm, manifest in an eagerness to establish an Arthur Griffith Society, was wasted on idle memories. Seán Ó Lúing had lamented in 1953 that there was no enthusiasm for the placing of a plaque on the office of the *United Irishman* in Fownes Street.[85] The society had no real cause to think that anything had changed in the fifteen years between. Lone calls for statues meant and yielded nothing.[86] The centenary of Griffith's birth, 1971, came and passed, unheralded but for a few articles, a wreath on Leinster Lawn and a token from Fine Gael on 5 December that commemorated the signing of the Treaty more than the man.[87] And even that was overshadowed. On the same day the Old Dublin Brigade prayed for Rory O'Connor,

[77] Letter from Con Sheehan to Richard Mulcahy, 25 Sept. 1968, Richard Mulcahy MSS, UCDA, P7D/76.

[78] Con Sheehan, 'True patriot – a Dubliner to remember', n.d., *ibid.*

[79] 'Wants tribute to Griffith', letter to the editor from Patrick O'Brien, no title, n.d., *ibid.*

[80] Letter from Con Sheehan to Richard Mulcahy, 25 Sept. 1968, *ibid.*; extracts from Mulcahy's speech, *II*, 14 Oct. 1968.

[81] *IT*, 14 Oct. 1968.

[82] Letter from Con Sheehan to Richard Mulcahy, 14 Oct. 1968, Richard Mulcahy MSS, UCDA, P7D/76.

[83] *Ibid.*, 11 Sept. 1968.   [84] *Ibid.*, 14 Oct. 1968.

[85] Letter from Seán Ó Luing to Piaras Béaslaí, 22 June 1953, Piaras Béaslaí MSS, NLI, MS 33,919(3).

[86] One was mooted in Apr. 1969: Richard Mulcahy MSS, UCDA, p7c/2(14); another by Maire Comerford in Feb. 1970, *ibid.*, P7D/76.

[87] DT 99/1/35 s5734e, Griffith–Collins Cenotaph – general file, internal memo relating to the application of Fine Gael to hold a wreath-laying ceremony at the Cenotaph in connection with

Liam Mellows, Dick Barrett and Joe McKelvey. De Valera prayed with the Brigade for these 'four martyrs'. Invocations of Griffith were long forgotten; de Valera was not to be seen on Leinster Lawn.[88] Griffith went unnoticed, ignored but for the government's refusal to grant him the honour of a postage stamp: 'Griffith was a Civil War figure . . . it would be inappropriate to honour anyone of that period.'[89] Having lost two ministers to an arms trial, Jack Lynch's reticence to revel in talk of civil war could be understood. But some simply could not comprehend: 'For God's sake – and I say it prayerfully – give us *something* to be proud of.'[90] To Michael Hayes this just could not be excused:

Griffith never ceased to work for Ireland. He died in August 1922 head of an Irish Government with one half-penny in his pocket. If he left nothing to his family, his ideas and leadership left to Ireland the sovereign Irish parliament in which Mr Lynch now occupies first place. To Griffith, more than to any other man, the Taoiseach owes his honours and his emoluments. It is ungenerous of a young and prosperous successor to dismiss so glibly an outstanding national figure like Arthur Griffith.[91]

An Irish postage stamp had honoured Gandhi in 1968: why was there none for the only Irishman who could ever have influenced him? It was forgotten that many of Griffith's early pamphlets were published in Hindustani and circulated throughout India by nationalist newspapers; that *The resurrection of Hungary* and *The working of the policy* had been translated into several Indian languages.[92] That Griffith finally graced a stamp in 1986 was perhaps too little too late.[93] Like Collins and de Valera, he got his bridge in Cork in the 1980s, his bust for sale in the *Irish Times* collection.[94] Even the college that now inhabits his now redundant barracks still bears his name.[95] He is recalled if not remembered; his fleeting appearance in the Neil Jordan film is perhaps evocative of his marginal place in popular Irish memory: 'He died a peculiarly lonely unknown man.'[96] It would be foolish to say that anything has changed.

He was once mourned. His funeral was proof of that, proof that thousands stopped and watched and blessed themselves as the coffin of the President

the party's arrangements for the commemoration of the signing of the Anglo-Irish Treaty of 1921, 10 Nov. 1971. *IT*, 6 Dec. 1971. The Arthur Griffith Society made a similar application in May 1971.

[88] *IT*, 6 Dec. 1971.
[89] *IT*, 21 Apr. 1971; Brian Maye, *Arthur Griffith* (Dublin, 1997), p. 376; DT 2001/6/506, Civil War commemoration for victims.
[90] DT 2001/6/434 s18438, Death of Art Ó Griofa and Micheál Ó Coileáin, anniversary 1972, anniversary of Art Ó Griofa, 1971, letter from Margaret Ahern to Jack Lynch, 6 Feb. 1970.
[91] Letter to the editor by Michael Hayes, *IT*, 23 Apr. 1971.
[92] Seán Ó Lúing, 'Arthur Griffith, 1871–1922: thoughts on a centenary', *Studies*, 60 (Summer 1971), pp. 127–8.
[93] An Post, *Postage stamps of Ireland*, p. 35.
[94] Letter from Neil Fitzpatrick, Cork Corporation, 29 May 1998.
[95] Advertisement for Griffith College Dublin, *Sunday Independent*, 23 Aug. 1998.
[96] Frank O'Connor, *The big fellow* (Dublin, 1991), p. 210.

passed. The nation may have joined 'in the grief of his widow and family and prays that Almighty God may support them in their overwhelming trouble',[97] but it could never take the grief away, the grief that yearly laid a wreath, that left the same sad short newspaper message.[98] Maud Griffith's remorse, the remorse of forty-one years of loneliness, is writ large in her few remaining letters, in the struggles with her husband's colleagues that turned much of her sorrow to rage.[99] Because he died 'as poor as the first day he entered Irish politics',[100] the £289 2s. 1d. he bequeathed obliged the government to provide for the 'nervous and over-wrought' widow.[101] She had a child in delicate health; she knew nothing of business. The £100 from Dáil Éireann funds to meet the immediate expenses of his death had quickly gone.[102] By October 1922 Maud Griffith was forced to beg: 'I have been approached by 3 different people in America to get up a subscription for us, but refused, [Griffith] always told me, we'd be looked after as he'd given up all ties to work for Ireland and most people knew this, of course I feel it keenly.'[103] Apart from Michael Hayes' efforts to trace Griffith's creditors, little was done to alleviate the family's position. The government turned a deaf ear, and only because a penniless President's widow was bad for its reputation, because 'all kinds of rumours are going around which, of course, are quite untrue, but are very damaging to the Government', the Griffith Settlement Bill limped into the Dáil on 28 February 1923.[104] 'The provision proposed to be made is a modest provision, barely sufficient, I think, to meet the requirements of the case. I think that it would be, perhaps the best tribute to the memory of this great Irishman that no very elaborate statement should be made on the introduction of a measure of this sort.'[105] Fine words did not seem to mix well with poverty and pittance. Much as Thomas Johnson and Darrell Figgis demanded eulogies, Cosgrave spoke only in denials.[106] The late President's family was not left desolate or destitute; Griffith would not have wanted finery mixed with finances. Retreating soberly with the somewhat

---

[97] Cabinet minutes, G1/3, PG89, 12 Aug. 1922.

[98] *Good Counsel Magazine* (Autumn 1966), Richard Mulcahy MSS, UCDA, P7/D/76.

[99] Maud Griffith died in January 1963. She had never re-married. Obituary, *IT*, 24 Jan. 1963.

[100] O'Connor, *Big fellow*, p. 210.

[101] James O'Connor, solicitor, to Michael Hayes, n.d., Michael Hayes MSS, UCDA, P53/209.

[102] James O'Connor, solicitor, to Michael Hayes, n.d., *ibid.*; cabinet minutes, G1/3, PG90, 14 Aug. 1922, Vote of £100 to Mrs Griffith to meet immediate expenses; cabinet minutes, G1/3, PG90, 14 Aug. 1922.

[103] Letter from Maud Griffith to Michael Hayes, 15 Oct. 1922, Michael Hayes MSS, UCDA, P53/208.

[104] The Bill was drafted, but not acted upon, in January 1923. Hugh Kennedy MSS, UCDA, P4/990; letter from James O'Connor to Michael Hayes, 31 Jan. 1923, Michael Hayes MSS, UCDA, P53/214.

[105] W. T. Cosgrave, *DE, official report*, II, col. 1781 (28 Feb. 1923).

[106] Thomas Johnson, *ibid.*, cols. 2025–6 (6 Mar. 1923); Darrell Figgis, *ibid.*, cols. 2026–8.

inadequate *'Si monumentum requiris circumspice'*, Cosgrave sat down; the Bill became an Act.

Maud Griffith would receive £500 per annum for life, each of her children £200 until they were twenty-five and Griffith's sister £100 per annum for life.[107] If either child died before the age of twenty-one the money in trust would revert immediately to the Exchequer of Saorstát Éireann. In government terms Maud Griffith was doing well. A year later, limited funds convinced the Minister for Finance, Ernest Blythe, to reduce old age pensions by a shilling a week. If his department had had its way the people would have lost two.[108] But Maud Griffith was not mere 'people'; she was, as she insisted, a President's wife and Cosgrave was too obviously comfortable on £2,500 a year.[109] The government added insult to her injury by taxing every penny she received. *'Si monumentum requiris circumspice'* was all very well on the dome of St Paul's Cathedral. To Maud Griffith it could only have a rather hollow ring. Hurt, she wrote in fury to Ernest Blythe:

> it is a pity I'm so retiring but with a broken heart one cares for nothing ... I have my husband's children and must see to them – for *you* to do this thing to us, who for month's [sic] shared prison life with my boy and knew his sweet unselfish disposition is hard – one would have thought you would have helped us, not take with 2 hands, part of the very little pittance allowed by the men who through all our sacrifices are put in the good paid positions, miserable for a supposed President's wife and family, one a very delicate child.[110]

Dispirited, she pleaded with Cosgrave:

> for my fatherless children I'd do much. You ask Mr Blythe to give us the money. It is very little when it is considered what Arthur Griffith did. Only for his life work Mr Blythe would have nothing to do with Finance. I blame him much ... No honour or even a visit or thought to a desolate woman has ever occurred to one of my husband's associates.[111]

She had watched her husband work himself to death for Ireland, and now what she considered a meagre allowance was taxed. And she grew bitter, jealous of the mere 'soldier' Collins, whose 'very distant relations can be seen in every Dept.'; jealous while 'a President's family' was left to beg;[112] jealous of the

---

[107] William Cosgrave, *ibid.*, col. 2028 (6 Mar. 1923). The Bill passed through its final stage on 9 Mar. 1923. *DE, official report*, II, cols. 2230–6 (9 Mar. 1923).

[108] Ronan Fanning, *The Irish department of finance 1922–58* (Dublin, 1978), p. 111.

[109] The salary of the President of the Executive Council was £2,500 per annum until de Valera reduced it to £1,500. A Free State minister earned £1,700 per annum. Saorstát Éireann, *Estimates for public services for the year ending 31st March, 1924* (Dublin, 1924), p. 7.

[110] DF f13/3/26, Griffith settlement – payment of annuity, letter from Maud Griffith to Ernest Blythe, Feb. 1925 (emphasis in original).

[111] *Ibid.*, letter from Maud Griffith to W. T. Cosgrave, quoted in a letter from Cosgrave to Ernest Blythe, 5 May 1925.

[112] *Ibid.*

£20,000 that would later ease Brigid O'Higgins' bereavement.[113] It was only when she threatened 'for the children I must fight even if it means coming on a platform during elections' that 'the poor woman' received 'every possible consideration'.[114] The widow wailed; to silence her the tax was reduced. But she had become an embarrassment. Her grief was too brutal and too human for men who seemed to begrudge paying her their miserly estimation of her husband's worth.

But by then she had already been broken by the treatment of her husband's memory. The promised glories never bestowed that mocked the very desolation of her grief. Although it would spend £200 more on the burial of Collins, drape City Hall in 'a more extensive nature' for the dead Commander-in-Chief, the government had buried Griffith honourably, rich with speeches and mourners and countless sorrowful flowers.[115] Time promised to turn clay to stone: the earth that kept him into a monument worthy of him. But time only brought his wife news of neglect and the hint of consideration.[116] Inspection of Glasnevin Cemetery revealed the past's predilection for honouring its 'national leaders' with lavish circular plots. Parnell had an eighty-foot circle to parade in, so early plans to let Griffith tarry in a mere twenty-six were quickly cast aside, overwhelmed somewhat by a childish impulse to prove that 'anything you can do I can do better'.

Without in any way disparaging the greatness of Parnell...it would be generally conceded that if National Monuments are to be taken as a reflection of National esteem, and they are, then, a 'Griffith Circle' should never be inscribed or constructed that would be dwarfed for all time by the 'Parnell Circle'.[117]

His resting place would be worthy of a president, but more importantly worthy of the state that had the power to bestow it. That the plot in question came to £10,430, a sum reduced to £5,000 by a Cemetery Committee bargained and bludgeoned into kindness, threw something of a spanner in the laudable works. The Parnell plot had been given for free; the government simply assumed that Griffith would provoke the same sense of generosity in the Cemeteries Committee: 'I am of the opinion that if the Cemeteries Committee were approached in a diplomatic manner that a generous gesture on their part would

[113] DF f200/44/27, O'Higgins settlement.
[114] DF f13/3/26, Griffith settlement – payment of annuity, letter from Maud Griffith to W. T. Cosgrave, quoted in a letter from Cosgrave to Ernest Blythe, 5 May 1925.
[115] Collins' funeral cost £580 18s. 11d. as opposed to £378 9s. 9d. for Griffith's. Dáil Éireann departmental file 5/83, Correspondence and receipts for funeral expenses in connection with the deaths of President Griffith and General Collins.
[116] Letter from Maud Griffith to Michael Hayes, 15 Oct. 1922, Michael Hayes MSS, UCDA, P53/208.
[117] DF s004/0013/24, Proposed acquisition of burial plot for deceased members of the national army – Collins plot and Griffith plot, report by M. Ó hEamhthaigh, Land Settlement Commission, 17 Oct. 1922.

be forthcoming.'[118] That 'The Cemeteries Committee will not view the trans-
action from the point of view of L.S.D'[119] was purely wishful thinking. The fee
remained; the approach was clearly not diplomatic enough. The government,
with all its ambitious talk of eighty-foot plots, was now relying on the 'kindness
of strangers'.[120] The Americans rode to the rescue in December 1922, a cavalry
of promises pledging to pay for and present the plot to the Irish nation. Buoyant
on the prospect of reaping benefits of honour that it would not have to pay for,
the government snatched at Major Eugene Kinkead's offer of charity:[121] 'We,
who are charged with the work of Government established through the foresight
and wisdom of the late Arthur Griffith, feel that the kind action of our friends in
the United States in making this provision, is indicative of their full realisation
of the greatness of the man whose life was so tragically cut off on the day of
victory.'[122] 'We who are charged with the work of government' were also glad
of the cash.

A New York stockbroker and a former major in American military intelligence, Kinkead was active in Irish-American republican organisations.[123] In
June 1923 he became secretary of what was to be known as the 'American committee for the purchase of the Griffith plot'. Edward L. Doheny of Broadway was
chairman, Thomas J. Maloney of West 40th Street, treasurer. Maud Griffith did
not seem to mind; her husband was promised the honour he deserved. The exiled and the emigrant, the Irish-Americans remembered a different Griffith, the
Griffith that struggled before 1916 turned every second man into an Easter in-
habitant of the GPO. But while the committee may have regarded 'it a privilege
to participate in the work',[124] Irish-American memory guarded its money more
closely than its ambitions or intentions. Of the 120 'friends who are interested
in Irish affairs' that were requested to donate $250, only 18 obliged.[125] The
cheques were returned and 'the American committee for the purchase of the

[118] DT s3913, Griffith and Collins ownership and erection of memorials at graves, report by M. Ó
hEamhthaigh, Land Settlement Commission, 17 Oct. 1922.
[119] *Ibid.*, letter from Seoirse McGrath to W. T. Cosgrave, 8 Nov. 1922.
[120] Dáil Éireann departmental file 5/83, Correspondence and receipts for funeral expenses in connection with the deaths of President Griffith and General Collins, memo by M. Ó hEamhthaigh,
17 Oct. 1922.
[121] DF s004/0013/24, Proposed acquisition of burial plot for deceased members of the national
army – Collins plot and Griffith plot, letter from Major Kinkead to W. T. Cosgrave, 7 June
1923.
[122] DT s3913, Griffith and Collins ownership and erection of memorials at graves, letter from
W. T. Cosgrave to Major E. P. Kinkead, 25 June 1923.
[123] David Fitzpatrick, 'Commemoration in the Irish Free State: a chronicle of embarrassment', in
Ian McBride (ed.), *History and memory in modern Ireland* (Cambridge, 2001), p. 199.
[124] DT s3913, Griffith and Collins – ownership and erection of memorials at graves, letter from
Major E. P. Kinkead to W. T. Cosgrave, 7 June 1923.
[125] DF s004/0013/24, Proposed acquisition of burial plot for deceased members of the national
army – Collins plot and Griffith plot, letter from Major E. P. Kinkead to Timothy Smiddy,
Washington, 31 Jan. 1924.

Griffith plot' was dissolved. By March 1924 the Department of Finance was asking desperate questions, among them the plaintive 'is there any likelihood of us being asked to pay for it?',[126] answered only with the wearied 'we shall have to do the needful' ourselves.[127]

The government was placed in 'a rather awkward predicament'; 'the President' would not 'have allowed such an appeal to be mentioned if there were the slightest doubt of its success'.[128] And now the price was added to the humiliation of the failure. It was decided that 'the matter must be dealt with on a "business" as distinct from a patriotic basis':[129] 'national monuments' could reflect 'national esteem' but only at the luxury of someone else's expense. That which should never be 'dwarfed for all time by the "Parnell Circle"' now welcomed the shadow of Home Rule's finery.

Embarrassed, the government did nothing, nothing until a distraught Maud Griffith applied to remove the remains of her late husband to her family grave in 1924.[130] The Cemeteries Committee had told the government of her requests, just as it had done every other time she had written to plead about the grave before.[131] Tired of broken promises, she wanted to honour him herself. The Executive Council agreed to release the body, but only after the Cenotaph ceremony in August, only after the crowds had left Glasnevin, only when no one could see.[132] A Mr Bradley was sent to see her to try to talk her out of it. He advised the government to lie to her, to get the Cemeteries Committee to write to her and tell her that the purchase of the plot was in hand, that matters would be settled soon.[133] While Cosgrave was anxious that 'the matter... be completely settled before the date of the Griffith–Collins Commemoration' exposed the neglect,[134] Maud Griffith frightened them: it all became 'very urgent', 'extremely urgent',[135] and her 'threatened action... precipitated things'.[136] She wrote again in July 1924:

[126] *Ibid.*, Department of Finance memo, 14 Mar. 1924.
[127] *Ibid.*, letter from Seoirse McGrath to W. T. Cosgrave, 2 Apr. 1924.
[128] *Ibid.*, letter from Seoirse McGrath to Timothy Smiddy, 12 Mar. 1924.
[129] *Ibid.*, internal Finance memo from J. H. (J. E. Hanna) to Joseph Brennan, 3 Apr. 1924.
[130] *Ibid.*, letter from C. D. Coyle, Dublin Cemeteries Committee to M. J. Heavey, Irish Land Commission, 21 June 1924.
[131] For example, DT s3913, Griffith and Collins ownership and erection of memorials at graves, letter from John O'Connell, Secretary of the Dublin Cemeteries Committee to M. J. Heavey, Irish Land Commission, 23 Apr. 1924.
[132] *Ibid.*, memo by M. McDunphy to Paul Banim, 30 June 1924.
[133] *Ibid.*, memo by Paul Banim, 1 July 1924.
[134] *Ibid.*, letter from M. McDunphy to Paul Banim, 12 July 1924.
[135] Dáil Éireann departmental file 5/83, Correspondence and receipts for funeral expenses in connection with the deaths of President Griffith and General Collins, letter from George MacGrath, Comptroller and Auditor General to Michael Ó hAodha, TD, 24 June 1924; letter from George MacGrath to Joseph Brennan, Secretary of the Department of Finance, 24 June 1924.
[136] DF s004/0013/24, Proposed acquisition of burial plot for deceased members of the national army – Collins plot and Griffith plot, internal Finance memo, O'H to Joseph Brennan, 28 June 1924.

More than 2 months ago Prof. Hayes, wrote that my husband's grave was to be bought at last, it is only 6 feet of clay I want, not a big plot, as I could not keep it. After Mr Parnell's death a committee looked after his grave for years, my husband was a far greater man, but since his death, at least the last 12 months there is a mean jealous conspiracy (in all government circles) of silence for this wonderman ... I want prayers & my boy's clay home, as promised, the wife of the man who made you all has not been treated well, I must press for an immediate answer if you intend to give me this clay or not, one year and eleven months have passed since he left us & we are gone back centuries. Someday God, may give another good man to Ireland, but we never deserved the noble Arthur Griffith he was much to [sic] good & followed his Lord in poverty, charity, humility etc. Awaiting a reply.[137]

Her letter was read to the Executive Council and the reply eventually came. An eighty-foot circle had shrunk to an area twenty-four feet by twelve; £5,000 fell to £367 17s. 6d. The actual plot, eight feet by four, was granted directly to Maud Griffith – a cunning magnanimity that meant 'care of the grave is a matter for Mrs Griffith'.[138] It is unclear whether this course of action was chosen to obviate the awkward question of whether the government would pay for the care of the grave, but the issue of payment in perpetuity was not one the government wanted brought before the Dáil: 'It is difficult to gauge what the views of the House would be.'[139] Their greater fear, however, was that Maud Griffith thought the entire area was at her disposal. At this point they even feared dealing with her, getting the Cemeteries Committee to hand over the deeds because it was not 'advisable for us to see Mrs Griffith as ... she is inclined to act unreasonably'.[140] But maybe she had reason to be unreasonable. Two years after Griffith's death the government had not even paid the £5 10s. 0d. it had taken to bury him; when it did departments quibbled over who should bear the pitiable cost.[141] Throughout, they had patronised Mrs Griffith, sneered at her slightly ungrammatical letters. Seven years later they could not even bother to remember her name and wrote to her as 'Dear Mary'.[142] She had been promised a worthy monument to a great man; two years brought her a

---

[137] DT s3913, Griffith and Collins ownership and erection of memorials at graves, letter from Maud Griffith, 17 July 1924.

[138] DF s004/0013/24, Proposed acquisition of burial plot for deceased members of the national army – Collins plot and Griffith plot, Department of Finance memorandum, May 1931; Dáil Éireann departmental file 5/83, Correspondence and receipts for funeral expenses in connection with the deaths of President Griffith and General Collins.

[139] *Ibid.*, letter from George MacGrath, Comptroller and Auditor General to Michael Hayes, 1 July 1924.

[140] DF s004/0013/24, Proposed acquisition of burial plot for deceased members of the national army – Collins plot and Griffith plot, letter to M. J. Heavey possibly from Seoirse McGrath, 30 Apr. 1924.

[141] The Department of Finance questioned the appropriateness of the army paying for the burial. *Ibid.*, unsigned Finance memo, 18 Aug. 1924.

[142] *Ibid.*, Department of Finance memo, May 1931; DF – Supply s102/2/39, Memorandum for the government, 24 Feb. 1939; DT s8114a, Garden of Remembrance.

miserable patch of unmarked earth. 'President Cosgrave sent some time ago the certificate for my boy's grave, the plot that was to be like Parnell's, has dwindled to 8 feet! and only I applied to have him exhumed, I'd never have got this few crumbs of clay.'[143] It was left to her to mark the plot, to buy the monument, to care enough 'to see to it immediately and have it up for his birthday'.[144] 'My boy must have a simple stone in keeping with his life, letting everyone get the praise for all his brain fag.'[145] From her taxed allowance she bought 'a simple yet beautiful monument', a broken column, unfinished like his work, broken like his will and her own spirit.[146] On the base it listed all she wanted known and remembered:

Arthur Griffith, TD Cavan & Tyrone, First President Dáil Éireann of the Irish Free State, founder of Sinn Féin, editor of *The United Irishman, Sinn Féin, Éire (Ireland), Scissors and Paste, Nationality & Éire Óg (Young Ireland)*. Author of *The resurrection of Hungary* and *Ballad history of Ireland* etc. Died 12th August 1922 aged 50 years. Erected by his loving wife. RIP.

Years later she burned all of Griffith's letters; they would get nothing more of him, no more of her desolate grief.[147] She might have known that he 'is not forgotten by a faithful few';[148] she may have even guessed that some republicans regretted the loss of him, 'that he was dear to my heart and when I broke with him in 1922 the loss to me was terrible'[149], but it was just never enough. The little that was done was simply too little, and it came only after too hard and squalid a fight.

[143] DF f13/3/26, Griffith settlement – payment of annuity, letter from Maud Griffith to Ernest Blythe, Feb. 1925 (emphasis in original).
[144] *Ibid.*   [145] *Ibid.*   [146] *The Nation*, 3 Aug. 1935.
[147] Notes by Michael Hayes following an interview with Mrs Arthur Griffith, 29 Aug. 1950, Michael Hayes MSS, UCDA, P53/222(11).
[148] Letter from Maud Griffith to Piaras Béaslaí, 4 Dec. 1945, Piaras Béaslaí MSS, NLI, MS 33,966(20).
[149] Letter from Riobárd Ó Breandáin to George A. Lyons, 5 Apr. 1950, George A. Lyons MSS, NLI, MS 33,675/A/2/(111).

4   'Who is the fool Pat?' Soldiers and the selective memory of civil war

William Doyle, Patrick O'Connor, Christopher Kierans and Peter Behan: to most these names mean nothing. To most they have no reason to. Little is known or can be known of them. Different routes had taken them to a back road in Wexford: two from Flanders, one from Irregular ranks, one simply a raw recruit. They shared little but their youth, the uniform that they wore and their death early one Sunday morning in October 1922. There are of course other details: an inquest listed wounds, lost limbs, the how and why and which organs failed in the process of their dying. But there is no need to know this or that their bodies had been scarred past recognition. No need to know because they are just names, names that never signed a treaty or a proclamation, that never danced across the pages of Dáil debates, names that mean nothing at all. For a couple of days their deaths were a staple of the country's diet of column inches: four young soldiers murdered defending 'the will of the people'; four young soldiers cut down in their prime by barbaric republicans. The next days brought the next course of tragedy turned indignation. In this there was nothing unusual or unfair. The news was obliged to carry on.

But for some these anonymous deaths were more than just a passing outrage; theirs the pain hidden in the parade of factual or well-meaning newspaper words. Local reports spoke of tearful congregations; of the grief of families and friends; of the mourning, the sadness, the loss of a fine young player from an obscure Gaelic team.[1] They spoke of large funerals, of wreaths and pallbearers, of the month's minds that followed, like any other death.[2] They told that these young men were missed.

Three years later soldier comrades still spoke of remembrance. Demobilised, they gathered under the grandeur of the 'Ex-Army Officers and Men's Association, Wexford', and bought a simple Celtic cross. In June 1925 they intended to unveil it, to mark the place in Ferrycarrig where an ambush had taken four lives: to honour the men who had once soldiered and been billeted by their sides. They had asked for no assistance, just for the President of the Free State to spare a few moments as he passed through the county, to pay these men the

[1] *The People*, 25–8 Oct. 1922.   [2] *Ibid.*, 4 Nov. 1922.

courtesy of a few dignified even grateful words.[3] They had no reason to think that the President would refuse. They had buried their comrades with guards of honour; tricolours proudly covered the coffins; 'They shall be remembered forever' still rang in their ears.[4] But Cosgrave never came. A ditch in Wexford was no place for a President.

Haughtiness had not kept the President from this place. That honour instead went to Richard Mulcahy. Learning of the Wexford men's plans he quickly dispatched letters to Cumann na nGaedheal activists in the county, and to the Department of Defence which had reacted enthusiastically to Wexford's requests for a firing party, a bugler and an army band.[5] Apparently 'the proposal was contrary to the policy that the political organisation would desire to have pursued in the matter of such memorials, in that it was proposed to erect it at the scene of the ambush rather than in religious surroundings'.[6] Even though the Cumann na nGaedheal party could only 'express the pleasure of the Organisation at the step proposed . . . to commemorate the memory of those four brave men' at their place of death,[7] it was all 'a bit political' for Mulcahy's now peaceable tastes.[8] Ostensibly he made the right noises and said the right things. Casting himself as one above reproach, he pleaded that 'both religion and politics would be damaged by endeavouring to associate parties, or party interests, with such matters'.[9] He could not see how 'as democratic Head of State here, he [Cosgrave] could allow himself to be put in the position of unveiling a monument which would perpetuate anything like the Ferrycarrig ambush or the other things that it recalls'.[10] But, behind his new and seemingly acute democratic sensibilities, his sudden and quite touching desire to be fair to 'all parties in the country', there lurked something not quite so worthy in Mulcahy's words.[11] Closer to the truth was that 'personally, I very much dislike the idea of . . . erecting a monument at the site of an ambush between Irishmen',[12] a truth which seemed to have more to do with shame than democracy. This may of course be unfair: an indictment of one man's heartfelt attempt to put the bitterness of civil war aside. But a sentence qualified his statement as it did his seemingly noble intention: 'the erection of a Cross where General Collins was killed is really a different matter'.[13] In other words the death of Michael

---

[3] W. T. Cosgrave was due to address a meeting in Enniscorthy.

[4] *Young Ireland*, 15 July 1922.

[5] Letter from Richard Mulcahy to the Minister for Defence, 10 June 1925, Richard Mulcahy MSS, UCDA, P7B/62(38–41).

[6] *Ibid.*

[7] Letter from Liam Burke, Chief Executive Organiser, Cumann na nGaedheal, to Laurence Grannell, Honorary Secretary of the Ex-Army Officers and Men's Association, Wexford, 15 Apr. 1925, *ibid.*, P7B/62(45–8).

[8] Letter from Richard Mulcahy to the Minister for Defence, 10 June 1925, *ibid.*, P7B/62(38–41).

[9] Letter from Richard Mulcahy to Kathleen Browne, 29 May 1925, *ibid.*, P7B/62(53–5).

[10] *Ibid.*   [11] *Ibid.*   [12] *Ibid.*   [13] *Ibid.*

Collins was a different matter. He was after all 'a great man': a rotting wooden Cenotaph on Leinster Lawn could unsteadily attest to that. At Béalnabláth the cross marked not a place of death, but a 'sacred spot'. Béalnabláth was indeed a different matter. Béalnabláth was a shrine. People stopped there to pray; men and women blessed themselves as they journeyed past. By comparison the men of Ferrycarrig were irrelevant, just four casualties of a routine ambush, unknown names turned statistics, simply soldiers, nothing sacred.

In Mulcahy's opinion the Wexford monument 'should be made a purely religious matter and that such monuments should be erected in religious surroundings, namely graveyards etc., rather than at places where there had been conflict'.[14] Graveyards were safe and solemn, not the place for fault and blame and accusations. All were as one again in the grave, at one before God: failure and defeat swept neatly under a convenient religious carpet. In October 1922 Richard Mulcahy had led the Free State forces against the republicans. As Commander-in-Chief he was ultimately responsible for the deaths of these four young men. It would never be 1916 again. There was a lower premium on the triumph of failure in a Free State uniform. The republicans maintained their rebel air: men turned martyrs for a still longed-for republic; monuments a reminder of what remained to be done. But the soldiers of the new state had something to defend: an orthodoxy, however ill defined; an establishment, however fragile. To die now was to fail. In 1925 the Free State could ill afford to revel in its failures.

Eager to oblige, the men of Wexford conceded to Mulcahy's demands. They had never meant to place the President in an 'awkward situation';[15] they chose a grave in Crosstown Cemetery and commemorated all the dead soldiers of Wexford. Mulcahy prised £15 from the Cumann na nGaedheal coffers, paying for the necessary alterations to the monument which the largely unemployed group of demobilised soldiers could not afford. He promised them marching bands and orations, bread and circuses, anything to take them from the side of the road, from the brazenly public commemoration of an army defeat.[16] The monument was finally unveiled on 6 September 1925 and 3,500 people attended the simple ceremony.[17] They listened to four speeches, each one adamant that they 'did not want to make political capital' out of the event.[18] One speaker was a Cumann na nGaedheal stalwart, one a lowly minister for fisheries. Two were, conveniently, candidates in the following week's Senate elections. They spoke of reconciliation, of 'the mothers, brothers, sisters, wives and sweethearts of

[14] *Ibid.*
[15] Letter from Richard Mulcahy to Kathleen Browne, 9 June 1925, *ibid.*, P7B/62(49).
[16] *Ibid.*, P7B/62.   [17] *The People*, 5 Sept. 1925.
[18] Kathleen Browne, Batt O'Connor, Senator Irwin and Fionan Lynch each expressed this sentiment in a slightly altered form, but each used the words 'political capital'. *The People*, 5 Sept. 1925.

those boys who were gone'.[19] 'May God reward them for their heroism and may God comfort their relatives.'[20] For the 'many women who were visibly affected', for the parents who laid wreaths 'in loving memory of my dear son', it was an honourable day.[21] For the ex-soldiers of Wexford it had been an instructive one. Free State soldiers could be honoured once honour did nothing to hint at inadequacy or defeat. The people 'could be baptized lightly with the blood of martyrs, but there was nothing to be gained from advertising its total immersion' in the blood of sons that an efficient young state should never have lost.[22]

In 1796 Wolfe Tone marvelled at the Panthéon Français. Envisaging a glorious revolutionary dawn in Ireland, he spoke not of graveyards or ditches but of a similar pantheon for his homeland, for the dead who would give their lives for Ireland. He warned only against France's volatile regard for the dead, against the indecent haste that had filled the Panthéon's vaults in 1793, only to empty them again after the Terror.[23] When the time came the rebel upstarts paid no heed to the man they eagerly adopted as the father of revolution. Though the French may have been fickle, slaves to the latest whim of revolutionary fashion, their will to commemorate was, at least, constant. It was the nature of the Irish Free State to suppress, to remember selectively, to try to forget. And civil war made sure of that. Violent antecedents were troublesome to a government that clung nervously to power, that met terrorism with terrorism in uniform. As revolutionaries the Treatyites had failed: there was no thirty-two county Ireland, no republic. There was an oath that made rebel songs difficult to sing. The dead could not be celebrated; they accused more than they inspired. Granted, Collins was honoured; he had to be. His position demanded it and his position made it worthwhile. In honouring Collins there was plenty of potential for propaganda. That he was honoured in a derisory fashion is another matter. The greatest test of this will to forget, however, is the case of the Free State soldiers, the men of the many Ferrycarrigs. Unknown, they present none of the duty and deference due to Collins, none of the required posturing in the direction of 1916–21. There was no obligation. There was possibly a little more honesty.

Because Maud Griffith believed that common soldiers were valued more than her dead President her jealousy uttered: 'all Ireland will subscribe for a memorial to the National Soldiers (someday)'.[24] Years of an unmarked army

[19] Senator C. J. Irwin quoted in *ibid.*   [20] *Ibid.*

[21] *Ibid.*; *Enniscorthy Guardian*, 5 Sept. 1925; *New Ross Standard*, 5 Sept. 1925.

[22] Catherine Merridale, 'War, death and remembrance in Soviet Russia', in Jay Winter and Emmanuel Sivan (eds.), *War and remembrance in the twentieth century* (Cambridge, 1999), p. 70.

[23] Theobald Wolfe Tone, *The autobiography of Theobald Wolfe Tone*, ed. R. B. O'Brien, 2 vols. (Dublin, 1867), I, pp. 267–8.

[24] DF f13/3/26, Griffith settlement – payment of annuity, letter from Maud Griffith to Ernest Blythe, Feb. 1925.

plot were to prove her wrong. Nameless, the soldiers had done the dirty work, carried out the orders, killed at another's bidding and taken the guilt with the welcome pay. Dying was part of the risk and at least eight hundred were lost.[25] In July 1922 Michael Collins wanted their broken bodies, their funerals, shown in every cinema, shown to remind the nation that they 'were shot in maintaining the People's supremacy'.[26] They were useful then; they could make republicans repulsive. By 1924 they were just statistics, bodies that no one had ever even bothered to count. By 1924 they were dead figureheads of a mutinous brigade: the less said the better.

To die in 1916, 1919, 1920 or 1921 was to die a martyr for old Ireland. To die in a Free State uniform was to die a mere soldier. Republicanism, though it hijacked the mantle of martyrdom, cannot be blamed entirely for this demotion. Dying is as much a part of soldiering as it is of insurrection. And payment does not always preclude ideals. Maybe it is enough to say that 'if you join the army you have to soldier': that because death is considered a risk or a consequence it is no longer the stuff of sacrifice, and martyrdom is nothing without sacrifice. But even if a soldier can expect death, that expectation should not devalue his memory. The republicans said that they were foolish, their heads turned by Lloyd George's wizardry, by wages and the promise of a false peace. To the purists the Free State soldiers were pro-British; to support the Treaty was to turn one's back on Ireland, to no longer believe in the notion or the possibility of the Republic. They may have fought for what the republicans called a compromise, but there were too many memoriam notices lamenting a dead son who died for Ireland for it to be as simple as that. Maybe 'dying for Ireland' just made sense of these lost young lives. Maybe 'there were equally brave and idealistic men and women on the Free State side, acting as they thought best in the interests of the newly established state'.[27] Maybe they were republicans too. The revolution, such as it was, had changed. For many it had ended; for those willing to risk the unsteady stepping stones it had entered another phase, a new beginning. No one can know why men fought and died for the Free State. Calling them counter-revolutionaries is as blinkered as calling them traitors or mercenaries.[28] They may have been all of these things and none. They may have been pro-British, indifferent, loyal to a personality or its infamy, poor, hungry, battle weary. Maybe they just wanted to fight. It would be convenient to say they died defending the state established by the Treaty – a little too convenient. 'Dying

[25] There is no precise figure available for military casualties. Eight hundred was a figure quoted by the government covering the period January 1922 to April 1924. Hopkinson, *Green against green*, pp. 272–3.

[26] DT s595, Propaganda: suggestions by Michael Collins, July 1922, memo to Desmond FitzGerald, 12 July 1922.

[27] Séamus Mac Suain, *County Wexford's Civil War* (Wexford, 1995), p. 7.

[28] See, for example, John M. Regan's *The Irish counter-revolution 1921–1936* (Dublin, 1999).

for Ireland' was as valid a reason as any other. The republicans' condemnation can be understood; they had supposedly sung of gallant callings since 1798. To them there was nothing of commitment or ideal; these soldiers did a treacherous and ignoble job of work. Republicanism had staked its claim on martyrdom, on dying the noble death for the country it refused to compromise. 'Dying for Ireland' had changed, but none changed it more than the men who had led these soldiers to their deaths. Nothing robbed the Free State soldier of his dignity more than his government's treatment of his memory.

Granted, wars leave too many casualties to celebrate the life of each and every soldier, and it would be foolish to expect that much from a government which had reservations about the commemoration of its own President and Commander-in-Chief. But the soldiers were treated badly and it is not enough to blame the somewhat revisionist years of Fianna Fáil power. At least Fianna Fáil had its reasons. The soldiers were the obstinate rank and file of opposition, a mixture of fools and traitors who sold their republican souls for the uniform and the shilling. Although the pro-Treatyites did not have the luxury of this excuse, they did have some excuses. It was the soldiers' duty to fight and die for their country and army; duty was reward in itself. Their monument was the state, democracy their eulogy. And of course the shortage of money was always a reliable defence. However, the excuses were never good enough, especially for their comrades, especially when £50,000 flowed to Islandbridge, when £25,000 was readily allotted to the care of British military graves that held the bodies of 1919 to 1921's enemies,[29] when the eloquence of Cosgrave's '*si monumentum requiris circumspice*' was nothing but an empty turn of phrase.[30] Yet maybe they were right to forget, to turn a blind eye to the casualties of a war that no one wished to fight. There was little to celebrate in winning an internal struggle against former friends, in killing compatriots with a greater hunger and alacrity than were ever expended on the British. Maybe they had to forget because forgetting suppressed the memory of war, the memory of weakness, of a violent enemy that condemned the pro-Treatyites for the corruption of compromise. The Free State was to be a beginning; to revel in the memory of the ordinary men who died for it made it an end in itself, an end to which an uncertain Cumann na nGaedheal government could never concede.

But this forgetting came later, when the army had mutinied, when commemoration was no longer useful. Dead soldiers had once served a purpose; their deaths filled 1922's and 1923's approved column inches, the dying proof of evil republican ways. Alive they were just soldiers; dead they were lost young lives spent in the protection of the state; they were tragedy turned propaganda.

[29] The amount was allotted for the care and maintenance of British military graves from 1914–21. DF s004/0013/24, Proposed acquisition of burial plot for deceased members of the national army, Department of Finance memorandum, May 1931.
[30] W. T. Cosgrave, *DE, official report*, II, col. 2028 (6 Mar. 1923).

This may be unfair. Some were not so callous. When nine men had been killed in Kerry in August 1922 Michael Collins wrote that 'we have had a hard few days here – the scenes at the Mass yesterday were really heartbreaking. The poor women weeping and almost shrieking (some of them) for their dead sons. Sisters and one wife were there too, and a few small children. It makes one feel I tell you.'[31] But maybe Collins was different. He was their leader; he was one of them. He might even have cared enough to pay for their grave. The nine soldiers that Collins lamented were praised. Newspapers tripped over themselves to report how big their funerals were, to speak of their 'valour' and their 'worth'.[32] But more was said about the 'group of desperate men', of those 'who have misled and murdered'.[33] Gratitude was due to 'these soldiers of Ireland' because they 'fell in Ireland protecting us from tyranny and the flouting of all law'.[34] An t-Óglách spoke of 'young lives ... sacrificed', of dying for Ireland, of 'desolated' homes.[35] It said: 'Dublin honours the brave.'[36] The graves of these men remained unmarked until 1967.

In the beginning there was talk of American money: a charitable bequest that begot big ideas and an easy extravagance. The same Major Kinkead, buoyant on his committee's plans for the Griffith plot, was also eager to bestow the recommended honour of an eighty-foot circular plot on Michael Collins and the soldiers who had been blessed for eternity by being buried by his side.[37] Collins was the object of the glory. The circle was for him, for him to rival Parnell. The soldiers were simply lucky enough to be close by. But unlike the republican monuments that were later built largely through the generosity of American donations, the money never came.[38] At America's idealised remove, the Free State soldiers had none of the republicans' purported promise. The republic had statues of IRA men with guns pointing purposefully North (see figure 4); it had graves with tricolour wreaths and headstones proclaiming that 'his task remains unfinished'.[39] Its banners still declared 'The 32 are ours'.[40] By comparison the Free State had little to offer, just the grave of the men who had apparently stood in the republic's way. In the absence of American assistance, the government quickly forgot what extravagance meant. Concerns for a Collins circle, for the possibility that 'any outsider' could purchase a grave

[31] Ó Broin, In great haste, p. 213.   [32] Free State – An Saorstát, 12 Aug. 1922.
[33] Ibid.   [34] Ibid.   [35] An t-Óglách, 4, 10 (12 Aug. 1922).   [36] Ibid.
[37] The offer to pay for both plots was accepted by W. T. Cosgrave. DF s004/0013/24, Proposed acquisition of burial plot for deceased members of the national army, letter from W. T. Cosgrave to Major Kinkead, 8 May 1923.
[38] Among the many republican monuments which received American aid are the Ballyseedy monument, the Tullamore Courthouse monument, the East Clare IRA memorial, the Shankill monument, the Cahirsiveen monument, and the Newcastlewest monument.
[39] IRA monument, Bruff, Co. Limerick; headstone of George McDermott, killed in action 5 July 1922, 'Faithful unto death but his task remains unfinished', Ardbracken Cemetery, Co. Meath.
[40] Banner observed outside the '98 Memorial Hall, Ballyshannon. Donegal Democrat, 27 Apr. 1935; Mary MacSwiney MSS, UCDA, p48a/453.

within twelve feet of the blessed Commander-in-Chief, were submerged in a long and squalid struggle for land with the Dublin Cemeteries Committee.[41] The half price of £7,708 was haggled down to £6,000. It was agreed but never paid. The year 1924 brought the mutiny and the army plot suddenly became a matter of 'the greatest urgency': keep the soldiers happy, 'purchase . . . to be settled at once'.[42] But soured by the impudent soldiers, £6,000 became £2,700 7s. 6d. and the plot shrivelled to a mere seventy-two by twenty-eight feet.[43] Future casualties would be buried four to a grave; no need to waste money on their mutinous remains, no need to keep civil war's expensive promise to close the plot with that tragic struggle's dead[44], no need when government files could not even recall how many men were already buried there: 115, 133, 189, possible figures never precise, 'about 115', 'about 133'.[45] No one thought enough to count. Over a year and a half after the war the government had not even paid for the burials.[46] The sum of £1,035 5s. 0d. was still due for payment in August 1924. In December 1925 there was talk of trying to get the £2,700 back: 'I think it is still not too late to raise the matter', to seek from the beleaguered Cemeteries Committee a charitable bequest.[47]

For some 'the privilege of being buried near the late Commander-in-Chief' may have been enough.[48] For others the reality of a much 'trampled and unsightly' grave said more.[49] Calls for attention to the plot were made and ignored from 1924 onwards. The condition of the graves was only of concern once a year. The anniversaries of Griffith's and Collins' deaths brought pilgrims; the summer brought tourists. Concern only came when the neglect could be found out. Seán Lester wrote to the Executive Council in July 1923:

it was reported that the graves of the late President Griffith and late General Collins required immediate attention, as they are at present appear little cared for . . . an instruction to have the graves properly dressed should be sent immediately to the Cemetery

---

[41] DF s004/0013/24, Proposed acquisition of burial plot for deceased members of the national army, Department of Defence memo regarding negotiations for the plot, 11 Jan. 1924.

[42] *Ibid.*, letter from the Secretary to the President to the Army Finance Office, 12 July 1924 (emphasis from original).

[43] The payment was sanctioned in Aug. 1924, *ibid.* DF Supply s102/2/39, Memorandum for the government, 6 Mar. 1939; DT s8114a, Garden of Remembrance.

[44] DF s004/0013/24, Proposed acquisition of burial plot for deceased members of the national army, memo from Joseph Brennan, Department of Finance to W. T. Cosgrave, 5 Aug. 1924; Dáil Éireann departmental file 5/83, Correspondence and receipts for funeral expenses in connection with the deaths of President Griffith and General Collins, letter from Richard Mulcahy to Timothy Healy, 3 Mar. 1923.

[45] DF s004/0013/24, Proposed acquisition of burial plot for deceased members of the national army, memo from Joseph Brennan, Department of Finance to W. T. Cosgrave, 5 Aug. 1924; Department of Defence memos 11 Jan. 1924 and 19 Oct. 1924; plan of army burial plot, n.d.

[46] *Ibid.*, letter from D. O'Sullivan, Army Finance Office, 18 Aug. 1924.

[47] *Ibid.*, memo from the Department of Finance, dated 10 Dec. 1925.

[48] *Ibid.*, letter from Seoirse McGrath, Accountant General to W. T. Cosgrave, 9 Jan. 1923.

[49] *Ibid.*, letter from Joseph Brennan, Department of Finance to W. T. Cosgrave, 5 Aug. 1924.

authorities, especially in view of the fact that a large influx of visitors is expected during this month and next month, many of whom will, no doubt, visit Glasnevin.[50]

Otherwise, there was no need to do what others could be shamed into doing for free; no need when the Cemeteries Committee is 'unlikely to let it fall into neglect due to its prominent position'.[51] The artificial wreaths with the weathered inscriptions of 1922 and 1923 would do. A gardener was grudgingly hired to cut the wayward grass, the Cemeteries Committee having refused the work because the government was not prepared to pay for 'maintenance carried out on the best possible lines'.[52] The committee did not want the responsibility for the government's meanness. But in 1931 the government gave in. It balked at the cost of an OPW gardener and settled a reduced fee of £50 per annum with the Cemeteries Committee. With plants and flowers, the plot was tidy, never ostentatious; all the government could do was ask for a reduction.[53] Although the Cemeteries Committee did what it could, a few flowers were not what honour promised; the grave was still neglected. 'The Plot is not marked in any way to identify it as the Army Plot and there is nothing on the spot to show where the remains of any particular soldier (even of the late Commander-in-Chief) are buried. Compare this with what is being done in the case of British military graves.'[54] This was written in May 1931. In 1957 the plot was enclosed by a concrete curb. It was graced by a memorial ten years later: 'To the memory of deceased officers and men of Oglaigh na hÉireann – Requiescant in pace'; some names, some dates of death, plain slabs, cheaply placed. 'Gravestones through their simplicity and uniformity, like soldiers in battle, lead into a serious and reverential mood.'[55] That may be true of the cemeteries scattered across Europe, lovingly maintained to the honour of the dead of two world wars. It was not so with this mean and dreary plot hidden behind the gravediggers' shed. Islandbridge shames it by comparison, a comparison which places the alleged neglect of the Great War dead in a new and rather altered context[56] (see figure 5).

---

[50] DT s3913, Griffith and Collins – ownership and erection of memorials at graves, letter from Seán Lester to the Executive Council, 3 July 1924.

[51] DF s004/0013/24, Proposed acquisition of burial plot for deceased members of the national army, letter from Thomas Gorman, Department of Defence to Finance, 10 Mar. 1924.

[52] DF s004/0098/25, Army burial plot, Mount Prospect Cemetery, Glasnevin, sanction for maintenance by the army, letter from M. J. Beary, Assistant Secretary, Department of Defence to Doolin, Department of Finance, 13 Oct. 1930.

[53] The committee refused on the basis that £50 was already a vastly reduced sum which omitted all overhead charges. *Ibid.*, letter from M. J. Beary to the Department of Finance, 19 Dec. 1931.

[54] DF s004/0013/24, Proposed acquisition of burial plot for deceased members of the national army, Department of Finance memo, May 1931.

[55] Emil Högg, *Kriegergrab und Kriegerdenkmal* (Wittenburg, 1915), p. 29, quoted in George L. Mosse, 'National cemeteries and national revival: the cult of the fallen soldiers in Germany', *Journal of Contemporary History*, 14, 1 (1979), p. 9.

[56] Keith Jeffery has referred to this as 'the amnesiac tendency of Southern Ireland' to the Great War. Jeffery, *Ireland and the Great War*, p. 73.

Figure 5 The National War Memorial, Islandbridge, Dublin.

If the relative splendour of Islandbridge can be conceived as neglect, what were these overlooked decades, what was this cheap and uninspiring plot? Etched with a uniformity that probably befits the army's encouraged anonymity, it was a mere list of names. We know only that they were soldiers. We can imagine their youth, their families and their loss. Yet they can be mourned more for their forty-five unmarked years, for the pitiable monument that people presumed would honour Michael Collins.[57]

In 1931, one man recognised that a trampled grave was not good enough. His anonymous voice was raised in the Department of Finance: 'The condition of things...is amazing and shows neglect of the feelings of relatives of the deceased soldiers buried in the Plot. Unless remedied, there will be an outcry one of these days.'[58] Needless to say his objections fell on the deafest ears. The 'feelings of relatives' were not a priority; they were merely a consequence, an inconvenience. Grief meant little to a government that spoke in terms of 'regulating the activities...of the relatives of the deceased soldiers buried in

[57] An article in the *Irish Independent*, 13 Nov. 1967, entitled 'Government planning Collins memorial', led to confused questions in Dáil Éireann. *DE, official report*, CCXXXI, cols. 721–2 (23 Nov. 1967).

[58] DF s004/0013/24, Proposed acquisition of burial plot for deceased members of the national army, Department of Finance memo, May 1931.

the Plot'.[59] Maybe it should be no surprise. What more could be expected from
a government that had to be threatened with legal action in 1926 before it paid
a meagre £28 12s. 0d. for its dead soldiers' wreaths?[60] Once weeping mothers
and wives had been good for the cause, when there was a war to be won, when
republicans could be taunted by the visions of their pathetic grief. But while
republicanism continued to revel in the last emotive letters of the executed,
in the touching tales of 'boy martyrs', of 'gentle inoffensive lads',[61] 'Soldiers
Have Mothers Too' was just the stuff of 1922.[62] There was no place for pity in
the illusory confidence of peace. This may be unjust. Perhaps the government
felt and continued to feel the bereavement, to grieve for their men with a passion
that bureaucracy hides. But its actions, or more appropriately lack of action,
betray a government that no longer needed or wished to care. Money alone
moved it to act. In July 1922 an insurance company failed to redeem three
policies on the life of Private Gerald O'Connor, a soldier killed that month in an
ambush in Gort. The Prudential Insurance Company had not been informed that
he had joined the army. The contract had clauses protecting the company from
indemnity in war and it had no obligation to pay. The prospect of countless other
cases like O'Connor's, of countless other families left without insurance and
looking to the state for support, prompted the Free State to a type of expedient
magnanimity. One hundred and fifty-six insurance companies were bombarded
with a letter from the secretary to the Provisional Government. He proclaimed
that the insurance companies were acting

as a deterrent on men who would otherwise gladly offer their services in this crisis. In
the cause of ordered Society and Stable Government. It is not necessary to remind you,
– it has not yet passed from the public mind – that insurance companies throughout
Ireland and Great Britain waived clauses of this kind in favour of men joining the Allied
Armies in the European War. It was a recognition of the individual's self-sacrifice for
the public safety, happiness and welfare. The spirit impelling to arms is in both cases
essentially the same and I am directed by the Irish Government to bring the matter before
the companies with a view to a like relief being conceded to the members of the Irish
National Army during the present operations. It is confidently felt that the matter has
only to be mentioned, and that the companies will spontaneously waive clauses of the
type already referred to.[63]

The Provisional Government was right to feel confident. Most did waive the
clause. Most were British companies to whose patriotic sentiments this analogy

---

[59] DF s004/0098/25, army burial plot, Mount Prospect Cemetery, Glasnevin, sanction for maintenance by the army, letter from Secretary of the Department of Defence to the Department of
Finance, 1 May 1925.
[60] DF s004/125/26, Army Finance Office – claim for wreaths supplied.
[61] *Wolfe Tone Weekly*, 1, 4 (25 Sept. 1937), p. 5; *ibid.*, 1, 7 (16 Oct. 1937), p. 5.
[62] *The Free State – An Saorstát*, 14 Oct. 1922.
[63] DT s1703, Insurance of lives of national troops killed in action, general letter to insurance
companies, 25 Oct. 1922.

with the Great War must have appealed. But the men of this Provisional Government had stood against conscription in 1918; now when it served a practical purpose all seemed changed, or forgotten: 'the spirit impelling to arms is in both cases essentially the same'. This was a self-serving, sensible measure for the benefit of the troops, for the benefit of the drive for a larger army, and for the benefit of the government itself. Nothing appealed to this same practicality once the fighting stopped. Dead soldiers were of no more use.

The mother of Private Daniel Savage wrote politely in November 1924: 'Will you kindly let me have a permit to place a small marble monument over my boy's resting place in Military Plot Glasnevin. It is a very small one to Rest on top of Earth not a fixture.'[64] Letters circled the Department of Defence. Her dead son was eighteen years old, she had nine other children, she had been given ten pounds in compensation for his life. She was replied to courteously and quickly: 'The matter of marking the graves is under consideration. Pending a decision it would be inadvisable for her to incur expense on a monument even of the kind she mentions. The design might be out of keeping with the general arrangement. It would be better to postpone her application.'[65] It was kind of them to consider her financial position, but the woman probably never lived to see the proposed 'general arrangement'. They thought of her needlessly incurring expense; she, like every other soldier's parents, thought only of a dead son who could never be forgotten. Hers was the same mother's instinct that inscribed the plot with small metal crosses and artificial wreaths, anything to keep alive a memory that the government seemed to prefer to forget. In 1922 and 1923 soldiers were fighting and dying for Ireland, for democracy: 'they shall be remembered forever'.[66] The government broke a promise it could never keep to every father, mother and son. The shame was that it never even tried.

'An insecure and inexperienced elite found itself presiding over a population that wanted unheroic things'; perhaps it was simply time to make promises to the living instead of the dead.[67] The deceased were now simply irrelevant: the letters to their relatives were proof of that. The barrack graves that scarred the counties were left unattended: nothing was done until a sister complained of, their 'very poor state', that she would prefer her brother to be 'buried with his own people',[68] until parents asked for their sons' bodies back. Though peace may have brought the power that these men had fought for, brought the

---

[64] Department of Defence A13221, Applications by relatives to erect memorials on graves of deceased soldiers, letter from Mrs D. Savage to 'the Army', 25 Nov. 1924.

[65] *Ibid.*, letter from O'Connor to Cassidy, Department of Defence, 29 Nov. 1924.

[66] *Young Ireland*, 15 July 1922.   [67] Garvin, *1922*, p. 62.

[68] Department of Defence A12779, Exhumation of the remains of Maurice Ahern, buried at Bruff, for re-interment at Midleton, Co. Cork, letter from Mary Coughlan to the Adjutant General, Parkgate Street, 9 Sept. 1924.

government the prerogative to forget them, to forget the war, there was no need to leave a father waiting on a Kerry railway platform for a body that never arrived,[69] no need to deny a mother access to her own son's neglected grave. Boasting of victory for democracy and democratic institutions was all very well, but it was of little comfort to the father of Private Mulhall as he stood waiting in that railway station or to Mrs Cregan who had to wait for over a year for permission to tend her son Francis's neglected grave in St Joseph's cemetery, Cobh.[70]

And 1924 brought even less comfort. As barracks closed across the country, as the army moved its men, the bodies of the executed prisoners were brought too.[71] With brandy, whiskey, cigarettes and an extra 1s. 6d. for the soldiers forced to dig the bodies up, the army performed these macabre manoeuvres often without ever notifying the dead men's families.[72] There were objections: resolutions passed at earnest council meetings, letters of complaint.[73] But the government stayed staunch:

it is not desirable to exhume and hand over the remains of executed prisoners to their relatives for the purpose of re-interment. The re-interment of an executed Irregular would almost to a certainty be made the occasion for a demonstration for the purpose of attracting the sympathies of the general public towards the bereavement of the relatives at a time when the necessity for the executions has to a certain extent faded from the minds of the people.[74]

The bodies were brought from barracks to barracks; furtively dug up and reburied in the middle of the night. But in September a letter came. Reminding

---

[69] Private Mulhall, shot in Kerry on 19 Dec. 1922, was initially buried in Dingle Cemetery. The inefficiency with which the exhumation was dealt with provoked Labour leader, Thomas Johnson, to complain on Mulhall's parents' behalf. Department of Defence Secretary's Office A11233, Remains of Pte Mulhall, re-interred at Glasnevin, letter from Thomas Johnson to the Secretary, Department of Defence, 12 Jan. 1924.
[70] Pte Francis Cregan, died 11 Nov. 1922. Over a year later his mother was still left without claim to the grave and was not permitted to tend it or erect a monument. She was finally granted access in December 1923. Department of Defence A13221, Applications by relatives to erect memorials on graves of deceased soldiers.
[71] DJ H197/45, Executed Irregulars – exhumation and re-interment. For example, with the closure of the outpost at Drumboe Castle the bodies of the four men executed there were taken to Athlone Military Barracks.
[72] DF s004/0215/24, Army Finance Office – exhumation of remains of executed Irregulars – extra pay for men engaged in the work, memo from Thomas Gorman, Army Finance Office to the Department of Finance, 26 July 1924. The officers supervising got an extra £5 or £15.
[73] The Republican Convention at Letterkenny condemned the act on the grounds that none of the families were informed. Realt a Deiscirt, 6 Sept. 1924; letter to the editor by John Burke, Martin Cooney and Martin J. Walsh, FJ, 15 Aug. 1924. The actions were also condemned by Waterford No. 2 Rural District Council, Waterford News, 3 Oct. 1924; Mary MacSwiney MSS, UCDA, p48a/454.
[74] DT s1884, Executions by Provisional Government 1922–4, Letter from W. T. Cosgrave to Eoin O'Duffy, 27 June 1924.

Cosgrave of five pending by-elections, the secretary of the Cumann na
nGaedheal Coiste Gnotha wrote:

The Coiste Gnotha believe that the Ministry of Defence must surely have had good and
sufficient reason for their action in digging up the remains of recently executed men at
Tuam and elsewhere and unceremoniously disposing of them in some fashion which can
only have been satisfactory to the official who gave the order, but which certainly has
produced violent indignation amongst even our members, and is regarded throughout
the country as nothing short of an atrocity.[75]

The letter continued, comparing the treatment of the remains of British soldiers
in Cork, that the people were able to read a very full account of the proper
treatment received by the British, that 'the contrast has been bitterly commented
on throughout the country, but nowhere more than in Cork, where we are saddled
with the task of winning 2 important bye-elections [sic]'.[76] The government
had never shown itself dreadfully eager to listen to the party in the past. Indeed
another month would bring the 'October Manifesto' from a standing committee
frustrated with the government's haughty disregard for its own party's wishes.
That the party had sent the letter was possibly irrelevant; mention of the five
November by-elections was all that mattered. The electorate was not to be
further upset.

The bodies would be returned, all of them, all on the same day, 24 October
1924. Sometime between the hours of 9.00 a.m. and 4.00 p.m. the remains would
be handed over. Families were asked to come at 9.00 a.m., to stand and wait.[77]
After the days and nights of sending a son to stand at Beggar's Bush Barracks
because there was a rumour that the uncoffined remains of Erskine Childers
might be moved, another day would not matter.[78] For Childers in particular a
republican gathering was to be avoided at all costs. The discourtesies shown
these men's families, the year and a half that kept these bodies from them,
the secrecies and the prohibitions were at least alleviated by the promise of
republican pomp and circumstance. In only one case the family did not want
it. The parents of Joseph Hughes were quite averse to republican attempts to
organise his funeral. They wanted to bury their son in their own way, without
politics and party lines. Naturally the police report saw nothing more than the
fact that 'The Republican party are endeavouring to use this young man as a
"pawn" purely for propaganda purposes.'[79] And maybe the report was right.
But no other objections were raised against the tricolours and the volleys fired

[75] *Ibid.*, letter from the Coiste Gnotha to W. T. Cosgrave, 15 Sept. 1924.   [76] *Ibid.*
[77] Letter from Major General Aodh MacNeill to Mrs Childers, 22 Oct. 1924, Childers MSS, TCD, MS 7829/36.
[78] Letter from M to P., A.P., C.S., D.I., M.F., A.M.F., D.P. and D., 15–16 Sept. 1924, *ibid.*, MS 7829/32.
[79] DJ H197/45, Executed Irregulars – exhumation and re-interment. Report by Superintendent John Farrell, Dundalk, 1 Nov. 1924.

over these dead sons' graves. They were at least being buried with the honour the republic had promised them. The families of the Free State soldiers were left with nothing but the indignity, nothing but the knowledge that they were treated little better than the enemies of their dead sons. It would not have seemed so bad if the government had not made its hollow promises, if it had not gone out of its way to honour an anti-Treatyite with a military funeral in 1924.

Pro-Treatyite relatives squabbled with republicans over the right to bury Patrick Harte's anti-Treatyite body.[80] While his family got the military funeral they wanted, the government got to rub salt in the raw republican wound:

That the ceremony connected with the burial should have been conducted by the National Army has greatly mortified the Irregular leaders, who had made all arrangements for a big display. The incident humiliated them in the extreme, as the hundreds of released prisoners present saw, for the first time, the absolute helplessness of their erstwhile leaders, who failed in the attempt made even at the last moment to take charge of the arrangements. The effect too on the civil population of the towns in West Cork... has been good. Though only a small incident it has had a big effect here.[81]

It was a childish victory; it was playing politics with Patrick Harte's family be they pro- or anti-Treaty. It could only serve to insult the soldiers' families left to mourn at unmarked army plots.

But by 1924 these families should perhaps have known better. When letters came from the Duke of Devonshire, from Andy Cope in Dublin Castle asking for the return of the bodies of British soldiers who had been killed in the War of Independence, the replies were always prompt:

Every facility will be afforded to relatives of the deceased who wish to visit the burial places, and, should there be any desire on the part of the relatives to have the bodies removed for re-interment, either in England or any existing British military cemeteries in Ireland, every possible facility will be granted for the purpose, including the transfer of the bodies to the cemetery or nearest port of embarkation. Full military honours will, unless the relatives express a wish to the contrary, be tendered by the Free State National Forces during the removal of the bodies, and, in the case of re-interment in the Free State during the interment.[82]

The response should not have been otherwise. In 1926 the promise was made to honour all the British military graves in Ireland: 'to meet the cost of providing and erecting headstones over the graves'. This was sent with the hope that 'the

---

[80] Department of Defence A11118, Military burial – query; DF s004/0103/24, Funeral expenses of Commandant P. Harte.

[81] Department of Defence Chief of Staff Department MS34, Anniversaries ceremonies, letter from Col. M. Costello, Director of Intelligence to the Chief of General Staff, 26 Feb. 1924.

[82] DT s3827, Applications from British government for exhumation of bodies of persons buried in the Irish Free State, letter from General Richard Mulcahy to N. J. Loughnan, on behalf of the Governor General, Timothy Healy, 12 Oct. 1923.

British Government will find this proposal acceptable'.[83] The task, perhaps predictably, was never completed. The local authorities in Sligo and Clare could not bear the sight of regimental badges in their graveyards.[84] But the thought, the intention, seemed genuine. The £25,000 was actually put aside.[85] There was never the same concern for the Irish army. In January 1924 the government received a letter from England from Dr R. A. Dove. He wrote: 'it has been a great consolation to my wife and myself to have our boy's body brought back to England, and for the way in which you have met our every wish we are most grateful'.[86] There are no letters like this from the families of Free State soldiers, only disappointed letters of complaint.

Remembrance was a family's burden. That was clear from the start. It was left to the men and women, the families and friends, to the comrades and companions, to those photographed in prayer at pathetic makeshift mortuary chapels. In the case of the men of Ferrycarrig 'the only thing that has really aroused public interest with regard to the memorial' was the promise of a performance by the army band.[87] There was no other interest, just the spectacle of the unveiling. An t-Óglách, the army journal, made brief notes of monuments, crosses erected over the graves of a couple of captains.[88] Their rank earning them a paragraph's attention, insignificant in comparison to the crowds, albeit on St Patrick's Day, drawn to the unveiling of a monument in Cork to the allegedly forgotten Great War dead.[89] Of the anonymous privates there was nothing. Their graves were marked silently over the years; marked with the same silence as any other grave, with the same variety of what a family could afford. Some were never marked: one, the grave of Pte Cornelius O'Sullivan, only seventy-six years later.[90] In many cases the graves were all these people had. 'The immemorial instinct to cradle and cosset the lifeless bodies of loved ones has often been denied by the sheer ferocity of the violence.'[91] They had

[83] Timothy Healy to the Secretary of State for Dominion Affairs, 11 Feb. 1927, PRO, DO 35/1229.
[84] David Fitzpatrick, 'Commemoration in the Irish Free State: a chronicle of embarrassment', in Ian McBride (ed.), History and memory in modern Ireland (Cambridge, 2001), pp. 191–2.
[85] DT s3913, Griffith and Collins – ownership and erection of memorials at graves, Subhead B of Public Works and Buildings Estimate for 1931–2.
[86] DT s3827, Applications from British government for exhumation of bodies of persons buried in the Irish Free State, copy of a letter from Dr R. A. Dove to the Irish government, sent by the Duke of Devonshire to Timothy Healy, 1 Jan. 1924.
[87] Letter from Kathleen Browne to Richard Mulcahy, June 1925, Richard Mulcahy MSS, UCDA, P7b/62(20).
[88] For example, Captain T. Walsh's grave was marked by a Celtic cross in November 1922, An t-Óglách, 1, 18 (new series), (17 Nov. 1923), p. 9; Captain Philip O'Doherty's monument was erected in Buncrana cemetery in July 1926, An t-Óglách, 5, 2 (17 July 1926), p. 6.
[89] Illustrated London News, 66, 4484 (28 Mar. 1925), p. 558.
[90] A stone cross was erected over the grave in Templin graveyard, Bruff, Co. Limerick, in July 1998. O'Sullivan was killed in action at Gortboy, Kilmallock, on 16 July 1922. Letter from Pat Quilty, Bruff, 10 July 1998.
[91] Fintan O'Toole, 'All we can do is remember', IT, 6 Nov. 1999.

nothing but a grave, possibly a simple cross, sometimes a persistent memoriam notice, a printed inch that kept a memory alive.

Republicanism's foot soldiers never knew such anonymity. Although 'the period that immediately followed the black tragedy of Ireland's Civil War, when the morale of the nation seemed broken and the instinct of patriotism seemed blighted', brought the 'disgraceful neglect' of the graves of the men of 1922 and 1923, this disgrace and neglect quickly ended in 1926.[92] Abandoned by de Valera and his followers, Sinn Féin, at its most uncompromising, founded the National Graves Association to stake its claim to the republican dead. Tidied graves and roadside plaques became the means to bring 'home to the rising generation that the young men of to-day had a duty to fulfil by seeing to it that the sacrificial deaths so honoured were not in vain'.[93] Neglect gave way to the hope of new recruits to the beleaguered Sinn Féin, to the fledgling Fianna Fáil. As republicans squabbled amongst themselves, there could never be neglect again. In its varied shades, the movement was regularly chronicled paying its respects. Small towns chose Celtic crosses and statues as their centrepieces; civil war names added to the lists of War of Independence dead. Names consumed in the ecumenism of an 'all who died for Ireland' that never seemed to include the Free State dead. The Garden of Remembrance was all very well; it was erected on a grand scale of cross-party consensus and the fervour of 1966. The monument in Newcastlewest to the dead of both sides of the civil war gave a more accurate definition of what ecumenism really meant. Although the committee, like the one formed for the 1690–1921 monument in Bruff, Co. Limerick (see figure 4), brought former civil war opponents side by side, the monument itself was not quite so accommodating.[94] The one Free State soldier that the monument honours had not been struck down by a republican hand. He had simply blown himself up. At the monument in Shankill, Co. Roscommon, it was even clearer. 'All who died for Ireland' only meant the men of Roscommon 'who lost their lives ... in upholding the idea of a Republic'.[95] Criticism of the omission of Michael Dockery's name needed no more justification than that he was a brigadier in the Free State army.[96] The National Graves Association may have had masses said regularly for 'all who died for Irish freedom', but on 'such solemn occasions continued fealty to the same cause for which our

---

[92] National Graves Association pamphlet, 'Forty-three years of national service', Gerald Tighe MSS, NLI, MS 25,583(54).

[93] Ibid., 'Thirty-three years of worthy service to the nation', Gerald Tighe MSS, NLI, MS 28,894(b)1.

[94] Letter from Pat Quilty, Bruff, 10 July 1998; Restoration programme (Newcastlewest, 1992); letter from John Cussen, Newcastlewest, 22 July 1998.

[95] Roscommon Herald, 21 Sept. 1963.

[96] Gerald Tighe MSS, NLI, MS 25,583(91), MS 25,583(95); National Graves Association pamphlet, 'Thirty-three years of worthy service to the nation', Gerald Tighe MSS, NLI, MS 28,894(b)1.

dead patriots had endured martyrdom' was strictly affirmed. For many years several members of the association refused to recognise the legitimacy of the Free State, much less the lives of its misguided soldiers. The country towns and villages, which scrimped and saved and bought their Celtic crosses and limestone Volunteers, did not and could not share the Garden of Remembrance's haughty and detached luxury. A gallant idea, Dublin's distant garden could never mean as much as a cross in Taghmon, a Virgin Mary in Ballylanders, a Volunteer in Newport, in Killarney, in Cahirsiveen.[97] The Garden of Remembrance was a place visited, passed by, bought and paid for by the state, undoubtedly trying to set a fine example. It could never be like the simple statue in the middle of a small town, bought by the pounds, shillings and pence that had taken years to save; the statue standing as a daily reminder, invoking the memory of the local men who had died for Irish freedom. The crosses that mark many country roads, the strange and almost unexpected dignity of Ballyseedy's much politicised bronze figures, these could never really be expected to be quite so forgiving. Although politics was quick 'to commemorate the murder of a republican; not his memory',[98] and speeches at Ballyseedy were possibly eloquent proof of that, republicanism had the comfort of never compromising, the assumption that 1798, that 1916 were theirs, that the easy glance North still proved they were right. The Free State soldiers had nothing. The state, that many presumed would, never took up the burden of remembrance. It had neither the money, the inclination, the security nor the taste for it. In the presumption no one else bothered.

There were, of course, some exceptions. Three thousand gathered in the graveyard in Knockananna, Co. Wicklow on 6 November 1924.[99] None had been discouraged, possibly more encouraged, by the republican demonstration in Tinahealy the day before.[100] 'Erected in memory of Colonel Commandant Tom Kehoe, by his old comrades in the Fight for Irish Freedom', a large Celtic cross and a marble likeness of the dying Kehoe, clutching his heart and his revolver, were unveiled by ex-Major General Liam Tobin (see figure 6). In his oration, ex-Major General Piaras Béaslaí spoke of Tone, Thomas Davis, Arthur Griffith, Michael Collins. He echoed the portrayals of 1798, 1867, 1916, carved on the side of the pedestal, the depictions that desperately insisted that Treatyites could be republicans too.[101] The gravestone and statue, costing more than £600, a fortune in the context of 1923's miserly Cenotaph, had been paid for by the army mutineers, by the 150 former soldiers who formed a guard of honour, and by the columns of men listed in the newspaper reports with their revealing former ranks.[102] They were there to remind 'many who had lost their old enthusiasm'

---

[97] This is merely a random selection of republican monuments.
[98] Letter to the editor by 'Nemo', *II*, 13 Oct. 1926.   [99] *Wicklow People*, 8 Nov. 1924.
[100] *Ibid.*, 8 Nov. 1924 and 22 Nov. 1924.   [101] Piaras Béaslaí MSS, NLI, MS 33,920(1).
[102] *Wicklow People*, 22 Nov. 1924. The gathering also included the TDs who had resigned over the army mutiny.

Figure 6 Tom Kehoe's grave, Knockananna, Co. Wicklow.

that 'the end of the path to freedom was not yet reached',[103] that ''tis the soldier's sword alone can reap the harvest when 'tis grown'.[104] They were there to taunt a seemingly indifferent government with the patriotism and the death

[103] *FJ*, 17 Nov. 1924; *II*, 17 Nov. 1924.   [104] Piaras Béaslaí MSS, NLI, MS 33,920(1).

of Tom Kehoe. They were there to indict, to rebuke even with the monument itself, to encourage a return to the rather laboured symbolic union of the heart and the gun. That the families of the Free State soldiers had so little made the exploitation of what they had for political gain seem so much worse. What mutineers began in 1924, time would soon continue with a sordid politics that made fascist salutes over dead boys' graves.[105]

But Kehoe was not the only exception. There were others. A plaque in Sligo town recalls the five men killed in an ambush in July 1922.[106] A cheap and simple plaque honours Christopher McGlynn in Abbeyleix. Easily missed, it prays that his twenty-one-year-old soul should rest in peace.[107] A small memorial in the Ox Mountains remembers the death of Brigadier General Joseph Ring, the only leading IRA officer in Mayo to side with the Treatyites.[108] Ring had an illustrious War of Independence past. He was a high-ranking officer and he left an active political family that still boasts a Teachta Dála, a family with force and money enough to commemorate him. Like Seán Hales, Ring was possibly one of the predictable exceptions; he had fought enough Englishmen to commend his immortal soul to even the most virulent republican. But these monuments were almost deviations. The more anonymous Free State soldier was rarely commemorated at his place of death. In the case of Macroom, the town had more republican priorities. Six officers and two privates of the Free State army were killed by a mine there in September 1922. Because some of the men were from the area, a small cross marked their obscure place of death. It was erected in September 1923 by the men's comrades in the 32nd Battalion. The crowd that watched the ceremony was made up of army men.[109] In the centre of Macroom a large obelisk remembers the men of the 7th and 8th Battalions of the Cork No. 1 Brigade IRA who died for Ireland between 1920 and 1923. It was unveiled by George Gilmore on 19 August 1928. At the ceremony he spoke of waging war on England; he called on the young men of Cork to join Fianna Éireann and the IRA. Unlike the soldiers' cross, this time 'a large attendance of the general public' came.[110]

But other places could not even make Macroom's concession to the Free State dead. Often the soldiers were strangers in a hostile place and the hostility that survived them had no wish to remember them. There is nothing to the men who died at Knocknagoshel; the land just bears the marks of a fatal explosion. There is nothing to the nine men killed in Kerry in August 1922, nothing to the O'Connor Scarteen brothers shot in their own home in Kenmare. Perhaps it is foolish to expect otherwise. Kerry especially had run too red with republican blood; there were too many Ballyseedys to speak well of the soldier dead. Naïve,

[105] See chapter 5.   [106] Letter from Michael Farry, Sligo, 29 May 1999.
[107] Letter from Vera Quinn, Abbeyleix Branch Library, 3 June 1998.
[108] Letter from Michael Farry, Sligo.   [109] CE, 17 Sept. 1923.
[110] An Phoblacht, 1 Sept. 1928.

Dan Nolan lamented to Richard Mulcahy that 'one never hears mention of the five men who were blown up at Cordal', the soldiers killed before the trap mine at Ballyseedy Wood.[111] The outpost of the republic had no place on its roads for simple crosses to the soldier dead. But the whole country should not be judged by Kerry's particularly bloody standards. Elsewhere, where people had faced the republicans 'sullenly, as if we had belonged to a hostile invading army', the soldiers were welcomed.[112] In Ferns 'the local people greeted the triumphant Free State soldiers with cheers and congratulations'.[113] And Ferns was not alone. Towns welcomed the soldiers as liberators, freeing them from the unruly clutches of republican occupation, giving them back a longed-for normality. At Westport and Castlebar, they 'were received with great enthusiasm by the people'.[114] Night-long celebrations met them in Claremorris, 'great cheering' in Waterford, 'huge crowds' in Tipperary town.[115] By Lil Conlon's own admission the unfortunates who took Cork, after being 'hailed with joy and thankfulness by the citizens who welcomed them as deliverers', were then smothered by an all-singing, all-knitting brigade of Cumann na mBan.[116] And there were the photographs to prove it.[117] There were gifts for the wounded from the merchants of Cork city, gifts for Christmas and to celebrate the new year; collections were made by 'Comforts Committees' for the ease of the national troops.[118] Appealing to the women of Cork to 'remember the generous welcome you gave the National troops on their entry into your city, and forget not the government who sent them there. This same government which has done so much for you, now asks for your votes. Support them and save the country from destruction' was all very well in the fraught election days of 1923.[119] Remembering afterwards was never as important. There were no crosses plain or lavish, no plaques, no monuments, nothing; welcomed men simply forgotten. Partisan areas did not have Kerry's excuse.

Wexford, or more precisely the Ferrycarrig of earlier pages, may explain it all. The reticence of Richard Mulcahy to allow the monument to grace his soldiers' place of death was almost an admission that such monuments were more a glorification of republican victory than his own troops' sacrifice. As the stronger power, gathered under the authority of the very word army, there was no longer the macabre credit of being done to death by the cruel oppressor. To die fighting when there was no hope of winning was now only the republicans'

---

[111] Letter from Dan Nolan to Richard Mulcahy, 27 Apr. 1965, Richard Mulcahy MSS, UCDA, P7c/2(23).
[112] Robert Brennan, *Allegiance* (Dublin, 1950), p. 352.
[113] Mac Suain, *County Wexford's Civil War*, p. 48.
[114] DT s567, Civil war 1922, post office reports, 27 July 1922.   [115] Garvin, *1922*, p. 103.
[116] Conlon, *Cumann na mBan and the women of Ireland*, pp. 276–98.
[117] Many of these pictures appear in the Desmond FitzGerald photograph collection, UCDA. They were later alleged to have been staged for propaganda purposes.
[118] Conlon, *Cumann na mBan*, pp. 277, 283–4.   [119] Cumann na mBan poster, *ibid.*, p. 291.

prerogative, hence the legion of small plaques and crosses that easily commemorate a republican death, that only define death and bravery as an act of rebellion. The Free State soldiers, like Islandbridge's 49,400 Great War dead, were dying for an orthodoxy, an authority, a compromise. Whether it called itself home rule or dominion status no longer mattered. Death was now a failure that no monument could be allowed to concede.

The Seán Hales monument that gazes over the famous 'Bridge at Bandon', although something of an exception, still testifies to this cruel logic. Hales was a brigadier general; he had died for the glory and good of the Free State; his was martyr's blood. Republicanism had capitalised so much on the deaths of the four men executed as a reprisal for his murder for it possibly to be provocation enough. A monument would stand in his home town, a town which gloried in his family's heroics during the War of Independence. It was the least his comrades could do. 'The Hales family embraced revolution',[120] but the Treaty broke them. Brothers parted: Seán followed Michael Collins' lead; Donal and Tom took the republican side, fighting the very men their brother led. Yet Donal reportedly commissioned the statue in Genoa in 1928.[121] A brother's sorrow was complemented by a large local committee that was comprised of a plethora of solicitors, doctors and TDs.[122] From 1926 the appeals were phrased in terms 'of doing justice to that heroic figure of the Anglo-Irish War'.[123] The glorious past appealed more to sensitive generosity. The Gárdaí were encouraged to subscribe, pounds and shillings buying a place in a proudly published list of eager subscribers.[124] But despite the Gárdaí's enthusiasm, it took four years to pay for the monument, four years until 'a large gathering'[125] watched Eamon Duggan unveil the six-foot uniformed figure of Seán Hales. People were welcomed 'irrespective of any political opinions they might hold' and people of diverse opinion came.[126] Like Collins, Hales was one of their own; many believed he was shot by mistake, that the real target was his companion Pádraig Ó Máille. 'In life he had been beloved of all, in death he had not been forgotten, not even by his enemies.'[127] That Seán Collins spoke from the platform was proof of that; he only worked to end the bitterness that took his brother's life.[128] There was none of the newspaper talk of 1922, of a man 'foully slain', of the heartless 'assassin's bullet'.[129] There were countless members of Cumann na nGaedheal, but there was no Cosgrave, no Mulcahy: none of

---

[120] Peter Hart, *The IRA and its enemies: violence and community in Cork, 1916–1923* (Oxford, 1998), p. 199.

[121] Eunan O'Halpin, *Defending Ireland: the Irish state and its enemies since 1922* (Oxford, 1999), p. 34.

[122] Memorial appeal, *An t-Óglách*, 4, 19 (22 May 1926), p. 2.

[123] *Ibid*, 4, 20 (29 May 1926), p. 2.

[124] *Gárda Review*, 2, 2 (Jan. 1927), p. 137; *ibid.*, 2, 5 (Apr. 1927), p. 456.

[125] *Realt a Deiscirt*, 25 Jan. 1930.   [126] *Ibid.*   [127] *Ibid.*   [128] *CE*, 20 Jan. 1930.

[129] *An t-Óglách*, 4, 27 (16 Dec. 1922), p. 1.

the men the Hales family had to beg for money in 1923.[130] There was just a simple inscription that looked to a more accommodating past: 'Erected by a grateful people in proud and loving memory of Brigadier General Seán Hales, TD: Volunteer, Soldier, Statesman and Patriot.'

The hurling clubs named in his honour, the poems and the laments, set Seán Hales apart.[131] He was a dead hero of the War of Independence, a convenient figure who could still appeal across civil war's divide. That he could do so may have made the unveiling ceremony an uncomfortable occasion for Richard Mulcahy and W. T. Cosgrave. Nineteen-thirty was just too soon for these men to stand shoulder to shoulder with Seán's staunchly republican siblings. But others shared the President's and Mulcahy's discomfort; they understood it from their own republican point of view. Twenty-three years later Bandon was graced with another monument, this time on the other side of the river. It remembered the men of the West Cork Brigade IRA who died for Ireland from 1916 onwards. Seán Hales, who had been a battalion commandant in the West Cork Brigade, was not included; he was never mentioned at the unveiling ceremony. In 1953, it was still clear that the sin of the compromise was not yet forgiven.

Civilian casualties shared the forgotten soldiers' fate. They were remembered only by those closest to them, those who felt more than the temporary shock of a newspaper report. One, Dr Thomas O'Higgins, killed by republicans in February 1923, was honoured by a monument in Stradbally, Co. Laois, but it was a monument to his entire family, an expression rather of local regard. The fundraising appeal for this rather ugly edifice even removed the possibly contentious 'killed by raiders in defence of his home'.[132] No monument recalled the loss of Emmet McGarry, the TD's son burnt to death in an attack on his father's home. If 'there is assuredly a special heaven for such little martyrs', there was no memorial on this crueller earth.[133]

Maybe this neglect was right. Maybe it was not a war for monuments: the enemy was within and too many had died. It was more convenient to forget, to overlook, to let the soldiers march away with their uniformed companions who lingered in the comparatively splendid isolation of Islandbridge: victims too of another war that it had become unfashionable to fight. In the name

130 The family home had been destroyed during the War of Independence. Seán Hales' father had been driven insane and had to be confined to an asylum. Department of Defence A/7749, Seán Hales, TD, personal file.
131 Seán Hales Gaelic Club still exists in West Cork. 'Lament for Seán Hales' by 'Carbery Ranger', *Realt a Deiscirt*, 18 Jan. 1930. The final verse of the lament, 'Let him sleep in the breast of his dear land, Wrapped in sward from his own native dales, For the fame of his valour shall garland, With glory the tomb of Seán Hales', appears on the pedestal of the monument.
132 O'Higgins memorial appeal (July, 1955), Richard Mulcahy MSS, UCDA, P7C/2(30). The large obelisk, possibly the most dominant feature of the town, was unveiled on 20 Apr. 1958. *Irish Press*, 21 Apr. 1958; *II*, 21 Apr. 1958; *IT*, 21 Apr. 1958; *Offaly Independent*, 26 Apr. 1958; *Leinster Leader*, 3 May 1958.
133 *Young Ireland*, 23 Dec. 1922.

of a fragile peace there had to be silence. In some ways Islandbridge was a memorial to this awkward type of silence. Although the National War Memorial Committee commended de Valera and his government for their 'spirit of toleration, co-operation and mutual goodwill',[134] the men who blew up the statue of George II in St Stephen's Green, the men who rioted at screenings of the film *Gallipoli*,[135] who disrupted every Armistice Day, did not do the same. With the announcement that conscription might be extended to Northern Ireland in 1939, an opening ceremony at Islandbridge became impossible for de Valera: 'instead of having a good effect a ceremonial opening of the War Memorial Park in the altered circumstances might evoke hostility and give rise to misunderstanding'.[136] An IRA campaign began in Britain on 12 January 1939. An Irish leader opening a memorial to Irish men who died in the British army constituted a risk that leader was not prepared to take. There could be no such 'misunderstandings'. Irishmen might be conscripted in the North, someone might wave a Union Jack, the IRA might be upset and the extremes of Fianna Fáil might agree with them. Silence was easier all round. But then it always had been. Remembering the Great War dead had always caused trouble. The £50,000 donated by the Cumann na nGaedheal government was welcomed by the Memorial Committee, but to the opposition it was nothing more than a sop to the old order to prop up pro-Treatyite power.[137] To the IRA it was anathema; even to Dublin Corporation it was objectionable. The donation only applied to former soldiers and left a mere £5,000 for all other relief work schemes.[138] Remembrance of the Great War could only be remote: a wreath at the Cenotaph in London, a wreath at the tomb of the unknown soldier left by the first athletes to represent the Free State when they went to the Paris Olympics in 1924.[139] Even the Irish Peace Tower at Messines is sufficiently distant, sufficiently remote to cope with the weight of North–South relations that seem to have been foisted onto and filtered through the memory of Ireland's Great War dead.

While Kevin Myers might be correct in assuming that 'we are extremely uneasy with memorials which are not strictly our own',[140] while Islandbridge remains testimony to the neglect of the Great War dead, Myers does not take account, indeed no one does, of the unease with the memory of 'our own'. The dead of the civil war could not 'be honoured and memorialised without implicitly demanding vengeance'.[141] The Free State dead could not be honoured

---

[134] *IT*, 16 Apr. 1937.   [135] *Connaught Telegraph*, 30 Sept. 1933.
[136] DT s4156c, War Memorial, Islandbridge, report of meeting of Major Tynan and A. P. Connolly of the British Legion and Eamon de Valera, 28 Apr. 1939.
[137] For example, front page cartoons in the *Irish Press*, 12 Dec. 1931 and 14 Jan. 1932.
[138] *Republican File*, 6 Feb. 1932.   [139] *Sunday Tribune*, 30 July 2000.
[140] Kevin Myers, 'It is not all over', *IT*, 18 Apr. 1998.
[141] Fintan O'Toole, 'All we can do is remember', *IT*, 6 Nov. 1999.

because they were proof of a state's military inadequacy, because they were perceived as fighting to compromise the republic. But political practicalities make no allowance for the instinct of memory, for the sorrow of a family that seeks refuge in an honour that compensates for an otherwise futile young death. Parents left wreaths 'In memory of our patriot dead'.[142] Some would have called their son a traitor, some a fool. Alone they had to honour him because honour was not convenient to a government that feared to take pride in its dead. There was no glory in rattling the bones of men who seemed to embody the defence of a disappointing compromise. The men who died suppressing Irish republicans were merely carrying out an unpleasant task. The government had battled once for the souls of 1916's dead. In the midst of civil war it had no choice; acceptance of the Treaty was not treachery to these noble men whose Spirits were summoned so forcefully by republican relatives during the Treaty debates. Nods were made in the direction of 1798, of 1919–21, but revolutionary violence no longer sat well with the top hats and tails of government and the 'wild men screaming through the keyholes'.[143] It was simply easier to forget. And civil war made sure of that. The Free State soldiers are just the most obvious casualties of this more comfortable forgetting.

The ideal was never achieved; it never could be. Granted, Fianna Fáil's chosen moral high ground was a darker shade of green, but the dead were less welcome company when the 'slightly constitutional party' turned executioner.[144] The dead are cherished most by the rebellious, by the grievance yet to be appeased. Sacrifice suits the separatist best; that is why Eoin O'Duffy targeted the Cenotaph in 1933, why Blueshirts chanted over forgotten Free State soldier graves, why the more extreme shades of republicanism still walk to hidden graves. Authority is uneasy with the violence of these deaths, a violence that authority can no longer countenance. It still doffs its cap: the glorious beginnings have to be found somewhere. The men of Wexford got their cross, their speeches and their marching band. But like Messines 'we had our day. We opened our tower. Now let us get on with what we do best: forgetting.'[145] In 1922 the Free State soldiers were promised that 'they shall be remembered forever'.[146] In the same year a republican, Padraig O'Brien, wrote to a former friend and comrade who had joined the Free State army:

Your name and cause will fade like last year's snow, for that is ever the fate of the Imperialist in this country, whether he calls himself a Cromwellian, a Yeoman, a Constabularyman, or a National Soldier. For you flying flags, banners waving, cannon,

---

[142] *The People*, 5 Sept. 1925.
[143] Kevin O'Higgins, *Three years hard labour: an address delivered to the Irish Society at Oxford University on the 31st October, 1924* (Dublin, n.d.), p. 7.
[144] Seán Lemass, *DE, official report*, XXII, col. 1615 (21 Mar. 1928).
[145] 'An Irishman's diary', *IT*, 2 Apr. 1999.   [146] *Young Ireland*, 15 July 1922.

and press plaudits – and FORGETFULNESS. For me a Fenian's grave and remembrance forever, in the company of Tone, Emmet, MacSwiney and Brugha. WHO IS THE FOOL PAT?[147]

The government broke a promise it could never keep; maybe the irredentist O'Brien was just a little more honest.

[147] 'Open letter from Padraig O'Brien of the "Irregular" forces to his former friend and comrade, Pat O'Brien of the "National" Army', NLI, ILB 300p3, item 13 (emphasis from original).

5 'Shows and stunts are all that is the thing now': ceremony and the collective memory of conflict

In 1922 John Crowley was ten years old. In August a soldier burst into his home and ordered the boy outside. There was something the child had to see. Outside was the 'greatest man that Ireland has ever produced'; outside was the corpse of Michael Collins.[1] The child had to see the body. He had to see the value of the sacrifice: all that had been given for him and others like him. The child would never see his like again. Eyes wide with fear and fascination, the boy looked and remembered for the rest of his life.

Whatever there was of pride and despair that compelled this soldier made a certain sense. Hours before, his 'Chief' had died and he had failed to save him. Now even the children had to see the bloodied wrong; even the children had to mourn. What made no sense is that the same soldier, gratified by the contrite child, should leave the precious carcass on the roadside, unguarded and alone.[2] It seems the soldier and his companions were hungry. And the 'Big Fella' was not going anywhere anymore.

Over eighty years later this soldier is perhaps an easy target. Nothing can be known of the man's misery, of what made for rational or irrational on that trip from Béalnabláth. But there was something ominous, however ridiculous, in this grief that stopped for tea, that seemed to come and go at practicality's command. The pattern seemed set within hours of death: there was a time for sadness, for respects to be paid and heads hung low, and there was a time for moving on, for drinking tea and running the country and forgetting that there were ever bodies to bury or soldiers to mourn. The dead could be useful, but the dead could also exceed their usefulness. It was all very well to build statues; it was another thing to return, to stand in the rain year after sodden year when there was nothing to be gained, when a politician at the side of the road no longer made the news.

It is to this 'returning' that this chapter will attend. Who returned, why, how often: the ceremonies, the pilgrims, the users and abusers, the eighty years of

---

[1] Recounted by John Crowley in Twohig, *The dark secret*, p. 166.
[2] It makes no sense, especially in the context of the removal of the body by sea from Cork to Dublin because of fears of a republican ambush. *Emmet Dalton remembers*, RTÉ 1, 22 Aug. 1978.

Free State dead. There is no definition, no restriction. Returning is as much a memoriam notice or a cheap broken wreath as it is a lavish ceremony with manicured phrases and marching bands. Stripped of the impetus that built cenotaphs and crosses, of bodies not yet cold, the years of anniversaries tell of a different devotion. There is none of the same compunction that builds and celebrates; there is never that urgency again. There is instead a will to remember; to return and honour a life lost; to pay what convenience vaguely calls 'our respects'. However, it would be foolish to imagine that crowds marched eagerly to monuments and statues year after year, that generation replaced sorrowful generation on well-worn paths to martyrs' graves. It would be naïve to suggest that all who went went with bowed heads and sorrowful hearts. There was a novelty in seeing, a benefit in being seen. There were years when it was useful, when it was embarrassing, when it suited best to say nothing at all. There were fashionable and fickle years, controversial and inconsequential years. But there were always some who never noticed or cared about the difference, some who refused to trade their grief for column inches. There were always some who went because they wanted to, not because they had to.

The Cenotaph's is a dispiriting story, the cross at Béalnabláth cheap and uninspiring. The monuments are few, the graves unmarked, ignored, grudgingly adorned. It is not easy to be hopeful about the ceremonies. In the last pages of *The plague* there is a conversation about a monument to the plague's dead. 'I can almost hear them saying, "Our dear departed..." And then they'll go off and have a good tuck in.'[3] The cynicism is almost tangible, almost appropriate. Knowing how meanly the Free State built, block upon penurious block, it is easy to envy Camus his cynicism. After all, men who erected rotten wooden cenotaphs to their illustrious dead could not be counted on for years of heartfelt and unswerving devotion. Granted, if money is a measure of grief theirs was but a trifling sorrow. If money is a measure of grief then they mourned uncontrollably for the Great War dead that they allegedly overlooked. The right thing to say would be that money does not matter; rotten wood means as much as the most lavish edifice if erected for the right reasons. And it was a mean, careful state anyway. The republicans did not call the Free Staters shopkeepers for nothing.[4] Patrick McGilligan contemplated letting people starve.[5] But then other countries were poor, other regimes wrought from revolution had to scrimp and save, but still they celebrated. France changed its commemorative mind with the revolutionary weather, yet it spent even as its people starved.[6] And the Free State did not have the excuse of a more pragmatic century. Finland was proof

[3] Albert Camus, *The plague* (London, 1960), pp. 250–1.
[4] Francis Stuart, *Things to live for: notes for an autobiography* (New York, 1938), p. 245.
[5] *DE, official report*, XI, cols. 557–62 (30 Oct. 1924).
[6] Mona Ozouf, *Festivals and the French Revolution* (Cambridge, Mass., 1988).

of that and Islandbridge confirmed it.[7] Islandbridge would always confirm it. Its £50,000 of Free State money would always shout it even from the loftiest senator's rooftop.[8] The Free State had shamed itself with its paltry and its miserly monuments. The ceremonies were its only chance of redemption. Yet to judge the years of coming and going, kneeling and genuflecting with the same jaundiced eye that contemplated the erection of these monuments would be unfair. Ceremonies were convenient and not necessarily costly. By the Free State's own tight-fisted logic it should have excelled itself.

For Michael Mac Liammoir matters were clear, black and white, unaffected: Ireland would have been a paradise 'if it had as much affection and respect for the living as it has for the dead'.[9] In the face of the republican tradition he might have a point. There 'the image is one of a succession of soldier-heroes sacrificing themselves in bloody efforts to unshackle the mystical "Republic" ';[10] there, consolation was 'Cheer up boy! You are dying for Ireland!';[11] there one advertised to the flatulent and constipated readers of An Phoblacht with 'IF YOU ARE A MARTYR' in large bold print.[12] The Free State perspective could never be so simple. From 1922 it could never be simple again. It was torn. For the government and 'the majority of the people in 1922 the time had come to halt. Pearse's clarity of vision was a luxury the nation could no longer afford.'[13] The people 'were worn out, exhausted, fed up with ... the crusade for the Republic of Virtue',[14] fed up 'living in the explosion'.[15] The civil war 'woke us up from the mesmerism of the romantic dream. It set us asking questions about political institutions, international relations, financial reform, economics, education, about the pre-sanctified dogmas of our history.'[16] The air once thick with martyrs was clearing. The past was of no use to the working man who wanted to live rather than die by treaties and formulas.[17] Even the war by its very nature fought the instinct for ceremony. 'There had been something glorious and holy

---

[7] Mandy Lehto, 'The unfinished civil war and the politics of remembrance in Finland, 1918–1928', unpublished Ph.D. thesis, University of Cambridge (2000); Lee, *Ireland 1912–1985*, p. 69.

[8] DT s4156b, War Memorial, Islandbridge.

[9] Quoted in T. P. O'Mahony, *The politics of dishonour: Ireland 1916–1977* (Dublin, 1977), p. 18.

[10] *Ibid.*, p. 17.

[11] Elizabeth MacCurtain to Thomas MacCurtain, 20 Mar. 1920, quoted in Hart, *The IRA and its enemies*, p. 72.

[12] 'IF YOU ARE A MARTYR to indigestion, flatulence, constipation, liver complaints etc. TRY PEPTO', *An Phoblacht*, 20 June 1925.

[13] Margaret O'Callaghan, 'Language, nationality and cultural identity in the Irish Free State, 1922–7: the *Irish Statesman* and the *Catholic Bulletin* reappraised', *Irish Historical Studies*, 24, 94 (Nov. 1984), p. 227.

[14] Quoted in Margery Forester, *Michael Collins – the lost leader*, p. 346.

[15] W. B. Yeats, May 1922, quoted in F. S. L. Lyons, 'Yeats and the Anglo-Irish twilight', in Oliver MacDonagh, W. F. Mandle and Pauric Travers (eds.), *Irish culture and nationalism, 1750–1950* (London, 1983), p. 218.

[16] '1916–1941: tradition and creation', *The Bell*, 2, 1 (Apr. 1941), p. 11.

[17] George O'Brien, *The village of longing* (Belfast, 1993), p. 31.

in the fight against the British but now – .'[18] Now there were hundreds maybe thousands dead and thousands injured. And the British had not fired a shot. No one was to blame but themselves; no one was more bloodthirsty than Irish men in Irish uniforms, than a desperate Irish government. There was shame in civil war, shame in winning. There could be nothing 'glorious' or 'holy' in celebrating the victory.

But while the government was busy 'delivering us from obsession',[19] ushering in the new rational independent dawn, there was still the lure of the past, the instinct for ceremony that was still stronger than shame. If the government had inherited anything from Arthur Griffith, it was the determination that it 'should not go down in history as "the greatest set of poltroons" ever to control Irish destinies'.[20] Ceremonies would have their uses. There was the lure of popular legitimacy, an image to piece together out of the wreckage: the Free State was the 'guardian of Ireland's newly won freedom'.[21] Republican fantasies of carrying on the fight, of provoking another war with England, looked all the more irresponsible at the foot of an Irish soldier's grave. If, as in its own language, the government was 'a force for good against evil in Irish society', the years of ceremony, the glorification of the men who had given their lives for this 'good', would do no harm.[22] And, after all, was ritual not the continuation of war by other means?[23] Beaten on the battlefield, republicans were vanquished again and again with every march to Glasnevin, with every pilgrimage to Béalnabláth. With power de Valera proved it; the marches stopped. But there were other reasons for ceremony. Geertz calls them 'the realities of postcolonial life'; freedom had to be lived in instead of merely imagined.[24] 'The sacred leaders of the national struggle are either gone, replaced by less confident heirs or less theatrical generals, or have been diminished to mere heads of state'.[25] The ceremonies at least maintained the fiction, maintained the link with all that was once thought honourable. Ordinary men remembered men who had done extraordinary things; they basked in whatever there was of glory. They had to because IRA men spoke in terms of waking 'up some morning to find ourselves members of the civil population, with peace made and our occupation and our power gone. Then I'll go back to the poorhouse and I suppose you'll start selling collars again.'[26] If the

[18] Brennan, *Allegiance*, p. 351.   [19] W. B. Yeats, quoted in Lyons, 'Yeats', p. 221.
[20] Richard Davis, *Arthur Griffith* (Dundalk, 1976), p. 41.
[21] Graham Walker, 'Propaganda and conservative nationalism during the Irish Civil War, 1922–1923', *Éire-Ireland*, 22, 4 (Winter 1987), p. 101.
[22] John Regan, 'The politics of reaction: the dynamics of treatyite government and policy, 1922–33', *Irish Historical Studies*, 30, 120 (Nov. 1997), p. 553.
[23] Peter Burke, *The fabrication of Louis XIV* (New Haven and London, 1992), p. 65.
[24] Clifford Geertz, *The interpretation of cultures* (New York, 1973), p. 235.
[25] *Ibid.*
[26] Florence O'Donoghue to 'G', 8 May 1921, Florence O'Donoghue MSS, NLI, MS 31,176.

ceremonies made them sleep sounder in their poorhouse beds, then ceremony was worthwhile.

Ceremony was also worthwhile because it was part of a tradition that the Free State could not afford to ignore. Denied the means of protest, the nineteenth century 'inaugurated a movement which may be said to be the parent of every other agitation ... a plant which in truth can be said to have been watered by the blood of martyrs, and grew to immense proportions – namely the funeral procession'.[27] A growing emphasis upon the rituals of death developed alongside Irish nationalism; funerary signs became political signs, funerals a political ritual.[28] Schooled in the spectacles of the funerals of O'Connell and the Young Irelanders, mock funerals for the Manchester Martyrs set in motion the annual practice of publicly commemorating their deaths.[29] An empty grave in Glasnevin drew 'young people of Fenian proclivities on almost every Sunday in the year'.[30] Thousands came in November and in a kind of 'Fenian stations of the cross, proceeded to the grave sites of other separatist heroes'.[31] As the years passed they added to their sorrowful and glorious mysteries: Parnell, Pearse, Kevin Barry. The nation could not be born without blood and suffering.[32] While Ireland was not alone in this – Mexico 'nationalised' by its bloody war with France, some Italians longing for the suffering of the Great War to make an Italian nation out of the mere Italian state – the dead had a special place in Ireland.[33] Nina Witoszek even goes so far as to claim that Ireland's fascination with death is 'the most evident hallmark of the Irishness of Irish culture'.[34] Death was writ too large in Irish folklore and religious beliefs, and the rituals of death had undergone a century of politicisation. A new government could not turn away from ritual even if it wanted to. Ritual was instinctive and ceremony could make up for the compromise.

In death the compromise took on heroic status. In ceremony the Free State could choose a past. Unintended consequences could become conscious aims, as if the main purpose of the past, the intention of the dead, had been to bring about this present, this dominion status.[35] Excluded from the republican pantheon by

---

[27] Quoted in Gary Owens, 'Constructing the martyrs: the Manchester executions and the nationalist imagination', in Lawrence McBride (ed.), *Images, icons and the Irish nationalist imagination* (Dublin, 1999), p. 31.

[28] *Ibid.*; Nina Witoszek, 'Ireland: a funerary culture?', *Studies*, 76 (Summer 1987).

[29] Owens, 'Constructing the martyrs', p. 31; Breandán Mac Giolla Choille, 'Mourning the martyrs: a study of a demonstration in Limerick city 8 December 1867', *North Munster Antiquarian Journal*, 10, 2 (1967), pp. 173–205.

[30] Owens, 'Constructing the martyrs', p. 33.

[31] *Ibid.* The Manchester Martyrs were executed in November 1867.

[32] Daniel J. O'Neil, 'The cult of self-sacrifice: the Irish experience', *Éire-Ireland*, 24, 4 (Winter 1989), p. 93.

[33] *Ibid.*, pp. 92–3.   [34] Witoszek, 'Ireland', p. 207.

[35] Peter Burke, 'History as social memory', in T. Butler (ed.), *Memory: history, culture and the mind* (London, 1989), p. 110.

virtue of the Treaty, the Free State had, as stated in chapter 1, to construct one of its own: a rival pantheon, one that justified actions, that legitimised, but one that would always do what was never intended, one that made the Treaty a disappointing end in itself. It would always be troublesome. By its very nature it had to be. On the one hand the Free State dead had won. There was no longer 1916's triumph of failure; Collins was the exception that proved that. Failure was an integral part of Irish martyrdom – the more inevitable the failure, the more precious the martyr. On such terms the Free State was just too successful for that pathetic constituency. On the other hand, the rituals that blamed and accused republicans would always imply that the dead had died for something other than the republic. An alternative pantheon insinuated another objective, a lesser one, one tainted by a British seal of approval. It made no difference if these men accepted the Treaty as a means to a republican end. Not all spoke in Cosgrave's disparaging tones, questioning whether 'the Republic is the great thing you say it is';[36] not all went, like Kevin O'Higgins, 'into the Empire... with our heads up'.[37] Many entered 'with no love and great frustration'.[38] But that did not matter any more. The rival republican pantheon was too strong; the Free State had been too eager to fill it.

Though bound by pride in the dead, by the need to cling to the nationalism that death implied, the state was also repulsed by death. The dead may have proved that the Treaty was worth fighting for, the Free State worth dying for, but in power there was no glory in dying. Casualties suggested inefficiency, uniformed bodies that competency should never have lost. To die now was a type of defeat and the Free State had too much to lose and too little to gain from wallowing in its failures. Ceremony and ritual could only be confusing: blaming republicans yet still claiming to be republican; proud of the dead yet ashamed of the conflict. Commemoration could never be simple again.

In one of the many frenzied end-of-millennium polls, the coveted position of 'person of the century' went to an Irishman.[39] It may be fair to say that a poll conducted by an Irish newspaper would naturally lean towards an Irish winner and that a certain film loomed large in the public mind, but there is no way of being sure of that. For whatever reason, Michael Collins won. He won because, despite the confusion, despite seventy-eight years of mixed motives and party politics, the ceremonies and the rituals worked. Collins is remembered, revered, even celebrated. Much troubled, the instinct to commemorate seems to have survived.

At times commemoration incriminates the living more than it reveres the dead. In this there is nothing particularly Irish, nothing particular to the Irish Civil War. But while acts of remembrance are often used as symbols of unity and

---

[36] DT s585, Attempted reorganisation of people of old Sinn Féin tendencies, 1924, letter from W. T. Cosgrave to Richard Mulcahy, 1 Feb. 1924.
[37] *DE, treaty debate*, p. 45 (19 Dec. 1921).   [38] Regan, *The Irish*, p. 48.
[39] *IT*, 31 Jan. 2000.

common interest, in Ireland they divide.[40] 'Commemorations are as selective as sympathies. They honour our dead, not your dead.'[41] They cherish a civil war mentality, always aggravating, always nurturing the memory of the conflict as much as, if not more than, the memory of the dead. Desmond O'Malley recalled his first days in Dáil Éireann in 1968: 'The Dáil still had figures who had played a prominent part in the War of Independence and in the Civil War. For some of them, the Civil War had never really ended. Their conversation was often backward looking and historical events exercised them more than current events.'[42] In 1968 there was revolt in Europe; closer, there was violence erupting on the streets of Northern Ireland. But still they spoke of 1922's rights and wrongs. It may be all very well for O'Malley to place himself above all this, to inhabit the higher moral ground furrowed by Noël Browne in the late 1940s when he was disillusioned by the Dáil's 'white hot hate', by the shouts of 'seventy-seven' and 'Ballyseedy'.[43] They were not part of this first generation, this civil war generation that dominated the Dáil well into the 1960s. Sheer longevity may have been the excuse: hale and hearty old men defying the 'shelf life' of memories.[44] But in 1996 deputies Mary O'Rourke and Michael McDowell did not have the same excuse as they chided each other with their own ancestors' allegiances.[45] This bitterness was as much political device as it was political reality. It was easier to appeal to old hatreds than to devise new ones. In the face of fundamental social and economic differences,[46] in spite of a Fine Gael Cenotaph erected by a Fianna Fáil government, bitterness had learned to be obedient. For over seventy years ceremony came when it was called.

As a minister in the Provisional Government, as Ceann Comhairle of the Free State Dáil, Michael Hayes should have known something of this bitterness. 'The bitterness engendered was great but it has been exaggerated both as to depth and duration.'[47] Hayes wrote this in 1969. However coloured by Northern Ireland, by the recent reissue of the republican reminiscences of Tom Barry and Dan Breen,[48] by the knee-jerk revisionism of a Treatyite, Hayes spoke of pre-1922 friendships preserved. Although Hayes failed to mention Cumann

---

[40] Brian M. Walker, *Dancing to history's tune: history, myth and politics in Ireland* (Belfast, 1996), pp. 74–5.

[41] Edna Longley, *The living stream* (Newcastle-upon-Tyne, 1994), p. 69.

[42] *Sunday Times*, 17 Oct. 1993; Walker, *Dancing*, p. 65.   [43] Browne, *Against the tide*, p. 228.

[44] Jay Winter and Emmanuel Sivan, 'Setting the framework', in Jay Winter and Emmanuel Sivan (eds.), *War and remembrance in the twentieth century* (Cambridge, 1999), p. 16.

[45] *DE, official report*, CDLXI, col. 424 (7 Feb. 1996).

[46] William Murphy, 'In pursuit of popularity and legitimacy: the rhetoric of Fianna Fáil's social and economic policy 1926–34', unpublished MA thesis, University College, Dublin (1998).

[47] Hayes, 'Dáil Éireann and the Irish Civil War', p. 22. J. J. Barrett's book *In the name of the game* (Bray, 1997) would seem to support Hayes' conclusion. He details the sense in which men were reunited through the GAA.

[48] Both Dan Breen's *My fight for Irish freedom* and Tom Barry's *Guerilla days in Ireland* were reprinted in 1968.

na nGaedheal's continued contempt for de Valera, Cosgrave's wariness of O'Higgins, or Mulcahy's contempt for the haughty triumvirate of O'Higgins, FitzGerald and Hogan, although the same article goes on to blame Britain for most, if not all, of Ireland's twentieth-century ills, it does not devalue the point.[49] Bitterness 'exaggerated' and bitterness fostered; the years of ceremony and ritual oscillated between the two. The 'first Taoiseach of the post-civil war generation', Jack Lynch, recalled that 'his earliest memories of politics were not of Fianna Fáil and Fine Gael but of the divisions in Cork between the followers of John Redmond and William O'Brien'.[50] Division predated the civil war; division was an integral part of the political landscape. The 'glorious unity' that supposedly broke the British was a sham. The civil war was the next, granted the bloodiest, round of an endless, and possibly an inevitable, struggle. The Redmondites became Cumann na nGaedhealers, the O'Brienites joined Fianna Fáil. The civil war was another attraction, another curiosity on the back of the party bandwagon. Bitterness had its time and its place, its functions and its uses. It enlivened speeches dulled by economics; it made for more eye-catching election posters. In a country where many people found it difficult to define their political allegiances beyond the preferences of their parents, political capital had to be made from anything that reaffirmed that devotion. Thus one generation inherited another's bitterness; however real, however much a political device, it was in the party interest to keep it alive.

Together, party interest and private grief ensured that ritual would go on. But ritual was a stolen thing. Republican, Free Stater, it made no difference. Both pilfered from the same source, from a British military blueprint. A volley of shots, the Last Post, both copied the only things they knew. Like the pillar boxes painted green, there was just a different uniform, a few words in Irish, later balaclavas instead of braided caps. Otherwise nothing changed: year after year the same. The same sombre, melancholy affairs: homage to the death more than celebration of the life. Granted, religion imposed its dignities; the ceremonies were often conducted in religious surroundings, always in religious terms. And death was never the gayest host, especially when the memory was of violent death. But there was a doleful air about these ceremonies that defied even death and dignity and religion's proprieties. There seemed to be a sorrow for something almost as great as death. Every monument embodied regret, every ceremony was a reminder not only of the life lost but the nature of its ending, the nature of civil war itself and all its bitter, wasteful ends. Republicanism

---

[49] Maryann Gialanella Valiulis' 'The man they could never forgive' was a particularly apposite choice of title. '"The man they could never forgive". The view of the opposition: Eamon de Valera and the Civil War', in J. P. O'Carroll and John A. Murphy (eds.), *De Valera and his times* (Cork, 1986), pp. 92–100.

[50] Stephen Collins, 'He did the state some service', *Sunday Tribune*, 24 Oct. 1999; Patrick Maume, *The long gestation: Irish nationalist life 1891–1918* (Dublin, 1999), pp. 110–11.

still took some sort of vicarious comfort in blaming Britain, but ashamed and possibly frightened by its thirst for compatriot blood, the state could never revel in its glorious beginnings. Civil war saw to that. It loomed like a great bloody embarrassment, and ceremony broached it again and again. 1922's 'the sooner over the better' had swept it neatly under a carpet of order and efficiency;[51] ceremony stripped it bare, speaking of the chances never taken, of a state born kicking and screaming and murderously gasping for breath, of men who had to die because men could not agree. Ceremony in its every funereal aspect mourned this very fall to civil war.

Whether it was high mass for a dead president in a Pro-Cathedral, high mass with ministers and foreign dignitaries, or whether it was mass on a weekday morning in a small parish church with a lonely family, with a clutch of pious women and a few stragglers standing in from the rain, ceremony's constant was religion. Indeed religion was often ceremony in itself. Before the march to monument or grave there was always mass. At the grave there was always prayer, always the rosary. Religion was constant because religion was familiar; it was the comfort of well-known words and rituals, it was consolation, it mediated loss. And this was what religion was supposed to do: what it did for every other death. Religion defined the ritual of remembrance, gave it form, expression, maybe even meaning. But religion was a type of retreat. It was sombre and dignified; it was the solemnity of church and graveyard. In theory it refused to entertain man's squabbles over treaties and oaths and dominion status. Such matters were petty and inappropriate. Religion only countenanced death. In practice religion was a type of approval. God is on our side, and we have the bishops' pastoral letter to prove it.

There is nothing unusual about the anniversary masses, the rosaries; death brought them regardless. Unusual, rather, is that religion dominated so much of civil ceremony. Without it, there is little but the Last Post and marching soldiers and the occasional political speech. At more anonymous gatherings, there is nothing else at all. In the same way that 'those in mourning who turned to the churches for aid in their sorrow were bound to dwell on traditional devotional art and sculpture',[52] the men and women who repeatedly nailed their grief to Celtic crosses took yearly refuge in predictable prayer. Yet there was more to this predictability than Catholic instinct. Following the executions of 1916, masses for the dead became political events. To attend was to declare an allegiance, to voice an opinion, to strengthen a show of strength. That mass replayed the sacrifice, one man dying to take away the sins of the world, was not lost on a populace schooled in Pearse's visions of redemption and gorged on pictures and

---

[51] Ernest Blythe, quoted in Eoin Neeson, *The Civil War in Ireland 1922–1923* (Dublin, 1966), p. 11.
[52] Winter, *Sites of memory, sites of mourning*, p. 92.

postcards and relics of the saintly dead.[53] Prayer had become part of patriotism and civil war did not put an end to that. But prayer was also a form of atonement. These men had died with the blood of their countrymen on their hands; civil war was a type of fratricide that had none of the glory of the 'just wars' of 1916 or of 1919–21. For the civil war dead, prayer was the only refuge of this greater sin.

The masses began in 1922: ceremony within days of death. From the Pro-Cathedral in Dublin to the Cathedral in Enniscorthy to novenas in Lough Rea, the country prayed for Griffith and Collins.[54] The declared day of mourning, 28 August 1922, was only the beginning.[55] Mass across the country was dedicated to its leaders' honour; men stopped work, businesses closed.[56] Councils and organisations passed resolutions, others had masses said.[57] People with nothing in common but the street on which they lived gathered and invited others there to pray:

As a mark of fidelity and gratitude to the bravest and best, the residents of Great Brunswick Street and Brunswick Place have arranged for a novena of Masses for the late President Arthur Griffith to be said in the Abbey, Lough Rea, Co. Galway, and a novena of Masses for the late General Michael Collins, to be said in the Church of St Teresa's, Clarendon Street, and four masses to be said in the Church of St Andrew's Westland Row, for the officers and men of the National Army who have bravely died that Ireland may live.[58]

Mass was their only means, their only ceremony, of consolation. And so it continued: consolation, duty, obligation. With Griffith and Collins observance was publicised. First-anniversary masses were advertised and well attended. Throughout Dublin city, throughout the country, Derry, Athlone, Wexford, Cork, Belfast, Sligo, Kenmare, Killarney, Mayo, Donegal and Limerick, even in London and Sussex, heads bowed and prayed.[59] The Pro-Cathedral welcomed the capital to requiem mass.[60] Ministers, dignitaries and foreign consuls led the crowds who made their way to Marlborough Street and 'knelt on the steps and the street outside', to the mass that officially marked the first anniversary and

---

[53] Hart, *The IRA and its enemies*, p. 207; Lyons, *Ireland since the famine*, p. 382.

[54] *Young Ireland*, 9 Sept. 1922; *The People*, 26 Aug. 1922.

[55] DT s2967, Civil war press cuttings, *II*, 26 Aug. 1922.

[56] *Ibid*. In Dublin the cessation of all work apart from essential services was ordered, while in other parts of the country business was to be suspended between the hours of 11.00 and 12.00.

[57] One local newspaper contained resolutions from the following bodies: Cumann na Saoirse, Wexford Corporation, Enniscorthy Urban Council, the *Ard Craobh* of Sinn Féin, the Irish National Foresters and the National Teachers. *The People*, 26 Aug. 1922.

[58] *Young Ireland*, 16 Sept. 1922.

[59] These are merely some of the many places where mass was dedicated to the two men. *An t-Óglách*, 1, 13 (new series), (11 Aug. 1923), p. 9; *FJ*, 14 Aug. 1923; *IT*, 14 Aug. 1923; *II*, 14 Aug. 1923; *CE*, 14 Aug. 1923; *II*, 13 and 23 Aug. 1923; *CE*, 22 Aug. 1923; *FJ*, 25 Aug. 1923; *United Irishman*, 1 Sept. 1923.

[60] *II*, 14 Aug. 1923.

the unveiling of the Cenotaph.[61] As the years passed, as the pilgrims returned to the Cenotaph, they retraced these steps to Marlborough Street. The government always paid its respects; mass always began the return to Leinster Lawn.[62] Naturally future years did not share the first anniversary's enthusiasm. Castlebar, Wexford, Tralee, Dublin – 1924 saw fewer observances.[63] The task fell to family and government, to the IRAO whose mass in Dublin made its own mutinous point.[64] Decline was gradual and understandable. Griffith's Dublin and Collins' Cork remained vigilant; family lovingly persevered. Party took the place of government in 1932; with Fianna Fáil power the state-orchestrated praying predictably stopped.[65] But Cumann na nGaedheal remained devout; Fine Gael still prays each August for the repose of these men's souls.[66] Indeed opposition encouraged prayer; urgency returned and Blueshirtism went to mass in August 1933 and 1934. Of course there was always the encouragement of 'satisfactory' church door collections. Collins anniversary masses could be lucrative and Cumann na nGaedheal naturally made the most of them.[67] Yet in spite of the heavy collection boxes there was never the same urgency again. The Blueshirts preferred to march than to pray: it was enough that one journalist commented on a mass with the surprised 'there was no disturbance . . . of any kind'.[68] But when Blueshirtism waned, the stalwarts remained. The families continued and continue to pray. The Association of the Old Dublin Brigade paid its respects until it was incorporated into the 1916–21 Club in the 1980s. Made up of men from both sides of the conflict like its ecumenical predecessor, Cumann 1916, the association has had a mass said each year for Griffith and Collins since 1927.[69] In 1968 it even persuaded Eamon de Valera to attend. Encouraged by Seán Lemass's 1966 attendance at a mass for all the dead of the civil war,[70] de Valera prayed. It was difficult for a President to counsel peace in Northern Ireland when he could not even bend a knee to pray for an old adversary. Or maybe in his eighty-sixth year it was just his time to make peace. He had, after all, ended his bitter feud with Cosgrave, welcoming the

---

[61] Christopher Hassall, *Edward Marsh, patron of the arts* (London, 1959), p. 489.

[62] Although mass was not always celebrated on the same day as the Cenotaph ceremony, it remained an integral part of the annual ritual.

[63] *CE*, 22 Aug. 1924; *FJ*, 12, 13 and 21–3 Aug. 1924; *Realt a Deiscirt*, 23 Aug. 1924; *Cork Weekly Examiner*, 16 Aug. 1924; *IT*, 13 and 23 Aug. 1924. These are merely some of the more widely publicised masses.

[64] *FJ*, 21 Aug. 1924.

[65] The Fianna Fáil paper, the *Irish Press* happily reported on the masses, however. *Irish Press*, 19 and 22 Aug. 1932.

[66] Letter from Patrick O'Meara, Policy and Research Officer, Fine Gael, 8 July 1998.

[67] Collections for Cumann na nGaedheal funds were taken at all Cork city churches. *CE*, 21 Aug. 1933; *IT*, 21 Aug. 1933.

[68] *IT*, 14 Aug. 1933.   [69] Piaras Béaslaí MSS, NLI, MS 33,946(1–20).

[70] Mass was held at Dublin Castle as part of the 1916 celebrations. *Michael Collins memorial foundation supplement*, 20 Aug. 1966, NLI, ILB 05p8.

man he only spoke to on the floor of the Dáil to Áras an Uachtaráin to meet the papal nuncio and to come afterwards for 'a private chat'.[71] For whatever reason, it still made headlines; another end to civil war politics, another 'grand gesture to [mark] the end of an unhappy era',[72] another scoop to enliven a tired and useful caption.[73] And there were more headlines in June 1973: de Valera attended again fifty years after the end of the civil war.[74] The masses continue, regardless of the congregation, regardless of the headlines. In 1956 prayer even included a Protestant service, ecumenically 'in memory of those who gave their lives in the struggle for Irish independence'.[75] But the occasional ecumenism aside, mass remains the beginning and often the end of ritual.

For the more anonymous casualties, mass was the most important ritual. Granted, the army was a willing supplicant. The men of Wexford and Baldonnel and Clonmel paraded and prayed;[76] the army turned the feast of All Souls into a day of mourning for deceased officers and men;[77] it spent £121 on a year of requiem masses.[78] The captains, the colonel-commandants, the brigadier generals; their masses made the pages of An t-Óglách; troops joined relatives, swelling paragraphs and congregations in polished formation.[79] But though it was 'pleasing to note that the memory of our humbler heroes is not neglected by their old comrades', that pleasure passed with time.[80] The Brigadier Ruanes, the Captain Walshes, the Brigadier General Rings, soon went undocumented like all the rest.[81] With new concerns, and especially after the mutiny, An t-Óglách chose to overlook them. Increasingly awkward and no longer newsworthy, the burden of ceremony fell to the families of the dead. With or without the army, with or without the Blueshirts, there was always mass. At eight o'clock on a Tuesday morning in Kenmare seventy-five years later there was still mass.[82]

---

[71] Coogan, De Valera: long fellow, long shadow, p. 684; Longford and O'Neill, Eamon de Valera, p. 456; T. Ryle Dwyer, Eamon de Valera: the man and the myths (Dublin, 1991), p. 192.

[72] Nenagh Guardian, 20 July 1968.   [73] Clonmel Nationalist, 20 July 1968; IT, 23 June 1969.

[74] Irish Press, 11 June 1973, Department of Foreign Affairs, Washington Embassy 1966–70, p8/5 General.

[75] Invitation to service in St Werburgh's Church, Dublin, 24 Apr. 1956, Ernest Blythe MSS, UCDA, p24/1719.

[76] FJ, 2 Aug. 1923 and 11 Aug. 1924; CE, 13 Aug. 1923; An t-Óglách, 1, 18 (new series), (17 Nov. 1923), p. 9.

[77] An t-Óglách, 2, 21 (22 Nov. 1924), p. 14.

[78] DF s0004/0097/24, Payment for requiem masses celebrated for deceased members of the national army, 31 Mar. 1924.

[79] An t-Óglách, 1, 11 (new series), (14 July 1923), p. 9; ibid., 1, 13 (new series), (11 Aug. 1923), p. 9; ibid., 1, 15 (new series), (6 Oct. 1923), pp. 10, 18; ibid., 1, 16 (new series), (20 Oct. 1923), p. 12; ibid., 2, 12 (new series), (19 July 1924), p. 3.

[80] Ibid., 1, 14 (new series), (1 Sept. 1923), p. 2.

[81] Ibid., 1, 11 (new series), (14 July 1923), p. 9; ibid., 1, 16 (new series), (20 Oct. 1923), p. 12; Iris an Ghárda, 1, 31 (24 Sept. 1923), p. 3.

[82] Mass was said for brothers General Tom and Captain John O'Connor Scarteen, killed in their home in 1922. Sunday Independent, 14 Sept. 1997.

Yet mass was generally the beginning, the start of a pageant that replayed bereavement again and again. Instinct seemed to revert to the most familiar ritual, and year after year, in small numbers or in throngs, these men and women retraced their funereal steps and stood at the foot of a grave.[83] That civil war had brought them to such mourning made mourning the most appropriate ritual. 'We knew there was nothing left, that everything was gone';[84] ceremony could be triumphant but ceremony was always a type of sadness. Although the dead of other struggles were commemorated in a similar fashion, Tone celebrated at Bodenstown, 1916's dead worshipped at Arbour Hill, there was never the same sense of regret, never the sense that death and ceremony were so plainly intended to divide. At civil war graves it was a solemn return, a return to the death of 1916's type of hope, a return to the incessant persistence of this regret.

Granted, there were different types of returning. The family that returned alone came for different reasons from the marching platoons, from the political parties, from the processions of posturing O'Duffys. There was a difference between Mrs Griffith and her two children coming quietly to lay a wreath year after year and the 800 soldiers, the 300 Gárdaí, the 200 DMP men who marched from Cenotaph to grave with their heads held high and their buttons polished.[85] Theirs was a '*Bothar Buadha*' or 'Road to Victory' parade, with well-phrased speeches, with the best buglers and bands, with obedience and discipline and military strength[86] (see figure 1). Every footfall proclaimed triumph, because it was 1923 and triumph still had to be proclaimed. Ita Griffith just left a heart-shaped wreath that said 'To Daddy'.[87] Wherever soldiers marched, however much they may have grieved and sympathised individually, they bespoke power and authority; they were a state-sanctioned presence, a marching, clanging, bugling seal of approval. Law and right and power were on the side of these dead men; law and right and power because de Valera was quick to take the soldiers away. With Fianna Fáil in government the army stopped going to the graves, to the Cenotaph, to Béalnabláth. With inter-party government they returned; marching pawns in some childish symbolic game, made to look ridiculous by their supposed parliamentary betters. March 1957 brought a Fianna Fáil administration and the Minister for Defence refused the Old Dublin Brigade the military guard of honour which the six combined years of inter-party government had led it to expect at its annual visit to Griffith's and Collins' graves. Instead it offered them the use of twelve rifles, even though the army command objected to firing parties at commemorations, together with two

[83] Owens, 'Nationalist monuments in Ireland, c. 1870–1914', p. 114.

[84] Joe Dolan, one of Collins' pall-bearers quoted in Forester, *Michael Collins*, p. 345.

[85] *II*, 21–5 Aug. 1923; *FJ*, 23–5 Aug. 1923; *An t-Óglách*, 1, 14 (new series), (1 Sept. 1923), p. 13; *Iris an Ghárda*, 1, 26 (20 Aug. 1923), p. 2; 1, 28 (3 Sept. 1923), p. 3; 1, 29 (10 Sept. 1923), pp. 3–5.

[86] *An t-Óglách*, 1, 14, (new series), (1 Sept. 1923), pp. 12–13.   [87] *FJ*, 14 Aug. 1923.

buglers and a drummer on condition they attended in civilian attire.[88] Naturally
the Old Dublin Brigade regarded this as 'an insult to our organisation and to
the memory of two great Irishmen, one of whom was Commander-in-Chief
of the National Army'. Naturally they had no desire to have men at the grave
'disguised as civilians'.[89] The army stayed away just as the government had
conspired and desired. The new rules were to be strictly enforced. Mass could
be heard in military chapels for Griffith and Collins but Fianna Fáil would no
longer concede the public imprimatur of the state.[90]

Foolishly, Fianna Fáil insulted indiscriminately. At least 'people of every
party and view' took part in the Old Dublin Brigade's pilgrimage to Glasnevin.[91]
The same could not be said of other pilgrims. The IRAO, in the mutinous enthusiasm of 1924, prayed and paraded to the graves in Glasnevin. A 'thronged'
church, 'impressive scenes' – they served a purpose; they were a show of
strength.[92] The dead legitimised: a memoriam notice called them Collins'
'comrades in the fight for freedom'[93], Griffith's son lent some sort of vicarious approval.[94] The dead were on the side of the IRAO; commemoration made
mutiny more honourable than a struggle for position and pensions. And Cumann
na nGaedheal knew it. The party promptly took up the strain in this symbolic tug
of war. 'Several hundred' party members met at Glasnevin; wreaths staked their
claim to the graves, to the men in them, to their legacy, and the well-chosen
chaplain of the disciplined army forces obediently led the day's praying.[95]
One hundred duteous guards loyally followed suit. That it was in the hands of
Cumann na nGaedheal 'to enable the general public to lay wreaths and otherwise pay tribute at the graves', said it all.[96] Nineteen twenty-four was a year
for doing the party's bidding.

But this assumes too much; it assumes that politics or obedience were the
only reasons for ritual. Grief was not only a family's prerogative. The soldiers
may have righteously marched in their 'Road to Victory' parade, but the fresh
wreaths left daily on the graves of Griffith and Collins for 1923's ten designated
days of commemoration bespoke a less publicised and perhaps a more honest

[88] F. M. Clarke, Rúnaí Cúnta, Department of Defence to Piaras Béaslaí, 2 Aug. 1957, Piaras Béaslaí MSS, NLI, MS 33,946(9).
[89] Piaras Béaslaí to F. M. Clarke, 8 Aug. 1957, *ibid.*; *II*, 16 Aug. 1957.   [90] *II*, 16 Aug. 1957.
[91] Association of the Old Dublin Brigade to Peadar Mac Mathghamhna, Rúnaí, Department of Defence, 24 July 1957, Piaras Béaslaí MSS, NLI, MS 33,946(9). The association was founded as a non-political group for pre-Truce members of the IRA. It endeavoured to foster the unity of pre-Treaty days.
[92] *FJ*, 21 and 23 Aug. 1924; *Realt a Deiscirt*, 30 Aug. 1924; *CE*, 18 Aug. 1924.
[93] *FJ*, 22 Aug. 1924.
[94] Nevin Griffith attended representing his mother. The Griffith family attended most of the commemorative masses.
[95] *FJ*, 19 Aug. 1924; *IT*, 19 Aug. 1924; *II*, 19 Aug. 1924.
[96] Minutes of the Griffith–Collins Anniversary Committee meeting, 11 July 1924, Richard Mulcahy MSS, UCDA, p7/b/330.

grief.[97] Joseph McKelvey had no reason to lie when he wrote from Mountjoy prison in November 1922 that 'the Free Staters here are terribly cut up about Mick – they seem absolutely lost'.[98] Nor does politics necessarily have to belie sincerity. Years of strict mass attendance had to count for something more than the annual inclusion of one's name among the newspaper lists of prominent attenders. In many cases the politicians mourned the loss of friends and did so as they would any other lost companion. Ceremony had political potential; they would be fools not to realise or capitalise. Had Collins himself not suggested the emotive value of showing funerals of Free State soldiers in Irish cinemas?[99] But these politicians also remembered the loss of him: on hearing of his death Kevin O'Higgins, 'unable to speak, cried with the painful, terrible intensity of a man unaccustomed to the refuge of tears'.[100] Indeed, seven years after Collins' and Griffith's death, Hugh Kennedy still mourned: 'The Dead march in Beethoven's Symphony *Eroica*, released floods of memory of murdered leaders and tramps to Glasnevin and that sense of despair for irreparable loss which has swept over me in these years of sullied freedom. Why that mood so grippingly today?'[101] The families of the dead men never had to ask such questions; they needed no symphonies to be swept along by these 'floods of memory'. The daily or weekly visits to the graves of Griffith and Collins went unnoted; the newspapers had only understandable space for the 'touching' anniversary scenes that would somehow school a nation in the etiquette of mourning. The families were described, but more effectively they were photographed: the Griffith family in prayer, a brother praying at an open coffin, a brother and a sister kneeling at the grave of Michael Collins.[102] In the first years their pain was public, writ large like some sort of allegory of the nation's loss. A widow and two fatherless children, a boy photographed with his father's companions standing pathetically where his father should still have been: these were the human faces of the loss of a 'great man'.[103] When Nevin Griffith was later called to the bar, the newspapers wished him every success; the boy had succeeded without his father; the allegory had a happy ending after all.[104]

However, the families were not alone. Those who had made 'a constant and daily pilgrimage' to Glasnevin in the days after Griffith's and Collins' death,[105] the woman who pushed through Dublin's mourning crowds to cry

[97] *An t-Óglách*, 1, 14 (new series), (1 Sept. 1923), p. 12.
[98] Letter from Joseph McKelvey (possibly to Ernie O'Malley), 28 Nov. 1922, Richard Mulcahy MSS, UCDA, P7/B/88.
[99] DT s595, Propaganda: suggestions by Michael Collins, July 1922, memo to Desmond FitzGerald, 12 July 1922.
[100] De Vere White, *Kevin O'Higgins*, p. 103; Simone Tery, 'As others see us III – Ireland honours the memory of Kevin O'Higgins', *Irish Statesman*, 11, 6 (13 Oct. 1928), p. 109.
[101] Hugh Kennedy diary, 9 Feb. 1929, Hugh Kennedy MSS, UCDA, P4/41.
[102] *II*, 23 Aug. 1924; *CE*, 15 Aug. 1923; *CE*, 6 Sept. 1922.   [103] *II*, 23 Aug. 1924.
[104] *United Ireland*, 13 July 1935.   [105] Hassall, *Edward Marsh*, p. 489.

out 'Why did you leave us?'[106], they returned in the years that followed. Anonymously they came and went, leaving flowers, wreaths, prayers, whatever they could afford. They came 'inspired with a pilgrim's motive'[107], nameless admirers, forgotten but for the stray utterance of a newspaper that felt touched by elderly men 'with tears in their voices', by the overheard 'Arthur, you're not forgotten.'[108] Of course there were more prominent pilgrims. Lady Lavery, who had excelled her ordinarily theatrical self at Collins' funeral by repeatedly flinging her pearl rosary beads on the grave, naturally made a dramatic return. Tempered by a husband's practicality that knew grief could not save her pearls from being pilfered, she charged a soldier with the task of placing them securely there.[109] When the grave was deserted and the flowers gone, her husband painted her the scene.[110] Returning for the first anniversary with another selection of 'magnificent rosary beads',[111] she added prayers and flowers to the scrapbooks and mortuary cards, to the shamrock she took from Béalnabláth, to the poems she wrote, to the private grief that adds fuel to the fire of biography's fascination. But she was different. Because she grieved with a flamboyant enthusiasm that was worthy of a tawdry melodrama, she stood apart. She broke the unwritten stoical rules. In grief there was supposed to be reserve. Kitty Kiernan, a silent figure, left her single white lily on Collins' coffin and disappeared;[112] Mrs Griffith merely returned to Glasnevin year after year with sombre resolve. Grief was a silent unwritten thing; it was spoken in prayers, performed in these pilgrim walks to hallowed graves. Grief craved ceremony because there was nothing else; relatives prayed and went to mass, they brought wreaths, they visited graves. Ceremony was traditional; it did what was supposed to be done. Ceremony said what hardened fighting men often could not bring themselves to say.

And it was the same throughout the country, the same for those who died known or unknown. Notoriety just brought newspapers and bigger crowds. But that the dead were mourned was not dependent on newspaper coverage. Understandably, the newspapers favoured the Seán Haleses and the Brigadier-General Rings. Men kept pictures of Hales in their homes; comrades spoke lovingly of this 'truly great man' who fired blanks at an enemy he had no wish to fight.[113]

---

[106] Quoted in Forester, *Michael Collins*, p. 344.

[107] James Barry, *Glasnevin cemetery: a short history of the famous Catholic necropolis* (Dublin, 1932), p. 20.

[108] *FJ*, 14 Aug. 1923. 'Micheál – Thank you, C.' written on a small card currently adorns the grave of Michael Collins (7 Aug. 2000).

[109] McCoole, *Hazel*, p. 100.   [110] *Ibid*.   [111] *II*, 15 Aug. 1923.

[112] Although she reportedly took to 'swooning and behaving in a most dramatic way' on the day of Collins' removal to the Pro-Cathedral, this incident took place in the privacy of St Vincent's hospital. Kathleen Galvin quoted in Mulcahy, *Richard Mulcahy*, p. 117.

[113] John L. O'Sullivan quoted in Kenneth Griffith and Timothy E. O'Grady, *Curious journey: an oral history of Ireland's unfinished revolution* (London, 1982), pp. 289–90.

That he had been shot down in cold blood only added an emotive last verse to a life immortalised in song by the very Black and Tans.[114] Without question ceremony wended its way to his Innishannon grave.[115]

An t-Óglách, the army journal, was more obliging to the more anonymous, particularly in 1923, but even its obligation never fell below the rank of captain. It reported anniversaries on a regular basis, telling of 'striking military displays', 'fitting solemnity' and 'impressive' ceremonies.[116] It reported primarily to a captive military audience, stressing marches and formations, guns and volleys and guards of honour. It recounted this with all the feeling of a tedious report on routine manoeuvres. Yet its function was to impress military men, to laud their bearing and efficiency in a still tenuous 1923, to impress that a soldier's life was a valued thing of honour. 'Civilian' activity at these sprightly military affairs was another, secondary matter; an aside that *An t-Óglách* toyed with to demonstrate a public allegiance and an army's popularity. 'There was a big attendance of military and laity', 'there was a large assembly of civilians, amongst whom were many relatives of the deceased': these are typical of the rare insights, insights that implied that volume was all that mattered.[117] A few relatives around the paltry grave of a mere private were not going to impress anyone; they were not worth the ink. The case of the O'Connor Scarteen brothers was an exception. Although as a captain and a brigadier general, the brothers would have their marching escort, their military bands, their paragraph in *An t-Óglách* anyway, it was the 'one thousand civilians' that spilled out onto Kenmare's streets that seemed to surprise the soldierly scribe. 'That their memories were revered by the people as well as their comrades in the National Army was evidenced by the vast concourse of civilians who took part in the commemoration ceremony.'[118] Granted, this was republican Kerry, but these two young men, one twenty, the other twenty-five, were shot dead in their own home on the main street of Kenmare. The man who led the attack had been Tom O'Connor Scarteen's best friend. It is the 'as well as' that gives this *An t-Óglách* reporter away: the surprise that 'civilians', particularly Kerry civilians, cared at all. The soldier thought only of soldiering; the people of Kenmare instead remembered two young brothers who were part of them long before talk of killing and civil war.

---

[114] 'Who killed John Hales?' was penned by soldiers of the Essex Regiment in Bandon during the war of Independence. Hart, *The IRA*, p. 187. Hales' escapades are also immortalised in the song 'There is a bridge at Bandon'.

[115] As part of General Seán MacEoin's trip to Béalnabláth as Minister for Defence in August 1954, he laid a wreath at the Seán Hales monument in Bandon. *II*, 23 Aug. 1954.

[116] *An t-Óglách*, 1, 11 (new series), (14 July 1923), p. 9; *ibid*., 1, 15 (new series), (6 Oct. 1923), pp. 10, 18.

[117] *Ibid*., 1, 13 (new series), (11 Aug. 1923), p. 9; *ibid*., 1, 11 (new series), (14 July 1923), p. 9.

[118] *Ibid*., 1, 15 (new series), (6 Oct. 1923), p. 10.

Scene at the graveside on the occasion of the Anniversary of the late Brigadier General Joe Ring. In the background are Major General Hogan, G.O.C., Claremorris Command, and Chief Superintendent McCarthy, Commandant, Depot.

Figure 7 Ceremony at the grave of Brigadier General Ring, *Iris an Ghárda*, 24 September 1923 (courtesy of the Gárda Representative Association).

And all over the county of Kerry,
Wherever those heroes had been;
The rosary rang out from the people,
For the sons of O'Connor Scarteen.[119]

The same was true of Brigadier General Joe Ring when the first anniversary of his death was covered with effusive detail by the comparatively prosaic *Iris an Ghárda*. There, there could not be enough of grief: no shutters were raised, no blinds pulled; it was a day of mourning. Women in their eighties who never left their homes made their way to mass to pray for him; the children even gathered along the route, their 'little faces showed that even they understood and realised the tragedy'.[120] From the photographed scene, the heads bowed, the solemn faces, it could be believed that this grave would 'be a place of pilgrimage', that 'when the history of our country comes to be written the name of Brigadier General Ring will hold a foremost place amongst the great and the glorious'[121] (see figure 7). The next year *Iris an Ghárda* made no mention of him. Now he is a short entry in a *Who's who*, not mentioned in the latest account of the civil war in Connacht, a curiosity at most for

[119] From 'The sons of O'Connor Scarteen', quoted in the *Sunday Independent*, 14 Sept. 1997.
[120] *Iris an Ghárda*, 1, 31 (24 Sept. 1923), pp. 2–4.
[121] *Ibid.*, 1, 31 (24 Sept. 1923), pp. 2, 4; *United Irishman*, 22 Sept. 1923.

a few local historians.[122] He may 'have joined the martyr band of Ireland's sons with Pearse, McDonagh [sic], Connolly', but that was 1923 when the Free State was desperate to have even the most tenuous membership of that particular republican club.[123] It was left to those with heads bowed beneath the photographed brims, to the woman he was to marry whose photographed face indicted death more than any graveside speech, and to the people of Westport who mourned him.[124] If the grave was a place of pilgrimage, after 1923 the Free State no longer needed this martyr's intercession.

Regardless of the state's needs, remembrance continued. The unknown privates and sergeants were prayed for, their graves visited, wreaths laid. But there was duty in death, a duty that leaves no way of knowing how deeply a family grieved or how much the dead were missed. Having a mass said, tending a grave; it had to be done. If it was not there would be talk, eyebrows raised, criticism of the neglected grave, anger at those who took exception to what was expected. The right thing had to be done but it also had to be seen to be done. The ritual of mourning, even at its most private, still had to be a public thing. But whatever the motivation, families still mourned the men who were not illustrious enough for An t-Óglách's or any other newspaper's attention. The evidence is scant, granted, but there is proof enough. That the government periodically considered the neglect of the army plot in terms 'of the feelings of relatives of the deceased soldiers' implied nothing if not the constant presence of grieving families and friends.[125] However, there is proof more tangible than this. Despite the yearly ceremonies at Leinster Lawn, the constant masses, Maud Griffith inserted a memoriam notice in the newspaper each year. It said the same thing every time: 'All loving thoughts to Arthur, whose great heart broke 12th August 1922.'[126] It was Maud Griffith's own message to her husband.[127] This was private grief expressed in a most public fashion. But it was democratic. Or at least as democratic as cost would allow. For the same price, for the same column inch, president or private could be remembered. To Witoszek, these notices attest to 'the dead living their public afterlife in the columns of the dailies'; they represent 'the Other-world which is an immanent part of contemporary Irish reality'.[128] This may be true, but the point is not as ethereal as she may think.

---

[122] Padraic O'Farrell, *Who's who in the Irish war of independence and civil war 1916–1923* (Dublin, 1997), p. 191; Nollaig Ó Gadhra, *Civil war in Connacht* (Cork, 1999).

[123] *Iris an Ghárda*, 1, 31 (24 Sept. 1923), p. 3.   [124] *Ibid.*, p. 7.

[125] Department of Finance memo, May 1931, DF s004/0013/24, Proposed acquisition of burial plot for deceased members of the national army.

[126] *IT*, 12 Aug. 1925; *Good Counsel Magazine* (Autumn 1966), Richard Mulcahy MSS, UCDA, P7/D/76.

[127] In the same fashion the men of the Four Courts Garrison inserted the same message each year to Rory O'Connor, Liam Mellows, Dick Barrett and Joe McKelvey in the *Irish Press*; see, for example, *Irish Press*, 8 Dec. 1932.

[128] Witoszek, 'Ireland', p. 213.

The following notice appeared in a local Wexford newspaper in 1925:

> In memory of our patriot dead:
> With martyr's blood they paid the price,
> And gloried in the sacrifice.
> We'll keep enshrined their memory
> Who fought and died to Ireland free.
> From the parents, brothers and sisters of Vol.
> Patk. C. Behan, Martinstown, Curragh.[129]

The Behans clearly missed their son and brother; they grieved for him, otherwise they would not have bothered. But most of all the Behans were proud. They were tired of the republican pamphlets that promised that their son's 'grave will be surrounded forever with dishonour'.[130] They were tired and they were proud, and perhaps they even protested too much. This soldier son was no mercenary, no traitor. He was a 'patriot' and a 'martyr' and maybe the words themselves made some sort of sense of his lost young life. The same words haunted a Miss M. Duggan's poem to Seamus Dwyer in 1927:

> Patriot facing deadly fire;
> For the people's right a martyr,
> Ireland blesses Seamus Dwyer.[131]

Denis Galvin too had spent his life for 'Erin's sake'.[132] Dying for Ireland maybe made it easier to understand; after all their government had said so: 'THESE ARE THE MEN WHO ARE DYING FOR IRELAND ... they are your own kith and kin. Give them your full support.'[133] And there were too many republican songs to damn them,[134] too many IRA men who revelled in labelling them 'the Drunkard, the Traitor, the wife deserter, the wife beater, the Tramp, the tinker and the brute'.[135] The memoriam notices were different; they were pride and memory and most of all a type of redemption.

And the soldiers had to be redeemed. While towns 'greeted the triumphant Free State soldiers with cheers and congratulations',[136] while one woman 'shook hands with each of us and said how proud she was to be able to cook a meal for Irish soldiers in Irish uniforms',[137] while 'the ordinary decent people

---

[129] *The People*, 12 Sept. 1925. Behan had been killed in Oct. 1922.

[130] 'Free State soldiers', Republican pamphlet, NLI, ILB 300p4, item 73.

[131] *The Freeman*, 24 Dec. 1927.

[132] 'In Memoriam, General Denis Galvin' by Vol. Seán Morrison, *An t-Óglách*, 2, 8 (24 May 1924), p. 12.

[133] 'Saorstát na hÉireann', Free State pamphlet, NLI, ILB 300p3, item 96 (emphasis from original).

[134] For example 'The National Army' quoted in Hart, *The IRA*, p. 149.

[135] Intelligence Officer, Cork No. 4 Brigade, to Intelligence Officer, 1st Southern Division, 8 Sept. 1922, Irish Military Archives, A/0991/4 (capitalisation from original).

[136] Mac Suain, *County Wexford's Civil War*, p. 48.

[137] Pinkman, *In the legion*, p. 161.

whom we met in the country were proud of us and supported us',[138] that popularity soon perished in the face of 'indiscipline and heavy drinking'.[139] The soldiers who lived in many ways damned those who had died. The acts of cruelty were simply more memorable than liberated towns and the eaten dinners soon forgotten. 'No better and often worse behaved than their predecessors'[140] with a predilection 'for taking the law into their own hands' and 'doing you in',[141] the soldiers had taken war in Ireland to a new and particularly grotesque level. Even Michael Collins wrote that 'we have no Army; we have only an armed mob'.[142] The horrors of too many Ballyseedys and the efficiency of republican propaganda, especially Dorothy Macardle's regularly republished *Tragedies of Kerry*, made it difficult to perceive the soldiers as anything more.[143] 'An armed mob' they would remain. *An t-Óglách* spoke of a stand-off at the Clashmealcon Caves as a 'Dramatic story of heroic deeds on the wild Kerry Coast'.[144] More were inclined to believe Macardle's account, with its pictures of grieving mothers. That even the usually unyielding Kevin O'Higgins was moved to criticise maybe says it all.[145] Granted, this was guerrilla warfare; comrades were being killed by faceless men who seemed to fade into the landscape, by former friends whose enmity was all the bitterer because of the disappointment of that once-valued regard. But now the soldiers represented a state; now they wore a uniform. They were supposed to be a force of law and order and law and order does not tie men to trap mines in Ballyseedy Wood. Although the entire Free State army was not made up of men determined to bomb and bludgeon a people into submission, the men of the Dublin Brigade cast a long shadow over the reputations of their comrades in arms. Pat Butler's recent documentary on Ballyseedy Wood cast it further still.[146] A swift end to the violence may have been desired, but nothing had prepared the people for the torture and murder of unarmed men. That the 'demands for the most hard-line measures came not from the military leadership but from their counterparts in the civilian government',[147] that politicians 'drunk with this sudden greatness their one idea is to revel in human blood',[148] meant little, may be nothing. The soldiers did

---

138 *Ibid.*
139 Michael Hopkinson, 'Review of *1922: the birth of Irish democracy* by Tom Garvin', *Irish Historical Studies*, 30, 120 (Nov. 1997), pp. 628–9.
140 Regan, *The Irish*, p. 103.
141 David L. Robinson to George Gavan Duffy, 10 Oct. 1922, Desmond FitzGerald MSS, UCDA, P80/338.
142 Ernest Blythe MSS, UCDA, P24/1783.   143 Macardle, *Tragedies of Kerry*.
144 *An t-Óglách*, 1, 9 (new series), (16 June 1923), pp. 3–5.
145 O'Higgins unleashed a strong attack on standards in the army in early 1923. Hopkinson, 'Review', p. 629.
146 *Ballyseedy*, written by Pat Butler, screened by RTÉ 1, 8 Mar. 1998.
147 Regan, *The Irish*, p. 106.
148 Peter Magennis, superior general of the Calced Carmelites, quoted in Keogh, *The Vatican, the bishops and Irish politics*, p. 97.

the dirty work; it was easier to remember them for that than the gallant giving of an honourable life.

Remembering that was the task of family and friends, of those who still came when the marching bands had gone. In some ways it is foolish to expect otherwise. While men like Colonel Commandant Tom Kehoe had funds established in their honour,[149] while the wounded soldiers could count on the proceeds of regular army balls and concerts,[150] remembrance had more fickle fancies when it came to the dead rank and file. Richard Mulcahy remembered Desmond FitzGerald, a man who would later hold the Defence portfolio, 'coming in from mass with the bodies of Kerrymen lying around, almost holding his nose'.[151] FitzGerald was a thwarted writer, a failed philosopher; soldiers meant nothing to him. They were menial men who simply did his menial tasks. Unlike Collins, who privately wrote of 'the splendid men we have lost on our side ... there is no one feels it more than I do',[152] there were others, like FitzGerald, who felt nothing at all. 'They [O'Higgins, Hogan and FitzGerald] had a superior feeling with regard to the whole of us [the army]';[153] they had a country to run and decisions to make. They had no time to waste on soldiers, fighters, 'Trucileers'; on men who had swapped unemployment for army uniforms, on men who were paid to do what they were told. In fairness the FitzGeralds and the Hogans had no real reason to regard the army with any special affection. And of course the army mutiny did nothing to commend the soldiers' immortal souls. Like the leaders of the army and the mutiny, the dead 'were victims of the fear of the power attained by the army during the civil war and of the government's anti-military spirit that had developed as a reaction to the horrors, the excesses and the very fact of the civil war'.[154] The once part-time revolutionaries were now gentlemen in government. Praying and parading for one's presidential peers was part of the flattering etiquette of statesmanship. Standing unnoticed at the unmown

---

[149] The Keogh Memorial Fund (many used this version of the spelling of his name) was a short-lived and strictly army-orientated affair. All donations, totalling £1,570 3s. 3d., were from fellow soldiers. The fund closed on 31 Dec. 1923. An t-Óglách, 1, 19 (new series), (1 Dec. 1923) – 1, 21 (new series), (29 Dec. 1923). A similar fund was inaugurated for the benefit of Seán MacCaoilte's family. Although open to the public, it elicited £5 and £10 donations from more prosperous and prominent Cumann na nGaedhealers. The money was spent on the education of MacCaoilte's three sons. Young Ireland, 2 Dec. 1922; 9 Dec. 1922.

[150] The Wounded Soldiers' Fund or The Wounded Soldiers' Comfort Fund began its appeals in mid-1922. Irish People, 2, War Special (23 July 1922); An t-Óglách, 1, 2 (new series), (10 Mar. 1923), p. 2; Invitation to an army concert, 10 May 1925, Richard Mulcahy MSS, UCDA, P7/C/90.

[151] The 'Kerrymen' in this instance are the nine soldiers killed in Kerry in early Aug. 1922. Granted, Mulcahy may not be the most unbiased commentator on Desmond FitzGerald. Transcript of a conversation between Mulcahy and General Michael Costello, 25 Mar. 1967, Richard Mulcahy MSS, UCDA, P7/D/3. Regan, The Irish, p. 91.

[152] Letter 234, Michael Collins to Kitty Kiernan, 4 Aug. 1922, in Ó Broin, In great haste, p. 212.

[153] Transcript of a conversation between Mulcahy and General Michael Costello, 25 Mar. 1967, Richard Mulcahy MSS, UCDA, P7/D/3. Regan, The Irish, p. 91.

[154] Maryann Gialanella Valiulis, 'The "army mutiny" of 1924 and the assertion of civilian authority in independent Ireland', Irish Historical Studies, 23, 92 (Nov. 1983), p. 364.

army plot was not. The mutineers had burned a portrait of Michael Collins in the middle of Collins' Barracks in 1924.[155] It was their protest against a government that had turned its back on his republican ideals. In many ways they had burnt the wrong painting. Collins would always matter to the government; his name was convenient if nothing else. They were the unimportant ones. The time for soldiers and soldiering had past.

Obedient to a government's indifference, the soldiers faded away, their duty done, gratitude softly spoken. The soldier dead retreated to the far-flung towns that bore them, their anniversaries remembered only 'at their native place', mass only in 'their native parish'.[156] The people who had watched them die had no wish to recall them; the towns they were once said to have liberated wanted normality more than martyrs.[157] In 1919 and 1921 they were rebels; they died as heroes. In a Free State uniform they were paid soldiers and fighting was just work, no longer the rebel's vocation. For many this was their first time to fight, for more it was the only job the Great War and the British army had left them able to do. What there was of regard was reserved for those with a War of Independence past, for those who had made their republican reputations firing bullets at Black and Tans. There was a respectability about the Brigadier General Rings, an undisputed republican pedigree that lent itself well to the disappointment of dominion status. Ring was still 'the bravest of the brave', Seán Hales 'a gallant patriot'.[158] Colonel Commandant Tom Kehoe was still remembered at a graveside commemoration as 'a model of patriotism' in 1953.[159] The 'young people' still came, even if it was 'out of curiosity to watch' the same ceremony ten years later.[160] They were part of a past that was never questioned, a past that inferred nationalism and republicanism merely by association. Because 'there would be no going back to revolutionary unity', no 'hope of a rapprochement'; because the executions had made sure of that,[161] that very 'revolutionary unity' became a weapon of war. The past was just something else to hold against men who had once shared it.

Dead soldiers were called to arms only if their deaths embellished the Free State with 1916's seal of approval. Nineteen twenty-two read of the death of Volunteer Doyle. The report cared little about how or why he died. More important was that he 'was the son of a gallant Irishman who died fighting in 1916'; that 'father and son have given up their lives to ensure that the Irish people shall be masters in their own land, and Ireland will ever cherish and honour their memory'.[162] That Volunteer Doyle's memory was cherished for as long as it took the ink of the *Free State War Special* to dry was another

---

[155] Duggan, *A history of the Irish army*, p. 129.
[156] *An t-Óglách*, 1, 16 (new series), (20 Oct. 1923), p. 12; 1, 13 (new series), (11 Aug. 1923), p. 9.
[157] Garvin, *1922*, p. 103.   [158] *Iris an Ghárda*, 1, 31 (24 Sept. 1923), p. 5; *II*, 20 Jan. 1930.
[159] *Wicklow People*, 19 Sept. 1953; Piaras Béaslaí MSS, NLI, MS 33,937(3).
[160] Letter from Seán Caffrey to Richard Mulcahy, Jan. 1963, Mulcahy MSS, UCDA, P7/C/2(15).
[161] Regan, *The Irish*, p. 113.   [162] *Free State War Special*, 13 July 1922.

matter. His death was an opportunity; the fashion of his father's demise was of the utmost convenience. They were cherished because they provided the chance to say that 'the men who fought for Ireland in 1916 and who survived the fight are – 90 per cent of them – with the men who are fighting for Ireland today against the mad and wicked attempt to override the National will and throw away the glorious fruits of the sacrifices of the past'.[163] The soldiers may well have been following 'in the footsteps of Pearse, Tom Clarke and Seán MacDermott',[164] they may have believed the wartime articles that drew 'the real comparison' between 1916 and 1922,[165] but what really mattered was that enough of the people seemed convinced. *Poblacht na hÉireann*, meanwhile, continued to raise the awkward point: 'As if the heroes of 1916 died for the fiction of a Free State.'[166] It was difficult to claim Pearse's legacy when Free State soldiers raided his mother's home, when his mother damned you in the Dáil, when his family refused to stand beside you at his grave.[167] The Free State marches that honoured 1916, the early pilgrimages to Bodenstown, even the routine army marches that went out of their way to Wolfe Tone's grave to symbolise a 'show of strength':[168] the harder it tried, the more ridiculous the Free State government seemed. And the Minister for Defence, Peter Hughes, only made it worse: 'were Wolfe Tone alive today he would be proud to carry a rifle in the Free State Army'.[169] At Terence MacSwiney's grave his sister Annie smashed the army wreath as soon as the officer laid it down.[170] The 'hayroes of the Four Courts' were said to have nothing in common with the men of 1916 simply because none of them had the foresight to die.[171] By its own deranged logic the Free State, at worst, had taken the place of General Maxwell. At best, it was a very poor shot.

Nineteen sixteen and all that followed was slipping from them; the posters of 'Irregulars' hiding under beds when it mattered in 1921, the occasional newspaper articles recalling increasingly distant fighting days meant nothing. Awkward as it may have been to claim Pearse's legacy while engaged in the repression of Irishmen who called themselves republicans, it became nigh impossible when the last vestiges of the Free State's republican illusions were thwarted by the Boundary Commission. By 1935 this legacy was lost to them. Cosgrave and his party refused to attend the unveiling of a statue to Cuchulainn in the GPO dedicated to the men of 1916. Retreating apparently with Emmet's good grace,

---

[163] *Ibid.*   [164] *Poblacht na hÉireann War News*, 167, 26 Feb. 1923.

[165] '1916–1922 The real comparison', *The Free State-An Saorstát*, 29 July 1922; NLI, LOp117, item 51.

[166] *Poblacht na hÉireann War News*, 167, 26 Feb. 1923.

[167] 'Holy places in Ireland have been violated by vandals', NLI, ILB 300p13, item 38.

[168] Pinkman, *In the legion*, p. 113.

[169] Letter from Liam [Billy Judge] to Liam Corrigan, 24 June 1925, quoted in Fitzpatrick, 'Commemoration in the Irish Free State', pp. 188–9.

[170] *IT*, 27 Oct. 1927.   [171] *The Free State, Special War Number*, 5 July 1922.

Cosgrave admonished de Valera: the time was not yet right for 'an adequate commemoration';[172] 'it is not possible to hide these national limitations today or to cover them with a veil lifted from the bronze statue of Cuchulainn'.[173] According to his own terms his ten years in government had achieved nothing; the state he had forged was not worthy of Pearse or of 1916. Neither, by a lesser implication, were de Valera's three years of power. But there was a hollow ring to Cosgrave's greener shade of rhetoric, a desperation, a resentment that de Valera had appropriated 1916 as his own. That the new leader had chosen the pre-emptive nineteenth rather than the predicted twentieth anniversary for his lavish display was not lost on his opponents. Cosgrave had fought in the GPO; he was there even if some alleged that he spent most of his time praying. The legacy was conceivably as much his and his party's as it was Fianna Fáil's or Sinn Féin's. Yet on his lips, after civil war, Cosgrave's lament for 1916 now seemed a rather tuneless air. For de Valera, for his followers, for all their sheer bloody-minded opposition in 1922, it would always be an easier song to sing. But 1916 was nationalism's only idiom; Cosgrave had no choice but to persevere. The price of perseverance was the soldier dead of an unwanted civil war.

And so they were forgotten. Government continued, conscience clear, free of what was now only a family's despair. But 1932 changed all that. Defeat left plenty of time for recollection. Granted, there had been intimations. The elections of 1927 and 1932 suggested the outpourings that defeat could induce: the posters taunting de Valera with 'the dead who died for an "empty formula"', the constant references to shadows and gunmen.[174] There was no mention of the Cumann na nGaedheal TDs who, dispirited by the party's economic policies, had defected to Fianna Fáil. It was easier to play the emotive civil war card, to script 'Fighting points for Cumann na nGaedheal speakers and workers' that dwelt on 'Fianna Fáil's opposition to the Treaty', its 'responsibility for the dumped arms', its 'antagonism to the army', and its 'record during 1922 and 1923'.[175] But like the posters that found Fianna Fáil cavorting with the few reds who huddled under the bed, it was all a ploy, a dramatic appeal – just clever posters in a difficult election campaign. The dead were a means to a victorious end: their death an indictment of the dangers of Fianna Fáil power. The precedent had been set by the electioneering of 1923, by Cosgrave's 'many a grave in many a graveyard…many a home with a vacant chair'.[176] With destitute pensioners penalised a shilling, the dead were more congenial company at the hustings.[177] 'The Free State party survived, up to the last election, by

[172] Bhreathnach-Lynch, 'Commemorating the hero', p. 158.   [173] *Irish Press*, 18 Apr. 1935.
[174] O'Kennedy-Brindley Ltd., *Making history – the story of a remarkable campaign* (Dublin, 1927); Cumann na nGaedheal posters, Richard Mulcahy MSS, UCDA, P7/A/172.
[175] Hugh Kennedy MSS, UCDA, P4/1398.   [176] *CE*, 20 Aug. 1923.
[177] In 1924 the old age pension had been cut by a shilling a week for certain categories.

virtue of the calamities of the Civil War! These it recited to the electors *ad nauseam*. The whole case of Cumann na nGaedheal consisted in a recapitulation of the burnings, shootings and depredations of Republicans in 1922–1923.'[178] Although the *Catholic Bulletin* was never one to understate its case when it came to berating Cumann na nGaedheal, the party's sudden timely concern for the dead it had begrudged the cost of burying was sanctimonious to say the least. There was also something derisory in blaming de Valera for the deaths of Rory O'Connor and Liam Mellows as one election poster seemed to imply.[179] That Patrick Hogan even went so far as to claim that the disciples of Liam Mellows, the man who had been executed by a Cumann na nGaedheal government, could now be counted among the members of Cumann na nGaedheal proved just how desperate the party had become.[180]

Defeat only made matters worse. In August 1932, irked by the absent soldiers at Leinster Lawn, the Army Comrades' Association, later to become known as the Blueshirts, drafted its confused constitution. It was decided that the association 'must link itself to the heroes of the past by celebrating in every district the memory of local Fenians and of pre-Truce IRA men and National Army men who died in action'.[181] This was one of twelve objectives; it vied for prominence with the ambition of corporatism and resisting the illusory threat of communism. There is no consensus on Blueshirtism. One school sees a genuinely fascist leadership; another sees only the indelible mark of civil war.[182] Mike Cronin concludes that it was all of these things and none.[183] Though somewhat dated, F. S. L. Lyons makes the most eloquent assessment of this most inarticulate movement: 'The coshes and knuckledusters, the programmes and slogans, the posturing of O'Duffy, the gang warfare between the Blueshirts and the IRA, these were not the death-agonies of a Gaelic Weimar, they were rather the last convulsive spasm of the fever that had been wasting the land since 1922 – they were the nemesis of Civil War.'[184] The dead should have been proof of that. As Cronin goes on to question their fascist credentials, he speaks of 'the

[178] *Catholic Bulletin*, 17, 9 (Sept. 1927), p. 925. J. J. Walsh, former Postmaster General in the Cumann na nGaedheal government, concurred: 'we had endless and nauseating abuse of de Valera': Walsh, *Recollections of a rebel*, p. 72. Even after ten months of Fianna Fáil government, the *Bulletin* still considered that 'it would seem as if hell itself were raked for inspiration that would suggest ways and means of getting rid of President de Valera's party'. *Catholic Bulletin*, 23, 2 (Feb. 1933), p. 96.
[179] The particular poster 'The dead who died for Ireland' featured Erin showing de Valera the graves of the dead of the Irish Civil War, the implication being that he was responsible for the deaths of the men buried before him: Rory O'Connor, Liam Mellows, Cathal Brugha, Erskine Childers, Seán Hales, Emmet McGarry and Seamus Dwyer.
[180] *CE*, 12 Sept. 1927.
[181] Draft suggestions ACA constitution, Aug. 1932, Richard Mulcahy MSS, UCDA, P7C/44(1).
[182] Paul Bew, Ellen Hazelkorn and Henry Patterson, *The dynamics of Irish politics* (London, 1989); Maurice Manning, *The Blueshirts* (Dublin, 1970); Lyons, *Ireland*.
[183] Mike Cronin, *The Blueshirts and Irish politics* (Dublin, 1997).
[184] Lyons, *Ireland*, p. 536.

absence of the "hero" in the pantheon of Blueshirt man'.[185] But he, like every other historian of the Blueshirts, has taken no notice of the movement's attitude to the dead: a curious oversight given its constitution, given that a march to the Cenotaph was to be O'Duffy's momentous 'March on Rome'.

In August 1933 the *United Irishman* rallied the dead to its mast with the greatest indignation:

In every county in Ireland the grass grows green over lonely graves where rest brave hearts who answered the call to defend their Motherland against Mr de Valera's private army. In crowded city and quiet village there are homes that are desolate and hearts that are broken and mothers that grew old with waiting for their soldier sons who never came back. They died, these gallant Irish boys of 1922 to save their country from *your* private army, Mr de Valera; do not their ghosts arise to haunt you now?[186]

For the life of the Blueshirts, in their many and varied institutional guises, uniformed men and women marched to these 'lonely graves'. Collison and McCurtain were honoured at Moneygall; Matt Pender at Ferns; Thomas and John O'Connor Scarteen at Kenmare; the Lehans at Lahinch; Healy and Higgins at Foxford; John Kileen at Ballinrobe; Paddy Kennedy at Ballinure; Galvin and O'Connell at Dromtariffe.[187] In groups of fifty and three hundred, in flocks of 2,000 they descended on the soldiers' graves. Anything the IRA could do, the Blueshirts could do better. There were 'great parades',[188] 'magnificent indications of the spirit of the Blueshirts of the Division';[189] there were belligerent shows of strength that were often offensive in staunchly republican areas. Granted, there were rosaries muttered in Irish over the graves; granted, some locals joined in the pageant and listened to how an Irish soldier 'had been killed by a . . . follower of Mr de Valera',[190] but the songs and the shirts and the salutes had come to say something else. The orations, generally given by the touring luminaries Commandant Cronin or Captain Quish, usually culminated in an arrogant promise that 'the Blueshirts are . . . determined to redeem the Irish people and secure for them that ultimate freedom which will bring peace, happiness and prosperity'.[191] 'It was up to the Blueshirts to perfect their organisation and to ensure that victory would not be long delayed.'[192] There was no mention of the relatives of these dead soldiers, no consideration that the dead themselves might have detested these very men and women who came dressed in fascist costume, spouting a reactionary creed that longed for the days of 1926 when there was no such thing as Fianna Fáil. They came 'cycling, in lorries, and in

---

[185] Cronin, *The Blueshirts*, p. 39.
[186] *United Irishman*, 12 Aug. 1933 (emphasis from original).
[187] *United Irishman*, 8 July 1933; 22 July 1933. *United Ireland*, 16 Sept. 1933; 29 Sept. 1934; 6 Oct. 1934; 17 Nov. 1934; 5 Oct. 1935; 20 Oct. 1934; 14 Apr. 1934; 23 Mar. 1935; 6 Apr. 1935; 28 Mar. 1936.
[188] *United Irishman*, 8 July 1933.   [189] *United Ireland*, 28 Mar. 1936.
[190] *Ibid.*, 29 Sept. 1934.   [191] *Ibid.*   [192] *Ibid.*, 28 Mar. 1936.

every possible type of conveyance';[193] the dead were an excuse. They came to show, as the notice for the Dromtariffe ceremony clearly stated, 'that the "Boys in Blue" have the upperhand'.[194] That was all that mattered. Standing knee deep in unmown grass in Enniscorthy showed just how much they cared about the memory of Commandant Peter Doyle.[195] Commemoration was convenient, a chance to upset all the Fianna Fáil 'Kildangan "77" Cumainn' around the country, to irritate the men and women who were driven to beg the Department of Justice to ban such marches because 'there was nine Republican solgers [sic] belonging to the town executed in the year of 1922 and on that account alone the proposed demonstration is likely to lead to serious disturbance...it is only in the interists of pease [sic] we write'.[196] It was in the same 'interests of peace' that the Gárda commissioner advised the Department of Justice to refuse the application for the use of six rifles at the 1934 commemoration of Denis Galvin. Days before, four men had been brought before the military tribunal for firing shots over a grave. Denis Galvin was merely a means to test the mettle of the Attorney General. For eleven years no one had come near the grave of this man who had blown himself up in the civil war. In the commissioner's own words the commemoration was 'not bona fide';[197] in less diplomatic terms it was nothing but 'a "try-on"'.[198] The messages to 'boys' units' that 'if a local volunteer was killed the juvenile Blueshirts might be taken to visit his grave and might even, with the consent of his relatives, agree to take care of it' were all very well. That 'care...should be taken to instil no bitterness amongst the boys' was almost admirable. That 'with all this should go a certain amount of instruction in present day politics' was nearer the truth.[199] Like the forbidden dances and the provocative marches, the dead were enslaved to these 'present day politics'.

The civil war dead may have been truly missed by these be-shirted men and women. It would be callous and unfair to say otherwise. But much as the many ex-soldiers who swelled Blueshirt ranks may have grieved for their erstwhile comrades, the sincerity of the movement's regard for the dead can only be questioned by the manner in which it waned and by the way it disposed itself so deliberately to the whims of a largely social and economic battle with Fianna Fáil. For every republican celebrated, a bigger brasher march would wend its way to a Free State soldier's grave. For every Blueshirt dance disrupted

[193] *Ibid.*   [194] *Ibid.*, 23 Mar. 1935.   [195] *Ibid.*, 14 Oct. 1933.
[196] Mary Byrne, secretary of the Kildangan 77 Cumann, Monasterevin, to the Minister for Justice, 20 Feb. 1934, DJ H306/31, Resolutions protesting against the Army Comrades' Association and National Guard.
[197] Gárda commissioner to the Secretary, Department of Justice, n.d., DJ Jus8/351, Application for use of rifles at commemoration ceremonies.
[198] Memo by S. A. Roche, n.d., *ibid.*
[199] *United Ireland*, 8 Dec. 1934. Boys' units were also encouraged to take the name of a 'national leader or hero of the past', *ibid.*, 17 Mar. 1934.

tonight, a republican one would be ruined tomorrow. Commemoration, like violence, was just another means to compete. But because civil war was the most demonstrative reference point, the dead of that war were an integral part of this battle for hearts and minds. Kitted out in the familiar colours of civil war, the squabbles of the 1930s fell naturally, almost viscerally, into place: republicans killed these men in 1922; they had the audacity to defeat us ten years later. Denis Galvin meant nothing to Eoin O'Duffy in 1932. For all the speeches and salutes, for all the talk of nemesis, he meant nothing in 1936.

The Denis Galvins may not have measured up to Mike Cronin's definition of 'the hero', but neither, it seems, did the former President and Commander-in-Chief. Clutching the two firmly to its blueshirted bosom, the movement was not quite as choosy as Mike Cronin. Indeed, verging on the indiscriminate, it aimed long-windedly 'to foster patriotic idealism by honouring the memory of all the heroic dead who worked and suffered for Ireland and especially of Griffith, Collins and O'Higgins under whose leadership a free and independent state controlled by the common people of Ireland was, for the first time in history, brought into being'.[200] On one level this devotion was as harmless as the army officers who pitched and putted under the auspices of the Collins Golfing Society.[201] There were dances and picnics – innocent days out for the Blueshirts who had formed themselves into the Collins Social and Dance Club.[202] There were even Blueshirt 'socials' held at Sam's Cross, with dancing and singing at the very hallowed 'birthplace of Michael Collins'.[203] But when singing turned to saluting, when Collins social clubs became 'Collins Units', everything changed.[204] The 'Blue Blouse' who raised her right arm in the 'victory salute' as she passed the Cenotaph was just a little more demonstrative than her dancing and golfing companions.[205] Collins had been conscripted by the Blueshirts, consumed by them, uniformed in blue and sent out to spread the good corporatist news. Flag days exchanged his memory for money: his picture on a lapel pin, he was sold in the streets as a 'propagandist task', as 'a demonstration of the strength and efficiency of the ACA'.[206] Collins himself was irrelevant. Like Desmond FitzGerald who would take his place 'in a great fellowship with those architects of the new Irish State, Griffith and Collins and O'Higgins',[207] the Blueshirt leaders, men like Commandant Cronin who

[200] Suggested constitution, Army Comrades Association, n.d., Richard Mulcahy MSS, UCDA, P7C/44(11).
[201] Captain Tomás Ó hUiginn, honorary secretary of the Collins Golfing Society to Richard Mulcahy, 24 Feb. 1931, Richard Mulcahy MSS, UCDA, P7B/87(64–5).
[202] *United Irishman*, 8 July 1933.   [203] *United Ireland*, 9 June 1934.
[204] *Ibid.*, 17 Mar. 1934.   [205] *Ibid.*, 23 Dec. 1933.
[206] 'Flags for collection', *United Irishman*, 8 Apr. 1933; 29 Apr. 1933.
[207] Richard Hayes, 'Desmond FitzGerald, some memories of him', n.d., Desmond FitzGerald MSS, UCDA, P80/1450. Similar utterances were made about several other leading Cumann na nGaedheal figures; for example, Seán MacEoin's 'name will go down in history inextricably

now apparently 'had single handed won the Civil War', joined O'Duffy in allying themselves closely to Michael Collins, knowing now what he would have thought, doing what Collins would have done.[208] That they suffered badly by the comparison did not seem to concern them.

Less was said about O'Higgins, the high profile of his family in the movement said enough; that he inspired hatred more than heroics said even more. With Griffith, on the other hand, there was little real concern. Granted, nods were made in his direction each and every August; lip service was a cheap and worthy endeavour, but Griffith was lost to them or rather lost by them. That Fianna Fáil had happily taken up his protectionist mantle, that many of its TDs now called themselves 'sincere adherents of Griffith', did little for the former President's cause.[209] But then the President's cause had been ailing for some time. By 1926 Kevin O'Higgins had already dismissed his protectionism as the ravings of an otherwise eminent man: 'the propagandist political writings of any man cannot be accepted simply as revealed truth'.[210] Cumann na nGaedheal clearly had no time for his inconvenient verities. Yet political ploy or not, it is a good measure of the legacy of civil war bitterness that a Fianna Fáil government could go out of its way to emulate the enemy of 1922. That a former Cumann na nGaedheal minister could commend Fianna Fáil's adherence to Griffith's policies,[211] that he, along with several other Cumann na nGaedheal TDs and a member of the party's standing committee, defected to Fianna Fáil suggests even more.[212] In December 1931 de Valera even went as far as to speak in Collins' own words: 'The object of founding Fianna Fáil was to try to enable the forces that had been divided by the Treaty to come back and begin over again the forward march and to bring back those who believed the Treaty was a stepping stone to freedom.'[213] The more Cumann na nGaedheal maligned them as the troublemakers of 1922, the more Fianna Fáil 'pledged to wipe out "past dissensions"': 'those who have most opposed us are Irishmen like ourselves... we will need their help in building up the virile, prosperous Ireland of the

linked with Arthur Griffith and Michael Collins', quoted in Padraic O'Farrell, *The blacksmith of Ballinalee, Seán MacEoin* (Mullingar, 1993), p. 132.

[208] *The Blueshirt*, 24 Nov. 1934.

[209] D. F. Flynn declared himself so at a Fianna Fáil meeting in Cork, *Irish Press*, 11 Feb. 1932.

[210] Quoted in Seán Milroy, *The tariff commission and Saorstát economic policy* (Dublin, 1926), p. 40.

[211] Walsh, *Recollections*, p. 90.

[212] Rejecting Cumann na nGaedheal's economic policies and its treatment of its backbenchers, Hugo Flinn, T. P. Dowdall, Andrew O'Shaughnessy, J. J. Walsh and Professor O'Rahilly defected to Fianna Fáil. Fr Malachy Brennan resigned from the standing committee of Cumann na nGaedheal in 1927 and offered public support for Fianna Fáil at both the 1932 and 1933 elections. Richard Dunphy, *The making of Fianna Fáil power in Ireland 1923–1948* (Oxford, 1995), pp. 113–14.

[213] *Munster Express*, 11 Dec. 1931. Lemass also allegedly admitted that his economic policies were based on Collins' *The path to freedom*. Coogan, *Michael Collins*, p. 422.

future'.[214] In the Dáil, Seán Lemass presented himself and his party as veritable paragons of peaceful reason:

however we disagree as to the names we shall call ourselves or matters of that kind, we can at least work together in the things we have in common. If we want to get that co-operation and that sense of unity of effort we have got, even at the sacrifice of a little pride, to cut out everything that is likely to militate against it.[215]

That two days before he had admitted that Fianna Fáil was only 'a slightly constitutional party' seems to have slipped his mind.[216] The 'great bitterness' of civil war came and went at practicality's command.

In this respect none were more practical than the Blueshirts. It was all very well to take Griffith's *United Irishman* title; it had resonances beyond him to 1798. It was another matter to glorify him when fighting Fianna Fáil had become a squabble for tariffs and cattle, when he epitomised Fianna Fáil's more popular economic creed. But the Blueshirts were doing nothing new. To suggest otherwise would simply be foolish. Nurtured by the more belligerent wing of Cumann na nGaedheal, the shirted movement sang from the same party hymn sheet. That Cumann na nGaedheal had swapped its top hats for knuckledusters was indicative of a desperation; that some were uneasy in their new garb was clear from the inauspicious start of Fine Gael. But the gentlemen of government taught the so-called corner boys a thing or two. The dead were good in a fight and they had known that since 1922. Theories on the necessary 'soldierly spirit, with its patriotism and love of country, which impels a man to sacrifice himself for the good of his fellow countrymen, may be developed by ceremonial parades, on the occasion of national festivals, and on anniversaries of great events, such as the victories by which the nation asserted its rights' had served them well.[217] And Cumann na nGaelheal had learned from its mistakes. The dead had proved more amenable than these fickle 'anniversaries of great events'. Declaring the anniversary of the signing of the Treaty 'Independence Day' had not been a roaring success. 'Pressure of other business' interceded and it was not repeated after its lukewarm reception in 1924.[218] It would seem that 'Ireland's most notable day was notable mainly for its gloom'.[219] It was welcomed more enthusiastically by republicans; it was a yearly opportunity to rub a little more salt in the compromising wound.[220] The anniversary of the Truce was a little more agreeable. It still stood for a type of victory, for the type of hope of July 1921. It remains, with the anniversaries of the Easter Rising and the death of Michael Collins, as one of the special holidays

---

[214] Fianna Fáil statement quoted in Dunphy, *The making of Fianna Fáil power*, p. 128.
[215] *DE, official report*, XXII, col. 1799 (23 Mar. 1928).   [216] *Ibid.*, col. 1615 (21 Mar. 1928).
[217] *An t-Óglách*, 4, 28 (23 Dec. 1922), p. 1.   [218] DT s4178, Independence Day, 6 December.
[219] W. T. Cosgrave, quoted by Tom Garvin, 'A difficult birth', *IT*, 6 Dec. 1997.
[220] See, for example, *An Phoblacht*, 6 Nov. 1925; 8 Jan. 1926.

observed by the Irish army.[221] Some, however, could never be satisfied. To Tom Barry celebrating the Truce was an insult, an insult to the dead of the civil war, an insult to a troubled Northern Ireland which that Truce had apparently abandoned.[222] The anniversary is now linked with what is known as the National Day of Commemoration, the day of celebration of the dead of all wars.[223] That a speaker at the Kilmichael monument in 1998 could still make a call for a national day of commemoration 'to honour those who died for Irish freedom' is indicative of a persistent contempt for the dead of other 'mere wars'.[224] The definition of 'all who died for Ireland' clearly remains a contentious thing. Indeed the army was much more taken with the anniversaries of great events. Occupying Dublin Castle was recalled;[225] landing at Fenit was relived with martial glee.[226] Although ten men had been lost at Fenit, restaging the battle in Kerry's hostile and bloody lands seemed particularly thoughtless, even for the Dublin Guards.[227] Civil government was never quite as inconsiderate or adventurous. The dead were less contentious than the 'events' that few could be convinced to call 'great'. When the Dáil opened in 1922 the newspapers 'looked in vain for cheering crowds'.[228] The dead were simply more reliable; Leinster Lawn and Béalnabláth could always draw a crowd.

Standing in the rain at Leinster Lawn in August 1924 W. T. Cosgrave uttered the following words:

Twelve months ago we met here to offer to their memory a symbol of Ireland's reverence and sorrow, of Ireland's pride and gratitude. Today we return to recall our associations with them, to renew our faith in the work to which they put their hands and our determination to contribute to its completion . . . We, gathered here today to pay tribute to your memory, still vivid and fresh in our hearts, can garland your Cenotaph with the offerings of realisation of your hopes, honouring of your promises, unbroken progress of your work, steadfastness of your successors carried along by the impulse you gave to the National being.[229]

'Thousands of citizens' listened to him; 'large numbers formed avenues along the route' marched by 2,000 soldiers.[230]

---

[221] Leonard, *The culture of commemoration*, p. 17.   [222] *Western People*, 12 June 1971.
[223] Instituted in July 1985, the National Day of Commemoration is held in the Royal Hospital, Kilmainham. It is not recognised by the 1916–1921 Club.
[224] *IT*, 7 Dec. 1998.   [225] *An t-Óglách*, 4, 35 (10 Feb. 1923), p. 4.
[226] *Ibid.*, 1, 13 (new series), (11 Aug. 1923), p. 9; *ibid.*, 1, 15 (new series), (6 Oct. 1923), pp. 12–13; *ibid.*, 2, 14 (16 Aug. 1924), p. 7.
[227] As part of the ceremonies in 1924 the troops marched to the places where their comrades fell, carrying a banner with the names of the ten who died inscribed in Irish. *An t-Óglách*, 2, 14 (16 Aug. 1924), p. 7.
[228] *II*, 7 Dec. 1922; *Poblacht na hÉireann* (Scottish edn.), 23 Dec. 1922.
[229] W. T. Cosgrave's speech at the Cenotaph, 17 Aug. 1924, DT s5983/38. The speech was also quoted in full in each of the national newspapers and two Cork papers.
[230] *FJ*, 18 Aug. 1924; *CE*, 18 Aug. 1924.

Founders of the State! The State lives and grows:
Leaders of the people! The people are faithful:
Revivifers of the Gael! The pulse of the Gael throbs with life:
Great pair! Your work is doing – Rest in Peace.[231]

The people may have been 'faithful', they may indeed have come out in the rain to mourn. Maybe it was, as the newspapers declared, 'an inspiring tribute of the nation's abiding reverence and deep affection', maybe 'not one heart but was moved by the solemnity of this ceremony'.[232] But the newspapers failed to mention that the inter-provincial hurling and football finals of the Tailteann Games were to be played on the same afternoon, that the ceremony had been brought forward so as not to clash with the day's real attraction for many of the men, women and children who had come, buoyant with their teams from the four provinces, who lined the streets eager to see Dublin and its sights.[233] Commemoration was no rival for a football or a hurling match and commemoration gave in.[234] Two years after the deaths of Griffith and Collins the government could not afford to be naïve. The increased anti-Treatyite vote in the August 1923 election had taught it that. Neither could it risk the pictures of depleted crowds. 'The people are faithful', Cosgrave said so. There were mutineers to convince now as well as republicans.

And 'to convince' was what it was all about. On receipt of her ticket to what she called 'the Cenotaph show', Maud Griffith remarked that 'shows and stunts are all that is the thing now. When something is done to honour my husband alone, I'll help and take part, but I'm still waiting.'[235] 'Surely nothing is to take place there this year.'[236] She was never to attend the ceremony which the Department of Finance clinically called 'a Public Service'.[237] She sent her children though; she was keen that they were shown the same courtesies she thought were lavished on the Collins family. She had hated what she called Collins' 'mean and underhand way of working his own will behind Griffith's back',[238] and now she resented his relatives: 'When one thinks of a President's family and a soldier's very distant relations can be seen in every Dept. it makes one think how dreadful we were not country people.'[239] So year after year her

---

[231] W. T. Cosgrave's speech at the Cenotaph, 17 Aug. 1924, DT, s5983/38.

[232] *FJ*, 18 Aug. 1924; *II*, 18 Aug. 1924.

[233] Minutes of the second meeting of the Griffith–Collins Anniversary Commemoration Committee, 3 July 1924, Richard Mulcahy MSS, UCDA, P7/B/330.

[234] Originally planned for 3 p.m., the ceremony was brought forward to 12.30 p.m. so that it would not clash with the sporting fixtures. *Ibid.*

[235] Transcript of note from Maud Griffith, 10 Aug. 1924, Richard Mulcahy MSS, UCDA, P7/B/330.

[236] DT s3913, Griffith and Collins ownership and erection of memorials at graves, letter from Maud Griffith, 17 July 1924.

[237] Leydon to McElligott, 17 June 1926, DF s200/0027/24, Publicity department – Griffith–Collins commemoration 1924, formation of a committee: authority for expenditure.

[238] Maud Griffith to Piaras Béaslaí, n.d., Piaras Béaslaí MSS, NLI, MS 33,930(14).

[239] Maud Griffith to W. T. Cosgrave, n.d., DF f13/3/26, Griffith settlement – payment of annuity.

children went, to get what they were entitled to, almost out of spite. There they sat, alongside a handpicked selection of all who were considered great and good: a collection of politicians, foreign dignitaries, the judiciary, councillors, churchmen, educators, artists, writers, newspaper editors – an adequate assortment of the men and women who had managed to convince Desmond FitzGerald of their worth.[240] They were 'people in a position to emphasise the coming into the heritage of nationhood', whatever that means: people who had little in common with Griffith and even less with Collins[241], a 'representative attendance' that sounded impressive in the column inches the following day.[242] Ceremony was building an edifice of approval: a national pageant that reflected as much on the administration of the Free State as it did on the commemoration of these two men. Great nations orchestrate great pageants; that is why the rough wooden benches of 1923 were covered in expensive cloth,[243] why the graves were hastily tended,[244] why 'we can hardly raise any question on this expenditure of £260'.[245] That the Free State ministers objected to paying for the Cenotaph's wreath themselves put the memory of Collins and Griffith firmly in its paltry place.[246] But they had been no better the year before. For the unveiling on 13 August 1923 the five-guinea laurel wreath was to be paid for with 15 shillings from each minister: Ramsay & Son, the florists, were not paid until 4 October.[247] John Devoy, for all his Fenian renown, could make as many statements as he wanted about the 'fine, sturdy lot of men' of the national army,[248] Desmond FitzGerald could choose only the finest to bow their well-coiffeured heads at Leinster Lawn, but an article on the 'Plight of Ex-National Soldiers' printed next to a report on the ceremony put it all in perspective.[249] Convincing the nation that 'the State lives and grows', that 'the people are faithful' was all

---

[240] The guest list was compiled by a committee chaired by Desmond FitzGerald and including Senator Wyse-Power, General MacMahon, Seán Lester and Richard Mulcahy. Contributions were also made by General Eoin O'Duffy, Senator P. W. Kenny, Seamus Ó hAodha and F. T. Cremins. Richard Mulcahy MSS, UCDA, P7/B/330. The pattern of the first year was largely followed.

[241] The Governor General Timothy Healy was a habitual fixture at the ceremony despite the fact that Griffith had been firmly opposed to his appointment on the grounds that Healy had 'betrayed Parnell'. Gogarty, *As I was going down Sackville Street*, p. 97; Seán Ó Lúing, *Art Ó Gríofa* (Dublin, 1953), p. 399. Collins' draft constitution had omitted the office of Governor General altogether. Frank Callanan, *T. M. Healy* (Cork, 1996), p. 596.

[242] *CE*, 18 Aug. 1924; *FJ*, 18 Aug. 1924.

[243] Minutes of the first meeting of the Griffith–Collins Commemoration Committee, 27 June 1924, Richard Mulcahy MSS, UCDA, P7/B/330.

[244] Minutes of the second meeting of the Griffith–Collins Commemoration Committee, 3 July 1924, *ibid.*

[245] Patrick O'Kelly to T. S. C. Dagg, 15 Aug. 1924, DF s200/0027/24, Publicity department – Griffith–Collins commemoration 1924, formation of a committee: authority for expenditure.

[246] F. T. Cremins, Department of External Affairs to the Department of Finance, 30 Oct. 1924, *ibid.*

[247] DT s8358, Griffith–Collins commemoration 1923, receipt from Ramsay & Son, 4 Oct. 1923.

[248] *II*, 19 Aug. 1924.   [249] *Realt a Deiscirt*, 23 Aug. 1924.

very well, but the unemployed men who had to kill other Irishmen to defend a flawed dominion status was a reality that could not be covered over with a fancy cloth or upstaged by a gaggle of ambassadors or professors. That the Free State government carried on trying is possibly admirable in itself.

Cinematographers were there to capture the next year's attempts; newsreels brought the good news to those who were not lucky enough to have been numbered among the 50,000 which *An t-Óglách* extravagantly counted.[250] 'Many citizens' was the *Irish Times* more sedate estimate, a 'many' again 'swelled by excursionists from the provinces'.[251] Four thousand soldiers marched for the entertainment of tourist and dignitary alike; numbers doubled on 1924; numbers desperate to convince that mutiny was a thing of the past. Invoking the injunction of 'Holy Writ', Cosgrave had two things to say: firstly, 'The heroic soul of Collins rose supreme above disappointment and failure. Disappointment daunted him not – nor did failure deter him. Herein lay the secret of his greatness' and, secondly

to dwell in the slums when you might have lived in the light laughing places of the world; to go clad as the very poor are clad when purple and fine linen might have been yours; to eat dry bread, and not much of that, when you might have feasted full; to act thus and not for one year, not for ten, but for more than a generation – that is heroism of which few but God's Great are capable, and that was the heroism of Arthur Griffith.[252]

As Cosgrave spoke, the Boundary Commission was in the midst of its year-long deliberations. By February 1925 the government was already faced with the prospect of losing territory to Northern Ireland; by August 'disappointment' and 'failure' were inevitable. The government had fallen so very badly at Collins' first stepping stone. It was to set the 'boundary to the march of a nation'. It was being forced to recognise the reality of Northern Ireland, to concede that twenty-six counties would never become thirty-two. Amid the secrecy of those discussions there was something desperate, something ominous in this appeal to emulate the man it would betray most.

As for Griffith living heroically on 'dry bread', Maud Griffith, with what she termed her taxed 'little pittance', could have told them a thing or two about that.[253] That the government taxed her children's allowance put its hollow admiration of Griffith's self-denial firmly in its place. It was not that long since Patrick McGilligan's 'people may have to die in this country and die of starvation'.[254] It was no coincidence that in 1925 Griffith had taken on the persona of some saintly ascetic, happy to put his country before his personal

250 *An t-Óglách*, 3, 17 (22 Aug. 1925), p. 10.   251 *IT*, 17 Aug. 1925.
252 Department of Defence A12371, Collins–Griffith commemoration ceremony – text of speech, 1925.
253 Maud Griffith to Ernest Blythe, Feb. 1925, DF f13/3/26, Griffith settlement – payment of annuity.
254 Patrick McGilligan, *DE, official report*, XI, cols. 557–62 (30 Oct. 1924).

wealth. While this had always been true of Griffith, only now was it laudable, now when the workers and the labourers, the landless and the unemployed had begun to seek the fruits of this great independence. Standing in his morning suit, speaking to his well-fed hand-picked gathering on Leinster Lawn, Cosgrave was a poor advocate of poverty's temperance. And biased though *An Phoblacht* may have been, it made its point well:

But already many Free Staters know that they are far from the policy Griffith really preached in his poverty, and most of them did not trouble to attend the official tribute to his memory. According to the Press reports only seven of the eleven F. S. Ministers were present; only nine of the 105 F. S. Deputies and barely three of the whole F. S. Senate. Four thousand soldiers were there, but Griffith knew well what value is to be placed on the machine-made demonstrations of military sympathy.[255]

The same 'machine-made demonstrations of military sympathy' were oiled and polished for 1926. Four thousand soldiers again thrilled 'the thousands who thronged the line of the march',[256] making another well-made pro-Treatyite point. But the novelty had worn off and the point was no longer clear. The Commemoration Committee of previous years happily consigned its duties to the Office of Public Works; Desmond FitzGerald was tired of his new toy.[257] And so were the newspapers. That the next days gave several column inches to the unveiling of a monument in Wytschaete, to the supposedly embarrassing Great War dead, shows just how much the lure of the '*Bothar Buadha*' had faded.[258] Even the *Gárda Review* and *An t-Óglách*, which naturally spoke well of the men who marched, lacked their previous unquestioned acclaim.[259] Reference to the President's speech was terse; granted, the *Gárda Review* quoted it in full, but there was no comment, no praise, just the spoken words verbatim.[260] That Cosgrave's 'articulation was perfect' was the best they could do.[261] But given that the President had degenerated to the metaphorical depths of 'a man kneading the bread in a dark oven may suddenly remember the sun which ripened the grain out of which the bread is made ... we turn our minds to Griffith and Collins as we may to the sun which ripens the grain whereof our bread is made', reticence must have been a welcome retreat.[262] In many ways remembrance was

---

[255] *An Phoblacht*, 21 Aug. 1925.   [256] *IT*, 23 Aug. 1926.

[257] Letter from P. L. Banim, President's Office to Comdt O'Hegarty, Diarmuid O'Hegarty, and Seán Lester, 24 July 1926, Department of an Taoiseach s5098, Griffith–Collins commemoration, 1926.

[258] *IT*, 23 Aug. 1926. There was also detailed coverage of 'a pilgrimage to the battlefields' three days before the Cenotaph ceremony, *ibid.*, 19 Aug. 1926. The *Irish Independent* was the only paper to give the Cenotaph ceremony more attention: three columns to the Wytschaete ceremony's one. *II*, 23 Aug. 1926.

[259] *Gárda Review*, 1, 10 (Sept. 1926), pp. 693, 707; *An t-Óglách*, 5, 8 (28 Aug. 1926), pp. 10–11.

[260] *Gárda Review*, 1, 10 (Sept. 1926), p. 707.   [261] *Ibid.*, p. 693.

[262] DT s5983/38, Cosgrave's speech at the Griffith–Collins annual commemoration ceremony, 1926.

too awkward for anything else. Ireland 'has shaken off the death clothes'[263]; more appropriately, the government had 'shaken off' the beliefs of its dead. Standing at the foot of a monument to one who personified republicanism, to another who embodied economic self-sufficiency, when the government had balked at the first stepping stone, when the economics of Griffith were adopted to its shame by the newly founded Fianna Fáil, was nothing if not embarrassing. Ideologically these men were strangers to the free-trading Free State, to the 'imperialisms' of the O'Higginses. Imperial conferences were all very well, but words on a page meant little when the hope invested in the Boundary Commission had been dashed, when there was no territorial change, no immediate hope of advance, when there was a new party which promised to do what the government had seemingly lost the will to do. The Cenotaph had become an embarrassment, an annual reminder of the thwarted promise of two men, of the increasing failure to live up to them. It suggested that civil war, that bitterness had been pointless. There was nothing left to Cosgrave but his empty phrases and his asinine baking metaphors; anything more would have exposed too much. That *An Phoblacht* could mischievously write an article on the ceremony in praise of both Griffith and Collins may have been a cynical campaigning exercise, but there is a great deal to be said for its candour.[264] *An Phoblacht* possibly said what the other newspapers' increasingly muted coverage implied:

The commemoration last Sunday, of the deaths of Arthur Griffith and Michael Collins lacked the spontaneity which marks a people's veneration. The demonstration would have entirely failed if the F. S. Army and the Civic Guard were not present in their marshalled mourning. How both Griffith and Collins would have . . . sighed for one unordered heart-beat from the common people! Mr Cosgrave's oration was eloquent and empty. Obviously he dare not refer in any detail to the Griffith or Collins policy, the Free State Party being now too fundamentally divided as to what that policy was . . . The party whose head delivered the oration does not stand for the ideals of Collins or Griffith . . . There is no need to particularise what has happened [to] that ideal. Its ashes are under Mr Cosgrave's feet wherever he walks. Yet this man who deliberately abandoned his leaders' dearest ambitions now names those leaders as his inspiration. It is a piece of political humbug as threadbare as it is shockingly out of place.[265]

An Phoblacht was no stranger to political humbug; it knew the importance of its implications. Honouring the dead, even if they were 'their' dead, was not a thing to be taken lightly; there was value in the blasphemy, the disrespect. But as Cosgrave waxed lyrical about dark ovens and kneading dough, respect does not come too readily to mind.

---

[263] *Ibid.*
[264] 'At the Cenotaph: Griffith–Collins Anniversary, 1926', by Maghnus Ó Tuathail, *An Phoblacht*, 27 Aug. 1926.
[265] 'Events of the week', *ibid.*

Nineteen twenty-seven was different. Snatched back from the OPW, the ceremony was important again, important enough for Desmond FitzGerald to write the President's speech.[266] There would be no more 'meeting ostensibly to honour the dead...to preserve the sham of life in a government',[267] no more 'officers wearing patched and disreputable uniforms', smoking cigarettes, fraternising with the street traders.[268] There had been complaints: 'not infrequently were soldiers noticed looking at the spectators in whom they appeared to be more interested than in the Parade'.[269] Before they had marched for 'a forgotten sorrow. The faces were only formally sad.'[270] This year it would be different; this year's Leinster Lawn would be 'a rallying of the Free State establishment in the aftermath of O'Higgins' assassination'.[271] A type of fear had built the wooden edifice, and a type of fear brought the government back to Leinster Lawn with a vengeance in 1927. 'The ways of war' had not faded as Cosgrave had said in 1926;[272] the government needed another show of strength. Security had been taken for granted; this year the buttons would be polished, the soldiers keen, alert, a fighting force to be reckoned with. Murder had shaken the government's complacency. And cynical though it may seem, there was merit in martyrdom; the pension reduction could be put to one side, mistakes at least temporarily overlooked in the sympathy that any death inspires. Nineteen twenty-seven was more honest, more comfortable, because it was O'Higgins the ministers mourned, one closer to themselves, one who epitomised everything they had become, everything of Griffith and Collins they had betrayed. Without devaluing Timothy Healy's grief for his nephew, O'Higgins was not a prime candidate for martyrdom. Assassination elevated him to the heights of men who had died for the Free State: 'another of our nation's great ones' had given his life for it. It was worthy again. Divergence from the policies of Griffith and Collins made no difference now. It stood a government wronged yet again by the foul agents of extreme republicanism.

There was no harm in using the ceremony to thwart the advance of republicanism's more moderate shades; the second election of 1927 was proof of that. As genuine as their grief may have been for the former Vice-President, ritualised grief had its uses. Only four of the sentences which Desmond FitzGerald wrote for the President referred to Kevin O'Higgins. There was greater emphasis on how Griffith 'pursued with cheerful courage his self-appointed task' 'without

[266] Speech by Desmond FitzGerald for the Griffith–Collins memorial ceremony, 1927, Kathleen McKenna Napoli MSS, NLI MS 22,626.
[267] 'At the Cenotaph', *An Phoblacht*, 27 Aug. 1926.
[268] Department of Defence memo, 4 Aug. 1927, Department of Defence 2/12418, Griffith–Collins anniversary, 1927.
[269] *Ibid.*   [270] F. Scott Fitzgerald, *Tender is the night* (London, 1955), p. 252.
[271] *Weekly Irish Times*, 27 Aug. 1927; Callanan, *Healy*, p. 619.
[272] DT s5983/38, Cosgrave's speech at the Griffith–Collins annual commemoration ceremony, 1926.

money for a meal'; how 'we' have been faithful, despite 'trials and obstacles' to the work of Griffith and Collins.[273] Despite O'Higgins' sizeable funeral, he was never popular enough to forgo the old priorities. But there were too many Count Plunketts calling the ceremony 'a demonstration against the people',[274] too 'many of the men wore the silk hat and frock coat' to make bearing poverty with 'cheerful courage' anything more than the glibbest consolation.[275] 'Our best monument to their memory will be unceasing devoted effort to preserve the great trust they bequeathed: to build on the sound foundations they laid, to follow the noble plan they sketched.'[276] Unsettled by assassination and terrified by the electoral reality of Fianna Fáil, there was little left, just an old allegiance that seemed to protest too much.

By 1928 that was clear. The speeches stopped. It was better to say nothing at all than to pander to the increasingly incessant republican voice that mocked the government's departure from Griffithite policies whenever it could. Seán Lemass sent his regrets typed in green ink: he, like the other opposition deputies, would not attend.[277] Caught between the growing embarrassment of the comparisons and the determination to honour, ceremony became a silent imitation of the once proud display that went before. The new O'Higgins medallion appeared unannounced;[278] suggestions that without an oration 'the ceremony at the Cenotaph falls very flat' had no effect.[279] Enthusiasm had declined to the point where it was feared that the billiards, the chess and the golf competitions of the Tailteann Games might draw bigger crowds.[280] Nineteen twenty-seven had been the last hurrah; even the effusive *An t-Óglách*, the proud *Gárda Review* retreated from two pages to two wordless photographs.[281] After 1928 *An t-Óglách* never mentioned the ceremony again. Utterance instead became the preserve of the more partisan press, *The Freeman* and *The Star*: party papers, read by the loyal and the converted, precursors both of the Blueshirt press.[282] The first year of real opposition in the Dáil had taught the government something. A speech at the Cenotaph was now ammunition: words to be probed and examined and

[273] Speech by Desmond FitzGerald for the Griffith–Collins memorial ceremony 1927, Kathleen McKenna Napoli MSS, NLI, MS 22,626; *An t-Óglách*, 1, 1 (new series), (Oct. 1927), pp. 8–10; *Gárda Review*, 2, 11 (Oct. 1927), pp. 1080–1.
[274] *Kerry News*, 22 Aug. 1927.   [275] *IT*, 22 Aug. 1927.   [276] *The Freeman*, 27 Aug. 1927.
[277] DT s5706, Griffith–Collins–O'Higgins commemoration ceremony 1928, letter from F. Nic Dhomhnaill, private secretary to Seán Lemass to the President's Office, 15 Aug. 1928.
[278] DF s200/0006/28, Commemoration ceremony 1928 – addition of medallion portrait of the late Vice-President, Mr Kevin O'Higgins to Cenotaph.
[279] Department of Defence memo, 16 Aug. 1928, Department of Defence 2/16304, Griffith–Collins–O'Higgins anniversary 1928, *Bothar Buadha* parade.
[280] DT s5706, Griffith–Collins–O'Higgins commemoration ceremony 1928, letter from Paul Banim to Diarmuid O'Hegarty, 13 July 1928.
[281] *An t-Óglách*, 1, 4 (new series), (July–Sept. 1928), pp. 6, 7; *Gárda Review*, 3, 11 (Oct. 1928), pp. 1078, 1080, 1083; *ibid.*, 4, 11 (Oct. 1929), p. 1125; *ibid.*, 5, 10 (Sept. 1930), p. 964; *ibid.*, 5, 11 (Oct. 1930), p. 1101; *ibid.*, 6, 11 (Oct. 1931), p. 1191.
[282] *The Freeman*, 25 Aug. 1928; *The Star*, 17 and 24 Aug. 1929.

used at Fianna Fáil's convenience. Increasingly the ceremony became a matter of celebrating the foundation of the state rather than the men who died for it. The installation of the new Governor General, James McNeill, in February 1928, set what was to be the new stately civic tone. An eminent cast was pictured making its way across Leinster Lawn. There McNeill laid a wreath at the foot of the Cenotaph, sealing an ostensibly civil ceremony with an apparently courteous reference to the illustrious dead.[283] In truth, the dead had become part of the etiquette of power. By laying a wreath McNeill sought Collins' and Griffith's approval, their imprimatur, he allied himself to their cause, devoted himself to the state for which they died. Without another monument the Cenotaph to their deaths had become an edifice to the state's beginnings. As the dead became more inconvenient, celebrating the state was a welcome release. From 1929 army memos spoke of the march past the Cenotaph as 'closely connected with the establishment of the State'.[284] Complimentary letters even wrote in terms of the 'splendid demonstration of the State's forces', of 'the popularity of our magnificent little army'.[285] The dead seemed incidental.

Blythe officiated in 1929, silently laying a solitary wreath on behalf of 'Mhuintear na h-Éireann'.[286] As usual Mrs Griffith was invited, as usual she refused to go. This year, however, she replied a little more forcefully to her hosts: 'I want several tickets for this, they were not enclosed, so please forward. Some of my husband's friends might go . . . it is time to give up this show, I expected last year to be the end.'[287] Her well-chosen emphasis was pointed enough; the opinion of Griffith's closest friends was clear. She was tired of the façade, tired of the insincerity: 'it was maddening at the Cenotaph to see Mr Milroy stuck upon the platform'.[288] She had always felt that the ceremony never really honoured her husband, but now it had become a long drawn-out pretence. To her 'he has escaped them all, so called friends, bitter enemies'.[289] That his 'so called friends' had to receive the annual prompting – 'It is suggested that the Minister should attend' – proved her point.[290] *The Nation*, biased like *An Phoblacht*, could only convince her of what she knew already:

[283] *IT*, 2 Feb. 1928; DF s200/0003/28, Installation of Governor General – purchase of wreath for placing on Griffith–Collins Cenotaph; Ernest Blythe MSS, UCDA, P24/144; Hugh Kennedy MSS, UCDA, P4/1256.
[284] Major General Seán MacEoin to the Minister for Defence, 4 Apr. 1929, Department of Defence ceremonial box III, 2/19270, Wolfe Tone anniversary, Bodenstown, 1929.
[285] Copy of letter from P. J. Cahill to the *FJ*, 26 July 1928, Department of Defence 2/16304, Griffith–Collins–O'Higgins anniversary 1928, *Bothar Buadha* parade.
[286] *IT*, 19 Aug. 1929. Cosgrave was absent to one of his periodic 'illnesses'.
[287] Maud Griffith to the Department of the President, 9 Aug. 1929, DT s5906, Griffith–Collins–O'Higgins commemoration ceremony, 1929.
[288] Maud Griffith to Desmond FitzGerald, 5 Sept. 1929, Desmond FitzGerald MSS, UCDA, P80/512(1).
[289] Maud Griffith to Sr Angela Mulcahy, n.d., Richard Mulcahy MSS, UCDA, P7C/13.
[290] P. J. Banim to the private secretaries of all ministers, 16 Aug. 1929, DT s5906, Griffith–Collins–O'Higgins commemoration ceremony 1929.

Abandoning their leaders

The most striking thing about this ceremony at Leinster Lawn was the way Cumann na nGaedheal boycotted it. At election times we are never done hearing of those 'Fathers of the Free State'; but at heart the Free State party cares so little for them that on the one day a year that they are publicly honoured only five Cumann na nGaedheal deputies and one Cumann na nGaedheal Senator troubled to be present. Four ministers, including President Cosgrave, were absent. Of the judiciary only two high court judges and two district court justices put in an appearance. Nobody seemed to feel surprised at this. It is evidently widely understood that Mr Cosgrave and his Party are mentally about as far away from Griffith's teaching today as the Tories were in Griffith's day. It is hard to mourn for a man in whom one has ceased to believe.[291]

Cumann na nGaedheal's adversaries had more in common with the men the party honoured than the party did itself. Honour was no longer a weapon, it was an incrimination. Yet, caught between the embarrassing comparisons and the ignominy of giving up the great pageant of state, the ceremony limped on. The army files, the civil servants' reports were as efficient as ever; every last penny counted, every bugler and foot soldier well trained and carefully chosen.[292] But the enthusiasm had gone; the crowds had dwindled. That a routine address by Seán Lemass in 1931 received more attention than the Cenotaph ceremony from the haughtily pro-government *Irish Times* said it all.[293] In 1932 de Valera put Cumann na nGaedheal out of its misery; ceremony ended. Predictably the Army Comrades Association and the *United Irishman* quickly vented their spleen: 'the blind unceasing hatred which burns at this man's breast against all, whether living or dead, who opposed his attempt to strangle the new-born Irish State in 1922' had cradled this 'attempt to deprive the great dead of the annual tribute of respect from the State which their heroic sacrifices and splendid national services did so much to establish'.[294] There were even verses to remind the new President that 'jealousy thou art a shameful thing'.[295] What the *United Irishman* failed to mention was that the Cumann na nGaedheal government had been considering abandoning the ceremony since 1927. On 21 July 1927 the following note was sent to each cabinet minister: 'The President wishes to have the question of the Griffith–Collins Commemoration Ceremony discussed at the next meeting of the Cabinet with a view to deciding whether the Ceremony should take place this year.'[296] De Valera's departmental secretary had reviewed the files, the years of formal pageantry, and came to the following conclusion: 'Though there is no record of a formal decision to that effect I

---

[291] *The Nation*, 24 Aug. 1929.
[292] DF s200/0006/30, Griffith–Collins–O'Higgins commemoration ceremony, 1930; Department of Defence ceremonial box III, 2/23403, *Bothar Buadha* parade 1930; DF s200/7/31, Griffith–Collins–O'Higgins commemoration ceremony, 1931; DT s3115, Griffith–Collins–O'Higgins commemoration ceremony, 1931.
[293] *IT*, 17 Aug. 1931.   [294] *United Irishman*, 20 Aug. 1932.   [295] *Ibid.*, 27 Aug. 1932.
[296] DT s8362, Griffith–Collins–O'Higgins commemoration, 1932.

am aware that there was a general feeling in favour of the abandonment of the elaborate ceremonial and the reduction of the commemoration to a minimum consistent with respect to the dead.'[297] In effect de Valera did what the Cumann na nGaedheal government had lacked the courage to do for five years, what Maud Griffith had wanted since 1924.

Yet to say that with Fianna Fáil power ceremony ended is not correct. Admittedly 'official' ceremony ended; there were no more soldiers, no more dignitaries, no more marching bands. It was possibly foolish to expect a republican government to subscribe to a '*Bothar Buadha*' that celebrated its defeat in civil war, that enshrined a state it intended to dismantle. But there was no 'Cenotaph Ceremony Ban' as was writ large by the *United Irishman*. Thousands of people still witnessed a procession to the Cenotaph; thousands watched a wreath laid to the honour of the three dead men.[298] Organised by the Association of the Old Dublin Brigade IRA and held 'with the concurrence of the Oireachtas authorities', an illustrious procession made its way to the foot of the Cenotaph.[299] Former soldiers, members of the Army Comrades Association, walked with relatives and a former President: apathy gone in the heightened sensibilities of opposition.

> Strange that the State you founded
> Should even by seeming, spurn you,
> Humbly we lay these flowers
> That Ireland may know we mourn you[300]

was the only message on the wreath: pique more than heartfelt emotion or distress, an ache for the pomp and circumstance that was inherent in leadership and ceremony. A mass in every military barracks was dedicated to the memory of the three men; that never changed. It was just never public enough. Cumann na nGaedheal had grown used to government, had taken for granted the authority that could command an army to march. The Cenotaph was the party's symbol of power and victory; it ill behove the party leader to ask permission to visit it. Cumann na nGaedheal may have grown tired of it, even embarrassed by it, but now it symbolised the party's powerlessness. The impotence of opposition made ceremony important again; the shabby monument staked Cumann na nGaedheal's claim to the state. The dead were emotive, useful; 'de Valera won't let us honour our dead'. But de Valera was not the one who refused to pay for their graves.

The plans for 1933 were made early; the Blueshirts prepared.[301] Groups were to descend on Dublin in tens and twenties, in hundreds and thousands:

---

[297] Memorandum from the Secretary of the Department of the President, 2 Aug. 1932, DT s8362, Griffith–Collins–O'Higgins commemoration, 1932.
[298] *IT*, 22 Aug. 1932.   [299] DT 99/1/35 s5734E, Griffith–Collins Cenotaph – general file.
[300] *Irish Press*, 22 Aug. 1932.
[301] The first announcement was made in the *United Irishman*, 13 May 1933.

twenty from Portarlington, forty from Lahinch, forty-five from Ferns, fifty from Cashel, one hundred and fifty from Listowel, two hundred from South Meath, 'as many comrades as possible from Shanballymore', from Leitrim, from Bullaun, from Cork, from Tralee, Emly, Limerick, Clonmel, Nenagh, Birr, Waterford, Galway, Ballina, Westport, Sligo, Cavan.[302] The indignity of 1932 was not to be repeated. As many men and women as possible would be 'got into uniform'; there were warnings to 'Order Shirts in Time'.[303] For months commands circled the country, to 'consolidate co-operation on the part of all county units', to co-ordinate local marches with the march to the Cenotaph.[304] The Blueshirts spoke in terms of 'companies' and 'ranks', 'divisions' and 'units'[305]; their members were 'Volunteers' marching, receiving 'orders for the parade'.[306] It was, throughout, the language of a military campaign. The shirts, the salutes, the whispered 'March of the Comrades', the appropriated idioms of the March on Rome: none of it went unnoticed.[307] There had been talk of trouble since 1932, anonymous information 'that they are preparing for a fight...that they claim a big following in the Regular Army'.[308] De Valera could not fully trust the security forces, particularly the police, to suppress a coup, especially if it was led by O'Duffy, especially since Cumann na nGaedheal was to form an integral part of the procession. In 1931 O'Duffy admitted that

The Garda, individually and collectively, has been for the past nine years more loyal and faithful and constant in its support of the present government than any other state service. It has been recruited 99 per cent from supporters of Cumann na nGaedheal, and up to date Cumann na nGaedheal organisers rely upon the local sergeants for hints and advice to enable them to carry out their organising work...the Gardaí grew up in the belief, because of circumstances, that they were servants of the Government Party rather than of the State itself.[309]

Denied their beloved master and now subject to an enemy, the Gardaí were not to be trusted in 1933.[310] They made the march impossible. Despite promises that the 'civilians' were to give 'the proceedings a quality of spontaneity and popularity',[311] the prospect of 30,000 Blueshirts marching on the capital and the remainder targeting the towns of Ireland, did little to reassure the Fianna Fáil government.[312] De Valera knew all about codified orders to parade; Easter 1916 must have played heavily upon his mind. That O'Duffy chose the day

[302] *United Irishman*, 3 June 1933; 10 June 1933; 17 June 1933; 15 July 1933; 8 July 1933; 29 July 1933. *The Blueshirt*, 5 Aug. 1933.
[303] *United Irishman*, 3 June 1933; 24 June 1933.   [304] *Ibid.*, 24 June 1933.
[305] *Ibid.*, 15 July 1933.   [306] *The Blueshirt*, 12 Aug. 1933.
[307] *United Irishman*, 20 May 1933.
[308] DJ H306/23, Personal objections etc. – Army Comrades Association, letter from Bill Quirke TD to the Minister for Defence, 9 Aug. 1932.
[309] Memo from General Eoin O'Duffy, Commissioner of the Gárda Síochána to the government, 1931, Ernest Blythe MSS, UCDA, P24/488.
[310] Such was the level of distrust, the Broy Harriers were recruited as an emergency measure.
[311] *United Irishman*, 24 June 1933.   [312] Cronin, *The Blueshirts*, p. 22.

before the proposed march to make his pronouncements on the future of Irish politics only made the situation worse. As far as he was concerned the current system of government was un-Irish and, despite the declared 'will of the people', unrepresentative. He proposed that future elections should be held on a limited franchise based on vocational and professional groups; he ordered Ireland to emulate fascist Italy.[313] The march was banned under article 2A of the constitution, and armoured cars enclosed Leinster Lawn. Bitter as he may have been, de Valera had no option. The IRA was mobilising; violence was inevitable. With the 'eruption from the rat holes of the country of an usurping army', matters had gone beyond commemoration; this was possible rebellion, promised civil war.[314] In the Blueshirts' own words, it was 'the march of a nation against Fianna Fáil'.[315]

On the eve of the proposed march the *United Irishman* made the following statement:

Today we may not even honour the memory of the great Irishman whom Mr de Valera's private army slew in the prime of his life; the bitter vendetta which Mr de Valera waged against Collins in life is to be carried across the grave. The man who sits in the seat of Government erected by the sacrifices of Griffith, Collins and O'Higgins threatens to suppress any attempt to honour them fittingly in the capital city of the State for which they gave their lives. We may leave the National Guard to deal with this threat; for ourselves we can rest serenely confident that the names of Griffith, Collins and O'Higgins will be known and honoured in Irish history when the name of de Valera is but an evil memory and his story a tale to frighten children.[316]

But again honour was never suppressed: only the threatened parade. Access to Leinster Lawn had been granted to the one hundred individuals who had applied for entry. It was not the fault of the Fianna Fáil government that only two anonymous women availed themselves of tickets, that the other ninety-eight were in favour of the march.[317] The following week the Old Dublin Brigade IRA paraded past the Cenotaph 'without incident';[318] the Blueshirts marched freely in Clonmel, Kanturk, Kilkenny, Nenagh, Rathcormac, Rathkeale, Glengariff, Monaghan and Macroom.[319] Marches in Limerick, Dublin, Wexford and Cork provoked some of the violence that could have convulsed Dublin the week before.[320] Commemoration and honour were never the issue, however much O'Duffy and his comrades might pose with their wreaths of blue

[313] *IT*, 12 Aug. 1933; Cronin, *The Blueshirts*, p. 22.
[314] *Catholic Bulletin*, 23, 2 (Feb. 1933), p. 96.   [315] *United Irishman*, 19 Aug. 1933.
[316] *Ibid.*, 12 Aug. 1933.   [317] DT 99/1/35 s5734E, Griffith–Collins Cenotaph – general file.
[318] Department of Justice Jus8/721, Old Dublin Brigade IRA 1933.
[319] *CE*, 21 and 22 Aug. 1933; *IT*, 21 and 22 Aug. 1933. Peadar Livingstone, *The Monaghan story* (Enniskillen, 1980), p. 414.
[320] *CE*, 21 Aug. 1933; there were some outbreaks around Dublin on the day of the proposed march, but these were confined to localised incidents among groups of young men. *CE*, 14 Aug. 1933; *IT*, 14 and 15 Aug. 1933.

cornflowers, however much Collins' sister spoke of 'enmity beyond the grave'.[321]

Nineteen thirty-three was about political chaos; it was to be the culmination of a festering collection of sporadic incidents with IRA men, of tussles at election booths and dances and cattle sales, of bigger marches to republican graves. It was about anger at the election result of January 1933, when de Valera was returned with an overall majority, when the same irate sister of Michael Collins, Margaret Collins-O'Driscoll, a TD for Dublin North since 1923, had failed to be re-elected. As much as she may have mourned her brother, as much as the banning of the parade may have seemed like an affront to the memory of Griffith, Collins and O'Higgins, the politicisation, the abuse of memory by the Blueshirts, by Cumann na nGaedheal who abetted them, did more to dishonour these men than anything the supposedly demonic de Valera could have conceived. Because of Fianna Fáil 'the ceremony is denuded of meaning'; there was a convenient hypocrisy in Cosgrave's hollow words.[322] That the years that followed provoked nothing more than predictable masses and marches, that they were peaceful, innocuous, inoffensive, explained what 1933 was all about.[323] As civilised as the handover of power may reputedly have been in 1932, there were elements of pro-Treatyite support, namely the most militarist, who could not countenance defeat in any form, defeat in itself, by the enemies of 1922, or by the socio-economic alternatives of 1932. The dead were a means to an end, cherished and vigorously championed maybe, but still an emotive and evocative rallying cry that had come to sound sickeningly shrill.

And Béalnabláth was no different. It too had suffered 1932's humiliation: the army taken away. In 1933 it was to be an integral part of the grand Blueshirt design to rise again. There had never been the same formality about this desolate place; remoteness had always contained the crowd, limiting it to locals, to those willing and financially able to make the journey. It was a place evocative purely of the man, with none of the Cenotaph's claims to statehood. It was a place of pilgrimage, of a morbid fascination that prompted question after question about his dying and the men who may have killed him. Without the Cenotaph's pompous selectivity, with no gilt-edged invitations, no top hats or morning suits, it was accessible to all, republican or Free Stater, who happened to pass along that narrow twisting road. Here grief was personal, not dependent on the eloquence of a President's speech: just wreaths laid with messages of ambition

---

[321] *United Irishman*, 19 Aug. 1933.   [322] *Connaught Telegraph*, 19 Aug. 1933.
[323] Parades were held by Blueshirt units throughout Wexford, Westmeath, Kilkenny, Tipperary, Mayo, Meath: *United Ireland*, 1 Sept. 1934; 22 Sept. 1934. Mass was held in Dublin: *ibid.*, 25 Aug. 1934; 31 Aug. 1935; 14 Sept. 1935. And a parade was held in Kilkenny, *ibid.*, 21 Sept. 1935.

or achievement like pleas for intercessions to a saint.[324] Even Lady Lavery, for all her sophistication, could speak only in terms of her 'pilgrimage' there.[325] In this respect, in the republican regret that brought men from both sides to Béalnabláth for the unveiling in 1924, the politicisation of this pathetic place seems so much worse. In Collins they had killed one of their own: the one, with the hindsight of trap mines and executions, who might have saved them from the worst excesses of civil war. Béalnabláth was as much a monument to republican remorse as it was to Free State grief. That here, where emotion was rawest, there was only the exploitation of him was too much for remorse to endure. Ritual had recruited him and Béalnabláth to the ranks of Cumann na nGaedheal, a party founded eight months after his death, to the boisterous brigades of the Blueshirts, to the more sober Fine Gael. Ritual could only complete the alienation of this republican regret. In 1932 Richard Mulcahy told the three thousand who had gathered at Béalnabláth that he was 'prepared in the doing of its work to shoulder arms in defence of your country again... that you cannot remove from influence in this country men who stood by the State in 1922, no more than you can remove the men and women who worked in order that they could build up a Government of the people'.[326] Most of the three thousand wore blue shirts, most came angry about the absent army, angry that de Valera was now in charge. This display had very little to do with Michael Collins.

In 1933 the procession at Béalnabláth was banned. The fears that gripped Dublin on 14 August were shared by Cork on the 27th.[327] A police cordon had never been honour's intention, but none could pass fear's firmly drawn line, not even the sister of Michael Collins, Mrs Collins-Powell, who only wanted to lay a wreath.[328] Her desperate attempt to break through the cordon only underlined the heartless cruelty of the exploitation of her brother's memory, the heavy-handedness of the ceremony's suppression. There was possibly more to it than fear; a republican commemoration passed unimpeded in Midleton on the planned day of the Béalnabláth procession.[329] The contrasting photographs from the *Cork Examiner* suggest that bias played its part. Ceremony was politics by other means. The *United Irishman* was happily indignant on Mrs Collins-Powell's behalf.[330] There was invaluable copy in the mourning woman wronged.

---

[324] On a visit to Béalnabláth in 1999, there was a wreath with a message from Kathleen Woulfe telling Collins that her father had had a Fine Gael Branch named after him.

[325] Quoted in McCoole, *Hazel*, p. 116; Lady Lavery to Edward Marsh, in Hassall, *Edward Marsh*, p. 489.

[326] Police Commissioner's report of Richard Mulcahy's address to the ACA at Béalnabláth, 21 Aug. 1932, DJ H306/23, personal objections etc. – Army Comrades Association; *Irish Press*, 22 Aug. 1932.

[327] A Blueshirt march to the grave of Brigadier General Ring's grave in Mayo was also proclaimed. *Mayo News*, 23 Sept. 1933.

[328] *CE*, 28 and 29 Aug. 1933.   [329] *Ibid.*, 28 Aug. 1933.

[330] *United Irishman*, 2 Sept. 1933.

Yet neither O'Duffy, who stood on the monument's platform in 1934 and spoke to 2,500 saluting Blueshirts of the selling of seized cattle,[331] nor the boys on the hill top who shouted 'Fuck Collins' and 'Up Dev', thought much of the men and women who had come there to mourn, who took comfort in the trappings of ceremony, ceremony that once claimed to honour the man they had lost.[332] 'The spirit of Michael Collins is abroad today, the nation is once more upon the march, who dares cry "Halt" to us?' were O'Duffy's last words to his assembled minions.[333] From the monument bedecked in its Blueshirt flags these minions marched to the nearest farmhouse. There they broke windows and terrified James Hennessy, his wife and his two daughters.[334] The 'spirit of Collins' was in safe hands.

By 1935 Blueshirtism had split. Fine Gael, now a rival for the legacy, had done the 'detestable thing' of using 'the dead for purposes of party propaganda'.[335] Citing Collins' 'If I fall you have O'Duffy' was, of course, an entirely different matter.[336] Béalnabláth's 'forget politics and petty jealousies . . . think only of the sacrifice of their dead Leader and emulate his example' was all very well.[337] Writing newspaper articles about Fine Gael's 'attempt to dishonour the memory of Collins' was more useful.[338] Béalnabláth was now all these factions had. In 1935 it was chosen to honour Griffith, Collins and O'Higgins because Leinster Lawn was lost to them.[339] And between them they ruined it. Ceremony became the rantings of bitter men and the people stayed away in disgust. 'Interest . . . lapsed for many years',[340] and the 1940s could have little respect for the icon of a shirted movement, little time for the divisive past when world war had fostered a fragile unity.[341] Men from both sides of the divide came together in Local Defence Force units:

It was heartening to see together again in their old companies the 'diehards' and the 'Free State' lads. Many friendships had been shattered by the unfortunate civil war; now they were coming together again, all willing to do their bit for their common country . . . I was indeed proud to be back with the old boys, and marched with my head held high.[342]

331 The *Cork Examiner* set the crowd at 8,000, 3 Sept. 1933; the Department of Justice report put the figure at 2,550. Report by Chief Superintendent M. McCarthy to the Chief Commissioner, 3 Sept. 1934, DJ JUS8/38, Commemoration ceremony held by League of Youth at Béalnabláth on 2 Sept. 1934.
332 Chief Superintendent M. McCarthy to the Chief Commissioner, 3 Sept. 1934, *ibid*. There was a similar incident between Blueshirts and local republicans at Foxford: *United Ireland*, 29 Sept. 1934.
333 *CE*, 3 Sept. 1934.
334 Chief Superintendent M. McCarthy to the Chief Commissioner, 3 Sept. 1934.
335 *The Nation*, 3 Aug. 1935.   336 *Ibid*.
337 *Northern Star*, Sept. 1935; Richard Mulcahy MSS, UCDA, p7c/45(3).
338 *The Nation*, 3 Aug. 1935.   339 *United Ireland*, 13 July 1935.
340 Twohig, *The dark secret of Béalnabláth*, p. 56.
341 *Seven Ages* by Seán Ó Mordha, part 3, screened by RTÉ 1, 6 Mar. 2000.
342 Joseph F. Coffey, 'The men who came back: memories of the "26th" ', *Capuchin Annual* (1948),

Indeed the indifference took its toll on republican ceremonies too. In 1940 in Kildare it was reported that 'locally these events have practically no support'; 'no member of the general public attended'.[343] More notably, at Benbulben in Co. Sligo, at a monument to six IRA men, the thirty-five who came in 1940 dwindled to five in 1942; there were eight in 1944, twelve in 1945, twenty-one in 1946.[344] There were sixty-three in 1947 only because a cross was unveiled.[345] Of the five, eight, twelve and twenty-one, most were known members of the IRA, most had come to serve, as the intensity of the police surveillance suggests, more pressing political ends.

It was the early 1950s before things changed. The first inter-party government, fuelled by the residual spite of 1932, ordered the return of the army to Béalnabláth.[346] Fianna Fáil returned in 1951 and the army was ordered home. The same thing happened again at the next change of government in 1954, and again in 1957.[347] Béalnabláth was political again, interesting again. Furious letters to editors, 'uproar at Council meetings', Dáil questions, party politics, bitterness, regard, spite – controversy brought the people back.[348] The local Collins Commemoration Committee, founded because of the years of indifference, simply welcomed the publicity and widened the road to cater for the numbers. And it carried on, into the 1960s; the annual Dáil question receiving the same refusal. The army would not return to Béalnabláth. Each Taoiseach was faced with his own version of 'His blood is on your hands and that is what is wrong with you',[349] with the irresponsible invective that infused the crowds at Béalnabláth with a renewed and invidious political fervour. That the most

---

pp. 122–3. There were tentative attempts to distract men away from the IRA and to integrate them into state forces in the 1930s through the Volunteer Force and the Broy Harriers. O'Halpin, *Defending Ireland*, p. 121.

[343] DJ Jus8/881, National Graves Association – general file, report by J. S. Flynn, Apr. 1940.

[344] DJ Jus8/865, IRA commemoration ceremony at Benbulben Mountain, Co. Sligo, report of Chief Superintendent Seán Liddy, 26 Sept. 1940 and 2 Oct. 1942; report of Superintendent Peter Fahy, 26 Sept. 1944, 21 Sept. 1945 and 1 Oct. 1946.

[345] *Ibid.*, report of Superintendent Peter Fahy, 26 Sept. 1947.

[346] Department of Defence 3/6427, Ceremonial – commemoration ceremony – General Michael Collins; Department of an Taoiseach s5734D, memo by N. S. Ó Nualláin to the Taoiseach, 10 July 1951.

[347] Department of Defence 3/6427, Ceremonial – commemoration ceremony – General Michael Collins; Department of an Taoiseach s15136A, Anniversary of the death of Michael Collins – army or government participation in annual ceremony at Béalnabláth.

[348] *II*, 21, 24, 27, 28, 29 Aug. 1951; 25 Sept. 1951; 4, 6 Oct. 1951; 23 Aug. 1954; 31 July 1957; 2, 3, 8, 9, 17 Aug. 1957; 16, 25 Sept. 1957; *IT*, 2, 5 Aug. 1957; *Irish Press*, 28 Aug. 1951; 3, 18 Sept. 1951; 1 Aug. 1957; *Evening Herald*, 24 Aug. 1957; *DE, official report*, CLXIV, cols. 264–5 (30 Oct. 1957); *ibid.*, CLXIV, cols. 660–8 (6 Nov. 1957); *ibid.*, CLXX, cols. 681–2 (16 July 1958); *ibid.*, CLXXVI, cols. 553–4 (2 July 1959); *ibid.*, CCVIII, cols. 971–2 (12 Mar. 1964); *ibid.*, CCXV, cols. 2178–9 (26 May 1965); *ibid.*, CCXXIII, cols. 2289–91 (7 July 1966); *ibid.*, CCXXVII, col. 1340 (11 Apr. 1967); *ibid.*, CCXXVII, cols. 1451–2 (12 Apr. 1967); *ibid.*, CCXXX, cols. 650–2 (21 July 1967); *ibid.*, CCXXXVI, cols. 724–6 (10 July 1968).

[349] Fintan Coogan, *DE, official report*, CCXXX, col. 652 (21 July 1967).

vocal, and the most insidious were Fine Gael TDs who had been elected in the
1950s and 1960s, who had no civil war record; that they could stoop to the
most superficial levels of 'What will the Americans think?',[350] inclines one to
question their sincerity.

It was easy to blame Fianna Fáil, to say that 'the man in the park is jealous of him'.[351] It was as lazy and destructive as the headlines that declared
that 'FF continue to slight Collins'.[352] In the 1950s anti-Treatyites had paid
their respects at Béalnabláth: 'I ... am proud to record the fact that men of all
political shades participated with me and in 1955, at the Béal na Bláth ceremony, I was singularly proud to be associated there with one of the officers
who was engaged on the opposing side of the fatal ambush.'[353] By 1967 Tom
Barry, who had happily unveiled a monument to Collins in 1965, was writing
to Jack Lynch to deny that he had ever been there. In the course of his letter
he told the Taoiseach 'some active Fine Gaelers have ... told me they were
completely against this attempt by FG to take over Collins, who if he were
alive would certainly not be associated with them or their activities'.[354] 'Most
people in Cork realise that this commemoration was used by a political party
for furthering its political programme and purposes.'[355] Collins, at a politically
barren period for Fine Gael, was again recalled by the more wilful elements
of the party. It made no difference that the Fianna Fáil Minister for Defence
responded to their entreaties with 'I want all who died for this country honoured
together';[356] that Jack Lynch was prepared to instigate 'an all-Party Committee
to see how best we could commemorate all those who fell in the Civil War'.[357]
Fianna Fáil's bitterness made better headlines; it had a more visceral electoral
appeal.

In the early 1950s the Fianna Fáil government had decided that

in view of the many anniversary commemorations and the difficulty of making any
selection which would not appear invidious and give rise to much heart-burning, the
best thing was to have one day set apart on which the State could celebrate the securing
of independence here and honour all who took part in the struggle to achieve it. Easter
Sunday was the day selected. I still think that that decision was a wise one, and the

[350] *Sunday Independent*, 25 Aug. 1968.
[351] Gerald L'Estrange, *DE, official report*, CCXXIII, col. 2291 (7 July 1966). At this stage de
Valera was President and therefore resident at Áras an Uachtaráin in the Phoenix Park.
[352] *II*, 27 Aug. 1967.
[353] T. F. O'Higgins, *DE, official report*, CLXIV, cols. 663–4 (6 Nov. 1957); Senator Victor Carton,
letter to the editor, *Evening Herald*, 24 Aug. 1957.
[354] Tom Barry to Jack Lynch, 30 Aug. 1967, DT 96/6/641 s15136B, Anniversary of the death of
Michael Collins – army or government participation in annual ceremony at Béalnabláth, Co.
Cork.
[355] Paddy McGrath, TD commenting at a meeting of Cork County Council, *Irish Press*, 19 Sept.
1951.
[356] Michael Hilliard, *DE, official report*, CCXXIII, col. 2291 (7 July 1966).
[357] Jack Lynch, *DE, official report*, CCXXXVI, col. 725 (10 July 1968).

best at any rate for the present generation. This position, of course, does not prevent the individual anniversaries being honoured by the friends of those who died. These anniversaries will naturally continue to be honoured as in the past, but for the State as such it is better to have one general commemoration.[358]

This was de Valera's own explanation to Seán Collins. Much as the decision may have disappointed him, Seán Collins accepted it without complaint. He had enquired about the army attendance only in the belief that it 'would be the means of healing the sores of the Civil War'.[359] He sent his wife Nancy's regards to de Valera, 'her old friend of Gaelic League days'.[360] His family had always been anxious to dispel the bitterness. That was why the monuments only bore Collins' name and his date of death, why Liam Collins never went to Béalnabláth, why he wanted to celebrate his uncle's centenary at Woodfield 'in a proper manner not at Béalnabláth, but in a totally apolitical manner'.[361] De Valera was possibly not the bitter old villain that Fine Gael, and latterly Tim Pat Coogan, wished to believe. That Béalnabláth was defaced for the first time during the presidential election of 1966 and again in 1968 during the referendum on proportional representation was no coincidence.[362] De Valera had not taken the army from Béalnabláth to stand at an Irregular's grave, but this made no difference. No one mentioned the years of taunts he had endured, the allegations that he had killed Collins,[363] that he was just 'jealous of a West Cork farmer's son',[364] that he himself was 'the bastard son of a Spanish Jew',[365] that he was the only deputy in the Dáil who ever had to defend his parentage.[366] Bitterness had its constituency on both sides. It was foolish to assume that abuse would not beget abuse, that the men and women who valued the ceremonial honour of Collins would not suffer as a consequence. One woman wrote in anger to the *Evening Herald*:

it is a disgrace that our Army will not be allowed to take part in the annual commemoration . . . As a girl I queued for hours to pay tribute to Ireland's dead President and ten days later to see the last of brave Michael Collins with the Army doing the Guard of

[358] Eamon de Valera to Seán Collins, 18 July 1957, DT s15136A, Anniversary of the death of Michael Collins – army or government participation in annual ceremony at Béalnabláth, Co. Cork; *Irish Press*, 1 Aug. 1957.
[359] Seán Collins to Eamon de Valera, n.d., *ibid.*
[360] *Ibid.* Nancy Collins née O'Brien, Seán's second wife, had worked in the castle during the independence struggle. She had carried messages to Michael throughout the war.
[361] *Southern Star*, 13 Oct. 1990.
[362] *DE, official report*, CCXXIII, cols. 1010–12 (22 June 1966); *IT*, 16 Oct. 1968; *II*, 16 Oct. 1968; *Irish Press*, 16 Oct. 1968; *CE*, 16 Oct. 1968. On the second occasion 'Vote Yes' had been painted in various places on the cross and platform.
[363] See, for example, an exchange of letters in 1927 alleging that de Valera had orchestrated the killing. Fianna Fáil wrote to the *Cork Examiner* demanding an apology for the libellous letters. *CE*, 13–15 Sept. 1927.
[364] P. J. Hogan election address, *CE*, 12 Sept. 1927.   [365] Dwyer, *Eamon de Valera*, p. 192.
[366] *DE, official report*, L, cols. 2514 (2 Mar. 1934).

Honour. I am the wife of a 1922 soldier and the mother of four sons wearing the Irish uniform and I feel ashamed that their right is taken from them. We will not forget the 11 o'c Mass at St Joseph's Church, Berkeley Road, on Sunday.[367]

Party politics never seemed to countenance that she and others like her would be hurt in the vindictive process. Maybe Seán Irwin was right; maybe Fianna Fáil would be damned for its 'consistent lack of magnanimity and generosity' in its dealings with Béalnabláth.[368] Maybe Jack Lynch was right when he called it 'a political ceremony'. Somewhere between the two, one generation's bitterness and regard became the stuff of another's convenience.

In more recent years, 'against the background of the Northern conflict, Béalnabláth orators have been doing some fancy footwork to deflect attention from Collins the man of violence, asking us rather to consider Collins the administrator and the man of ideas'.[369] Although his covert operations in the North in 1922 are indicative of where his instinctive sympathies lay, Mary Banotti was convinced that Collins would have voted for peace if he had had the chance in 1998's referendum on Northern Ireland.[370] In 1999 Maurice Manning concluded that Collins 'would have rejoiced in our membership of the European Union and the opportunities it has given us'.[371] In some respects this no longer matters. The manipulation of the dead is an inherent part of the commemorative process and possibly because of this hundreds still go to Béalnabláth. Unlike Griffith, whose memory limps on in the occasional lecture, in the work of a little-known Arthur Griffith Society, Collins endures often because and sometimes in spite of versions and revisions.[372] Over eighty years of poems, plays, exhibitions, films and biographies, over eighty years of ceremony, quickly belie the alleged conspiracy of Fianna Fáil silence.[373] Collins has defied 'the shelf life of memories'[374], survived as all things to all men with an alacrity that has often driven the people of Béalnabláth to change the signposts to the much-visited cross. Naturally memory has changed, matured, and, despite the heated response to Neil Jordan's film, become less emotional. There is little of his life that has not been probed and debated and infused with another generation's curiosity. Much can be explained by his fame and his infamy. Collins was the acceptable face of 1922: amenable to the honours that memory lavished upon him. The soldiers who died wearing his uniform would never be the same. Memory could afford to forget them because they evoked too much of a war that should never have been fought. They, like the men who had died in the

---

[367] *Evening Herald*, 23 Aug. 1957.
[368] Seán Irwin to Michael Hayes, 3 Nov. 1970, Michael Hayes MSS, UCDA, P53/396.
[369] *II*, 25 Aug. 1996.   [370] *IT*, 24 Aug. 1998.   [371] *Ibid.*, 23 Aug. 1999.
[372] Richard Mulcahy MSS, UCDA, P7/D/76; Piaras Béaslaí MSS, UCDA, MS 33,966(20).
[373] It was alleged in 1990, for example, that 'for seventy years politics had tried to ignore his name'. *Southern Star*, 20 Oct. 1990.
[374] Winter and Sivan, 'Setting the framework', p. 16.

Great War's trenches and battlefields, had become an embarrassment. They were the all-too-bloody reality of the Free State's disappointment, the constant reminder of republican regret. Memory was the burden and the indulgence of those closest to them. They were soldiers; nothing more. They were 'the young lieutenants' lying dead, the 'great pool of blood...covered simply by a rough potato sack'.[375] They did their duty, did what they were told. They were shadows, snatched remembrances – nothing more.

[375] Browne, *Against the tide*, p. 5.

Conclusion

In 1959 Emmet Dalton made a film about the erection of a monument to a dead IRA man. The monument, a large and rather distorted figure of a naked man, was eventually blown up by the 'blessed patriot's' illegitimate son. *This other Eden* was billed as a gentle comedy, a satire of rural Irish life.[1] It was neither very good nor very funny. Instead it was more of a strange indictment, a mischievous reproof of all those men who spoke of martyrs and marched with solemn faces to neglected crosses and untended patriot graves.

Almost in spite of itself, this film is possibly one of the finest contemporary assessments of civil war memory or, to be more precise, of the memory of Michael Collins. Collins and Dalton are mirrored in the characters of Carberry and Devereux, the patriot ambushed and the companion later suspected of complicity in his death. The civil war is, granted, a lesser player, tacitly alluded to in the joy of seeing 'all the parties united in his honour'.[2] But the film tells a sordid tale: a tale of elderly men eager to erect a monument because it 'would do the town a power of good', 'because the tourists will be flocking here . . . cramming your hotel, hiring your cars, buying your horrible souvenirs'.[3] It is a tale of men desperate to maintain the myth of the martyr, adept at exploiting the legend, but incapable of acknowledging the more brutal realities, the flaws, the faults, the inconvenient son. Here commemoration is only an abuse of memory, nothing more. Remembrance is a lucrative and self-serving hypocrisy.

Five chapters after asking how 'the survivors used the memory of the civil war to further their purposes', Emmet Dalton's dispiriting film seems an appropriate answer.[4] It is difficult to commend the Free State government for its attempts to commemorate. At the Cenotaph, at the army plot, compliments do not spring readily to mind. It would be easy to take refuge in sweeping statements, in versions of 'Civil War was the greatest curse with which this land has ever been blasted',[5] but that would be too easy. These words make forgetfulness seem like some noble retreat, as though silence was the proper price to pay for

---

[1] *This other Eden*, directed by Muriel Box and produced by Emmet Dalton, was released in 1959. It was based on a play of the same title by Louis D'Alton, *This other Eden* (Dublin, 1954).
[2] *This other Eden*, Irish Film Archive.   [3] *Ibid.*   [4] Lee, *Ireland 1912–1985*, p. 69.
[5] 'Naosc A' Ghleanna', 'Twenty years a-withering', *The Bell*, 3, 5 (Feb. 1942), p. 379.

future peace. With such phrases silence can never mean neglect; it takes on a significance far too honourable for the reality of overgrown graves and parents left waiting on railway platforms for their sons' remains. If it was indeed an episode best forgotten, let it at least be admitted that this forgetfulness appeased the Department of Finance as much as it did any tormented soul in Ballyseedy or Leinster House.

Peter Burke says that the victors can afford to forget; Peter Burke assumes too much about victory and forgetting.[6] The civil war was what military men would call a dirty war: victory by atrocity and execution, lacking the requisite laurels and blazes of glory. And it is glib to say that loss is so willingly overlooked.[7] Victors still feel a duty to their dead even if, and often because, that duty perpetuates the victory and the divide. Loss is not the preserve of the losers; there were enough empty spaces at cabinet tables and kitchen tables to challenge any Peter Burke. There could be no forgetting.

Although there could be no forgetting, there was a will to forget, a retreat to a type of silence that erased all but the victory. The end had been reached; there was no need to reminisce about the means. 'The revolutionaries of 1912–23 had to turn themselves into politicians: an evidently painful and confusing metamorphosis.'[8] The winners had to 'highlight their democratic credentials and to gloss over their revolutionary origins';[9] republicans were trying to do to them what they had once done to the British. Silence was better than hypocrisy.

Silence was also better than disgust. 'Both sides had done terrible things and both sides knew it.'[10] Left with 'the memory of the unspeakable', with the 'elements of our own humanity that we cannot bear to hear',[11] there was no need to recall 'that our deep-rooted belief that there was something in us finer than, more spiritual than, anything in any other people, was sheer illusion, and that we were really an uncivilised people with savage instincts. And the shock of that plunge from the heights to the depths staggered the whole nation.'[12] There was too much to be done to dwell on this Miltonic fall.[13] Points had to be proved: to the republicans, to the British, to themselves; the winners could afford no talk of any paradise lost. Memories were deliberately repressed because life

---

[6] Burke, 'History as social memory', p. 106.

[7] Tom Garvin has also concluded that the reasons for 'forgetfulness' during the seventy-fifth anniversary of the civil war 'are fundamentally healthy'. Tom Garvin, 'De Valera and the Tories failed to see reality of Republic', *IT*, 10 Jan. 1997.

[8] Tom Garvin, 'Civil war took several billion out of economy', *IT*, 6 Dec. 1997.

[9] Ronan Fanning, 'Michael Collins: an overview', in Gabriel Doherty and Dermot Keogh (eds.), *Michael Collins and the making of the Irish state* (Cork, 1998), p. 203.

[10] A quotation which Garvin attributes to Seán Lemass. Garvin, 'Civil war took'. J. J. Walsh also reminisced that 'Rough methods were used on both sides'; *Recollections of a rebel*, p. 57.

[11] Ronit Lentin quoted in Katrina Goldstone, 'Thanks for the memory', *IT*, 21 Jan. 1998.

[12] P. S. O'Hegarty, *The victory of Sinn Féin* (Dublin, 1924; 1998 edn.), p. 91.

[13] John Regan speaks of the recollection of civil war 'in almost Miltonic terms'. Regan, 'The politics of reaction', p. 563.

had to be rebuilt from the very 'ashes of the catastrophe'.[14] There could be no fanfare to mark the birth of the Free State on 6 December 1922; the labour had been too difficult.[15] There was just 'the most decorous meeting of the Dáil that I ever attended', because, 'the dead past apparently has buried its dead; gone for ever are the hectic nights and days of Earlsfort Terrace'[16], gone for ever in the hail of bullets that took the life of Seán Hales on 7 December, in the revenge that executed four leading republicans on the 8th.

But whatever there was of silence and confusion, there was also politics. It was soon taken for granted that 'the sharply antagonistic shape of party politics' owes its peculiar hostility to the fact that 'the civil war was fought anew on the floor of the Dáil with a venom all the more concentrated for having been distilled for five years'.[17] No one is disputing that de Valera was despised by certain members of the Cumann na nGaedheal cabinet. To Richard Mulcahy, Fianna Fáil could never 'safely be left unwatched'.[18] No one is denying the anecdotes, the Fianna Fáil party rule 'that members should not conduct any business with Cumann na nGaedheal Ministers or deputies in bar or restaurant and that fraternization under any circumstances be not permitted', because these were the men who ordered the execution of comrades in 1922.[19] But Ronan Fanning's statement takes too much for granted. Party politics was defined by more than civil war. Party politics was a complex mix of social and economic issues, of frustrations within parties, of divisions that predated 1922. Both Fianna Fáil and Cumann na nGaedheal went to the polls with more than a glorified encore of the Treaty debates. Civil war did divide them, but it quickly became a mechanism. Squabbles over economic policies took on the emotive rhetoric of civil war. Bitterness was obedient on election banners when the parties could think of no other way to reaffirm their supporters' devotions. Rehashing the old row seemed somehow more alluring than the reality that politics had retreated to the unheroic inanities of living the independence they had coveted for so long. And commemoration was proof of this. The parties could meet behind closed doors, discuss cenotaphs, complete each other's schemes of remembrance. They knew that 'some 200,000 people are on the register who never saw a Tan, never lived under the Cosgrave regime and who don't care one damn about where anyone

[14] Katrina Goldstone, 'Thanks'.

[15] The first anniversary of the signing of the Treaty in London marked the end of the period of Provisional Government.

[16] Impressions of an *Irish Times* reporter 'December 6: birth of Irish Free State', *IT*, 6 Dec. 1922; Tom Garvin, 'A difficult birth', *IT*, 6 Dec. 1997.

[17] Fanning, '*The four-leaved shamrock*', p. 10.

[18] Letter from Richard Mulcahy to George A. Lyons, 29 Apr. 1938, George A. Lyons MSS, NLI, MS 33,675/A/2(53).

[19] Rule proposed by Seán Lemass to the Fianna Fáil political party in 1928; Eunan O'Halpin, 'Parliamentary party discipline and tactics: the Fianna Fáil archives, 1926–32', *Irish Historical Studies*, 30, 120 (Nov. 1997), p. 589.

202 Commemorating the Irish Civil War

was in '16, '22 or '39'.[20] They knew it, but many preferred to overlook it. On the floor of the Dáil the civil war was a reliable retort in the repertoire; deputies could bait each other at convenience's command with the vehemence of 1922, with the names and the massacres of men many never even knew. That the hatred was evoked most by those who took no part in the civil war, by those too young, those never even born, says it all. That deputies were still doing so in 1996,[21] that August 2001 only brought 'Collins has more in common with F[ianna] F[áil] ideals', is proof that bitterness has its constituency still.[22]

Politics with its podium platitudes took no account of the men and women who always returned to monument and grave. Theirs was a type of remembrance that politics would never understand. Private grief had none of politics' misgivings. A son, a brother, a husband had died a hero, had died for Ireland. There was no talk of compromise, no mention of dominion status. Maud Griffith mourned her husband: she proudly mourned a president. Her husband's erstwhile colleagues found it all a little embarrassing and only reluctantly paid for his grave. When it was convenient, politics promised all types of honour. It was convenient to pay £50,000 towards the splendid neglect of Islandbridge. There were influential people to impress; it was a practical donation. To some Islandbridge represents a callous disregard for the memory of the Great War dead. It is hard to be so sure when for forty-five years parents mourned their sons at an unmarked national army grave.

In party hands, the dead were 'prostituted to the polemics of the present, and the gravediggers drag out the corpses with the sole purpose of hawking them around present battlefields'.[23] There was nothing of suffering, nothing of grief. After 1923 that was just too awkward to behold, too brutal a reminder of what was never achieved. Civil war made victory an awkward burden; the dead were a strange blessing, at times even a curse.

At the end of *This other Eden* an Englishman came to save the day. He vowed to buy the town a new monument so no one need ever know that the patriot's 'bastard came and blew his statue up'.[24] Disgusted by a rotting Cenotaph on Leinster Lawn, Maud Griffith must have understood why men blow statues up.

In the aftermath of civil war, memory is a contested thing. In Ireland, despite the occasional newspaper headline that attests smugly to the end of bitterness, the race is far from run.

---

[20] Letter unsigned from Fianna Fáil head office to Séamus Fitzgerald, 8 November 1947, Séamus Fitzgerald MSS, CAI, PR/6/521.

[21] *DE, official report*, CDLXI, cols. 413–24 (7 Feb. 1996).   [22] *IT*, 18 Aug. 2001.

[23] J. J. Lee, 'Keeping perspective in the commemoration stakes', *Sunday Tribune*, 25 Jan. 1998.

[24] *This other Eden*.

Bibliography

PRIMARY SOURCES

MANUSCRIPTS

Cork
Cork Archives Institute
Séamus Fitzgerald MSS

Dublin
Fianna Fáil Archives
Independence movement and Sinn Féin, 1915–28
Foundation of party and early years, 1926–28
Party minute books

Military Archives, Dublin
Department of Defence miscellaneous papers A/series
Department of Defence ceremonial box I–III

National Library of Ireland
Piaras Béaslaí MSS
John Devoy MSS
Joseph Fowler MSS
Kathleen McKenna Napoli MSS
Florence O'Donoghue MSS
Seán T. O'Kelly MSS
Seán Ó Lúing MSS
George A. Lyons MSS
O'Mullane MSS
Celia Shaw diary
Gerald Tighe MSS

Trinity College, Dublin
Robert Barton MSS
Childers MSS

University College, Dublin, Archives Department
Ernest Blythe MSS
Caitlin Brugha MSS

Margaret Burke and Fr Tom Burke MSS
Desmond FitzGerald MSS
Greene family MSS
Michael Hayes MSS
Healy/Sullivan family MSS
Hugh Kennedy MSS
Mary MacSwiney MSS
Richard Mulcahy MSS
Diarmuid O'Hegarty MSS
O'Rahilly MSS

Private Collections
Michael MacEvilly private collection
National Graves Association records

London
Public Records Office
Dominions Office

GOVERNMENT RECORDS

National Archives of Ireland
Dáil Éireann, cabinet minutes
Dáil Éireann departmental files
Department of an Taoiseach, S files
Department of an Taoiseach, President's Office files
Department of Finance files
Department of Foreign Affairs, Secretary's Office files
Department of Foreign Affairs, Washington and London embassies
Department of Justice files
Provisional Government, cabinet minutes

Official Publications
Dáil debates, September 1922 –
Iris Dháil Éireann: official report. Debate on the Treaty between Great Britain and Ireland signed in London on the 6th December, 1921.
Saorstát Éireann, *Estimates for public services for the year ending 31st March 1924* (Dublin, 1924).

OTHER PRIMARY PRINTED SOURCES

'1916–1922 The real comparison', NLI, LOp117, item 51.
'Advance publicity booklet for Piaras Béaslaí's *Michael Collins and the making of a new Ireland*' (Dublin, n.d.), NLI, p2467, item 18.
Antrim's patriot dead 1797–1953 (n.d.).
Ballyseedy Memorial Committee, *75th anniversary programme* (Kerry, 1998).
Cuimhníonn Luimneach Cásg 1966 (Limerick, 1966).
Eleven Galway martyrs: unveiling programme (Tuam, n.d.).
Emly IRA memorial – souvenir programme (Tipperary, 1955).

Fine Gael, *Éire Ireland 1922–1997: a salute to the founders of a free and independent Ireland* (n.d.).

Free State Freaks, NLI, ILB 300p24, item 7.

'Free State soldiers', republican pamphlet, NLI, ILB 300p4, item 73.

'Holy places in Ireland have been violated by vandals', NLI, ILB 300p13, item 38.

'Invitation to the unveiling of the Cenotaph', NLI, ILB 300p9, item 14.

Irish Republican Army Organisation, *The truth about the army crisis* (Dublin, n.d.).

'League Against Imperialism and for national independence', NLI, LOp115, item 41.

'Memorial fund appeal', NLI, p2467, item 8.

'Memorial to Arthur Griffith', NLI, LOp115, item 56.

'Memorial to the founders of the Irish state', NLI, IR94109m15.

'Michael Collins memorial foundation supplement', 20 Aug. 1966, NLI, ILB 05p8.

'More executions', republican handbill, NLI, ILB 300p3, item 6.

National Archives of Ireland, *'A nation and not a rabble': Ireland in the year July 1921–June 1922* (Dublin, n.d.).

National Graves Association, *Tour of Glasnevin Cemetery* (Dublin, n.d.).

Oglaigh na hEireann Iarthar Luimní 1916–22, Newcastlewest monument restoration programme (1992).

O'Higgins, Kevin, *Three years hard labour. An address delivered to the Irish Society at Oxford University on the 31st October, 1924*, foreword by Eoin MacNeill (Dublin, n.d.).

O'Kennedy-Brindley Ltd., *Making history – the story of a remarkable campaign* (Dublin, 1927).

'Open letter from Padraig O'Brien of the "Irregular" forces to his former friend and comrade, Pat O'Brien of the "National" Army', NLI, ILB 300p3, item 13.

Premiere programme 6 Nov. 1996, *Michael Collins* directed by Neil Jordan.

'Publicity department pamphlet (republican), 9 July 1922, NLI, LOp117, item 91.

'Saorstát na hÉireann', Free State pamphlet, NLI, ILB 300p3, item 96.

'Souvenir programme of the unveiling of the Liam Lynch tower wolfhounds', 28 July 1996.

The two leaders (Dublin, 1922).

NEWSPAPERS

The Blue Flag
The Blueshirt
Clonmel Nationalist
Connaught Telegraph
Cork Constitution
Cork Examiner
Cork Weekly Examiner
Daily Bulletin
Derry Journal
Donegal Democrat
Donegal People's Press
Drogheda Independent
Éire – The Irish Nation
Enniscorthy Guardian

Evening Echo
Evening Herald
Free State – An Saorstát
Free State War Special
The Freeman – An Saoránach
Freeman's Journal
The Guardian
The Independent
Irish Freedom
Irish Independent
Irish People – War Special
Irish Press
Irish Times
Kerry News
Leinster Leader
Limerick Chronicle
Limerick Leader
Mayo News
Morning Post
Munster Express
Munster News
The Nation (1842–97)
The Nation (1922)
The Nation (Oct. 1924 – Aug. 1925)
The Nation (Mar. 1927 – Sept. 1931)
The Nation (June – August 1935)
Nenagh Guardian
New Ross Standard
Northern Star (1935)
The Observer
Offaly Independent
The People (Wexford)
An Phoblacht
Poblacht na hÉireann (Scottish edn.)
Poblacht na hÉireann War News
Realt a Deiscirt/Southern Star
Republican File
Republican Leader
Republican War Bulletin
Roscommon Herald
Sinn Féin
The Star – An Réalt
Sunday Independent
Sunday Press
Sunday Times
Sunday Tribune
The Times
Tipperary Star

United Ireland
United Irishman
Waterford News
Weekly Irish Times
Western People
Wicklow People
Young Ireland

PERIODICALS

The Bell
Catholic Bulletin
Fine Gael Digest
Gárda News
Gárda Review
Good Counsel Magazine
Illustrated London News
Iris an Ghárda
Iris Fianna Fáil
Irish Builder
Irish Statesman
Monthly Film Bulletin
An t-Óglách
Revolt – Voice of Young Republican Ireland
Wolfe Tone Annual
Wolfe Tone Weekly

PHOTOGRAPHIC COLLECTIONS

Hulton Getty Picture Collection
R Series – National Photographic Archive, Dublin
Elinor Wiltshire Collection – National Photographic Archive, Dublin

FILM, RADIO AND TELEVISION PROGRAMMES

RTÉ Archive
Ballyseedy by Pat Butler
Emmet Dalton remembers
Ireland: a television history
The Pat Kenny radio programme, Radio 1 (27 May 1998)
Lee, J. J., 'Opening address', Collins Conference, University College Cork, 28 Feb.
    1997, *Looking south*, Radio 1 (13 Aug. 1997)
Looking south, Radio 1 (20 Aug. 1997)
The madness within, produced by Colm Magee, RTÉ 1 (21 Jan. 1998)
Prime time
Seven ages by Seán Ó Mordha

Irish Film Archive
Beloved enemy (1936), directed by H. C. Potter
Mise Eire

Saoirse?
This other Eden (1959), directed by Muriel Box
Topical Budget, item no. 575–1

SECONDARY SOURCES

BOOKS

Abbott, Richard, *Police casualties in Ireland 1919–1922* (Dublin, 2000).
Agulhon, Maurice, *Histoire vagabonde* 2 vols. (Paris, 1998).
Anderson, Benedict, *Imagined communities: reflections on the origin and spread of nationalism* (2nd edn, London, 1996).
Andrews, C. S., *Dublin made me* (Dublin and Cork, 1979).
  Man of no property (Dublin and Cork, 1982).
Augusteijn, Joost, *From public defiance to guerrilla warfare: the experience of ordinary volunteers in the Irish War of Independence, 1916–1921* (Dublin, 1996).
Bann, Stephen, *The inventions of history: essays on the representation of the past* (Manchester, 1990).
Barrett, J. J., *In the name of the game* (Bray, 1997).
Barry, James, *Glasnevin cemetery: a short history of the famous Catholic necropolis* (Dublin, 1932).
Barry, Sebastian, *Plays 1* (London, 1997).
  The whereabouts of Eneas McNulty (London, 1998).
Barry, Tom, *Guerilla days in Ireland* (Dublin, 1949).
Bartlett, T. and Jeffery, Keith (eds.), *A military history of Ireland* (Cambridge, 1996).
Béaslaí, Piaras, *Michael Collins and the making of a new Ireland*, 2 vols. (Dublin, 1926).
Beckett, J. C., *The making of modern Ireland 1603–1923* (London, 1966).
Behan, Brian, *With breast expanded* (London, 1991).
Behan, Dominic, *Teems of times and happy returns* (London, 1961).
Bew, Paul, Hazelkorn, Ellen and Patterson, Henry, *The dynamics of Irish politics* (London, 1989).
Blake, Frances M., *The Irish civil war and what it still means for the Irish people* (London, 1986).
Bowen, Elizabeth, *The last September* (London, 1987; 1st edn, 1929).
Brady, Ciaran (ed.), *Ideology and the historians, historical studies, XVII* (Dublin, 1991).
Breen, Dan, *My fight for Irish freedom* (Dublin, 1968 edn).
Brennan, Robert, *Allegiance* (Dublin, 1950).
Brown, Terence, *Ireland: a social and cultural history* (London, 1985).
Browne, Noël, *Against the tide* (Dublin, 1987).
Bunyan, J. J. (ed.), *A sense of Fermoy* (Freshford, n.d.).
Burke, Peter, *The fabrication of Louis XIV* (New Haven and London, 1992).
Butler, T. (ed.), *Memory: history, culture and the mind* (London, 1989).
Byrne, John Francis, *Silent years: an autobiography with memoirs of James Joyce and our Ireland* (New York, 1953).
Callanan, Frank, *T. M. Healy* (Cork, 1996).
Camus, Albert, *The plague* (London, 1960 edn).
Chubb, Basil, *The government and politics of Ireland* (Oxford, 1974).

Clifford, Brendan, *The Irish Civil War: the conflict that formed the state* (Cork, 1993).

Cobb, Richard, *Reactions to the French Revolution* (Oxford, 1972).

Colley, Linda, *Britons: forging the nation 1707–1837* (New Haven and London, 1992).

Collins, Michael, *The path to freedom* (Dublin, 1922).

Collins, Stephen, *The Cosgrave legacy* (Dublin, 1996).

Colum, Padraic, *Arthur Griffith* (Dublin, 1959).

Conlon, Lil, *Cumann na mBan and the women of Ireland 1913–25* (Kilkenny, 1969).

Connerton, Paul, *How societies remember* (Cambridge, 1989).

Connolly, Seán (ed.), *The Oxford companion to Irish history* (Oxford, 1998).

Coogan, Oliver, *Politics and war in Meath* (Dublin, 1983).

Coogan, Tim Pat, *Michael Collins: a biography* (London, 1990).

   De Valera: long fellow, long shadow (London, 1993).

Coogan, Tim Pat and Morrison, George, *The Irish Civil War* (London, 1998).

Cooney, James, *Macroom: people and places* (Macroom, 1983).

Corish, P. J. (ed.), *Radicals, rebels and establishments, historical studies, XV* (Belfast, 1985).

Crone, J. S., *A concise dictionary of Irish biography* (Dublin, 1928; expanded edn, Dublin, 1937; reprint, 1970).

Cronin, Mike, *The Blueshirts and Irish politics* (Dublin, 1997).

Cronin, Seán, *Frank Ryan: the search for the republic* (Dublin, 1980).

Dalton, Charles, *With the Dublin Brigade 1917–1921* (London, 1929).

D'Alton, Louis, *This other Eden* (Dublin, 1954).

Darnton, Robert, *The great cat massacre and other episodes in French cultural history* (London, 1984).

   The kiss of Lamourette (London, 1990).

Davis, Richard, *Arthur Griffith* (Dundalk, 1976).

Deane, Seamus, *Reading in the dark* (London, 1996).

Deasy, Liam, *Brother against brother* (Dublin and Cork, 1982; Cork, 1998).

De Fuiteóil, Nioclás, *Waterford remembers* (Waterford, n.d.).

Devaney, Rev. Owen, *Killoe, history of a County Longford parish* (n.p., 1981).

De Vere White, Terence, *Prenez garde* (London, 1986 edn).

   Kevin O'Higgins (Dublin, 1986 edn).

Devlin, Judith and Fanning, Ronan (eds.), *Religion and rebellion* (Dublin, 1997).

Doherty, Gabriel and Keogh, Dermot (eds.), *Michael Collins and the making of the Irish state* (Cork, 1998).

Dooge, James (ed.), *Ireland in the contemporary world: essays in honour of Garret Fitzgerald* (Dublin, 1986).

Duggan, John P., *A history of the Irish army* (Dublin, 1991).

Dunne, Tom, *The writer as witness, historical studies, XVI* (Cork, 1987).

Dunphy, Richard, *The making of Fianna Fáil power in Ireland 1923–1948* (Oxford, 1995).

Dwyer, T. Ryle, *Eamon de Valera: the man and the myths* (Dublin, 1991).

Elliott, Marianne, *Wolfe Tone: prophet of independence* (Yale, 1989).

English, Richard and O'Malley, Cormac (eds.), *Prisoners: the civil war letters of Ernie O'Malley* (Dublin, 1991).

Evans, Martin and Lunn, Ken (eds.), *War and memory in the twentieth century* (Oxford and New York, 1997).

Fanning, Ronan, *The Irish department of finance 1922–58* (Dublin, 1978).
   Independent Ireland (Dublin, 1983).
   'The four-leaved shamrock': electoral politics and the national imagination in inde-pendent Ireland (25th O'Donnell Lecture, Tuesday, 22 February 1983, University College, Dublin, 1983).
Farley, Fidelma, *Ireland into film – This other Eden* (Cork, 2001).
Farrell, Brian, *The founding of Dáil Éireann: parliament and nation building* (Dublin, 1971).
Farry, Michael, *The aftermath of revolution: Sligo 1921–23* (Dublin, 2000).
Feehan, John M., *The shooting of Michael Collins: murder or accident?* (3rd edn, Dublin, 1982).
Fitzgerald, F. Scott, *Tender is the night* (London, 1955).
Fitzgibbon, Constantine, *High heroic* (London, 1969).
Fitzpatrick, David, *Politics and Irish life 1913–1921: provincial experience of war and revolution* (Dublin, 1977).
Fitzpatrick, David (ed.), *Ireland and the First World War* (Dublin, 1986).
   Revolution? Ireland 1917–1923 (Dublin, 1990).
Forester, Margery, *Michael Collins – the lost leader* (London, 1971).
Foster, R. F., *Modern Ireland 1600–1972* (London, 1988).
   The Irish story: telling tales and making it up in Ireland (London, 2001).
Fraser, T. G. (ed.), *The Irish parading tradition: following the drum* (London, 2000).
Fraser, T. G. and Jeffery, Keith (eds.), *Men, women and war, historical studies, XVIII* (Dublin, 1993).
Friel, Maeve, *Here lies – a guide to Irish graves* (Dublin, 1997).
Fussell, Paul, *The Great War and modern memory* (Oxford, 1975).
Gallagher, Frank, *The Anglo-Irish treaty* (London, 1965).
Garvin, Tom, *The evolution of Irish nationalist politics* (Dublin, 1981).
   Nationalist revolutionaries in Ireland 1858–1928 (Oxford, 1987).
   1922, the birth of Irish democracy (Dublin, 1996).
Geary, Laurence M. (ed.), *Rebellion and remembrance in modern Ireland* (Dublin, 2001).
Geertz, Clifford, *The interpretation of cultures* (New York, 1973).
Gellner, Ernest, *Conditions of liberty: civil society and its rivals* (London, 1996).
Gerth, H. H. and Wright Mills, C. (eds.), *Max Weber – essays in sociology* (2nd edn, London, 1964).
Geyl, Pieter, *Napoleon for and against* (London, 1949).
Gildea, Robert, *The past in French history* (New Haven and London, 1994).
Gillespie, Raymond and Kennedy, Brian P. (eds.), *Ireland: art into history* (Dublin, 1994).
Gillis, John R. (ed.), *Commemorations: the politics of national identity* (Princeton, 1994).
Gogarty, Oliver St John, *As I was going down Sackville Street* (London, 1954 edn; 1st edn, 1937).
Greer, D., *The incidence of the Terror during the French Revolution, a statistical inter-pretation* (Cambridge, Mass., 1935).
Griffith, Kenneth and O'Grady, Timothy E., *Curious journey: an oral history of Ireland's unfinished revolution* (London, 1982).
Halbwachs, Maurice, *La mémoire collective* (Paris, 1950).
Hart, Peter, *The IRA and its enemies: violence and community in Cork, 1916–1923* (Oxford, 1998).

Harvey, D. and White, G., *The barracks: a history of Victoria/Collins barracks* (Cork, 1997).

Hassall, Christopher, *Edward Marsh, patron of the arts* (London, 1959).

Hill, Judith, *Irish public sculpture: a history* (Dublin, 1998).

Hobsbawm, Eric J., *Nations and nationalism since 1780: programme, myth, reality* (Cambridge, 1990).

Hobsbawm, Eric J. and Ranger, Terence (eds.), *The invention of tradition* (Cambridge, 1983).

Hopkinson, Michael, *Green against green: the Irish Civil War* (Dublin, 1988).

Horgan, John, *Seán Lemass: the enigmatic patriot* (Dublin, 1997).

Hugo, Victor, *Les misérables*, 2 vols. (London, 1994 edn).

Ingram, John Kells, *Sonnets and other poems* (London, 1900).

Irish political song and poem leaflets 1915–1932 (Dublin, 1933).

Jeffery, Keith, *Ireland and the Great War* (Cambridge, 2000).

Jordan, Anthony J., *Seán MacBride – a biography* (Dublin, 1993).

Kee, Robert, *The green flag*, III: *Ourselves alone* (London, 1989).

Kelleher, Margaret, *The feminization of famine: expressions of the inexpressible?* (Cork, 1997).

Keogh, Dermot, *The Vatican, the bishops and Irish politics 1919–39* (Cambridge, 1986).
Ireland and Europe 1919–1948 (Dublin, 1988).
Twentieth-century Ireland: nation and state (Dublin, 1994).

Kiberd, Declan, *Inventing Ireland: the literature of the modern nation* (London, 1995).

Kinsella, Thomas, *Nightwalker and other poems* (Dublin, 1968).

Laffan, Michael, *The resurrection of Ireland: the Sinn Féin party 1916–1923* (Cambridge, 1999).

Lagrou, Pieter, *The legacy of Nazi occupation: patriotic memory and national recovery in Western Europe, 1945–1965* (Cambridge, 2000).

Lankford, Siobhán, *The hope and the sadness: personal recollections of troubled times in Ireland* (Cork, 1980).

Lee, J. J., *Ireland 1912–1985: politics and society* (Cambridge, 1989).
The modernisation of Irish society 1848–1918 (Dublin, 1989 edn).

Lee, J. J. (ed.), *Irish historiography 1970–1979* (Cork, 1981).
Ireland: towards a sense of place, UCC-RTE Lecture Series (Cork, 1985).

Leerssen, Joep, *Remembrance and imagination: patterns in the historical and literary representation of Ireland in the nineteenth century* (Cork, 1996).

Le Harivel, Adrian (ed.), *National Gallery of Ireland – illustrated summary catalogue of drawings, watercolours and miniatures* (Dublin, 1983).
National Gallery of Ireland – illustrated summary catalogue of prints and sculpture (Dublin, 1988).

Leonard, Jane, *The culture of commemoration: the culture of war commemoration* (Dublin, n.d.).

Leslie, Shane, *Long shadows* (London, 1966).

Liddy, Pat, *Dublin be proud* (Dublin, 1987).

Lincoln, Colm, *Dublin as a work of art* (Dublin, 1992).

Litton, Helen, *The Irish Civil War: an illustrated history* (Dublin, 1995).

Livingstone, Peadar, *The Monaghan story* (Enniskillen, 1980).

Longford, Earl of and O'Neill, T. P., *Eamon de Valera* (London, 1970).

Longley, Edna, *The living stream: literature and revisionism in Ireland* (Newcastle-upon-Tyne, 1994).
Lowenthal, David, *The past is a foreign country* (Cambridge, 1985).
Lyons, F. S. L., *Ireland since the famine* (London, 1971).
    Ireland since the famine (London, 1973 edn).
    Culture and anarchy in Ireland, 1890–1939 (Oxford, 1979).
Lyons, George A., *Some recollections of Griffith and his times* (Dublin, 1923).
Macardle, Dorothy, *Tragedies of Kerry* (Dublin, 1924).
    The Irish Republic (London, 1937).
McBride, Ian (ed.), *History and memory in modern Ireland* (Cambridge, 2001).
McBride, Lawrence (ed.), *Images, icons and the Irish nationalist imagination* (Dublin, 1999).
McConkey, Kenneth, *A free spirit: Irish art 1860–1960* (London, 1990).
McCoole, Sinéad, *Hazel: a life of Lady Lavery 1880–1935* (Dublin, 1996).
MacDonagh, Oliver, *Ireland* (New Jersey, 1968).
MacDonagh, Oliver, Mandle, W. F. and Travers, Pauric (eds.), *Irish culture and nationalism, 1750–1950* (London, 1983).
McDonnell, Kathleen, *There is a bridge at Bandon* (Cork, 1972).
MacEoin, Uinseann, *The IRA in the twilight years 1923–1948* (Dublin, 1997).
McIntosh, Gillian, *The force of culture: unionist identities in twentieth century Ireland* (Cork, 1999).
Mackay, James, *Michael Collins: a life* (Edinburgh, 1996).
MacManus, Francis (ed.), *The years of the great test, 1926–39* (Cork, 1967).
Mac Suain, Séamus, *County Wexford's Civil War* (Wexford, 1995).
Maher, Jim, *The flying column – west Kilkenny 1916–1921* (Dublin, 1987).
Manning, Maurice, *The Blueshirts* (Dublin, 1970).
Maume, Patrick, *The long gestation: Irish nationalist life 1891–1918* (Dublin, 1999).
Maye, Brian, *Arthur Griffith* (Dublin, 1997).
Mays, J. C. C. (ed.), *Collected poems of Denis Devlin* (Dublin, 1989).
Milroy, Seán, *The tariff commission and Saorstát economic policy* (Dublin, 1926).
Morash, Christopher, *Writing the Irish famine* (Oxford, 1995).
Morrison, George, *The Irish Civil War* (Dublin, 1981).
Mosse, George L., *Fallen soldiers. Reshaping the memory of the world wars* (Oxford, 1990).
Mulcahy, Risteárd, *Richard Mulcahy (1886–1971): a family memoir* (Dublin, 1999).
Murphy, Imelda, *Clongeen through the ages* (n.p., n.d.).
Murphy, John A., *Ireland in the twentieth century* (Dublin, 1975).
Murphy, Seamus, *Stone mad* (2nd edn, London, 1966).
National Graves Association, *The last post: Glasnevin cemetery* (1st edn, Dublin, 1932; 2nd edn, Dublin, 1976; 3rd edn, Dublin, 1985; American edn, Dublin, 1986).
Neeson, Eoin, *The Civil War in Ireland 1922–1923* (Cork, 1966).
Nelson, Justin, *Michael Collins: the final days* (Dublin, 1997).
Ní Dhonnchadha, Máirín and Dorgan, Theo (eds.), *Revising the rising* (Derry, 1991).
Nora, Pierre, *Les lieux de mémoire*, 7 vols. (Paris, 1984–92).
    Realms of memory: the construction of the French past, III: *Symbols* (New York, 1998).
Nowlan, Kevin B. (ed.), *The making of 1916: studies in the history of the rising* (Dublin, 1969).

O'Brien, George, *The village of longing* (Belfast, 1993 edn).

Ó Broin, León (ed.), *In great haste: the letters of Michael Collins and Kitty Kiernan* (Dublin, 1983).

O'Callaghan, Michael, *For Ireland and freedom: Roscommon's contribution to the fight for independence, 1917–1921* (Roscommon, 1991 edn).

O'Casey, Sean, *Three plays* (London, 1980 edn).

Juno and the paycock (Dublin, 1988 edn).

O'Connell, Maurice R. (ed.), *Daniel O'Connell: political pioneer* (Dublin, 1991).

People power: proceedings of the third annual Daniel O'Connell Workshop (Dublin, 1993).

O'Connor, Frank, *The big fellow* (Dublin, 1991 edn).

An only child (Belfast, 1993 edn).

Guests of the nation (5th edn, Dublin, 1993).

My father's son (Belfast, 1994 edn).

O'Connor, Ulick, *Brendan Behan* (London, 1970).

O'Day, Alan and Stevenson, John (eds.), *Irish historical documents since 1800* (Dublin, 1992).

O'Donoghue, Florence, *No other law* (Dublin, 1954).

O'Farrell, Padraic, *The Seán Mac Eoin story* (Dublin and Cork, 1981).

The blacksmith of Ballinalee – Seán Mac Eoin (Mullingar, 1993).

Who's who in the Irish war of independence and civil war 1916–1923 (Dublin, 1997).

O'Flaherty, Liam, *Civil war* (London, 1925).

The informer (3rd edn, London, 1926).

The assassin (8th edn, Dublin, 1993).

Insurrection (5th edn, Dublin, 1993).

O'Flanagan, P. and Buttimer, C. G. (eds.), *Cork: history and society* (Dublin, 1993).

Ó Gadhra, Nollaig, *Civil war in Connacht 1922–1923* (Cork, 1999).

O'Halpin, Eunan, *Defending Ireland: the Irish state and its enemies since 1922* (Oxford, 1999).

O'Hegarty, P. S., *A bibliography of Arthur Griffith, Michael Collins and Kevin O'Higgins* (Dublin, 1937).

The victory of Sinn Féin (Dublin, 1998) (1st edn. 1924).

Ó Luing, Seán, *Art Ó Gríofa* (Dublin, 1953).

O'Mahony, T. P., *The politics of dishonour: Ireland 1916–1977* (Dublin, 1977).

O'Malley, Ernie, *On another man's wound* (Dublin, 1990).

Ozouf, Mona, *Festivals and the French Revolution* (Cambridge, Mass., 1988).

Pakenham, Frank (Lord Longford), *Peace by ordeal* (London, 1935).

Phelan, James D., *Travel and comment* (San Francisco, 1923).

Philpin, C. H. E. (ed.), *Nationalism and popular protest in Ireland* (Cambridge, 1987).

Pinkman, John A., *In the legion of the vanguard*, ed. Francis E. Maguire (Dublin, 1998).

Porter, Roy (ed.), *Myths of the English* (Cambridge, 1992).

Potterton, Homan, *The O'Connell monument* (Cork, 1973).

An Post, *Postage stamps of Ireland: 70 years 1922–1992* (Dublin, 1992).

Regan, John M., *The Irish counter-revolution 1921–1936* (Dublin, 1999).

Reynolds, Brian A., *William T. Cosgrave and the foundation of the Irish Free State, 1922–25* (Kilkenny, n.d.).

Richards, Michael, *A time of silence: Civil War and the culture of repression in Franco's Spain* (Cambridge, 1998).

Roche, Richard, *Here's their memory: a tribute to the fallen of republican Wexford* (Wexford, 1966).

Rockett, Kevin (ed.), *The Irish filmography: fiction films 1896–1996* (Dun Laoghaire, 1996).

Rockett, Kevin, Gibbons, Luke and Hill, John, *Cinema and Ireland* (London, 1987).

An Roinn Oideachais, *Report of the Department of Education for the school year 1930–31* (Dublin, 1932).

Rousso, Henry, *The Vichy syndrome: history and memory in France since 1944* (London, 1991).

Ryan, Meda, *The Tom Barry story* (Dublin, 1982).

The day Michael Collins was shot (Dublin, 1989).

Schama, Simon, *Landscape and memory* (London, 1995).

Scott, James C., *Domination and the arts of resistance: hidden transcripts* (New Haven and London, 1990).

Sheehy, Jeanne, *Kingsbridge station* (Cork, 1973).

Snoddy, Theo, *Dictionary of Irish artists – twentieth century* (Dublin, 1996).

Spillman, Lyn, *Nation and commemoration: creating national identities in the United States and Australia* (Cambridge, 1997).

Stuart, Francis, *We have kept the faith* (Dublin, 1923).

Things to live for: notes for an autobiography (New York, 1938).

Thelen, David (ed.), *Memory and American history* (Bloomington and Indianapolis, 1990).

Thompson, E. P., *The making of the English working class* (4th edn, London, 1980).

Tone, Theobald Wolfe, *The autobiography of Theobald Wolfe Tone*, ed. R. B. O'Brien, 2 vols. (Dublin, 1867).

Twohig, Patrick J., *The dark secret of Béalnabláth – the Michael Collins story* (4th edn, Cork, 1997).

Valiulis, Maryann Gialanella, *Portrait of a revolutionary: General Richard Mulcahy and the founding of the Irish Free State* (Dublin, 1992).

Vovelle, Michel, *Ideologies and mentalities* (Chicago, 1990).

Walker, Brian M., *Dancing to history's tune: history, myth and politics in Ireland* (Belfast, 1996).

Walker, Brian M. (ed.), *Parliamentary election results in Ireland, 1918–1992* (Dublin, 1992).

Walsh, J. J., *Recollections of a rebel* (Tralee, 1944).

Whaley, J. (ed.), *Mirrors of morality. Studies in the social history of death* (London, 1981).

Williams, T. Desmond (ed.), *The Irish struggle, 1916–1926* (London, 1966).

Wilson, Trevor (ed.), *The political diaries of C. P. Scott 1911–1928* (London, 1970).

Winter, Jay, *Sites of memory, sites of mourning: the Great War in European cultural history* (Cambridge, 1996).

Winter, Jay and Sivan, Emmanuel (eds.), *War and remembrance in the twentieth century* (Cambridge, 1999).

Wrong, Dennis (ed.), *Max Weber* (New Jersey, 1970).

Yeats, W. B., *The collected poems of W. B. Yeats* (New York, 1956).

Younger, Calton, *Ireland's civil war* (London, 1968).

A state of disunion – Arthur Griffith, Michael Collins, James Craig, Eamon de Valera (London, 1972).

Zeldin, Theodore, *An intimate history of humanity* (New York, 1994).

ARTICLES

'After 75 years – the force celebrates', *Gárda News*, 16, 6 (Aug. 1997), 7–9.

Aguilar, Paloma, 'Collective memory and the Spanish Civil War: the case of political amnesty in the Spanish transition to democracy', working paper CEACS, no. 185 (Madrid, 1996).

    'Agents of memory: Spanish Civil War veterans and disabled soldiers', in Winter, Jay and Sivan, Emmanuel (eds.), *War and remembrance in the twentieth century* (Cambridge, 1999), 84–103.

Akenson, D. H. and Fallin, J. F., 'The Irish civil war and the drafting of the Free State constitution – the drafting committee and the boundaries of action', *Éire-Ireland*, 5, 1 (Spring 1970), 10–26.

    'The Irish civil war and the drafting of the Free State constitution – the drafting process', *Éire-Ireland*, 5, 2 (Summer 1970), 42–93.

    'The Irish civil war and the drafting of the Free State constitution – Collins, De Valera and the pact: a new interpretation', *Éire-Ireland*, 5, 4 (Winter 1970), 28–70.

Alter, Peter, 'Symbols of Irish nationalism', *Studia Hibernica*, 14 (1974), 104–23.

Aughey, Arthur, 'What is living and what is dead in the ideal of 1916?', in Ní Dhonnchadha, Máirín and Dorgan, Theo (eds.), *Revising the rising* (Derry, 1991), 71–90.

Banotti, Mary, 'Introduction', in Doherty, Gabriel and Keogh, Dermot (eds.), *Michael Collins and the making of the Irish state* (Cork, 1998), 15–18.

Barrett, Cyril, 'Irish nationalism and art 1800–1921', *Studies*, 64 (Winter 1975), 393–409.

Barrington, T. J., 'Public administration 1927–36', in MacManus, Francis (ed.), *The years of the great test, 1926–39* (Cork, 1967), 80–91.

    'The civic deficit in Ireland', in O'Connell, Maurice (ed.), *People power* (Dublin, 1993), 1–18.

Barry, Peter, 'The boy from the cross', *Cork Review*, 4 (Oct. 1980), 48–9.

Behal, Risteard, 'Ballyseedy – 60th anniversary', *An Cumann Cabhrach testimonial dinner programme* (1983), 18–19.

Bendix, Richard, 'Reflections on charismatic leadership', in Wrong, Dennis (ed.), *Max Weber* (New Jersey, 1970), 166–81.

Bew, Paul, 'The real importance of Sir Roger Casement', *History Ireland*, 2, 2 (Summer 1994), 42–5.

Bhreathnach-Lynch, Sighle, 'Albert Power, RHA', *Irish Arts Review Yearbook* (1990–1), 111–14.

    'The church and the artist 1922–1945', *Irish Arts Review Yearbook* (1991–2), 130–4.

    'Public sculpture in independent Ireland 1922–1972: expressions of nationhood in bronze and stone', *The Medal*, 21 (Autumn 1992), 44–52.

    'Face value: commemoration and its discontents', *Circa*, 65 (Autumn 1993), 35–7.

    ' "Executed" : the political commissions of Albert G. Power', *Éire-Ireland*, 29, 1 (Spring 1994), 44–60.

    'The art of Albert G. Power, 1881–1945: a sculptural legacy of Irish Ireland', in Gillespie, Raymond and Kennedy, Brian P. (eds.), *Ireland: art into history* (Dublin, 1994), 118–31.

    'The Easter rising 1916: constructing a canon in art and artefacts', *History Ireland*, 5, 1 (Spring 1997), 37–42.

'Commemorating the hero in newly independent Ireland: expressions of nationhood in bronze and stone', in McBride, Lawrence (ed.), *Images, icons and the Irish nationalist imagination* (Dublin, 1999), 148–65.

Blau, Peter, M., 'Critical remarks on Weber's theory of authority', in Wrong, Dennis (ed.), *Max Weber* (New Jersey, 1970), 147–65.

Blight, David W., ' "For something beyond the battlefield": Frederick Douglass and the struggle for the memory of the Civil War', in Thelen, David (ed.), *Memory and American history* (Bloomington and Indianapolis, 1990), 27–39.

'Blueshirts and the IRA', *Quarterly Review*, 261 (July and Oct. 1933), 292–305.

Bolton, G. C., 'The Anglo-Irish and the historians', in MacDonagh, Oliver, Mandle, W. F. and Travers, Pauric (eds.), *Irish culture and nationalism, 1750–1950* (London, 1983), 239–57.

Boyce, D. G., 'Ireland and the first world war', *History Ireland*, 2, 3 (Autumn 1994), 48–53.

Brasted, H. V., 'Irish nationalism and the British empire in the late nineteenth-century', in MacDonagh, Oliver, Mandle, W. F. and Travers, Pauric (eds.), *Irish culture and nationalism, 1750–1950* (London, 1983), 83–103.

Broderick, Joseph, 'De Valera and Archbishop Mannix', *History Ireland*, 2, 3 (Autumn 1994), 37–42.

Bromage, Mary C., 'Image of nationhood', *Éire-Ireland*, 3, 3 (Autumn 1968), 11–26.

Bryan, Dominic, 'Interpreting the twelfth', *History Ireland*, 2, 2 (Summer 1994), 37–41.

Buckley, Vincent, 'Poetry and the avoidance of nationalism', in MacDonagh, Oliver, Mandle, W. F. and Travers, Pauric (eds.), *Irish culture and nationalism, 1750–1950* (London, 1983), 258–79.

Burke, Peter, 'Rethinking cultural history', *Cambridge Review* (18 Nov. 1983), 206–8.
  'History as social memory', in Butler, T. (ed.), *Memory: history, culture and the mind* (London, 1989), 97–113.

Bushaway, Bob, 'Name upon name: the Great War and remembrance', in Porter, Roy (ed.), *Myths of the English* (Cambridge, 1992), 136–67.

Butler, Pat, 'Interview with Séamus Murphy 15th July, 1975', *Cork Review*, 4 (Oct. 1980), 42–5.

Cannadine, David, 'War and death, grief and mourning in modern Britain', in Whaley, J. (ed.), *Mirrors of mortality. Studies in the social history of death* (London, 1981), 187–219.

Clive, Kitty, 'Albert Power, RHA', *The Leader* (7 Nov. 1942), 290–2.

Coffey, Joseph F., 'The men who came back: memories of the "26th" ', *Capuchin Annual* (1948), 121–6.

Coleman, Marie, 'Historians and the Irish civil war', *UCD History Review* (1994), 37–40.
  'Review of Pádraic O'Farrell's *Who's who in the Irish war of independence and civil war, 1916–1923*', *Irish Economic and Social History*, 24 (1997), 168–9.

Comerford, R. V., 'Patriotism as pastime: the appeal of Fenianism in the mid-1860s', *Irish Historical Studies*, 22, 87 (Mar. 1981), 239–50.

Confino, Alon, 'Collective memory and cultural history: problems of method', *American History Review* (Dec. 1997), 1386–1403.

Cooke, Francis, 'A recollection of a young man's civil war in the west of Ireland', *Galway Roots*, 4 (n.d.), 54–5.

Coote, Michael, 'In memory of a murdered colleague', *Gárda News*, 15, 9 (Nov./Dec. 1995), 26–7.

Courtney, Shay, 'Women active in IRA flying columns?', *History Ireland*, 4, 4 (Winter 1996), 11–12.

Crane, Susan A., 'Writing the individual back into collective memory', *American Historical Review*, 102, 5 (Dec. 1997), 1372–85.

Crawford Greer, Sammye, 'The poet's role in an age of emptiness and chaos: a reading of Yeats's *Meditations in time of civil war*', *Éire-Ireland*, 7, 3 (Autumn 1972), 82–92.

Cronin, Mike, 'Blueshirts, sports and socials', *History Ireland*, 2, 3 (Autumn 1994), 43–7.

'The Blueshirt movement, 1932–5: Ireland's fascists?', *Journal of Contemporary History*, 30, 2 (1995), 311–32.

Curtis, Louis Perry Jr., 'Moral and physical force: the language of violence in Irish nationalism', *Journal of British Studies*, 27, 1 (Jan. 1988), 150–89.

Dalton, G. F., 'The tradition of blood sacrifice to the goddess Éire', *Studies*, 63 (Winter 1974), 343–54.

Daly, Mary E., 'Review article: historians and the Famine: a beleaguered species?', *Irish Historical Studies*, 30, 120 (Nov. 1997), 591–601.

Daniel, T. K., 'Griffith on his noble head: the determinants of Cumann na nGaedheal economic policy, 1922–32', *Irish Economic and Social History*, 3 (1976), 55–65.

Davis, Eoghan, 'The guerrilla mind', in Fitzpatrick, David (ed.), *Revolution? Ireland 1917–1923* (Trinity History Workshop, Dublin, 1990), 43–59.

Deane, Seamus, 'Irish national character 1750–1900', in Dunne, Tom (ed.), *The writer as witness* (Cork, 1987), 90–113.

'Wherever green is read', in Ní Dhonnchadha, Máirín and Dorgan, Theo (eds.), *Revising the rising* (Derry, 1991), 91–105.

'Land and soil: a territorial rhetoric', *History Ireland*, 2, 1 (Spring 1994), 31–4.

De Valera, Sile, 'Dev and Collins were good pals', in Nelson, Justin, *Michael Collins: the final days* (Dublin, 1997), 115–17.

De Vere White, Terence, 'Social life in Ireland', in MacManus, Francis (ed.), *The years of the great test, 1926–39* (Cork, 1967), 19–29.

'The seeds of division', in *Eamon de Valera 1882–1975: the controversial giant of modern Ireland* (Irish Times, Dublin, 1976), 99–105.

Doherty, Gabriel, 'A Star Chamber affair: The death of Timothy Coughlan', *History Ireland*, 3, 1 (Spring 1995), 43–7.

Doherty, Gabriel and Keogh, Dermot, ' "Sorrow but no despair – the road is marked": the politics of funerals in post-1916 Ireland', in Doherty, Gabriel and Keogh, Dermot (eds.), *Michael Collins and the making of the Irish state* (Cork, 1998), 186–201.

Dooley, Dolores, 'Expanding an island ethic', in Lee, J. J. (ed.), *Ireland: towards a sense of place* (Cork, 1985), 47–65.

Duggan, J. P., 'Poltergeist pistol', *History Ireland*, 3, 3 (Autumn 1995), 27–8.

Dunne, Tom, 'A polemical introduction: literature, literary theory and the historian', in Dunne, Tom (ed.), *The writer as witness* (Cork, 1987), 1–9.

Fallon, Charlotte, 'Civil war hungerstrikes: women and men', *Éire-Ireland*, 22, 3 (Autumn 1987), 75–91.

Fanning, Ronan, ' "The great enchantment": uses and abuses of modern Irish history', in Dooge, James (ed.), *Ireland in the contemporary world: essays in honour of Garret Fitzgerald* (Dublin, 1986), 131–47.

'Michael Collins – an overview', in Doherty, Gabriel and Keogh, Dermot (eds.), *Michael Collins and the making of the Irish state* (Cork, 1998), 202–10.

Farrell, Brian, 'The new state and Irish political culture', *Administration*, 16 (1968), 238–46.

'A note on the Dáil constitution 1919', *Irish Jurist* (1969), 127–38.

Finney, Helen, 'Art of the state', *Sculptors' Society of Ireland Newsletter* (1997), 10.

Fitzpatrick, David, 'The geography of Irish nationalism 1910–1921', in Philpin, C. H. E. (ed.), *Nationalism and popular protest in Ireland* (Cambridge, 1987), 403–41.

'The futility of history: a failed experiment in Irish education', in Brady, Ciaran (ed.), *Ideology and the historians, historical studies, XVII* (Dublin, 1991), 168–83.

'Militarism in Ireland, 1900–22', in Bartlett, T. and Jeffery, Keith (eds.), *A military history of Ireland* (Cambridge, 1996), 379–406.

'Review of Pádraic O'Farrell's *Who's who in the Irish war of independence and civil war, 1916–1923*', *Irish Historical Studies*, 30, 120 (Nov. 1997), 626.

'Commemoration in the Irish Free State: a chronicle of embarrassment', in McBride, Ian (ed.), *History and memory in modern Ireland* (Cambridge, 2001), 184–203.

Fleischmann, Aloys, 'A Munster Phidias', *Cork Review*, 4 (Oct. 1980), 23–5.

Foley, Dermot, 'The rose in the stone', *Cork Review*, 4 (Oct. 1980), 16–18.

Foster, R. F., 'Remembering 1798', in R. F. Foster, *The Irish story: telling tales and making it up in Ireland* (London, 2001), 211–34.

Gallagher, Michael, 'The pact general election of 1922', *Irish Historical Studies*, 21, 84 (Sept. 1979), 404–21.

Garvin, Tom, 'The destiny of the soldiers: tradition and modernity in the politics of de Valera's Ireland', *Political Studies*, 26, 3 (Sept. 1978), 328–47.

'Priests and patriots: Irish separatism and fear of the modern 1890–1914', *Irish Historical Studies*, 25, 97 (May 1986), 67–81.

'O'Connell and the making of Irish political culture', in O'Connell, Maurice R. (ed.), *Daniel O'Connell: political pioneer* (Dublin, 1991), 7–12.

'The rising and Irish democracy', in Ní Dhonnchadha, Máirín and Dorgan, Theo (eds.), *Revising the rising* (Derry, 1991), 21–8.

'Political power and economic development in Ireland: a comparative perspective', in O'Connell, Maurice R. (ed.), *People power* (Dublin, 1993), 32–6.

'Review of Brian P. Murphy's *John Chartres: mystery man of the treaty*', *Irish Historical Studies*, 30, 120 (Nov. 1997), 627.

'Dev and Mick – the 1922 split as social psychological event', in Doherty, Gabriel and Keogh, Dermot (eds.), *Michael Collins and the making of the Irish state* (Cork, 1998), 146–54.

Gaughan, J. Anthony, 'Review of *The Cosgrave legacy* by Stephen Collins', *Studies*, 86, 344 (Winter 1997), 400–2.

Gearty, Margot, 'Michael Collins: the Granard connection', in Doherty, Gabriel and Keogh, Dermot (eds.), *Michael Collins and the making of the Irish state* (Cork, 1998), 38–44.

'General Liam Lynch national commemoration committee', in Bunyan, J. J. (ed.), *A sense of Fermoy* (Freshford, n.d.), 126.

Gibbons, Luke, ' "A shadowy narrator": history, art and romantic nationalism in Ireland, 1750–1850', in Brady, Ciaran (ed.), *Ideology and the historian, historical studies, XVII* (Dublin, 1991), 99–127.

Gibbs, A. M., 'Bernard Shaw's other island', in MacDonagh, Oliver, Mandle, W. F. and Travers, Pauric (eds.), *Irish culture and nationalism, 1750–1950* (London, 1983), 122–36.

Girvin, Brian, 'Making nations: O'Connell, religion and the creation of political identity', in O'Connell, Maurice, R. (ed.), *Daniel O'Connell: political pioneer* (Dublin, 1991), 13–34.

Glandon, Virginia E., 'Arthur Griffith and the ideal Irish state', *Studies*, 73 (Spring 1984), 26–36.

Griffiths, A. R. G., 'Finland, Norway and the Easter rising', in MacDonagh, Oliver, Mandle, W. F. and Travers, Pauric (eds.), *Irish culture and nationalism, 1750–1950* (London, 1983), 149–60.

Grogan, Vincent, 'Towards the new constitution', in MacManus, Francis (ed.), *The years of the great test, 1926–39* (Cork, 1967), 161–72.

Hart, Peter, 'Youth culture and the Cork IRA', in Fitzpatrick, David (ed.), *Revolution? Ireland 1917–1923* (Dublin, 1990), 10–24.

'Michael Collins and the assassination of Sir Henry Wilson', *Irish Historical Studies*, 28, 110 (Nov. 1992), 150–70.

'Class, community and the Irish Republican Army in Cork, 1917–23', in O'Flanagan, P. and Buttimer, C. G. (eds.), *Cork: history and society* (Dublin, 1993), 963–85.

'Review of *Prisoners: the civil war letters of Ernie O'Malley* edited by Richard English & Cormac O'Malley', *Irish Historical Studies*, 28, 111 (May 1993), 336–7.

'The geography of revolution in Ireland, 1917–1923', *Past and Present*, 155 (May 1997), 142–76.

Hawkings, F. M. A., 'Defence and the role of Erskine Childers in the treaty negotiations of 1921', *Irish Historical Studies*, 22, 87 (Mar. 1981), 251–70.

Hayes, Michael, 'Dáil Éireann and the Irish Civil War', *Studies*, 58 (Spring 1969), 1–23.

'Michael Collins', *Capuchin Annual* (1972), 251–85.

'Review of *Green against green: the Irish civil war* by Michael Hopkinson', *Studies*, 78 (Spring 1989), 110–12.

Healy, James, 'The civil war hunger strike – October 1923', *Studies*, 71 (Autumn 1982), 213–26.

Heaney, Seamus, 'The sense of the past', *History Ireland*, 1, 4 (Winter 1993), 33–7.

Hill, Myrtle and Pollock, Vivienne, 'Images of the past: photographs as historical evidence', *History Ireland*, 2, 1 (Spring 1994), 9–14.

Holohan, Francis, T., 'History teaching in the Irish Free State 1922–35', *History Ireland*, 2, 4 (Winter 1994), 53–5.

Hopkinson, Michael, 'The Craig–Collins pacts of 1922: two attempted reforms of the Northern Ireland government', *Irish Historical Studies*, 27, 106 (Nov. 1990), 145–58.

'Review article: biography of the revolutionary period: Michael Collins and Kevin Barry', *Irish Historical Studies*, 28, 111 (May 1993), 310–16.

'Review of *1922: the birth of Irish democracy* by Tom Garvin', *Irish Historical Studies*, 30, 120 (Nov. 1997), 628–9.

Inglis, K. S., 'The homecoming: the war memorial movement in Cambridge, England', *Journal of Contemporary History*, 27, 4 (Oct. 1992), 583–606.

'IRA monument at Charleville', *Charleville and District Historical Journal*, 3 (1988), 112–13.

Jackson, Alvin, 'The Larne gun running of 1914', *History Ireland*, 1, 1 (Spring 1993), 35–8.

Jeffery, Keith, 'The Great War in modern Irish memory', in Fraser, T. G. and Jeffery, Keith (eds.), *Men, women and war, historical studies, XVIII* (Dublin, 1993), 136–57.

'Irish artists and the first world war', *History Ireland*, 1, 2 (Summer 1993), 42–5.

Jørstad, Jonas, 'Nations once again – Ireland's civil war in European context', in Fitzpatrick, David (ed.), *Revolution? Ireland 1917–1923* (Dublin, 1990), 159–73.

Kearney, Richard, 'Revisualizing times past', *Studies*, 71 (Spring 1982), 85–93.

Kennedy, Brian P., 'The Irish Free State 1922–49: a visual perspective', in Gillespie, Raymond and Kennedy, Brian P. (eds.), *Ireland: art into history* (Dublin, 1994), 132–52.

Kennedy, David, 'Catholics in Northern Ireland, 1926–1939', in MacManus, Francis (ed.), *The years of the great test, 1926–39* (Cork, 1967), 138–49.

Keogh, Dermot, 'The Catholic church and politics in Ireland', in O'Connell, Maurice R. (ed.), *People power* (Dublin, 1993), 57–79.

'Review of *De Valera – long fellow, long shadow* by Tim Pat Coogan', *History Ireland*, 1, 4 (Winter 1993), 58–9.

'The Catholic church and the Irish Free State 1923–32', *History Ireland*, 2, 1 (Spring 1994), 47–51.

Kiberd, Declan, 'The elephant of revolutionary forgetfulness', in Ní Dhonnchadha, Máirín and Dorgan, Theo (eds.), *Revising the rising* (Derry, 1991), 1–20.

'Romantic Ireland's dead and gone', *Times Literary Supplement* (12 June 1998), 12–14.

Kinsella, Sean, 'The cult of violence and the revolutionary tradition in Ireland', *Studies*, 83 (Spring 1994), 20–9.

Kirkaldy, John, 'English cartoonists; Ulster realities', *Éire-Ireland*, 16, 3 (Autumn 1981), 27–42.

Kline, Benjamin, 'Churchill and Collins 1919–22: admirers or adversaries?', *History Ireland*, 1, 3 (Autumn 1993), 38–43.

Kotsonouris, Mary, 'Revolutionary justice: the Dáil Éireann courts', *History Ireland*, 2, 3 (Autumn 1994), 32–6.

Laffan, Michael, 'The unification of Sinn Féin in 1917', *Irish Historical Studies*, 17, 67 (Mar. 1971), 353–79.

' "Labour must wait": Ireland's conservative revolution', in Corish, P. J. (ed.), *Radicals, rebels and establishments, historical studies, XV* (Belfast, 1985), 203–22.

'Insular attitudes: the revisionists and their critics', in Ní Dhonnchadha, Máirín and Dorgan, Theo (eds.), *Revising the rising* (Derry, 1991), 106–21.

'Review of *Green against green: the Irish Civil War* by Michael Hopkinson', *Irish Historical Studies*, 28, 111 (May 1993), 335–6.

'The sacred memory: religion, revisionists and the Easter rising', in Devlin, Judith and Fanning, Ronan (eds.), *Religion and rebellion* (Dublin, 1997), 171–89.

Laquer, Thomas W., 'Memory and naming in the Great War', in Gillis, John R. (ed.), *Commemorations: the politics of national identity* (New Jersey, 1994), 150–67.

Lawlor, S. M., 'Ireland from truce to treaty: war or peace? July to October 1921', *Irish Historical Studies*, 22, 85 (Mar. 1980), 49–64.

Lee, J. J., 'In search of Patrick Pearse', in Ní Dhonnchadha, Máirín and Dorgan, Theo (eds.), *Revising the rising* (Derry, 1991), 122–38.

'The challenge of a Collins biography', in Doherty, Gabriel and Keogh, Dermot (eds.), *Michael Collins and the making of the Irish state* (Cork, 1998), 19–37.

Leonard, Jane, ' "Lest we forget": Irish war memorials', in Fitzpatrick, David (ed.), *Ireland and the First World War* (Dublin, 1986), 59–67.

'Facing "the finger of scorn": veterans' memories of Ireland after the Great War', in Evans, Martin and Lunn, Ken (eds.), *War and memory in the twentieth century* (Oxford and New York, 1997), 59–72.

Longley, Edna, 'The rising, the Somme and Irish memory', in Ní Dhonnchadha, Máirín and Dorgan, Theo (eds.), *Revising the rising* (Derry, 1991), 29–49.

Lukes, Steven, 'Political ritual and social integration', *Sociology*, 9 (1975), 289–308.

Lydon, Sean, 'The Harriers – another look', *Gárda Review*, 4, 3 (Mar. 1976), 13–15.

Lyons, F. S. L., 'The minority problem in the 26 counties', in MacManus, Francis (ed.), *The years of the great test, 1926–39* (Cork, 1967), 92–103.

'Yeats and the Anglo-Irish twilight', in MacDonagh, Oliver, Mandle, W. F. and Travers, Pauric (eds.), *Irish culture and nationalism, 1750–1950* (London, 1983), 212–38.

Lysaght, Charles, 'Review of Sinéad McCoole's *Hazel: a life of Lady Lavery, 1880–1935*', *Irish Historical Studies*, 30, 120 (Nov. 1997), 629–32.

McBride, Ian, 'Review article: reclaiming the rebellion: 1798 in 1998', *Irish Historical Studies*, 31, 123 (May 1999), 395–410.

McCabe, Ian, 'J. F. K. in Ireland', *History Ireland*, 1, 4 (Winter 1993), 38–42.

McCabe, Michael, 'Baptism of fire', *Gárda Review*, 20, 4 (May 1992), 20–1.

McCartan, Tom, 'The untouchable – the strange story of Michael Collins and Channel 4', *Irish Ways*, 1 (Winter 1991/92), 12–13.

McCarthy, Andrew, 'Michael Collins – Minister for Finance 1919–22', in Doherty, Gabriel and Keogh, Dermot (eds.), *Michael Collins and the making of the Irish state* (Cork, 1998), 52–67.

McCartney, Donal, 'The political use of history in the work of Arthur Griffith', *Journal of Contemporary History*, 8, 1 (Jan. 1973), 3–19.

McColgan, John, 'Implementing the 1921 treaty: Lionel Curtis and constitutional procedure', *Irish Historical Studies*, 20, 79 (Mar. 1977), 312–33.

McCracken, J. L., 'The political scene in Northern Ireland 1926–37', in MacManus, Francis (ed.), *The years of the great test, 1926–39* (Cork, 1967), 150–60.

MacElhinney, Liam, 'The Drumboe martyrs', *An Cumann Cabhrach testimonial dinner programme* (1983), 5–6.

Mac Giolla Choille, Breandán, 'Mourning the martyrs: a study of demonstration in Limerick city 8 December 1867', *North Munster Antiquarian Journal*, 10, 2 (1967), 173–205.

McGlynn, Pat, 'Prison conditions in the south of Ireland 1585–1985', *An Cumann Cabhrach testimonial dinner programme* (1985), (not paginated).

McIntosh, Gillian, 'Symbolic mirrors: commemorations of Edward Carson in the 1930s', *Irish Historical Studies*, 32, 125 (May 2000), 93–112.

McKeane, Ian, 'Michael Collins and the media: then and now', *History Ireland*, 3, 3 (Autumn 1995), 23–6.

McMahon, Deirdre, ' "A worthy monument to a great man": Piaras Béaslaí's Life of Michael Collins', *Bullán: an Irish Studies Journal*, 2, 2 (Winter/Spring 1996), 55–65.

'Michael Collins – his biographers Piaras Béaslaí and Rex Taylor', in Doherty, Gabriel and Keogh, Dermot (eds.), *Michael Collins and the making of the Irish state* (Cork, 1998), 127–33.

MacManus, Francis, 'Imaginative literature and the revolution', in Williams, T. Desmond (ed.), *The Irish struggle, 1916–1926* (London, 1966), 19–30.

'The literature of the period', in MacManus, Francis (ed.), *The years of the great test, 1926–39* (Cork, 1967), 115–26.

Malcolm, Elizabeth, 'Popular recreation in nineteenth-century Ireland', in MacDonagh, Oliver, Mandle, W. F. and Travers, Pauric (eds.), *Irish culture and nationalism, 1750–1950* (London, 1983), 40–55.

Mandle, W. F., 'The Gaelic Athletic Association and popular culture 1884–1924', in MacDonagh, Oliver, Mandle, W. F. and Travers, Pauric (eds.), *Irish culture and nationalism, 1750–1950* (London, 1983), 104–21.

Mannion, Orlaith, 'The nationalist monuments at Cork and Skibbereen', in Geary, Laurence M. (ed.), *Rebellion and remembrance in Ireland* (Dublin, forthcoming).

Mansergh, Martin, ' "The freedom to achieve freedom"? The political ideas of Collins and de Valera', in Doherty, Gabriel and Keogh, Dermot (eds.), *Michael Collins and the making of the Irish state* (Cork, 1998), 155–85.

Mansergh, Nicholas, 'Ireland: external relations 1926–39', in MacManus, Francis (ed.), *The years of the great test, 1926–39* (Cork, 1967), 127–37.

Martin, F. X., '1916 – myth, fact, and mystery', *Studia Hibernica*, 7 (1967), 7–126.

'The 1916 rising – a coup d'état or a bloody protest?', *Studia Hibernica*, 8 (1968), 106–37.

Martin, Patrick, 'The years of Ned Broy', *Gárda Review*, 2, 8 (Aug. 1974), 15–16.

'O'Duffy – man with a mission', *Gárda Review*, 2, 9 (Sept. 1974), 24–5.

Meenan, James, 'From free trade to self-sufficiency', in MacManus, Francis (ed.), *The years of the great test, 1926–39* (Cork, 1967), 69–79.

Merridale, Catherine, 'War, death and remembrance in Soviet Russia', in Winter, Jay and Sivan, Emmanuel (eds.), *War and remembrance in the twentieth century* (Cambridge, 1999), 61–83.

Moran, Seán Farrell, 'Images, icons and the practice of Irish history', in McBride, Lawrence (ed.), *Images, icons and the Irish nationalist imagination* (Dublin, 1999), 166–76.

Morrall, John B., 'Kathleen Ní Houlihan's new clothes: recent perspectives on Irish history', *Studies*, 63 (Autumn 1974), 243–9.

Morris, Ewan, ' "God save the King" versus "The Soldier's Song": the 1929 Trinity College national anthem dispute and the politics of the Irish Free State', *Irish Historical Studies*, 31, 121 (May 1998), 72–90.

Mosse, George L., 'National cemeteries and national revival: the cult of the fallen soldiers in Germany', *Journal of Contemporary History*, 14, 1 (Jan. 1979), 1–20.

Mulcahy, Risteárd, 'Michael Collins and the making of a new Ireland', *Studies*, 67 (Autumn 1978), 187–200.

Murphy, Brian, 'The first Dáil Éireann', *History Ireland*, 2, 1 (Spring 1994), 41–6.

Murphy, Paula, 'The politics of the street monument', *Irish Arts Review Yearbook*, 10 (1994), 202–8.

'John Henry Foley's O'Connell monument', *Irish Arts Review Yearbook*, 11 (1995), 155–6.

Murphy, Sean, 'Who was Molly Malone?', *History Ireland*, 1, 2 (Summer 1993), 39–41.

Needham, Andy, 'Force has it licked!', *Gárda Review*, 25, 3 (Apr. 1997), 12–13.

Nevin, Donal, 'Labour and the political revolution', in MacManus, Francis (ed.), *The years of the great test, 1926–39* (Cork, 1967), 55–68.

Nowlan, Kevin B., 'President Cosgrave's last administration', in MacManus, Francis (ed.), *The years of the great test, 1926–39* (Cork, 1967), 7–18.

O'Beirne-Ranelagh, John, 'The IRB from the treaty to 1924', *Irish Historical Studies*, 20, 77 (Mar. 1976), 26–39.

O'Bradaigh, Ruairi, 'Women in struggle', *An Cumann Cabhrach testimonial dinner programme* (1986), (not paginated).

O'Brien, Gerard, 'The record of the first Dáil debates', *Irish Historical Studies*, 28, 111 (May 1993), 306–9.

O'Byrne, Anne, 'Monuments, counter-monuments and memory in Ireland', *Art Bulletin*, 2, 57 (June/July 1994), 13–16.

Ó Cainte, Donal, 'A Trinity of martyrs', *Charleville and District Historical Journal*, 5 (1990), 7–16.

O'Callaghan, Margaret, 'Language, nationality and cultural identity in the Irish Free State, 1922–7: the *Irish Statesman* and the *Catholic Bulletin* reappraised', *Irish Historical Studies*, 24, 94 (Nov. 1984), 226–45.

Ó Catháin, Séan, 'Education in the new Ireland', in MacManus, Francis (ed.), *The years of the great test, 1926–39* (Cork, 1967), 104–14.

Ó Conaill, Dáithí, 'Republican plot Cork', *An Cumann Cabhrach testimonial dinner programme* (1983), 6.

Ó Corráin, Donnachadh, 'Legend as critic', in Dunne, Tom (ed.), *The writer as witness* (Cork, 1987), 23–38.

Ó Crualaoich, Gearóid, 'Responding to the rising', in Ní Dhonnchadha, Máirín and Dorgan, Theo (eds.), *Revising the rising* (Derry, 1991), 50–70.

O'Farrell, Patrick, 'History in Ireland: some comments and questions', *Quest*, 1 (1974), 4–11.

Ó Giolláin, Diarmuid, 'Heroic biographers in folklore and popular culture', in Doherty, Gabriel and Keogh, Dermot (eds.), *Michael Collins and the making of the Irish state* (Dublin, 1998), 134–45.

O'Halpin, Eunan, 'A savage chaos: review of *Green against green: the Irish Civil War* by Michael Hopkinson', *Irish Review*, 6 (Spring 1989), 147–9.

'Army, politics and society in independent Ireland, 1923–1945', in Fraser, T. G. and Jeffery, Keith (eds.), *Men, women and war, historical studies, XVIII* (Dublin, 1993), 158–74.

'Parliamentary party discipline and tactics: the Fianna Fáil Archives, 1926–32', *Irish Historical Studies*, 30, 120 (Nov. 1997), 581–90.

'Collins and intelligence 1919–1923', in Doherty, Gabriel and Keogh, Dermot (eds.), *Michael Collins and the making of the Irish state* (Cork, 1998), 68–80.

'Historical revisit: Dorothy Macardle, *The Irish Republic* (1937)', *Irish Historical Studies*, 31, 123 (May 1999), 389–94.

O'Keefe, Timothy J., 'The art and politics of the Parnell monument', *Éire-Ireland*, 19, 1 (Spring 1984), 6–25.

' "Who fears to speak of '98?" The rhetoric and rituals of the United Irishmen centennial', *Éire-Ireland*, 28 (1992), 67–91.

O'Leary, Cornelius, 'Review of Eoin Neeson's *The Civil War in Ireland*', *Irish Historical Studies*, 16, 63 (Mar. 1969), 358–61.

Oliver, Sean, 'Irish revolutionary nationalism: Tone to Pearse', in O'Connell, Maurice R. (ed.), *People power* (Dublin, 1993), 94–111.

Ó Lúing, Seán, 'Arthur Griffith, 1871–1922: thoughts on a centenary', *Studies*, 60 (Summer 1971), 127–38.

Ó Murchadha, Domhnall, 'The making of a sculptor', *Cork Review*, 4 (Oct. 1980), 4–5.

O'Neil, Daniel J., 'The cult of self-sacrifice: the Irish experience', *Éire-Ireland*, 24, 4 (Winter 1989), 89–105.

O'Neill, Thomas P., 'In search of a political path: Irish republicanism, 1922 to 1927', in Hayes-McCoy, G. A. (ed.), *Historical studies*, X (Dublin, 1976), 147–71.

Ó Riain, Mícheál, 'Queen Victoria and her reign at Leinster House', *Dublin Historical Record*, 52, 1 (Spring 1999), 75–86.

O'Sullivan, Gearóid, 'Gearóid O'Sullivan – friend and ally', in Doherty, Gabriel and Keogh, Dermot (eds.), *Michael Collins and the making of the Irish state* (Cork, 1998), 45–51.

O'Toole, Michael, 'Portrait of the artist as a young lady', *UCD Connections*, 1 (Spring/Summer 1997), 42–5.

O'Tuama, Aodh, 'Cork republican silver', *Irish Arts Review*, 1, 2 (Summer 1984), 52–3.

'Our patriot dead', *Studies*, 55 (Winter 1966), 337–8.

Owens, Gary, 'Constructing the repeal spectacle: monster meetings and people power in pre-Famine Ireland', in O'Connell, Maurice R. (ed.), *People power* (Dublin, 1993), 80–93.

   'Hedge schools of politics: O'Connell's monster meetings', *History Ireland*, 2, 1 (Spring 1994), 35–40.

   'Nationalist monuments in Ireland, c. 1870–1914: symbolism and ritual', in Gillespie, Raymond and Kennedy, Brian P. (eds.), *Ireland: art into history* (Dublin, 1994), 103–17.

   ' "A moral insurrection": faction fighters, public demonstrations and the O'Connellite campaign, 1828', *Irish Historical Studies*, 30, 120 (Nov. 1997), 513–41.

   'Constructing the martyrs: the Manchester executions and the nationalist imagination', in McBride, Lawrence (ed.), *Images, icons and the Irish nationalist imagination* (Dublin, 1999), 18–36.

Parnaby, J. E., 'Charles Gavan Duffy in Australia', in MacDonagh, Oliver, Mandle, W. F. and Travers, Pauric (eds.), *Irish culture and nationalism, 1750–1950* (London, 1983), 56–68.

Pašeta, Senia, '1798 in 1898: the politics of commemoration', *Irish Review*, 22 (Summer 1998), 46–53.

Phoenix, Eamon, 'American sculptures in the National Gallery of Ireland', *The Arts in Ireland*, 2, 4 (1974), 28–31 and 49–50.

   'Michael Collins – the northern question 1916–1922', in Doherty, Gabriel and Keogh, Dermot (eds.), *Michael Collins and the making of the Irish state* (Cork, 1998), 92–116.

Pyne, Peter, 'The new Irish state and the decline of the republican Sinn Féin party, 1923–1926', *Éire-Ireland*, 11, 3 (Autumn 1976), 33–65.

Rafroidi, Patrick, 'Imagination and revolution: the Cuchulain myth', in MacDonagh, Oliver, Mandle, W. F. and Travers, Pauric (eds.), *Irish culture and nationalism, 1750–1950* (London, 1983), 137–48.

Rearick, Charles, 'Festivals in modern France: the experience of the Third Republic', *Journal of Contemporary History*, 12 (1977), 435–60.

Regan, John, 'Looking at Mick again: demilitarising Michael Collins', *History Ireland*, 3, 3 (Autumn 1995), 17–22.

'The politics of reaction: the dynamics of treatyite government and policy, 1922–33', *Irish Historical Studies*, 30, 120 (Nov. 1997), 542–63.

'Michael Collins – the legacy and the intestacy', in Doherty, Gabriel and Keogh, Dermot (eds.), *Michael Collins and the making of the Irish state* (Cork, 1998), 117–26.

'Retaking the Castle', *Gárda Review*, 15, 6 (July 1997), 4–11.

Rolston, Bill, 'Contemporary wall murals in the north of Ireland: "drawing support"', *Éire-Ireland*, 23, 3 (Autumn 1988), 3–18.

Russell, Mark, 'The building of Hamburg's Bismarck memorial, 1898–1906', *Historical Journal*, 43, 1 (2000), 133–56.

Scott, David, 'Posting messages', *Irish Arts Review Yearbook* (1990–1), 188–96.

Sheehan, Aideen, 'Cumann na mBan – policies and activities', in Fitzpatrick, David (ed.), *Revolution? Ireland 1917–1923* (Trinity History Workshop, Dublin, 1990), 88–97.

Sheehy, Ruth, 'Richard King's Kevin Barry memorial window', *Irish Arts Review Yearbook*, 11 (1995), 208–9.

Sheridan, Niall, 'The action in Carrickbeg', *The Bell*, 1, 3 (Dec. 1940), 19–26.

Sherry, Ruth, 'The story of the National Anthem', *History Ireland*, 4, 1 (Spring 1996), 39–43.

Simms, J. G., 'Remembering 1690', *Studies*, 63 (Autumn 1974), 231–42.

Smyth, William, J., 'Explorations of place', in Lee, J. J. (ed.), *Ireland: towards a sense of place* (Cork, 1985), 1–20.

Staunton, Enda, 'The Boundary Commission debacle 1925: aftermath and implications', *History Ireland*, 4, 2 (Summer 1996), 42–5.

Sweeney, George, 'Irish hunger strikes and the cult of self-sacrifice', *Journal of Contemporary History*, 28, 3 (1993), 421–37.

'The teaching of history in Irish schools – report of the study group on the teaching of history in Irish schools', *Administration*, 15, 4 (Winter 1967), 268–85.

Thornley, David, 'The Blueshirts', in MacManus, Francis (ed.), *The years of the great test, 1926–39* (Cork, 1967), 42–54.

Tobin, Ned, 'Eoin O'Duffy – the leader I knew', *Gárda Review*, 4, 7 (July 1976), 16–19; 4, 8 (August 1976), 23–7.

Towey, Thomas, 'The reaction of the British government to the 1922 Collins–de Valera pact', *Irish Historical Studies*, 22, 85 (Mar. 1980), 65–76.

Townshend, Charles, 'The Irish railway strike of 1920: industrial action and civil resistance in the struggle for independence', *Irish Historical Studies*, 21, 83 (Mar. 1979), 265–82.

Turpin, John, 'Irish history painting', *Irish Arts Review Yearbook* (1989–90), 233–47.

'Oliver Sheppard's 1798 memorials', *Irish Arts Review Yearbook* (1990–1), 71–80.

'Cuchulainn lives on', *Circa*, 64 (Autumn 1994), 26–31.

'Portraits of Irish patriots by Oliver Sheppard, 1865–1941', *Éire-Ireland*, 32, 4 (Winter 1996), 134–53.

Valiulis, Maryann Gialanella, 'The "army mutiny" of 1924 and the assertion of civilian authority in independent Ireland', *Irish Historical Studies*, 23, 92 (Nov. 1983), 354–66.

' "The man they could never forgive" the view of the opposition: Eamon de Valera and the civil war', in O'Carroll, J. P. and Murphy, John A. (eds.), *De Valera and his times* (Cork, 1986), 92–100.

'Review of *Building democracy in Ireland: political order and cultural integration in a newly independent nation* by Jeffrey Prager', *Journal of Modern History*, 60 (1988), 587–8.

Walker, Graham, 'Propaganda and conservative nationalism during the Irish civil war, 1922–1923', *Éire-Ireland*, 22, 4 (Winter 1987), 93–117.

' "The Irish Dr Goebbels": Frank Gallagher and Irish republican propaganda', *Journal of Contemporary History*, 27, 1 (Jan. 1992), 149–65.

Wall, Maureen, 'Partition: the Ulster question (1916–1926)', in Williams, T. Desmond (ed.), *The Irish struggle, 1916–1926* (London, 1966), 79–93.

Walsh, James P., 'Terminal interviews: Arthur Griffith, Michael Collins, and James Duval Phelan of San Francisco', *Éire-Ireland*, 23, 4 (Winter 1988), 81–94.

Walsh, Oonagh, 'Testimony from imprisoned women', in Fitzpatrick, David (ed.), *Revolution? Ireland 1917–1923* (Trinity History Workshop, Dublin, 1990), 69–85.

Ward, Margaret, 'The League of Women Delegates and Sinn Féin', *History Ireland*, 4, 3 (Autumn 1996), 37–41.

Whitfield, Éimear, 'Another martyr for old Ireland: the balladry of revolution', in Fitzpatrick, David (ed.), *Revolution? Ireland 1917–1923* (Trinity History Workshop, Dublin, 1990), 60–8.

Williams, T. Desmond, 'From Treaty to civil war', in Williams, T. Desmond (ed.), *The Irish struggle, 1916–1926* (London, 1966), 117–28.

'The summing up', in Williams, T. Desmond (ed.), *The Irish struggle, 1916–1926* (London, 1966), 183–93.

'Conclusion', in MacManus, Francis (ed.), *The years of the great test, 1926–39* (Cork, 1967), 173–83.

'De Valera in power', in MacManus, Francis (ed.), *The years of the great test, 1926–39* (Cork, 1967), 30–41.

Winter, Jay and Sivan, Emmanuel, 'Setting the framework', in Winter, Jay and Sivan, Emmanuel (eds.), *War and remembrance in the twentieth century* (Cambridge, 1999), 6–39.

Witoszek, Nina, 'Ireland: a funerary culture?', *Studies*, 76 (Summer 1987), 206–15.

'Women's Prisoners' Defence League', *An Cumann Cabhrach testimonial dinner programme* (1990), (not paginated).

Young, Peter, 'Michael Collins – a military leader', in Doherty, Gabriel and Keogh, Dermot (eds.), *Michael Collins and the making of the Irish state* (Cork, 1998), 81–91.

UNPUBLISHED DISSERTATIONS

Browne, Pius J. A., 'A history of Bruff and district', 3 vols., unpublished MA thesis, University College, Cork (1977).
Coleman, Marie, 'County Longford, 1910–1923: a regional study of the Irish revolution', unpublished Ph.D. thesis, University College, Dublin (1998).
Keane, Adrian Thomas, 'Who fears to speak of Easter week? Reflections on the commemoration of the Rising 1924–1991', unpublished MA thesis, University College, Dublin (1996).
Lehto, Mandy, 'The unfinished civil war and the politics of remembrance in Finland, 1918–1928', unpublished Ph.D. thesis, University of Cambridge (2000).
Murphy, William, 'In pursuit of popularity and legitimacy: the rhetoric of Fianna Fáil's social and economic policy 1926–34', unpublished MA thesis, University College, Dublin (1998).

LECTURES AND SPEECHES

Fanning, Ronan, 'Conflict and consolidation: the foundation of the state', University College, Dublin (16 Apr. 1997).
Foster, Roy, 'A Trevelyan lecture to commemorate the 200th anniversary of the Irish rising of 1798', Cambridge University (4 Nov. 1998).
Kearney, Tess, 'Oration at Ballyseedy Cross – 75th anniversary' (7 Mar. 1998).

INTERVIEWS

Fr Boland, Church of St Vincent de Paul, Griffith Avenue, Marino (12 May 1999).
Tess Kearney, Secretary, National Graves Association (18 Apr. 1998).

LETTERS

Carrie Acheson, Secretary, Third Tipperary Brigade Old IRA Commemoration Committee (28 July 1998).
Kathleen Browne, County Librarian, Kerry County Library (2 June 1998).
Eileen Burgess, Assistant Librarian, Donegal County Library (23 July 1998).
Kieran Burke, Cork City Library (18 June 1998).
Mary Butler, County Librarian, Offaly County Library (29 June 1998).
Pat Canniffe, Cumann Seanachas na Banndon (n.d.).
Philomena S. Cavanagh Neavyn, Honorary Secretary, Birr Historical Society (15 July 1998).
Maureen Combes, Local Studies Librarian, Clare County Library (2 June 1998).
Elizabeth Connelly, Honorary Secretary, County Kildare Archaeological Society (10 June 1998).
Paddy Connolly, Cloncoolmore, Bandon (16 June 1998).
Moira Corcoran, Old Drogheda Society (19 June 1998).
Michael Costello, Assistant Librarian, Kerry County Library (10 June 1998).
John Cussen, Newcastlewest, Co. Limerick (22 July 1998).
Michael Farry, Trim, Co. Meath (29 May 1999).
Thomas G. Fewer, Dunmore East (24 Sept. 1998).

Neil Fitzpatrick, Town Planning and Building Department, Cork Corporation (29 May 1998).

Margot Gearty, Longford (12 May 1999).

B. Gilligan, Assistant Librarian, Roscommon County Library (20 May 1998).

Mary Guinan-Darmody, Local Studies Department, Tipperary Libraries (29 June 1998).

William Hayes, Clonmel (3 July 1998).

Patrick Holohan, Honorary Secretary, Cork Historical and Archaeological Society (10 June 1998).

John Houlihan, Kerry National Graves Association (22 Oct. 1998).

V. Hussey, Offaly County Council (21 May 1998).

Tina Hynes, Archivist, Fingal County Council (9 June 1998).

Bernadette Jordan, Ballaghaderreen, Co. Roscommon (18 June 1998).

Michael Kavanagh, County Librarian, Kildare County Library (10 July 1998).

John Kearney, Offaly Historical and Archaeological Society (11 June 1998).

Mary Kearns, Honorary Secretary, Clare Archaeological and Historical Society (28 June 1998).

Michael Kelly, Youghal Heritage Society (18 June 1998).

Pat Kelly, Lusk Heritage Society (n.d.).

Máire Kennedy, Senior Librarian, The Gilbert Library, Dublin (13 July 1998).

G. Lambden, Acting County Secretary, Westmeath County Council (4 June 1998).

Matt Lean, Tralee (n.d.).

Michael Leydon, Galway (n.d.).

H. Lyons, County Secretary, Kildare County Council (4 June 1998).

Declan Macauley, Assistant Librarian, Kilkenny County Library (16 June 1998).

P. McClean, Monaghan County Council (29 June 1998).

Donal McDonnell, West Wicklow Historical Society (9 Aug. 1998).

Liam McGlynn, Senior Administrative Officer, Fingal County Council (22 May 1998).

M. McLoone, Office of the Donegal County Manager (5 June 1998).

Mary McNamara, South Dublin County Council (25 May 1998).

Siobhán Maher, Dublin Corporation (18 May 1998).

Maureen Moran, Acting County Librarian, Galway County Library (24 Aug. 1998).

Seán Morgan, Glenamaddy, Co. Galway (n.d.).

Connie Murphy, Beara Historical Society (29 June 1998).

Donal Murphy, Nenagh (29 July 1998).

K. Murphy, Louth County Library (23 July 1998).

Rory Murphy, Bunclody Historical Society (9 June 1998).

Michael Nicholson, Assistant County Secretary, Wicklow County Council (20 May 1998).

Kathleen O'Connor, Raheny Heritage Society (n.d.).

M. O'Connor, County Manager, Carlow County Council (20 May 1998).

Michael O'Donnell, Tipperary Historical Society (8 June 1998).

Liam Ó Duibhir, Clonmel (6 July 1998).

Patrick O'Meara, Policy and Research Officer, Fine Gael (8 July 1998).

Noreen O'Neill, Reference Librarian, Limerick Corporation (4 Dec. 1998).

Muiris Ó Raghaill, County Librarian, Dun Laoghaire-Rathdown (25 May 1998).

Kathleen O'Riordan, Bantry (10 June 1998).

Seán Ó Suilleabháin, Leitrim County Library (n.d.).

Edwin Phelan, County Librarian, Laois County Library (9 June 1998).

J. Pierce, County Secretary, Wexford County Council (14 May 1998).

Rosemary Purcell, Tipperary South Riding County Museum (8 June 1998).

Pat Quilty, Bruff, Co. Limerick (10 July 1998).

Vera Quinn, Abbeyleix Library (3 June 1998).

Michael Quirke, Kerry County Council (2 June 1998).

Geraldine Reilly, Galway Corporation (10 June 1998).

Diarmuid Ring, Killarney (1 July 1998).

Noel Ross, Honorary Secretary, Co. Louth Archaeological and Historical Society (25 July 1998).

James Scannell, The Old Bray Society (8 Aug. 1998).

Colin Scudds, Dun Laoghaire Historical Society (8 July 1998).

Albert Siggins, National Museum of Ireland (n.d.).

W. P. Smith, County Librarian, Meath County Library (9 June 1998).

Tony Storan, Senior Library Assistant, Limerick County Library (28 May 1998).

P. Waldron, Ballinlough, Co. Roscommon (20 July 1998).

Oliver Ward, Meath Archaeological and Historical Society (31 July 1998).

Hugh Weir, Whitegate, Co. Clare (27 May 1999).

Anne Yeoman, Honorary Secretary, Thomond Archaeological Society (9 June 1998).

Index

Studies in the Social and Cultural History of Modern Warfare

Titles in the series:

12 *Life between Memory and Hope: The Survivors of the Holocaust in Occupied Germany*
Zeev W. Mankowitz
ISBN 0 521 81105 8

Printed in the United Kingdom
by Lightning Source UK Ltd.
116727UKS00001B/97